# Interpretive Lenses in Sociology

*Series editors:* **Thomas DeGloma**, Hunter College, City University of New York, and **Julie B. Wiest**, West Chester University of Pennsylvania

The *Interpretive Lenses in Sociology* series provides a unique forum for scholars using a wide range of interpretive perspectives to explore their approaches to uncovering the deep meanings underlying human actions, events, and experiences.

### Forthcoming in the series:

*Interpretive Sociology and the Semiotic Imagination*
Editors **Andrea Cossu** and **Jorge Fontdevila**

*Interpreting Contentious Memory*
*Countermemories and Conflicts over the Past*
Editors **Thomas DeGloma** and **Janet L. Jacobs**

*Interpreting Subcultures*
*Sense-Making From Insider and Outsider Perspectives*
Editor **J. Patrick Williams**

### Out now in the series:

*Interpreting Religion*
*Making Sense of Religious Lives*
Editors **Erin Johnston** and **Vikash Singh**

**Find out more at**
bristoluniversitypress.co.uk/interpretive-lenses-in-sociology

# International advisory board:

Jeffrey C. Alexander, Yale University, US
Marni A. Brown, Georgia Gwinnett College, US
Giuseppina Cersosimo, University of Salerno, Italy
Lynn S. Chancer, Hunter College, City University of New York, US
Erica Chito-Childs, Hunter College, City University of New York, US
Manase Kudzai Chiweshe, University of Zimbabwe, Zimbabwe
Jean-François Côté, University of Montreal, Canada
Emma Engdahl, University of Gothenburg, Sweden
Veikko Eranti, University of Helsinki, Finland
Emily Fairchild, New College of Florida, US
Gary Alan Fine, Northwestern University, US
Stacey Hannem, Wilfrid Laurier University, Canada
Titus Hjelm, University of Helsinki, Finland
Annemarie Jutel, Victoria University of Wellington, New Zealand
Carol Kidron, University of Haifa, Israel
Krzysztof T. Konecki, University of Lodz, Poland
Joseph A. Kotarba, Texas State University, US
Donileen Loseke, University of South Florida, US
Eeva Luhtakallio, University of Helsinki, Finland
Lisa McCormick, The University of Edinburgh, Scotland
Neil McLaughlin, McMaster University, Canada
Beth Montemurro, Pennsylvania State University, Abington, US
Kylie Parrotta, California Polytechnic State University, US
Laura Robinson, Santa Clara University, US
Andrea Salvini, University of Pisa, Italy
Susie Scott, University of Sussex, UK
Cristine G. Severo, Federal University of Santa Catarina, Brazil
Xiaoli Tian, University of Hong Kong, Hong Kong
Vilna Bashi Treitler, Northwestern University, US
Hector Vera, National Autonomous University of Mexico, Mexico
Gad Yair, The Hebrew University of Jerusalem, Israel
J. Patrick Williams, Nanyang Technological University, Singapore
Eviatar Zerubavel, Rutgers University, US

## Find out more at
bristoluniversitypress.co.uk/interpretive-lenses-in-sociology

# INTERPRETING THE BODY

Between Meaning and Matter

Edited by
Anne Marie Champagne
and Asia Friedman

First published in Great Britain in 2024 by

Bristol University Press
University of Bristol
1-9 Old Park Hill
Bristol
BS2 8BB
UK
t: +44 (0)117 374 6645
e: bup-info@bristol.ac.uk

Details of international sales and distribution partners are available at bristoluniversitypress.co.uk

© Bristol University Press 2024

British Library Cataloguing in Publication Data
A catalogue record for this book is available from the British Library

ISBN 978-1-5292-1156-6 hardcover
ISBN 978-1-5292-1157-3 paperback
ISBN 978-1-5292-1159-7 ePub
ISBN 978-1-5292-1158-0 ePdf

The right of Anne Marie Champagne and Asia Friedman to be identified as editors of this work has been asserted by them in accordance with the Copyright, Designs and Patents Act 1988.

All rights reserved: no part of this publication may be reproduced, stored in a retrieval system, or transmitted in any form or by any means, electronic, mechanical, photocopying, recording, or otherwise without the prior permission of Bristol University Press.

Every reasonable effort has been made to obtain permission to reproduce copyrighted material. If, however, anyone knows of an oversight, please contact the publisher.

The statements and opinions contained within this publication are solely those of the editors and contributors and not of the University of Bristol or Bristol University Press. The University of Bristol and Bristol University Press disclaim responsibility for any injury to persons or property resulting from any material published in this publication.

Bristol University Press works to counter discrimination on grounds of gender, race, disability, age and sexuality.

Cover design: blu inc, Bristol
Front cover image: Abstract Figure by Juana Almaguer, 2021
(www.juanaalmaguer.com)

To our children and students,
who inspire us to interpret the world anew.

# Contents

| | | |
|---|---|---|
| Series Editors' Preface: Interpretive Lenses in Sociology—<br>On the Multidimensional Foundations of Meaning in Social Life | | ix |
| Notes on Contributors | | xiv |
| Preface and Acknowledgments | | xviii |
| | Introduction: Between Meaning and Matter<br>*Anne Marie Champagne and Asia Friedman* | 1 |
| 1 | Toward a Strong Cultural Sociology of the Body and Embodiment<br>*Anne Marie Champagne* | 19 |
| 2 | Thinking the Molecular<br>*Ben Spatz* | 44 |
| 3 | Interpreting Africa's *Seselelãme*: Bodily Ways of Knowing in a Globalized World<br>*Kathryn Linn Geurts and Sefakor Komabu-Pomeyie* | 66 |
| 4 | Gender on the Post-Colony: Phenomenology, Race, and the Body in *Nervous Conditions*<br>*Sweta Rajan-Rankin and Mrinalini Greedharry* | 88 |
| 5 | Reinterpreting Male Bodies and Health in Crisis Times: From "Obesity" to Bigger Matters<br>*Lee F. Monaghan* | 109 |
| 6 | Beauty, Breasts, and Meaning after Mastectomy<br>*Piper Sledge* | 133 |
| 7 | "You Are Not the Body": (Re)Interpreting the Body in and through Integral Yoga<br>*Erin F. Johnston* | 155 |

| | | |
|---|---|---|
| 8 | Black Girls' Bodies and Belonging in the Classroom<br>*Brittney Miles* | 178 |
| 9 | Embodied Vulnerability and Sensemaking with Solidarity Activists<br>*Chandra Russo* | 202 |
| 10 | Our Bodies, Our Disciplines, Our Selves<br>*Annemarie Jutel* | 223 |

Index      238

# Series Editors' Preface: Interpretive Lenses in Sociology— On the Multidimensional Foundations of Meaning in Social Life

Sociology is an interpretive endeavor.[1] Whatever the approach taken to study and explain an aspect of social life—qualitative or quantitative, micro or macro—sociologists work to interpret their data to reveal previously unseen, or to clarify previously misunderstood, social forces. However, within the broad field of sociology, and under the purview of its kindred disciplines, there are many scholars who work to unpack the deep structures and processes that underlie the *meanings* of social life. These interpretive scholars focus on the ways in which social meanings constitute the core structures of self and identity, the ways that individuals negotiate meanings to define their shared situations, and the collective meanings that bind people together into communities while also setting any given group or context apart from others. From this perspective, meaning underscores social mindsets and personal orientations in the world, as well as the solidarities and divisions that define the dynamics and mark the boundaries of our social standpoints and relationships. Furthermore, such scholars are concerned not only with how the individuals and groups they study actively make and remake the definitions that are central to their lives, as well as how those understandings influence their behaviors, but also how they seek to impact the world with their meaning-making processes. In this regard, meaning is of paramount significance to both the extraordinary moments and the routine circumstances of our lives.[2]

In their efforts to illuminate the deep social foundations of meaning, and to detail the very real social, political, and moral consequences that stem from the ways people define and know the world around them, interpretive scholars explore the semiotic significance of social actions and interactions, narratives and discourses, experiences and events. In contrast to those who take a positivist or realist perspective and see the world—or, more precisely, argue that the world can be known—in a more direct or literal light,[3] they use various approaches and draw on different interpretive traditions to decipher their cases in order to better understand the deep social, cultural, and psychic foundations of the phenomena they study. From such interpretive perspectives, a fundamental part of any social phenomenon is not directly evident or visible. Rather, the core foundations of meaning underlying the cases scholars study need to be unpacked, analyzed, and interpreted—and then rearticulated—to comprehend their deeper essences.[4] And they do this work of interpretation from various angles and perspectives, using different "lenses." It is with such interpretive lenses, in sociology and beyond, that we concern ourselves here. How do the people we study make sense of the world? How do they cooperate with others to construct shared understandings, and how do such actors define their situations for various audiences? Furthermore, how do scholars understand their sense-making processes and interpret their actions and experiences? How do they get at the deep social forces, culture structures, and relationships underlying the topics and themes they study?[5] Finally, how do their interpretations allow scholars to construct new and powerful explanations of social phenomena? How do they "possess explanatory torque" with regard to various topics of widespread significance (Reed, 2011, p 11; see also Garland, 2006, pp 437–438)?

This is the perspective from which we organized a unique conference, *The Roots and Branches of Interpretive Sociology: Cultural, Pragmatist, and Psychosocial Approaches*, in Philadelphia, Pennsylvania, in August 2018. From this endeavor, we learned that many scholars were excited by our call to bring them to the table to discuss their interpretive lenses with one another. Many almost intuitively grasped the distinctions we made among traditions and camps in the field (the cultural, the pragmatist/interactionist, the psychosocial, and others) that could be gathered under the umbrella of a broader "interpretive" agenda in sociology. And why not? We make such distinctions between different camps, with their various theoretical and methodological traditions, when we teach. This is how we organize many of our journals, our professional societies and their sections, and other scholarly institutions. We also often use such categories to explain our scholarly identities. In line with these distinctions, qualitative interpretation has developed simultaneously along different paths and among a field of factional communities, and the proponents of these different camps make various claims to distinguish their respective approaches from others.

However, despite the fact that we use such distinctions to delineate our disciplinary field, they rarely sync neatly with the work scholars actually do when they interpret the cases, communities, and issues they study. Rather, in their practices of social research and in their acts of interpretation, scholars combine and integrate elements of different traditions and programs in various ways that help them to focus on and make sense of their experiences as scholars. In other words, the process of interpretation comes alive in the practice of research and, more particularly, in research situations that demand a range of theoretical and methodological tools to illuminate and articulate the social foundations of meaning central to the case at hand.[6] Thus, over the course of their work, scholars develop interpretive lenses that help them find answers to the questions that drive them. While this may not come as a surprise to many readers, we rarely interrogate or compare the nuances of these lenses explicitly.

The purpose of this series is to interrogate, explore, and demonstrate the various interpretive lenses that scholars use when they engage their areas of interest, their cases, and their research situations. Each volume is centered on a substantive topic (for example, religion, the body, or contentious memories) or a particular interpretive-analytic method (for example, semiotics or narrative analysis). The editors of each volume feature the work of scholars who approach their central topic using different interpretive lenses that are particularly relevant to that area of focus. They have asked each author to explicitly illustrate and reflect on two dimensions of interpretation in their work, and to explore the connections between them. First, they asked authors to address how the individuals and communities they study assign meanings and achieve shared understandings with regard to the core topic of their volume. In doing so, authors address the social and cultural forces at play in shaping how people understand their identities, experiences, and situations, as well as how they frame their accounts, motivations, and purposes while acting, communicating, and performing in the world. Second, volume editors asked contributing authors to explicitly reflect on their interpretive processes and approaches to unpacking the meanings of the social phenomena they study. Some authors present new material while others provide a reflexive overview of their research to date, but all illustrate and discuss the work of interpretation and the central significance of meaning. Such conscious reflection on our interpretive traditions and lenses—on how they shape our analytic foci (in terms of what cases we explore, at what levels of analysis, and with regard to which social actors) and the ways we find meaning in our cases—can illuminate under-recognized or unspoken choices we make in our work. Furthermore, it can expose blind spots and suggest new frameworks for dialogue among scholars. This reflexive dimension, along with the diversity of lenses featured together in each volume, is what makes this series unique. In this vein, and to these ends, we hope the volumes of this series will present arrays of interpretive lenses that readers can use while working to make sense of their own cases and to develop new perspectives of their own. In the process, we also hope to advance the dialogue about interpretation and meaning in the social sciences.

In this volume, Anne Marie Champagne and Asia Friedman present a collection of essays that advance the study of bodies and embodiment in important ways. With an overarching emphasis on the "*processes of interpretation and meaning production,*" the collection highlights the ways in which different theoretical and methodological traditions both diverge and converge in approaches to interpreting the body. Approaching a breadth of topics from a range of interpretive perspectives, the chapters in this book offer numerous insights that are masterfully tied together in the volume's introduction, which both explains and contextualizes the evolution of approaches to studying the body while offering a cogent discussion of the challenges and possibilities of interpretive scholarship in this broad area of study.

The scholars featured in this volume apply various combinations of analytic perspectives (including cultural, materialist, semiotic, discursive, interactionist, postcolonial, critical, performative, and psychosocial) to studies of the body within different social contexts while also addressing a wide variety of important issues and themes including those related to race, sex and gender, age, emotion and affect, religiosity, health and medicine, aesthetics, and more. All the while, with Champagne and Friedman's guidance, these authors work to illustrate and reflect on their particular interpretive lenses, considering how they allow us to understand how bodies take on meaning in various contexts and situations. All of these authors offer us interpretive tools with which to conduct research that addresses the social character of bodies and embodiment. Thus, with this collection, Champagne and Friedman demonstrate that paying explicit attention to how interpretive processes shape meaning, both at the level of everyday life and as part of the scholarly process, along with consideration of how these processes structure our attention within complex dynamics of power and inequality, raises a number of important issues that move the social analysis of the body in new and illuminating directions. The overlapping space between meaning and materiality, these scholars show in different ways, is where connections are forged between the body and larger cultural and semiotic systems of interpretation, which allow for both *having* and *making sense of* embodied experiences. We are thrilled to feature this important book as part of our *Interpretive Lenses in Sociology* series.

*Thomas DeGloma*
*Hunter College and the Graduate Center, CUNY*

*Julie B. Wiest*
*West Chester University of Pennsylvania*

## Notes

[1] An extended series introduction is available for open access download at: bristoluniversitypress.co.uk/interpretive-lenses-in-sociology. Shorter and slightly modified versions appear as prefaces to the different volumes of this series.

[2] On the centrality of meaning in interpretive social analysis, see Reed's (2011) important work on interpretation and knowledge, especially his discussions of the "interpretive epistemic mode" (pp 89–121) and the "normative epistemic mode" (pp 67–88).

[3] See Reed (2011), especially on the "realist semiotic and the illusion of noninterpretation" (p 52).

[4] Indeed, this is what Clifford Geertz (1973) meant when he called for "thick description" in ethnographic analysis.

[5] Alfred Schütz (1932, pp 205–206; 1970, p 273) recognized the layers of interpretation we point to here when he argued, "The thought objects constructed by the social scientist ... have to be founded upon the thought objects constructed by the common-sense thinking of [people], living their daily life within their social world. Thus, the constructs of the social sciences are, so to speak, constructs of the second degree, namely constructs of the constructs made by the actors on the social scene." Geertz (1973, p 9) made a similar distinction when he argued "that what we call our data are really our own constructions of other people's constructions." Also see Reed (2017, pp 29–31) on "interpreting interpretations." Such a distinction also informs the fundamental premises of psychoanalysis, as the analyst is always in the business of interpreting interpretations and unpacking layers of symbolism.

[6] See also Tavory and Timmermans (2014), who advocate engaging the process of research and interpretation armed with "multiple theoretical perspectives" (p 35).

## References

Garland, D. (2006) 'Concepts of culture in the sociology of punishment', *Theoretical Criminology*, 10(4): 419–447.

Geertz, C. (1973) *The Interpretation of Cultures*, New York: Basic Books.

Reed, I.A. (2011) *Interpretation and Social Knowledge: On the Use of Theory in the Human Sciences*, Chicago, IL: University of Chicago Press.

Reed, I.A. (2017) 'On the very idea of cultural sociology', in C.E. Benzecry, M. Krause and I.A. Reed (eds) *Social Theory Now*, Chicago, IL: University of Chicago Press, pp 18–41.

Schütz, A. (1932) *The Phenomenology of the Social World*, Evanston, IL: Northwestern University Press, 1967.

Schütz, A. (1970) *On Phenomenology and Social Relations*, Chicago, IL: University of Chicago Press.

Tavory, I. and Timmermans. S. (2014) *Abductive Analysis: Theorizing Qualitative Research*, Chicago, IL: University of Chicago Press.

# Notes on Contributors

**Anne Marie Champagne** is a doctoral candidate in sociology at Yale University and a junior fellow at the Yale Center for Cultural Sociology. In addition to serving on the advisory council of Not Putting on a Shirt (NPOAS), a nonprofit advocating for satisfactory aesthetic outcomes for mastectomy patients, she is a member of the Civil Sphere Working Group, an international forum of theorists and empirical social scientists engaging with and developing civil sphere theory. Her research interests include aesthetic power in social life, materiality and culture, and issues of body and embodiment. Her dissertation looks at how aesthetics and materiality inform legal, medical, and individual approaches to mastectomy and constructions of identity in transmen and female-identified breast cancer survivors.

**Asia Friedman** is Associate Professor of Sociology at the University of Delaware. Her research has primarily focused on developing a body of research in cognitive sociology unified around her interest in the mental and sensory mechanisms of the social construction process. This has included efforts to expand the vocabulary of the field by theorizing concepts such as perceptual construction, filter analysis, and cultural blind spots, as well as to apply analytic frameworks rooted in the sociology of attention and perception to other substantive areas, specifically, gender, race, the body, medicine, and sociological theory. Her first book, *Blind to Sameness: Sexpectations and the Social Construction of Male and Female Bodies* (University of Chicago Press, 2013), won the Distinguished Book Award from the Sex and Gender section of the American Sociological Association in 2016. A second monograph, *Mammography Wars: Analyzing Attention in Cultural and Medical Disputes*, is forthcoming in 2023 from Rutgers University Press.

**Kathryn Linn Geurts** is Professor of Anthropology and Chair of the Global and Area Studies Department at Hamline University in Saint Paul, Minnesota. Her research focuses on investigating bodily experience—not through a Western lens but through a West African perspective. She is the author of *Culture and the Senses: Bodily Ways of Knowing in an African Community* (University of California Press, 2003) as well as numerous articles and book chapters. She has been the recipient of fellowships from Fulbright-Hays, NIMH, the School for Advanced Research on the Human Experience in Santa Fe, New Mexico, as well as the Guggenheim and Rockefeller Foundations.

**Mrinalini Greedharry** is an associate professor in the English Literature, Media, and Writing program at Laurentian University, Canada. Her research focuses on how the practices, organization, and theory of studying English literature engender postcolonial subjects, which builds on her longstanding interest in the ways that postcolonial theory can generate new ways of thinking about subject formation in general. She is the author of *Postcolonial Theory and Psychoanalysis* (Palgrave Macmillan, 2008), chapters in collections such as *What Postcolonial Theory Doesn't Say* (Routledge, 2018), *The Oxford Handbook of Identities in Organizations* (Oxford University Press, 2020), *Towards Organization 2666: Literary Troubling, Undoing and Refusal* (Springer, 2020), and *Racial Dimensions of Life Writing in Education* (IAP, 2022).

**Erin F. Johnston** is a senior research associate in the Department of Sociology at Duke University, where she leads qualitative data collection and analysis for the Clergy Health Initiative's "Seminary to Early Ministry" study, the first longitudinal study of divinity school students. Johnston's research interests lie at the intersection of cultural sociology, social psychology, and the study of religion and education in the US context. She has written about conversion narratives among contemporary Pagans (*Sociological Forum*, 2013), the aspirational nature of identity in spiritual communities (*Religions*, 2016), the social dynamics of failure and persistence in spiritual disciplines (*Qualitative Sociology*, 2017), and emotion management through yoga and prayer (*Symbolic Interaction*, 2021).

**Annemarie Jutel** is Professor of Health at Te Herenga Waka—Victoria University of Wellington and a sociologist of diagnosis. Her research interests focus on how diagnosis, as a category and as a process, influences how health, illness, and disease are understood at an individual as well as a sociocultural level. She is the author of *Putting a Name to It: Diagnosis in Contemporary Society* (Johns Hopkins University Press, 2011) and *Diagnosis: Truths and Tales* (University of Toronto Press, 2019).

**Sefakor Komabu-Pomeyie** holds a PhD in educational leadership and policy studies from the University of Vermont, where she currently teaches their online "Global Disability Studies" course, which serves a national constituency. Her research focuses on the shortcomings and idiosyncrasies that underlie contemporary responses to disability-oriented human rights abuses in schools. She has held a Ford Foundation Fellowship in addition to winning awards from the Association of University Centers on Disabilities and the International Alliance of Women. She has coauthored a chapter in *Disability in the Global South: The Critical Handbook* (Springer, 2016).

**Brittney Miles** is a PhD candidate in sociology at the University of Cincinnati, where she is an Albert C. Yates fellow. She holds a graduate certificate in women's gender and sexuality studies and an MA in sociology from the University of Cincinnati. She also holds an MEd in social and cultural foundations in education from DePaul University. Her scholarship centers Black girlhood, specifically in the areas of sexuality, disability, and embodiment. Within her research she employs a strength-based approach to critical Black feminist examinations of social problems. She is the coauthor (with A. Linders et al) of "The Sounds of Executions: Sonic Flaws and the Transformation of Capital Punishment" (*American Journal of Cultural Sociology*, 2022).

**Lee F. Monaghan** is Associate Professor of Sociology at the University of Limerick, Ireland. He mainly teaches the sociology of health and illness, classical and contemporary sociological theory, and the sociology of the body. He has researched and published on topics such as illicit steroid use, private security work, the war on obesity, childhood asthma, and COVID-19. Monaghan's work has been published in numerous international journals. He has also authored or coauthored four monographs and four edited collections. His most recent books are *Rethinking Obesity: Critical Perspectives in Crisis Times* (Routledge, 2022, with Emma Rich and Andrea Bombak), and *Key Concepts in Medical Sociology*, 3rd edn (SAGE, 2022, edited with Jonathan Gabe).

**Sweta Rajan-Rankin** is Reader (Associate Professor) in Sociology and Social Work at the University of Kent, UK. Her research investigates embodiment and racialized belonging in diverse contexts, including transnational service work in Indian call centers, racialized imaginaries and old age in postcolonial imaginaries, and most recently material intimacies, touch biographies, and Black hair practices. An interdisciplinary scholar and radical social worker, her research brings together postcoloniality and embodiment through a historically situated understanding of everyday lives of diasporic, migrant, and marginalized communities. She is a UKRI Future Leaders Fellowship recipient (Round 6) and is currently exploring texture-based discrimination and embodied understandings of Black children and young people in social care and educational settings in the North and South of England. Rajan-Rankin is a long-serving member of the British Sociological Association Race and Ethnicity Study Group, and she is currently a general editor for the *Sociological Review*, Britain's oldest sociology journal.

NOTES ON CONTRIBUTORS

**Chandra Russo** is Associate Professor of Sociology at Colgate University, where she teaches courses in social movements and activism, the body, and (anti)racism. Her book *Solidarity in Practice* (Cambridge University Press, 2018) examines how justice-seeking solidarity drives activist communities contesting US torture, militarism, and immigration policies. Before earning a PhD from the University of California, Santa Barbara, she spent several years working on immigrant justice issues in New York State, Central Mexico, and Colorado. Her research and writing have been published in such venues as *Mobilization, Race and Class, American Quarterly, City, Interface*, and the *Denver Post*.

**Piper Sledge** is Associate Professor of Sociology at Bryn Mawr College. Her research and teaching interests include gender, race, and embodiment. Sledge's first book, *Bodies Unbound: Gender-Specific Cancer and Biolegitimacy* (Rutgers University Press, 2021), is a comparative study showing how ideologies of gendered bodies shape medical care and how patients respond to these ideologies through decisions about their bodies using three cases: transgender men seeking preventative gynecological care, cisgender men diagnosed with breast cancer, and cisgender women with breast cancer who elect to undergo prophylactic mastectomies. Her current book project explores the relationship between trans* and mixed-race embodied experiences as one imbued with the radical potential to help us better understand how racial and gender ideologies are reproduced, resisted, and reimagined.

**Ben Spatz** is a nonbinary scholar-practitioner working at the intersections of artistic research and critical race and gender theory. They are a leader in the development of new audiovisual embodied research methods and produce scholarly writing, video essays, and video art. Spatz is Reader in Media and Performance at the University of Huddersfield; the founding editor of the videographic *Journal of Embodied Research* and the Advanced Methods imprint from Punctum Books; and the author of *What a Body Can Do* (Routledge, 2015), *Blue Sky Body* (Routledge, 2020), and *Making a Laboratory* (Punctum, 2020). <www.urbanresearchtheater.com>

# Preface and Acknowledgments

The overarching theme of this volume grew out of The Roots and Branches of Interpretive Sociology: Cultural, Pragmatist, and Psychosocial Approaches, a conference organized and chaired by Thomas DeGloma and Julie B. Wiest that took place over the course of two days immediately preceding the 2018 Annual Meeting of the American Sociological Association. The conference, which was sponsored by the Society for the Study of Symbolic Interaction, the Psychosocial Scholars Group, and Yale University's Center for Cultural Sociology, brought together scholars from across the globe working in the traditions of American pragmatism, cultural and cognitive sociology, psychoanalytic sociology, semiotics, symbolic interactionism, and other schools of thought. The range of interpretive approaches represented in the conference program offered a unique opportunity for investigating the conjunctions and disjunctions between each tradition's respective approach to grasping the meaning and matter of social life.

Serving as a member of the Conference Programming Committee, Anne Marie Champagne, a doctoral student and junior fellow at Yale University's Center for Cultural Sociology, co-organized (with Piper Sledge) a featured thematic panel, The Fine Lines of Interpreting Bodies and Identities, which set out to explore how bodies and embodied identities are presented, represented, and interpreted in the social sciences. The panel title gave a nod to Eviatar Zerubavel's book *The Fine Line: Making Distinctions in Everyday Life* (University of Chicago Press, 1991), a study of the sociomental processes of differentiation, association, and perception that partition reality into islands of meaning. Alongside panel presentations on auditory perception and attributions of value (Whitney Johnson) and the embodied aesthetics of far-right extremism (Cynthia Miller-Idriss), Asia Friedman, a former student of Zerubavel, presented an overview of her research highlighting a cultural cognitive vision for the social construction of the body. She specifically emphasized selective attention as a key cultural cognitive process that links meaning with materiality and plays a significant role in the social construction of the body. Her cultural cognitive approach is reflected in this volume's broader focus on interpretation as a uniquely valuable approach for advancing the study of the body as a simultaneously material and semiotic entity.

## PREFACE AND ACKNOWLEDGMENTS

While none of the contributions to this volume specifically originated in the Fine Lines of Interpreting Bodies and Identities panel, the idea and proposal for a book on "Interpreting the Body" did, thanks to the encouragement of the Interpretive Lenses in Sociology book series editors, Thomas DeGloma and Julie B. Wiest, and Bristol University Press editorial director Victoria Pittman. We owe the genesis of this book to their foresight and its completion to the editorial and production teams at Bristol.

We are especially indebted to the series editors, who empowered us to seek out and gather together under one cover the critical selection of chapters published here by notable and up-and-coming social scientists whose research and writing illuminate the interpretive connections that link human experiences, meanings, and actions to the body. For this, our utmost appreciation goes to our contributors—Kathryn Linn Geurts, Mrinalini Greedharry, Erin F. Johnston, Annemarie Jutel, Sefakor Komabu-Pomeyie, Brittney Miles, Lee F. Monaghan, Sweta Rajan-Rankin, Chandra Russo, Piper Sledge, and Ben Spatz—who dared to entrust us with their work and without whom this volume would not be possible.

Book projects demand patience, extraordinary effort, and collective will and are tasking even when undertaken in optimal conditions. The development of *Interpreting the Body: Between Meaning and Matter* began mere weeks before the global spread of COVID-19 disrupted every facet of human life, thoroughly transforming the way we work, educate and learn, and care for each other. No one was spared. And over the course of the two years during which this book materialized, editors and members close to the project lost family, friends, mentors, and colleagues as either a direct or indirect result of the pandemic. The dear and loved ones who departed from us much too soon are also a part of this book's spirit and wider circle of support. We carry them forward across these pages and remember them in our everyday lives with gratitude and fondness.

We wish to acknowledge Juana Almaguer (www.juanaalmaguer.com) for granting permission for the use of the artwork Abstract Figure 50/100, 2021, on the cover.

We also would like to extend a special note of thanks to those whose ideas and theories have shaped our own and/or who generously offered comment, including Jeffrey C. Alexander, Philip Smith, Eviatar Zerubavel, and the book's reviewers.

Lastly, we thank our families, who buoyed us, and the many colleagues and friends who cheered us on.

*Anne Marie Champagne*
*Asia Friedman*
May 9, 2022

# Introduction: Between Meaning and Matter

*Anne Marie Champagne and Asia Friedman*

At minimum, sociological interpretation engages processes of analytical (cognitive and perceptual) selection and deselection and representational techniques. Whereas processes of analytical selection mark certain subjects as worthy or unworthy of study and certain data as more salient than others, representational techniques offer methods for explaining, visualizing, reconstructing, and comprehending subjects of study (narratives, network topologies, and statistical models are all stylized representations of selected underlying data). In this regard it can be said that the discipline of sociology has always been an *interpretive* human science, just not one foundationally concerned with interpreting the human body. Preoccupied with understanding the drivers and characteristics of capitalist societies and the atomizing effects of "modernity," classical sociologists sought to understand the collective actions, systems, and events that held humans together in the face of these disparate social forces (Durkheim, 1893; Weber, 1930; Parsons, 1948). Although not explicitly theorized, the body was nevertheless implicated in early sociology: it operated in the background as the taken-for-granted medium of action external to the decision-making social actor, and it served as an expedient natural symbol representing "society as an organism" and/or "the body politic" (Douglas, 1970; Turner, 1991; Shilling, 2012).

The relative absence of the body from early sociological thought is ascribable to the historical sensibility of the nineteenth century that inflected sociology's interpretive lens. The discipline of sociology emerged against the backdrop of the Industrial Revolution, a period that ushered in widespread rural-to-urban migration and ostensibly one of the most dramatic transformations of human social organization since the Middle Ages. The expansion of industrial capitalism across Europe and the United States coincided with technological innovations and the rise of modern science (Wallerstein, 1989; Taylor et al, 2008). During this time, bureaucracy, individualism, realism, and rationality were not only the hallmarks of the positivist "hard" sciences, which sought to objectively measure and quantify the observable world and discover its regularities and causal connections, they also were the perceived attributes of modernity itself (Weber, 1930; Giddens, 1991; Taylor, 1995). Shaped by this historical milieu, early sociology drew from economics, law, and even positivism to formulate its disciplinary methods (Durkheim, 1895; Comte, 1975) as well as its concepts of social "action, choice, and goals" (Turner, 1991, p 7). At the same time that sociology drew methodological inspiration from positivism, it also sought to distinguish itself in opposition to it, as a thoroughly social (contra physical) human science. This rejection of the physical, Bryan Turner argues, left little interpretive room within classical sociology for "the biological conditions of action or for the idea of the 'lived body'" (1991, p 7).

The durée of the early- to mid-twentieth century witnessed the growth of sociology departments and programs in higher education, in addition to professional associations and theoretical texts dedicated to the field. As sociology developed and evolved in response to shifting historical contexts and diversifying theoretical perspectives, the scope of its analytic lens expanded. Branching off from economic models that viewed social action as arising from rational choice, interpretively oriented perspectives considered the symbols and values to which social action is keyed. Extending back to social theorists Max Weber, Emile Durkheim, Georg Simmel, George Herbert Mead, Talcott Parsons, Erving Goffman, Herbert Blumer, and others, this interpretive branch of sociology sought to "penetrat[e] beyond ... external form" to access the "inner meaning of actions, events, and institutions" (Alexander, 2003, pp 465–467). Yet this aim did not extend to the so-called "brute facts" of the natural world. Physical matter, including the body, continued to be viewed as unsociological—matter strictly "subject to the empirical rules of biological science," fixed, inert, and therefore impervious to "the mutability and flux of cultural change" (Csordas, 1994, p 1).

Amid the ferment of shifting political, economic, cultural, technological, and philosophical currents in the latter part of the twentieth century, the naturalness, constancy, and materiality of the body were cast into doubt, making the body available for new lines of inquiry and action. Among other changes, the civil rights and women's movements and the Rehabilitation Act of 1973, which extended civil rights to persons with disabilities, called into question what kinds of bodies matter and made the private body political (Frank, 1990; Turner, 1991; Shilling, 2012). Medical and technological advances, such as organ transplantation and in vitro fertilization, intensified the commodification of body parts and increased awareness of the body's malleability (Crawford, 1984; Scheper-Hughes, 2001). The converging forces of late-capitalist consumer culture, the health and beauty industries, and mass media and marketing transformed the discipline and control of ascetic attitudes toward the body into the embodied practices of self-care, self-expression, and self-actualization (Featherstone, 1982; Foucault, 1988; Turner, 1992, 2008; Davis, 1997). With the body having been reimagined as the *mutable* outer representation of the inner self, "body work" (Gimlin, 2002), or the managing of the aesthetic dimensions of the body, took on new moral significance and heightened anxiety (Bordo, 1993; Davis, 1997; Young, 2005), invigorating various "body projects" (Shilling, 2012)—dieting, fitness routines, fashionwear, antiaging regimens, cosmetic surgery, and body marking, among others (Turner, 1991, 1992, 2008; Bordo, 1993; Davis, 1997; Pitts-Taylor, 2003)—intended to publicly telegraph one's identity (Goffman, 1959; Giddens, 1991).

Philosophical and theoretical reflection on—and contestation of—the boundaries between meaning and matter spurred new conceptions of subjectivity and the body. Structural linguistics along with the semiotic turn in sociology advanced the argument that categories of identity, which conflate form with essence, "are not determined by the objects of the material world, but operate, and derive their differentiation, solely in relation to the system of language" (Olssen, 2003, p 190). From this view, the body is a material symbol posited through structural relations of oppositional meaning. Maintaining an interest in the role of language, especially in the form of narratives, discourses, and performative speech acts, while at the same time rejecting the formalism of structuralism, post-structuralist scholarship brought critical attention to the relations of power within which language, bodies, and identities are constructed. Michel Foucault (1978) foregrounded how embodied subjects are constituted through the disciplinary powers of discourse. Seeking to problematize the corporeal essentialism of the binary sex-gender order, feminist philosophers and sociologists wrote against the fleshiness of the body (Witz, 2000), exploring instead how social processes of representation rooted in historically white, patriarchal, heterosexist institutions are "deployed to legitimate [gendered and racialized] social relations of domination and subordination" (Davis, 1997, p 8) through constructed categories of difference.

Judith Butler's theory of gender performance is influential here. The body in Butler's philosophy comes to matter as an epiphenomenon of repeated enactment that unfolds within normative constraints. For Butler, just as there is no subject, no "I," no essence except that which is "manufactured through a sustained set of acts" (Butler, 1990, p xv), there is no discrete substance to the body. Bodies, Butler writes, "indicate a world beyond themselves, [and] this movement beyond their own boundaries, a movement of boundary itself, … [is] central to what bodies 'are'" (1993, p 9). There is a tendency in Butler's philosophy, as well as in other post-structuralist/feminist constructions, to eliminate agency—to theorize self and body, meaning and matter, as nothing more than the effects of power. Yet there is also a kernel of agency to be derived from Butler's suggestion that open-ended movement serves as the ontological ground of the body. The notion that the body defies definition because it is always gesturing beyond itself is evocative of the current of play, plasticity, and the possibility for resistance that characterizes deconstructionist and postmodernist perspectives. Emphasizing the highly mediated, individualized, contradictory, and therefore open and undecidable nature of social reality, deconstructionism and other postmodern perspectives prioritize individual agency, experience, interpretation, and knowledge over suprastructural forces and systems of relations (Rosenau, 2015).

In emphasizing individual agency and the undecidability of meaning, post-structuralist, deconstructionist, and postmodern perspectives effectively challenge the naturalization of binary hierarchies underlying Western philosophy and classical social theory (mind/body, immaterial/material, masculine/feminine, rational/emotional, civilized/primitive), yet critics have rightly pointed out the bodily blind spot of such perspectives; they overwhelmingly focus on language and discourse without applying constructionist perspectives to the "fleshy" matter of bodies themselves (Prosser, 1998; Witz, 2000; Epstein, 2002; Barad, 2007; Alaimo and Heckman, 2008; Pitts-Taylor, 2016b). Feminist materialisms (or neomaterialisms), for example, have offered a particularly powerful critique of dematerialized understandings of the body in feminist thought, aiming to readdress the physical body but without totally abandoning the insights offered by cultural constructionism and postmodernism (Alaimo and Hekman, 2008, pp 1–6).

The "coconstitution of nature and culture" (Pitts-Taylor, 2016a, p 10) is taken as the starting point of feminist materialism, but materiality is explicitly understood "not simply in social-structural but also in physical, biological, and natural terms" (Pitts-Taylor, 2016b, p 10). Additionally, there is an emphasis on reconceptualizing agency to include material agency, "to find a way to talk about the body as itself an active, sometimes recalcitrant, force" (Alaimo and Heckman, 2008, p 4). It is argued that without this ability, feminism and social-scientific scholarship will fail to meaningfully address "lived experience, corporeal practice, or biological substance" or effectively "engage with medicine or science in innovative, productive, or affirmative ways" (p 4). Attending to material agency means grappling with bodily differences and how material specificity matters—influencing both how social representations shape the experience of the body and how the body is able to determine its social representations (Pitts-Taylor, 2008, pp 25–26). Materiality, Victoria Pitts-Taylor notes, is always "specifically enacted in actual and differentiating conditions and contexts" (2016b, p 11) and is thus inextricable from and mutually constitutive of power and privilege.

Although we are persuaded by these critiques, we also find that most lack a clear analytic framework for moving beyond the limitations of discursive perspectives without lapsing into simplistic materialism. Some researchers borrow theoretical frameworks from other disciplines, such as quantum physics (Barad, 2007), to move beyond discourse while also avoiding material determinism. In this volume, we employ the focal metaphor of interpretation to return the important questions raised by feminist materialists and other critics of constructionist accounts of materiality to more explicitly sociological frameworks and theories. Interpretation as a concept is valuable for advancing the study of the body as a simultaneously material and semiotic entity. It directs us to consider how and why some aspects or details of the body and embodiment emerge as more notable or important than others, thus revealing how patterns of social, moral, or political salience generate the attentional topography of the body's materiality. For example, due to our cultural investments in gender difference, those aspects of the body that reflect such differences are imbued with more salience and moral/political attention than those body parts that reflect no such difference (Epstein, 1988, p 39; Laqueur, 1990; Lorber, 1994, p 39; Dreger, 1998; Fausto-Sterling, 2000; Lorber and Moore, 2007, p 15; Fine, 2010; Jordan-Young, 2010; Friedman, 2013). A similar argument can be made about the heightened concern for and attention to bodily racial differences due to their moral and political salience (Omi and Winant, 1986; Schwalbe et al, 2000; Brekhus et al, 2010; Feagin, 2010; Banaji and Greenwald, 2013; Friedman, 2016). Because interpretation potentially offers ways to account for both matter and culture without sacrificing either, it avoids the disembodiment of representation- and discourse-focused approaches while retaining important insights about the productivity of power and the way bodies are always and only known within discursive frameworks.

By facilitating reflection on how the body—as structuring and structured by social configurations of relevance and irrelevance, attention and inattention—actively participates in the "patterning of selves ... actions, and social systems" (Shilling, 2012, p 33), we aim to bring renewed theoretical and methodological attention to *processes* of interpretation and meaning production, specifically as they are articulated within and across the divergent yet oftentimes overlapping lenses of different theoretical traditions. In their introduction to the Interpretive Lenses in Sociology book series, in which this volume is situated, series editors Thomas DeGloma and Julie B. Wiest write that "taking the metaphor of the 'lens' seriously means considering how various approaches to interpretive analysis focus our analytic attention," making "assumptions about the character of data ... and what it can reveal," and "tun[ing] our vision differently at different angles of sight" (2022, pp 4–5). DeGloma and Wiest parse the many interpretive branches that make up the field of sociology's arbor into three "root" frameworks:

1) *Collective-formative framework*: The focal angle of this mode of interpretation articulates macro–micro links between the collective norms and systems of meanings that orient social life and individual action. This approach

conceives of meaning as inhering in dominant cultural codes that pattern individuals' thoughts, feelings, and everyday activities. The socializing, formative power of meaning may be theorized as functioning in relation to or as having significant autonomy over and above material and psychic conditions. Within the scope of this tradition, interpretive analysis focuses on the *shared* cultural foundations of symbols, meanings, emotions, cognitive-perceptual processes, and practices. Erving Goffman's (1974) framing theory, Pierre Bourdieu's (1977) formulations of habitus and field, Norbert Elias' (1978) "civilizing process," Michel Foucault's (1978) work on discourse and power, and the Strong Program in cultural sociology (Alexander and Smith, 2003) are just a few examples of the orientations one finds under this tent. The collective-formative framework has its intellectual origins in the classical perspectives of Emile Durkheim (1915) and Max Weber (1930).

2) *Interactive-emergent framework*: This interpretive lens focuses analytic attention on the dynamic emergence of shared meaning in social contexts. In contrast to the collective-formative framework, which generally approaches meaning as a collective reservoir from which social actors can readily draw, the interactive-emergent framework emphasizes the situated, dialogic, and therefore unpredictable conditions of meaning-making. From this view, meaning is an ongoing interactive accomplishment, something that must be made and continually remade. Candace West and Don H. Zimmerman's (1987) model of *doing gender*, actor-network theory (Latour, 2005) and new materialism perspectives that conceive of objects as social actors in their own right, and intercorporeal and interaffective theories of the "looking-glass," "dramaturgical," and "socio-semiotic" body (Goffman, 1959; Waskul and Vannini, 2006; Fuchs, 2017) highlight the relational contingencies of meaning-making. American pragmatism, with its focus on observable practical effects, and symbolic interactionism, as initially developed by George Herbert Mead (1934) and later formalized by Herbert Blumer (1986), are foundational to this perspective.

3) *Psychosocial framework*: This interpretive angle concentrates on the interior processes of mental life, focusing on how cognition is socially patterned and emanates from and contributes to social identities and group membership. Drawing from psychoanalytic theory as well as neuroscientific and cultural cognitive traditions, psychosocial approaches attend to meanings manifest as psychic structures and their cognitive, perceptual, and emotional connections to the social world. Exemplars of the psychosocial framework include Eviatar Zerubavel's (1991, 1997, 2015) work on "social mindscapes," classification, and attention, Asia Friedman's (2013) concept of perceptual filters, Arlie Hochschild's elaboration of "emotional labor" in her classic text *The Managed Heart* (1983), and Omar Lizardo et al's (2016) Dual Process Framework for understanding individual learning,

memory, thinking, and acting. Phenomenology is a prominent theoretical tradition within this framework, as are Lacanian and Freudian feminist perspectives (see Chodorow, 1989; Goldenberg, 1990).

These three distinct orientations to meaning have at times resulted in significant differences in emphasis and understanding among different interpretive schools of thought. Bringing the analytic perspectives of 12 scholars of the body together under one cover, this volume seeks to illuminate underlying programmatic tensions and connections in approaches to interpreting the body. Rather than provide a genealogy of common themes in body and embodiment studies, map the intellectual boundaries of the field, or attempt to systematically answer metaphysical questions about what a body is, reflecting the thematic scope of the Interpretive Lenses in Sociology series, we have sought to draw attention to the processes and problems of interpreting bodies across different social contexts and analytical angles of sight. This explicit attention to *process* is part of what distinguishes interpretation from prior concepts of the social construction of the body, which, when centered in systems of language, tend to overlook the structural or material processes and mechanisms through which the social construction of the body takes place, or, when rooted in the strong pragmatist perspective of praxis, emphasize objective actions, performances, and doings over the more internal processes of meaning-making (cf Prosser, 1998; Epstein, 2002; Barad, 2007; Alaimo and Heckman, 2008; Pitts-Taylor, 2016b).

Within the established paradigm of the social construction of the body, directing attention to interpretation can shed new light on the mechanisms and processes that engender material conditions of inequality, not in the least by revealing the reciprocal links that exist between meaning and power and, by extension, the production of symbolic and structural asymmetries—for instance, of in-groups versus out-groups or the pure versus impure—that underpin forms of institutional power and violence. Furthermore, exploring interpretation as a framework for thinking about the body allows for a reengagement with the materiality of the body while at the same time steering clear of simplistic understandings of biology as somehow accessible outside of cultural frameworks of meaning, especially gender and race but also age, ability, and sexuality. Focusing on the processes, problems, and mechanisms of interpretation presents a critical opportunity to conceptually bridge gaps of difference by asking ourselves how various interpretive lenses structure our epistemological understandings of the body and how the body's meaning and matter might be construed otherwise. Indeed, these are questions that thread the corpus of this volume.

In order to realize the potential of the volume's substantive theme, we requested that all contributors consider or reveal, implicitly or explicitly, two dimensions of interpretation and meaning within their work. We asked contributing scholars to explore how the subjects of their studies, cases, or reflections assign meanings and arrive at convergent or divergent understandings of the body. We further enjoined them to reflect on the interpretive lenses that they apply analytically and methodologically from within their respective research traditions, and in relation to others, that allow them as researchers and authors to access and identify these understandings. Motivated by this reflexive engagement with interpretation, the chapters gathered here stress different dimensions of body/embodiment—its influence, meaning, and matter. In the description of the volume's plan that follows, we introduce each chapter and elaborate these dimensions. In addition to outlining the interpretive lenses and "root" frameworks each scholar employs in their research and reflections on the body, we draw attention to how they marshal these frameworks to support, critique, or bridge core perspectives and illuminate their various entailments of meaning and matter.

In Chapter 1, "Toward a Strong Cultural Sociology of the Body and Embodiment," Anne Marie Champagne views the body through the hermeneutic lens of the Strong Program in cultural sociology. From this vantage, the body comes into being as a phenomenal meeting of horizons, a fusion between, among other dualities, ideality–materiality and subjectivity–objectivity. According to Champagne, the horizon of the body and the symbolic and material elements that comprise it are structured by dominant cultural codes, which reflect the collective representations that give meaning to and shape individuals' perceptions of their and others' bodies. This structuration of bodily meaning, she cautions, is not unidirectional. Because the body entails a fusion of ideal and material matter, it presents a uniquely mediating, reversible relation between the body and its embodiment in society. Self and society, Champagne contends, are reciprocally "constituted through the sensuous and performative workings of [the] physical body." For Champagne, culture is what sensitizes and completes the body and society, bringing each to material life. Hence, just as meaning depends on interpretation if it is to be comprehensible and shareable, the body is dependent upon interpretation for "getting itself out into the social world." Foregrounding the relative autonomy that the symbolic dimension of social life exercises over individuals' lived experiences, the focal perspective of Champagne's interpretive lens hews closely but not exclusively to the *collective-formative* framework. Applying a strong cultural analysis to three different scenarios of body modification—turning brown eyes blue with contact lenses, breast cancer-related mastectomy, and ritualized tooth extraction—Champagne also draws on the *interactive-emergent* and *psychosocial* traditions to elucidate the mutually powerful hand that sensuous contact with the outer world and internal processes of interpretation have in how individuals make sense of the body in society.

Looking to what bodies and consequently identities are made of, in Chapter 2, "Thinking the Molecular," Ben Spatz emphasizes a similar mutual relationship between the body's meaning and its substance. Working within the traditions of critical race theory, performance studies, and embodied artistic research, Spatz crafts a material-semiotic perspective on the body, which is used to show how the molecules that make up human (and nonhuman) bodies are at once materially and socially constructed through an iterative interpretive process that loops between *technique* (eg, disciplinary, political, and technoscientific practices) and *identity* (eg, cultural-identarian forces such as racial imaginaries). Processes of knowledge production are central to this circular relationship. As Spatz theorizes it, molecules of technique and identity emerge from repeated enactments of what one knows. Knowledge forms who we are, and identity is made of technique in the same way that technique, arising from who we are, is made of identity. Theorizing the molecular material-semiotic construction of the body and identity gives Spatz the necessary analytic leverage to contest the *collective-formative* hegemony of the natural sciences in determining what fundamentally constitutes the matter and reality of the body. It also provides an avenue for critiquing constructionist perspectives that treat the body and other material objects as passive matter "swept up into social and cultural discourse." Bringing theories of technique, identity, and molecularity to bear upon theories of the body and embodiment opens a space for exploring the moral heft of the molecular. As Spatz reminds us, the quantification and qualification of matter is not a neutral enterprise but one that takes place within asymmetrical relations of power—in racialized, gendered, and othered contexts. While privileging neither the material nor the symbolic dimensions of the body, the front-footing of the material in Spatz' *material-semiotic* lens offers a critical theory of the body that accents the ways in which the molecular asymmetries of racial and other identities substantively matter.

In "Interpreting Africa's *Seselelāme*: Bodily Ways of Knowing in a Globalized World" (Chapter 3), Kathryn Linn Geurts and Sefakor Komabu-Pomeyie explore recent trends in the Western appropriation, commodification, and interpretive distortion of the Anlo-Ewe phrase *seselelāme*, a term that conveys a particular "sensory-emotional, embodied way of knowing" enjoyed by West Africans. Comparing what Anlo-Ewe people of southeastern Ghana say about *seselelāme* to how yoga centers, fitness gurus, and other commercial enterprises in the Global North use and individualize the term, Geurts and Komabu-Pomeyie illuminate, by way of interpretive contrast, the particular intersubjective, phenomenological ground of *seselelāme* among the Anlo-Ewe. As something that emerges sensorily in the shared emotional rhythms of life, *seselelāme* expresses a modal phenomenon mediated by local historical knowledge and the contingencies of lived experience. It is not, therefore, some kind of universal category of thought, fixed sign, or identity that can be readily exported. Highlighting this, while at the same time being careful not to essentialize Anlo-Ewe ways of knowing, Geurts and Komabu-Pomeyie foreground the dynamic interweaving of *psychosocial, interactive-emergent*, and *collective-formative* interpretive frameworks that underpin the sociophysiological meanings of *seselelãme*. They also employ and refer to these frameworks to interrogate the institutional and geopolitical asymmetries in interpretive authority and communicative power that can have polluting and far-reaching material-symbolic consequences.

Focusing on interpretations of gendered and raced bodies in the context of colonialism, in Chapter 4, "Gender on the Post-Colony: Phenomenology, Race, and the Body in *Nervous Conditions*," Sweta Rajan-Rankin and Mrinalini Greedharry supplement Frantz Fanon's phenomenal-psychoanalytic perspective on racism and Black consciousness with postcolonial feminist and gender theory to present an intersectional close reading of Tsitsi Dangarembga's novel *Nervous Conditions*. Fanon's phenomenology, which centers on Black men's bodies, does not adequately theorize how gender and race are "a product of colonial ambitions to categorize, tame, discipline, and shape the colonized body." Rajan-Rankin and Greedharry thus frame "the problem of being a colonized woman" as being "constantly under erasure between gender and race." The physical body, they argue, "must disappear in order to resolve the tensions of colonized womanhood." Using Dangarembga's novel as an "organic theory of the native woman's body," they analyze "how African womanhood is negotiated and how girls' bodies are made available for, and find ways to resist, colonial architectures of power." Their analysis demands attention to the material specificity of bodies. Since the physical characteristics of bodies are never neutral but always interpreted through and taken up in social dynamics of power, the material specificity of the body matters for how one is perceived and for the kinds of social worlds different materialities make possible and preclude. In addition to their intersectional phenomenological approach, Rajan-Rankin and Greedharry's analysis incorporates an *interactive-emergent* framework for meaning, as illustrated, for one, in the way that the characters Tambu and Nyasha both experience their bodily pleasures as structured by family interactions rooted in social relations of race, gender, and colonialism.

In Chapter 5, "Reinterpreting Male Bodies and Health in Crisis Times: From 'Obesity' to Bigger Matters," Lee F. Monaghan takes a *collective-formative* approach to the male "obesity crisis," challenging medicalized "obesity epidemic" interpretive frameworks and the use of "health" discourse as a means of controlling socially deviant bodies. These social discourses of "obesity alarmism" largely focus on individual behavior change. Yet, as medical sociologists have demonstrated, individual health behaviors play very little role in health inequalities, which are largely macrostructural in nature, situated in the nested social-structural and symbolic systems of gender, medicalization, and neoliberal capitalism (with its attendant social inequalities of socioeconomic status and structural racism). Highlighting the kaleidoscopic complexities of these layered systems of meaning and structural inequality, Monaghan points out that "hegemonic narratives are also subject to considerable contestation and reframing." For instance, just considering gender and work, he points out that men's health is disproportionately impacted by a competitive work-oriented system and unemployment, yet masculinity can also provide a "status shield" that allows men symbolic recourse to resist fat-phobic discourse by invoking masculine norms of "occupying space" and masculine largeness that are not available to women. In light of this, medical and health policy solutions at the individual level are inadequate. In order to properly make sense of weight, health, and the body more broadly, health scholars, professionals, and policymakers must analytically attend to the complex intersections of these macrostructural discourses.

Piper Sledge initially applies a *collective-formative* framework to gender and mastectomy in Chapter 6, "Beauty, Breasts, and Meaning after Mastectomy," engaging macrolevel discourses of normative feminine embodiment and beauty that are institutionalized in medicine and breast cancer activism and which define dominant narratives of recovery. While these dominant discourses structure microlevel interactions and interpretations of the body after mastectomy, Sledge also finds that her participants are able to complicate macrostructural frames of gender and beauty and shift their interpretations of their embodied experience (in this case, of living flat after breast cancer) through interaction in interpersonal "communities of experience and supportive daily interactions that create pathways for new interpretations of beauty." Particularly when the embodied experiences in question challenge normative cultural frameworks, new interpretive filters can emerge through social interactions to make sense of them. Sledge thus identifies *interactive-emergent* frameworks that resist and allow for reinterpretation of dominant conceptual frameworks of gender and beauty.

In "'You Are Not the Body': (Re)Interpreting the Body in and through Integral Yoga" (Chapter 7), Erin F. Johnston, like Sledge, combines *collective-formative* and *interactive-emergent* approaches, demonstrating that the study of religious life must attend as equally to the linguistic, conceptual, and symbolic aspects of religious life, particularly forms of talk and discourse in situ, as it does to the practical, experiential, and embodied dimensions of religion. This dual focus is especially important given the interplay of the symbolic and the somatic that occurs in religious practice. In "You Are Not the Body," Johnston examines this "symbolic–somatic interplay" in the context of Integral Yoga, identifying the interpretive frameworks that yoga practitioners and instructors use to make sense of the body, specifically to cultivate bodily detachment, which is understood as necessary to become aware of and experience the "True Self." This "theology of the body," Johnston notes, is conveyed through the yoga teachers' verbal directions. She describes how, for instance, early in her participant observation as a teacher trainee, she did not recognize certain embodied experiences as moments of experiencing her "True Self" because she was not yet equipped with the correct language or conceptual framework for interpreting the somatic experience. Johnston argues that talk, as a form of interaction in situ, links the body to broader symbolic systems of interpretation, thereby enabling certain kinds of embodied experiences and the transmission of shared interpretive frameworks for making sense of them.

With a focus on race and gender in educational settings, in Chapter 8, "Black Girls' Bodies and Belonging in the Classroom," Brittney Miles likewise calls for bridging *collective-formative* and *interactive-emergent* perspectives on interpreting the body. Highlighting a range of inherited misogynist and anti-Black discourses, by way of which the meanings of Black girls' bodies are read and misread, Miles shows how these interpretive frameworks are centrally implicated in the reproduction of structural relations of inequality in schools. She specifically examines teachers' misinterpretations of Black female students' voice and body work. Exploring Black talk, sass, loudness and quietness, and focusing on dress and appearance in schools, she illustrates both how dominant racialized and gendered discourses emerge interactionally *and* how interaction can take the form of "embodied reverse discourse," a bodily practice of reappropriation that shifts meanings of gender and race, opening "conceptual space for the production of discursive counternarratives." While the body's meaning derives in tension, in the oppositional space between dominant and counter discourse, Miles acknowledges that *collective-formative* discourses, which hold more institutional authority, continually "work their way through microlevel interactions." Yet directing attention to the "interactional maneuverability" that enables embodied reverse discourse to emerge also "allows us to consider how Black girls' bodily negotiations may be understood differently when interpreted from their own perspective." Miles argues that symbolic interactionism provides a useful theoretical framework for recognizing these alternate interpretations and interactional shifts in sensemaking while still attending to dominant meanings.

"Our manner of making sense often impacts our sense experience," writes Chandra Russo in Chapter 9, "Embodied Vulnerability and Sensemaking with Solidarity Activists." Reflecting on her experience as an observer-participant involved in solidarity witnessing, a form of political protest in which activists collectively engage in physically demanding, vulnerabilizing strategies of resistance to raise awareness around issues of state violence, she considers how the interpretive interplay between affect, emotion, and culture underlying embodied vulnerability "becomes … meaningful to the task of research" and to social movements as "sensemaking projects." Interview and ethnographic excerpts from Russo's participation in the annual Migrant Trail Walk (in protest of US immigration policies) are particularly illustrative, showing how bodily labors precipitate interpretive labors. Protestors' affective experiences of pain and struggle, as they push their bodies to their physiologic limits, trigger strong emotions, which they interpret through the *collective-formative* frameworks of shared culture as well as the *interactive-emergent* pathways of verbal and intercorporeal dialog with one another. Additionally, Russo shows how the embodied vulnerability that solidarity witnesses experience prompts them, herself included, to reinterpret their bodies (and ethnographic data) by bringing into their awareness the privilege of protection afforded to some but not others on the basis of race, gender, and/or class. Linking bodily experience to interpretation, she presents a distinctively sociosomatic phenomenological account of knowledge construction in research and social movement activism.

The volume concludes with a biographical chapter exploring how researchers embody their scholarship and how their scholarship embodies them in turn. In Chapter 10, "Our Bodies, Our Disciplines, Our Selves," Annemarie Jutel reflects on the embodied roots of the development of her research program in the sociology of diagnosis. Similar to Russo's exploration (in Chapter 9) of how bodily experience can direct the researcher's methodology, Jutel posits that the researcher's body provides an interpretive framework for their choice of academic discipline. That disciplines offer *collective-formative* frameworks for interpreting the body is well known in body and embodiment literature. Here, Jutel highlights instead the way that embodied experience can also lead us to our academic disciplines and to the adoption of the interpretive tools they provide. She explains, "From a particular embodied stance (illness, diagnosis, catharsis), the scholar finds their discipline: locating it as a way of understanding, celebrating, or theorizing their physical existence in the world." Jutel illustrates this by tracing the trajectory of her own research and methodology, paying close interpretive attention to the embodied experiences at its roots. For example, she describes how her embodiment and identity as a woman runner (and later a cyclist) provided the impetus for understanding the construction of feminine frailty as a self-conscious "presencing" of the body that precludes full attention to the task at hand, and further how feminine self-scrutiny inscriptively engages moral aspects of body work whereby the surface of the body is taken as a reflection of its inner depths. Reinforcing the idea that our embodied experience underlies our academic research, Jutel draws from the well of her own lived experience to critique the positivist assumption that valid, "objective" research requires the evacuation of the researcher's embodied subjectivity. "Whether we realize it or not," she writes, "as scholars our embodied experience is at the root of our academic disciplines."

The contributions curated and juxtaposed in this volume are intended to offer insight into the relationships among lived experience, meaning-making, corporeality, materiality, research, and social construction. Individually and together they challenge the limits of what we know about bodies and interpretation, crafting new interpretive lenses in the process. Broadening the panoramic landscape of body and embodiment theory, they set new terms for what a body is and can be as an object of study and what a body can be and do in the social world. They affirm, each in their own way, that to interpret the body is to define and redefine the imaginable, imagined, and not yet imagined *stuff of life*.

## References

Alaimo, S. and Hekman, S. (2008) 'Introduction: emerging models of materiality in feminist theory', in S. Alaimo and S. Hekman (eds) *Material Feminisms*, Bloomington: Indiana University Press, pp 1–19.

Alexander, J.C. (2003) *The Meanings of Social Life: A Cultural Sociology*, Oxford: Oxford University Press.

Alexander, J.C. and Smith, P. (2003) 'The Strong Program in cultural sociology: elements of a structural hermeneutics', in J.C. Alexander (auth) *The Meanings of Social Life: A Cultural Sociology*, Oxford: Oxford University Press, pp 11–26.

Banaji, M.R. and Greenwald, A.G. (2013) *Blindspot: Hidden Biases of Good People*, New York: Delacorte Press.

Barad, K. (2007) *Meeting the Universe Halfway: Quantum Physics and the Entanglement of Matter and Meaning*, Durham, NC: Duke University Press.

Blumer, H. (1986) *Symbolic Interactionism: Perspective and Method*, Berkeley: University of California Press.

Bordo, S. (1993) *Unbearable Weight: Feminism, Western Culture, and the Body*, Berkeley: University of California Press.

Bourdieu, P. (1977) *Outline of a Theory of Practice*, Cambridge: Cambridge University Press, 2013.

Brekhus, W.H., Brunsma, D.L., Platts, T. and Dua, P. (2010) 'On the contributions of cognitive sociology to the sociological study of race', *Sociology Compass*, 4(1): 61–76.

Butler, J. (1990) *Gender Trouble: Feminism and the Subversion of Identity*, New York: Routledge, 2010.

Butler, J. (1993) *Bodies That Matter: On the Discursive Limits of 'Sex'*, New York: Routledge, 2011.

Chodorow, N.J. (1989) *Feminism and Psychoanalytic Theory*, New Haven, CT: Yale University Press.

Comte, A. (1975) *Auguste Comte and Positivism: The Essential Writings*, edited by G. Lenzer, Piscataway, NJ: Transaction Publishers.

Crawford, R. (1984) 'A cultural account of "health": control, release and the social body', in J. McKinlay (ed) *Issues in the Political Economy of Health Care*, New York: Tavistock, pp 60–103.

Csordas, T.J. (1994) 'Introduction: the body as representation and being-in-the-world', in T.J. Csordas (ed) *Embodiment and Experience: The Existential Ground of Culture and Self*, Cambridge: Cambridge University Press, 1997, pp 1–26.

Davis, K. (1994) 'Embody-ing theory: beyond modernist and postmodern readings of the body', in K. Davis (ed) *Embodied practices: Feminist Perspectives on the Body*, London: SAGE, pp 1–27.

DeGloma, T. and Wiest, J.B. (2022) 'On the multidimensional foundations of meaning in social life: an invitation to the series *Interpretive Lenses in Sociology*', Bristol: Bristol University Press, available from: https://bristoluniversitypress.co.uk/asset/11003/de-gloma-wiest-series-editors-article.pdf.

Douglas, M. (1970) *Natural Symbols: Explorations in Cosmology*, London: Routledge, 2010.

Dreger, A.D. (1998) *Hermaphrodites and the Medical Invention of Sex*, Cambridge, MA: Harvard University Press.

Durkheim, E. (1893) *The Division of Labor in Society*, translated by W.D. Halls, New York: The Free Press, 1984.

Durkheim, E. (1895) *The Rules of Sociological Method*, edited by S. Lukes, translated by W.D. Halls, New York: The Free Press, 1982.

Durkheim, E. (1915) *The Elementary Forms of the Religious Life*, translated by J.W. Swain, New Orleans, LA: Quid Pro Books, 2012.

Elias, N. (1978) *The Civilizing Process: The History of Manners*, translated by E. Jephcott, New York: Urizen Books.

Epstein, C. (1988) *Deceptive Distinctions: Sex, Gender, and the Social Order*, New Haven, CT: Yale University Press.

Epstein, S. (2002) 'A queer encounter: sociology and the study of sexuality', in C. Williams and A. Stein (eds) *Sexuality and Gender*, Malden, MA: Blackwell, pp 44–59.

Fausto-Sterling, A. (2000) *Sexing the Body: Gender Politics and the Construction of Sexuality*, New York: Basic Books.

Feagin, J.R. (2010) *The White Racial Frame: Centuries of Racial Framing and Counter-Framing*, New York: Routledge.

Featherstone, M. (1982) 'The body in consumer culture', *Theory, Culture and Society*, 1(2): 18–33.

Fine, C. (2010) *Delusions of Gender: How Our Minds, Society, and Neurosexism Create Difference*, New York: W.W. Norton and Co.

Foucault, M. (1978) *The History of Sexuality: An Introduction*, translated by R. Hurley, New York: Vintage Books, 1990.

Foucault, M. (1988) *The History of Sexuality: The Care of the Self*, New York: Vintage Books.

Frank, A.W. (1990) 'Bringing bodies back in: a decade review', *Theory, Culture and Society*, 7(1): 131–162.

Friedman, A. (2013) *Blind to Sameness: Sexpectations and the Social Construction of Male and Female Bodies*, Chicago, IL: University of Chicago Press.

Friedman, A. (2016) '"There are two people at work that I'm fairly certain are Black": uncertainty and deliberative thinking in blind race attribution', *The Sociological Quarterly*, 57(3): 437–461.

Fuchs, T. (2017) 'Intercorporeality and interaffectivity', in C. Meyer, J. Streeck and J.S. Jordan (eds) *Intercorporeality: Emerging Socialities in Interaction*, Oxford: Oxford University Press, pp 3–24.

Giddens, A. (1991) *Modernity and Self-Identity*, Cambridge: Polity Press.

Gimlin, D (2002) *Body Work: Beauty and Self-Image in American Culture*, Berkeley: University of California Press.

Goffman, E. (1959) *The Presentation of Self in Everyday Life*, New York: Anchor Books.

Goffman, E. (1974) *Frame Analysis: An Essay on the Organization of Experience*, Boston, MA: Northeastern University Press, 1986.

Goldenberg, N.R. (1990) *Returning Words to Flesh: Feminism, Psychoanalysis, and the Resurrection of the Body*, Boston, MA: Beacon Press.

Hochschild, A.R. (1983) *The Managed Heart: Commercialization of Human Feeling*, Berkeley: University of California Press.

Jordan-Young, R. (2010) *Brain Storm: The Flaws in the Science of Sex Differences*, Cambridge, MA: Harvard University Press.

Laqueur, T. (1990) *Making Sex: Body and Gender from the Greeks to Freud*, Cambridge, MA: Harvard University Press.

Latour, B. (2005) *Reassembling the Social: An Introduction to Actor-Network-Theory*, Oxford: Oxford University Press.

Lizardo, O., Mowry, R., Sepulvado, B. et al (2016) 'What are dual process models? Implications for cultural analysis in sociology', *Sociological Theory*, 34(4): 287–310.

Lorber, J. (1994) *Paradoxes of Gender*, New Haven, CT: Yale University Press.

Lorber, J and Moore, L.J. (2007) *Gendered Bodies, Feminist Perspectives*, Los Angeles, CA: Roxbury.

Mead, G.H. (1934) *Mind, Self and Society from the Standpoint of a Social Behaviorist*, Chicago, IL: University of Chicago Press, 2015.

Olssen, M. (2003) 'Structuralism, post-structuralism, neo-liberalism: assessing Foucault's legacy', *Journal of Education Policy*, 18(2): 189–202.

Omi, M. and Winant, H. (1986) *Racial Formation in the United States*, New York: Routledge.

Parsons, T. (1948) 'The position of sociological theory', *American Sociological Review*, 13(2): 156–163.

Pitts-Taylor, V. (2003) *In the Flesh: The Cultural Politics of Body Modification*, New York: Palgrave Macmillan.

Pitts-Taylor, V. (2008) 'Introduction', in V. Pitts-Taylor (ed) *The Cultural Encyclopedia of the Body, Vol. 1*, Westport, CT: Greenwood Press, pp xvii–xxviii.

Pitts-Taylor, V. (2016a) *The Brain's Body: Neuroscience and Corporeal Politics*, Durham, NC: Duke University Press.

Pitts-Taylor, V. (2016b) 'Mattering: feminism, science, and corporeal politics', in V. Pitts-Taylor (ed) *Mattering: Feminism, Science, and Materialism*, New York: New York University Press, pp 1–20.

Prosser, J. (1998) *Second Skins: The Body Narratives of Transsexuality*, New York: Columbia University Press.

Rosenau, P.V. (2015) 'Postmodernism: methodology', in J.D. Wright (ed) *International Encyclopedia of the Social and Behavioral Sciences* (2nd edn), Amsterdam: Elsevier, pp 680–683.

Scheper-Hughes, N. (2001) 'Bodies for sale – whole or in parts', *Body and Society*, 7(2–3): 1–8.

Schwalbe, M., Holden, D., Schrock, D., Godwin, S., Thompson, S. and Wolkomir, M. (2000) 'Generic processes in the reproduction of inequality: an interactionist analysis', *Social Forces*, 79(2): 419–452.

Shilling, C. (2012) *The Body and Social Theory* (3rd edn), London: SAGE.

Taylor, C. (1995) 'Two theories of modernity', *The Hastings Center Report*, 25(2): 24–33.

Taylor, P.J., Hoyler, M. and Evans, D.M. (2008) 'A geohistorical study of "the rise of modern science": mapping scientific practice through urban networks, 1500–1900', *Minerva*, 46: 391.

Turner, B.S. (1991) 'Recent developments in the theory of the body', in M. Featherstone, M. Hepworth and B.S. Turner (eds) *The Body: Social Process and Cultural Theory*, London: SAGE, pp 1–35.

Turner, B.S. (1992) *Regulating Bodies: Essays in Medical Sociology*, London: Routledge.

Turner, B.S. (2008) *The Body and Society: Explorations in Social Theory* (3rd edn), Los Angeles, CA: SAGE.

Wallerstein, I. (1989) *The Modern World-System III: The Second Era of the Great Expansion of the Capitalist World-Economy, 1730–1840s*, New York: Academic Press.

Waskul, D. and Vannini, P. (2006) *Body/Embodiment: Symbolic Interaction and the Sociology of the Body*, New York: Routledge.

Weber, M. (1930) *The Protestant Ethic and the Spirit of Capitalism*, London: Routledge, 2008.

West, C. and Zimmerman, D (1987) 'Doing gender', *Gender and Society*, 1(2): 125–151.

Witz, A. (2000) 'Whose body matters? Feminist sociology and the corporeal turn in sociology and feminism', *Body and Society*, 6(2): 1–24.

Young, I.M. (2005) *On Female Body Experience: 'Throwing Like a Girl' and Other Essays*, Oxford: Oxford University Press.
Zerubavel, E. (1991) *The Fine Line: Making Distinctions in Everyday Life*, Chicago, IL: University of Chicago Press.
Zerubavel, E. (1997) *Social Mindscapes: An Invitation to Cognitive Sociology*, Cambridge, MA: Harvard University Press.
Zerubavel, E. (2015) *Hidden in Plain Sight: The Social Structure of Irrelevance*, New York: Oxford University Press.

1

# Toward a Strong Cultural Sociology of the Body and Embodiment

*Anne Marie Champagne*

> For the task of intellectuals is not only to explain the world; they must interpret it as well.
> — Jeffrey C. Alexander, *The Meanings of Social Life: A Cultural Sociology*

Formerly noteworthy for its muted absence from sociological theory, the body with which contemporary theory concerns itself is no less remarkable despite it no longer being silent or absent (Williams and Bendelow, 1998; Shilling, 2012). Since the corporeal turn in sociology in the 1980s, considerable attention has been given to body studies across multiple academic disciplines within the humanities and social sciences (Shilling, 2016). As with other epistemic shifts, this turn has led to a proliferation of approaches to understanding the social ontology of the body and its constitutive role in the embodiment and production of social life and the self. Many of these approaches—including, among others, the *culturally pragmatic* (see Champagne, 2018; Broch, 2020),[1] *phenomenological* (see Merleau-Ponty, 1945; Leder, 1990; Csordas, 1994; Young, 2005), *interactionist* (see Waskul and Vannini, 2006), and *praxeological* (see Goffman, 1959; Garfinkel, 1967; Bourdieu, 1977; Foucault, 1978b; Butler, 1990)—highlight the body's embedment in symbolic horizons of meaning.[2] Yet, in spite of sharing a common interest in the cultural dimensions of the body and embodiment, there is scarcely agreement among scholars working within these traditions about what culture is (is it a fairly stable system of shared meanings or an emergent property of social interaction?), where it is located (in the mind or among things?), and whether it has ordering power (does it play a powerful or feeble role in structuring social life?). Neither is there a settled consensus regarding the role interpretation plays in constituting the "landscapes of meaning" (Reed, 2011, p 92) that shape and transform a person's sense of the social world nor the bodies and embodiments that may co-constitute that landscape. Is the body a "sign-bearing, sign-wearing" (Bourdieu, 1984, p 190) surface off of which we unconsciously read social-symbolic value? Or is it also a fecund reservoir of sensibility and imagination from which culture's webs of signification are spun (Geertz, 1973)? Is the body determined by actions alone or is it something one completes through meaning-making (Turner, 1991)?

The dissensus I have outlined here, while hardly exhaustive, is representative of outstanding debates regarding the relative autonomy of culture (Alexander and Smith, 2003). At the heart of these debates are competing understandings of the degree to which symbols and meanings comprise an ideal (value-oriented), as opposed to an instrumental (task-oriented), resource capable of suffusing bodies and materialities with a motivational—nay, motifactional—moral significance that animates social actions, norms, and structures.[3] In this chapter, I leverage these intellectual tensions concerning the relative autonomy of culture to advance the possibility of a strong cultural sociology of the body, one that approaches the body as a unique hermeneutical situation—a fusion of subject–object, ideality–materiality, constraint–potential, and other continua—structured by cultural codes and dependent upon interpretation for getting itself out into the social world.

I begin, in the sections that follow, with a rudimentary but instructive review of how culture and the body have been thematized in modern, postmodern, and contemporary sociology, often along ideal versus instrumental (or material) fault lines inherited from early sociological thought. Then, following a brief description of how a strong cultural, meaning-centered approach to body and embodiment stands in contradistinction to softer cultural approaches that treat culture as an artifact, I outline the three methodological commitments that define Strong Program cultural sociology (SPCS): (1) recognizing the relative autonomy of culture; (2) hermeneutically reconstructing meaning structures; and (3) utilizing what Isaac Ariail Reed (2011) refers to as "maximal interpretations" to explain how culture shapes and directs social reality (see also Alexander and Smith, 2003). Since length limitations preclude a thoroughgoing analysis of a data-rich empirical study, in order to elaborate the theoretical power of SPCS relative to other approaches, I introduce brief empirical examples excerpted from my and others' accounts of embodied social phenomena that illustrate each methodological commitment, applying the tools of analogy and interpretation to draw out their implications for interpreting the body and embodiment.

## Culture and the body: modern, postmodern, and contemporary themes

*The "absent presence" of culture and the body in early sociology*

Both culture and the body, as general sociological topics, share a unique position within the history of social theory. Until the last quarter of the twentieth century, sociology paid little to no heed to the integral significance of either culture or the body in social life (Fraser and Greco, 2005; Shilling, 2012, 2016). This neglect is due in part to sociology's positivist legacy, which tended to reduce human action to instrumental behavior, the body to a brute fact, and, following Cartesian dualism, separated mind from body and reason from nature (Robertson, 1988; Turner, 1991; Williams and Bendelow, 1998; Alexander, 2003). Having located the social self in the reasoning mind, and having dismissed culture as either irrelevant or, worse, a primitive and ignorant adherence to tradition, early sociology conceived for its "modern" subject the disembodied, rational actor who responded and adapted to the pressures of social structures "'larger' and more 'powerful'" than themselves (Robertson, 1988; Seidman, 1994; Howson and Inglis, 2001; Alexander, 2003, p 4). Such a legacy not only blunted sociology to the meaningful interiors of social actors and social structures, it also occluded from its view the interpretive fasciae, or symbolic connective tissues, that fuse soma and other materialities with meaning.

This bare-bones sketch of early sociology's (dis)engagement with culture hardly conveys the subtlety of cultural thought alive and well among its foundational theorists, but its tenor nevertheless rings true. Certain fin de siècle classical sociologists did acknowledge the historical and structural importance of cultural phenomena such as ritual, totemism, and collective representations (Durkheim, 1915), ideological spirits (Weber, 1930), and cultural forms (Simmel, 1971), but after the 1920s, once sociology was thoroughly professionalized as a problem-solving, scientific discipline,[4] culture, narrowly conceived as either a *product of* (Mead, 1934) or a *resource for* (Bourdieu, 1977) social interaction, was cast to the periphery.

In a similar fashion, the body was inferred but not thematized in the culturally inflected theories of classical as well as pre- and early postwar sociology. In *Elementary Forms*, Emile Durkheim acknowledges the body's unique inscriptive capacity, in particular its receptivity to tattooing, which makes it an expedient surface for emblematizing collective social life (1915, pp 221–225). Georg Simmel's (1971) menagerie of social types—inter alia, the stranger, the miser, the spendthrift, and the adventurer—implicates distinctive bodies and embodiments. One glimpses, as Chris Shilling (2012) does, the body's performative dimension in the asceticism of the Calvinist "calling" described in Max Weber's (1930) writings on the protestant ethic. Talcott Parsons' psychoanalytic model of social internalization presumes an embodied social actor (O'Neill, 1998). And despite George Herbert Mead's (1934) relegation of the body to the world of objects, the gesturing body is an essential feature of symbolic interactionism.

The exclusion of both culture and the body from the foundational subject matter of sociology is emblematic of the disciplinary boundary work that historically served to distinguish sociology from other scientific disciplines such as anthropology, psychology, and medicine (Turner, 1992; Calhoun et al, 2009). The positivist epistemology undergirding this disciplinary boundary work likewise erected rigid divisions between the realm of ideas and spirit and the realm of matter and science. The resulting cleavage posed a subjectivist–objectivist dilemma regarding culture's, but also the body's, place in theories of social action: Was culture a relatively autonomous system of shared meaning providing motifactional ideals and context for social action? Was it an epiphenomenon of action providing an expedient set of cognitive tools for directing practices? Or was it, as the body came to be understood, merely a condition of action, something determined by "other structures—of a more material, less ephemeral kind" (Alexander, 2003, p 5)?

The *homo economicus* intellectual style of early twentieth-century sociology presupposed this dilemma.[5] As a "rational" science interested in explaining how *objective* social forces structure human action, sociology was resistant to meaning-centered explanations on the grounds that they dealt with *subjective* matter, notably the symbolic foundations of myth, narrative, imagination, and emotion, which putatively had no place in modern society (Robertson, 1988; Alexander, 2003). The human body in classical and modern sociology underwent a comparable process of dichotomization. The biological reductionism of viewing the body as raw material excluded the knowledge, experience, and intentions of the lived body; and the idea of the disembodied rational actor, emblematic of modern conceptualizations of subjectivity, neglected the myths, motifs, and metaphors through which individuals apprehend and articulate their and others' bodies. Setting reason on par with the divine, and giving it dominion over the natural world, this rational model of self and society imputed a dualistic mind-over-matter hierarchy to the human body, principally in the form of a differential physiognomy of the sexes.[6]

Positioning culture and the body on the side of subjectivity-idealism in counterpoint to reason-society established the symbolic and methodological boundaries against which classical, "modern" sociology defined itself as an impersonal, objective science concerned with social order (Turner, 1992; Grosz, 1994; Howson and Inglis, 2001; Alexander, 2003; Fraser and Greco,

2005). To approach either culture or the body as anything other than the incidental tools and products of rational actors and institutions would have been anathematic to the scientific logic of the discipline. Shoring up sociology's disciplinary borders therefore included defending them against the profanation of "unsociological" approaches. To study meaning, feeling, and the body-subject as formative social forces in their own right was tantamount to polluting and disordering the discipline.

What changed? Explanations of the turn in the late twentieth century to culture and the body emphasize sociopolitical, economic, and cultural shifts in modes of production, consumption, and identity construction. Among the drivers of these changes, scholars frequently cite postindustrialization, late capitalism, and globalization (Robertson, 1988; Jameson, 1991; Martin, 1992; Turner, 2008); commercialization, digitalization, and the rise of consumer culture (Featherstone, 2007; cf Woodward, 2012); second-wave feminism (Turner, 1992, 2008); and the linguistic turn (Alexander and Smith, 2003). Underscoring the symbolic basis of economic-cum-social action, these interpretive shifts precipitated new conceptualizations of subjectivity and the body that undermined Marxian materialist critiques of ideology that specified culture narrowly in terms of class and political interests (see Robertson, 1988; Haraway, 1994; Turner, 1995; Alexander, 2003; Featherstone, 2007). Reconfiguring the relationships between technology, economy, and the self, these theoretical shifts expanded sociology's disciplinary canopy while also calling the generalizing tendency of modern social theory into doubt. While the scope of this chapter prevents me from elaborating these shifts, more germane to the thematization of culture and the body within sociology is their shared challenge of having to contend with the conflicting intellectual "impulses" (Frank, 1991) or "moods" (Lyotard, 1984) of the modern and postmodern (cf Featherstone, 1989). To assert the possibility of a strong cultural sociology of the body, we must first assay certain key fractures and conjunctions between modern and postmodern thought—for the recovery of the body and culture in contemporary sociology, as well as the development thereafter of SPCS, presents, each in its own way, a countercurrent to and/or a reconfiguration of the foundational logics of the modern and postmodern.

*Interpreting modernity: the postmodern crisis of meaning and cultural thematization of materiality and the body*

When discussing postmodernity it is important to clarify that the prefix "post" does not signify a periodizing break with modernity so much as an interpretive break. Characterized by an attitude of incredulity toward the grand narratives and systematizing impulses of modern social theory, postmodernism favors the decentered authority of subjective interpretation (Lyotard, 1984; Featherstone, 1989, 2007; Seidman, 1994; Bordo, 1998;

Susen, 2015). Privileging the ever-fleeting present over historical continuity, postmodernism rejects cultural theories of text, meaning, and explanation rooted in notions of coherence and connectivity (Featherstone, 2007). Consequently, as with modern positivist thinking, it eschews tradition. It also dispenses with traditional hermeneutic interpretations, since these maintain that a singular moment or event becomes meaningful only when placed in relation to a greater whole (Dilthey, 1976; Alexander, 2008).

In the main, postmodernism polemicizes against the modern on two interrelated fronts, the epistemological and the temporal. In place of historically situated, discursively grounded knowledge, it posits a plurality of equally valid interpretations with no fixed or collective meaning. In place of a system of signs, it posits a protean landscape of image-impressions (Jameson, 1991), a hyperplastic reality of textual drift in which all is text but text that is free-floating. Instead of *a* text, *a* subject, or *an* object, we are given flows, networks, and assemblages—relational velocities and intensities (Deleuze, 1992). And instead of a meaning-filled history, we are given "a series of perpetual presents" (Featherstone, 2007, p 5), a horizon of unweighted differences and the enduring promise of interminable self-reinvention.

There is a striking, though flawed, egalitarianism to the idea of a social world comprised of boundless, decentered subjectivities, where everything can mean anything and no interpretation is judged correct or incorrect. Because postmodern *egalité* flattens out meaning through equivalency, it inadvertently exchanges one homogenizing impulse for another (cf Bordo, 1998). To wit, the interpretive interchangeability that distinguishes the kaleidoscopic postmodern mood imposes a sublime universalism, that of the inescapable irreconcilability of difference, which promulgates a "crisis of representation" (Susen, 2015, p 95). For a discipline that seeks to explain social action and primarily concerns itself with problems of order, postmodernism is untenable. This is not to suggest that postmodernism failed to transform sociological thought for the better. In making such a radical turn away from objectivity and collective meaning toward subjectivity and private knowledge, postmodernism challenged modernity's essentialist claims to a common world and the hegemony of solidaristic models of social stability. What is more, the ontological uncertainty that arose from this challenge inspired new directions for sociological thought, especially with respect to culture and the body.

Reconceptualizing the material and psychical phenomena that make up our social world in terms of subjective processes comprised of sensations and pleasures, affects and feelings, and styles and representations, postmodernism opened sociological thought to phenomenological, post-structuralist, and praxeological theories of subject formation. These approaches understand the self to be an "effect and function of … public and social discourse" and the "acts which constitute its reality" (Butler, 1990, p 185). Neither reducible to the mind nor to nature, neither exclusively a subject nor an object, the *social self* is an embodied *being in the world* (Merleau-Ponty, 1945), a *situation* (de Beauvoir, 1949) experienced and enacted in a given context and therefore constrained but not entirely determined by an array of guided doings (Merleau-Ponty, 1945; Goffman, 1974). Inseparable from the material world, the socially constructed self implicates an altogether different metaphysics, one in which self and body, being the co-constitutive products of an ongoing achievement (Garfinkel, 1967), are inherently malleable and multiple yet ontologically durable—the perfect nexus for self-cultivation through bodily practices, interactions, and projects (Gimlin, 2002), which, although sometimes personal and idiosyncratic, remain accountable to collective interpretation.

In addition to facilitating the thematization of the body as a social fact worthy of study, constructivist inquiry into how one becomes a socially embodied self insinuated culture's involvement. Given early sociology's general relegation of culture to the purportedly *nondeterminative* sides of the material–*ideal* and objective–*subjective* dualisms of the time, the postmodern impulse toward fragmentation that had spurred new questions about subject formation and the body also reinvigorated interest in the symbolic dimensions of social life. Extending beyond the confines of language and discourse, explorations into the culture structures underpinning self and society began to reconsider the material (physical, empirical, economic, etc) elements of meaning-making, especially with respect to how individual meanings become collectively shared facticities and thus "an essential part" of the description, interpretation, explanation, and materialization of "social facts" (see Berger and Luckmann, 1966, p 18; Reed, 2011, p 2).

This more reflexive examination of *how* culture operates on and through (and can even formulate) material forces amounted not so much to a nostalgic backlash against postmodernism as it did a neo-modern effort to overcome the material–ideal divide (Robertson, 1988; Alexander, 2003). Marking what some have dubbed "the cultural turn," social scientists involved in this effort sought to demonstrate the constitutive role of culture in all domains of social life (Alexander and Smith, 2003). Doing so called for liberating the internal, ideational dimension of social action from economic determinism and moral equivalency without reinstating an overly macro-social, *integrationist*, or micro-social, *voluntaristic*, view of social cohesion (Robertson, 1988; Alexander, 2003; Featherstone, 2007; Susen, 2015; Simko and Olick, 2021). For SPCS in particular, this meant reasserting, à la Durkheim, the understanding that society expresses an observable, concrete, living reality—a living reality constructed from categories of experience and thought that filter, represent, and activate underlying social relations and which take part in the ideas and symbols individuals use to describe those relations (see Durkheim, 1915, pp 17–19; Alexander and Smith, 2003).

If the objects and interpretive conceptual tissues that comprise collective human experience appear to be mere illusion, as the postmodernists and post-structuralists assert, it is not because there is no *there* there. Rather, it is because "to the immediate data given by the senses" something extra is added, and that *something* is the psychical force of moral sentiment and feeling that we draft from the society in which we live (Durkheim, 1915, pp 203, 225–226, 348).

At the heart of Durkheim's conception of culture lies an interdependent relationship between individual and society mediated by material objects. Individuals give expression to ideas and experience by "fix[ing] them upon material things which symbolize them" (Durkheim, 1915, p 228). Subjectively, these ideas and experiences may be idiosyncratic. However, if they are to be shareable, they must necessarily connect to the shared categories of meaning upon which social life is organized (Durkheim, 1915; Mead, 1934; Alexander, 2003). The perdurance of society depends upon this very process of signification. If not for the materialization of signs and institutions—those "entities that don't sleep" (Latour, 2005, p 70)—individuals would have to assemble the common ground of social sentiment anew, from scratch, moment to moment, interaction to interaction. This would hardly be efficient or conducive to the social coordination of meanings necessary to support complex collective organization and action. The process of signification that takes place through the interrelationship of individuals, objects, and background representations allows us to quickly reassemble the social in our daily interactions, give it material form, and circulate it beyond ourselves, so that, in transcending both time and place, we feel its enduring structure as something living, natural … real.

The symbolic foundation of society that Durkheim illuminates in *Elementary Forms* is a central feature of the Strong Program in cultural sociology. If society is a web of crystalized relations between material things (signifying surfaces) and collective sentiments (discursive depths), then culture is the skein from which that web and bodies are woven (see Durkheim, 1915; Alexander, 2003; Reed, 2011). Furthermore, each "crystallization" within this web presents not an object—or *the body*—as such but an articulation of our interpretive "grasp on the world," aka "situation" (de Beauvoir, 1949, p 68). The task of the cultural sociologist is to tease out this skein to reveal the interpretive-symbolic connections that structure and support every articulation of social life, including the conditions of body and embodiment that make articulation possible. It is with this charge in mind that I propose the possibility of developing a strong cultural sociology of the body and embodiment.

## Toward a strong cultural sociology of the body and embodiment

An SPCS of the body and embodiment acknowledges that self and society are constituted through the sensuous and performative workings of a physical body that is situated within a historically and geographically contingent symbolic order (cf Crossley, 1995; Champagne, 2018). Consequently, an SPCS approach to the body and embodiment concerns itself with the material-symbolic dimensions of the corporeal body and its lived experience (see Broch, 2020, for an example). The particular focus of this concern stands in contradistinction to behaviorally oriented approaches that view the symbolic dimension of the corporeal and lived body as either a background participant in or a byproduct of objective structures, behavioral practices, and power (Merleau-Ponty, 1945; Bourdieu, 1977, 1984; Swidler, 1986; Butler, 1990, 1993; Frank, 2012). By restricting the meaningfulness of the lived body to whatever lines of action external conditions and power structures permit, these approaches reduce the body (and culture) to an instrumental toolkit made up of techniques, capitals, and tropes that individuals strategically deploy to meet the demands of a given social context (Goffman, 1959, 1974; Bourdieu, 1977, 1984; Swidler, 1986; Frank, 2012), or they treat the body as a discursive tabula rasa upon which meaning inscribes and reveals itself through gestures, performances, and displays (Mead, 1934; Goffman, 1959, 1974; Foucault, 1978a, 1999; Butler, 1990).

Taking a different interpretive tack, I contend that neither the tasks of the body nor the practical rules of the social game alone can tell us what a body is or means. Barring some deeper anchorage to underlying collective sentiments or structures of feeling, routinized action lacks the emotional, moral valence necessary to serve as a structural basis for the shared system of ideas we call society. Since a strong cultural perspective views all forms of materiality and materially mediated experiences as being imbricated "to some extent in a horizon of affect and meaning" (Alexander and Smith, 2003, p 12), it seeks to reach beyond surface examinations of "what a body does" or "what is done to a body" (Crossley, 1995, p 43) to uncover the deeper meaning structures that situate the workings of the physical and lived body within broader discourses and narratives that are themselves part of a symbolic system that patterns interpretation *and* practice. Indeed, the interpretive lens of SPCS is particularly well suited to this type of work. If we consider embodiment to comprise a meaning-filled relation between the physical and the lived body and thus between the localized self and the social world, then to understand that relationship requires an interpretive sociology capable of teasing apart the symbolic ligatures that bind sensation to sense and, in turn, materiality to meaning. What is needed, I argue, is a strong cultural sociology of the body and embodiment.

*The interpretive methodology of a strong cultural sociology of the body and embodiment*

Three methodological commitments distinguish the interpretive impulse of a strong cultural sociology of the body. Drawing on Jeffrey C. Alexander and Philip Smith's (2003) Strong Program in cultural sociology and Reed's (2011) cultural work on meaning and interpretation, I characterize these three commitments as follows:

1. treating culture as an independent variable, thereby acknowledging its analytical autonomy from social-structural determinations of body and embodiment;
2. applying hermeneutic methods to reconstruct the underlying culture structures that contour the "landscapes of meaning" (Reed, 2011) in and out of which the body, qua embodied situation, is constructed; and
3. utilizing "maximal interpretation" (Reed, 2011) to explain how culture disrupts and directs social reality—its landscapes of meaning, social structures, and thus body and embodiment.

In the subsections that follow, I describe these three methodological commitments in greater detail, contextualizing each in relation to a specific example of body modification—changing brown eyes to blue with contact lenses (Bordo, 1998), breast cancer-related mastectomy (Champagne, 2018), and ritualized tooth extraction (Durkheim, 1915)—in order to further highlight their specific implications for research on body and embodiment and to illuminate, more generally, the explanatory purchase that a strong cultural sociology of the body can grant researchers and others interested in the theory and matter of the body.

*Cultural codes and the relative autonomy of culture*

One of the most distinctive characteristics of SPCS is its recognition of the relative autonomy of culture. It also is its most controversial and, I would argue, misunderstood characteristic. By treating culture as an independent and thus relatively autonomous variable (Alexander and Smith, 2003), SPCS seeks to interpret and explain how cultural codes, namely in the form of contrastive oppositions thought to be fundamental to meaning-making, shape social structures and action. Criticisms of SPCS generally take one of two forms: an argument against the bracketing out of culture from social structure, on the grounds that it ignores the behavior-restricting effects of systematic relations of power, or a question regarding the ontological validity and explanatory relevance of binary cultural codes.[7] I will address the second of these criticisms first, before turning to a discussion of their implications for the reciprocal production of meaning and power.

With respect to binary cultural codes, it is not the Strong Program's position that social phenomena must be slotted into mutually exclusive categories. Rather, SPCS contends that the *cultural meanings* that pattern social life are constructed through comparative relationships of difference. Some of these relationships are oppositional (*this*–not-this) while others are more associative (similar-to-but-different-from–*this*). We need only to look to the binary sex-gender order to find examples of each of these. For instance, whereas the marked (*not*-male) sex-gender category "female-feminine" is understood in opposition to the unmarked category "male-masculine," we find on either side of this binary an associative relationship between sex and gender (eg, masculine gender being associated with but different from male sex). And yet, as this example likewise shows, the affinity of meaning between corresponding sexes and genders (ie, *cis*gender) is conditioned upon this prior opposition between the marked and the unmarked. I must emphasize here that there is nothing inherently "real" about these categories. They are socially constructed through relational contrast. It is also important to note that despite being relatively stable, binary codes can lose their conventional meaning, become obsolete, or be replaced by new binaries. However, while they remain in play, binary codes constrain and enable the infinite number of possible divisions and affinities that can exist between them,[8] and it is this potential for arranging and containing the proliferation or collapse of salient divisions that speaks to issues of moral valence and power.

In *The History of Sexuality*, Michel Foucault (1978a, p 93) asserts that power is not something endowed within a given point or source, it is everywhere. Power, he argues, is a substrate (think creative matrix). Imagine tension evenly distributed across the threads of a stretched canvas. What happens when you tug or press on a section of the canvas? A redistribution of force creates puckers, warps, asymmetries—differences that develop into salient formations. These formal effects are what we come to interpret as power; power is still everywhere, just not evenly distributed. Foucault refers to these effects, these formations, as "force relations" (1978a, pp 92–94), but we could just as well apply the terminology of other analytical perspectives with little to no adulteration. We might, for example, think of them as symbolic "distinctions," as observable locations within a social-symbolic field (Bourdieu, 1984). Or we might think of them as perceived lines or poles of potential action (Mead, 1934; Merleau-Ponty, 1945; Goffman, 1959, 1974) whose forms are made intelligible through an interpretive framework such as a cultural schema or frame (Goffman, 1974), perceptual filter (Friedman, 2013), or cultural script (Alexander, 2004).

Terminology aside, what each of these propositions share in common is a reliance upon collective representations, or shared classificatory contexts.

Just as power is everywhere, so too is meaning. Neither power nor meaning is endowed. Each must be made, and meaning in particular is made through symbolization—through interpretive processes of classification (distribution) that cluster and divide human experience into the more or less crystalized force relations of meaning we come to know and share as categories of experience, feeling, and thought, significant gestures, and classifiable bodies. In short, one cannot divide the substrate of lived experience into socially intelligible, citable classifications without creating a contrastive boundary, an inside and outside, that copresents a relation of power. Like power in my analogy of tugging on an evenly stretched canvas, "the grip of culture" (Bordo, 1998) makes matter meaningful, but not equally meaningful; some matter is characterized positively and some negatively.[9] And so it stands to reason that meaning matters and that the hermeneutic reconstruction of meaning eschewed by postmodernism, but embraced by SPCS, offers an interpretation of the symbolic relations of power as well as their material stakes.

Consider Susan Bordo's (1998) plea for recognizing the perils of flattening out meaning when we ignore the historicity and cultural contexts of "beautifying" body projects. In "Material Girl," Bordo critiques a 1988 episode of the Phil Donahue Show in which the host asked a purposively diverse audience whether advertisements for DuraSoft colored contact lenses, which proposed to "get brown eyes a second look" by making them appear violet, were racist. The audience answered "No." Changing one's eye color was a "matter of creative expression," a form of free play no different than putting on makeup or styling one's hair (Bordo, 1998, p 48). Under the banner of "free play," the audience viewed "*all* cosmetic changes as … having equal political valence … and cultural meaning" (p 48), which is to say, as Bordo points out, no valence or meaning at all.

What the show's audience members may not be consciously self-aware of is exactly what the cultural sociologist seeks to bring to light: the *taken-for-granted* forms of meaning—the cultural codes—that scaffold social action and give materiality its negative or positive charge. The implication of the rhetoric of "free play"—that choice is free of connotation, that self-determination is unlimited, and that meaning-making is up for grabs—belies the cultural mediation of materiality that constrains and enables meaning as well as choice. The historicity of gendered and racialized codes of civility/incivility and the beautiful/sublime establishes, along with other background representations, a "pedagogy" of beauty that specifies different "requirements … for different groups" and ensures that not all body transformations are commensurate (Bordo, 1998, pp 48–49). The devaluation of dark skin and natural Black hair is one example of how racial discrimination relies on cultural signification to exploit the material affordances and limitations of the physical body. It also highlights that the meanings we impute to the body and bodily action are what give the body its moral weight. Material affordances and technology may, like culture itself, enable or constrain bodily agency, but, as Bordo notes, a white female celebrity's cornrows and a Black woman's hair straightening are not equivalent practices. She writes, "When Oprah Winfrey admitted … that all her life she has desperately longed to have 'hair that swings from side to side' … she revealed the power of racial as well as gender normalization, normalization not only to 'femininity,' but to the Caucasian standards of beauty" (p 49).

To heed Bordo's critique is to recognize that relations of power congeal between poles of meaning, which themselves delimit potential lines or poles of action (Merleau-Ponty, 1945). What is more, these meaning structures are often hidden beneath the surface of witnessable practices. Thus the cultural sociologist of the body must use the tools of interpretation to excavate the cultural forms of moral sentiment that bring us from sheer corporeality (body) to lived corporeality (embodiment), to that which is enfleshed rather than simply inflected with meaning.

*The hermeneutic reconstruction of meaning*

Strong Program cultural sociology employs the interpretive lens of hermeneutic reconstruction to show how the elemental structures of culture—myth, narrative, discourse, and symbols—form the basis of social life (Durkheim, 1915; Alexander and Smith, 2003; Woodward, 2012). Culture, like society, does not live alone in the mind. To be knowable and endure, it must be given form and put into relation. Wrought through and upon material and corporeal forms, culture allows us to locate meaning in, as well as impute it to, the body and lived experience, such that we "touch symbols when we think we are touching bodies and material objects, and vice versa" (Paz, 1969, p 69). This reversible fusion of materiality and meaning allows us to (re)make and "[re]finish ourselves" (Geertz, 1973) and our bodies by way of culture and thus to be embodied as well as have a body.

To better understand the phenomenology of reversibility, it is helpful to imagine the mutually implicative relationship that exists between the body and the embodied self in analogical terms. Both a material and symbolic form, object as well as subject, the embodied self conjoins the parallel figures of *somatics and semiotics*—of bodily surfaces conjoined with signified depths; of *sense and sensibility*—of physical sense impressions being bound to processes of symbolization; and of *text and textuality*—of the physical body-as-project, or work, and its ongoing interpretive entextualization (see Barthes, 1977; Csordas, 1994).

What each of these analogies conveys is the notion of an embodied self that at once experiences thingness and beingness, something that can touch as well as be subject to touch and that can interpret as well as be subject to interpretation. Most of the time we are not consciously aware of our bodies. Nor are we generally aware of, as my discussion of Bordo (1998) in the previous section suggests, the body's interpretive fusion with meaning, that is, its embodiment or the quality of being invested with a living value (Merleau-Ponty, 1945, p 52). This is because in the immersive flow of everyday life, the body, as Drew Leder describes it, "not only projects outward in experience but falls back into unexperienceable depths" (1990, p 53). The inexperienceability to which Leder refers brings to mind a related phenomenon common to processes of signification, and that is the sign's reliance upon the repression—the inexperienceability—of the relational gap between form and content. Regardless of the form in which it is given (be it a sense impression, a feeling, material surface, or image) the sign is not a thing in and of itself but rather an articulation of terms, most simply of a material signifier (form) and a signified (content).[10] When it successfully represses the relational gap between these two terms, the sign tricks us in a way to conflate form with content, content with meaning, and meaning with form. This is what allows us to transform an object into a subject-object, to fuse a physical body with a situated, meaning-filled embodied self—to throw together sense-cum-sensibility and text-cum-textuality and touch ideas when we think we are touching or engaging with material forms. We can identify this quite readily in binary gender systems of meaning wherein a soft, voluminous, curvilinear chest is interpreted normatively as feminine and constitutes a key marker for identifying female subjects in social space (Champagne, 2018).

In short, processes of signification and interpretation work together. A sign has meaning when it articulates an interpretative relation between a signifying surface and a signified depth. The elemental structures of culture are what help to fuse the relational gap between terms and make interpretations stick. They assist the interpretive process by forming a type of material-cultural fascia between "a living structure and its environment" (Dilthey, 1976, p 236) or, correspondingly, between self and society, body and embodiment, experience and meaning. Yet, just as we normally remain unaware of our individual body despite it being ever present (Leder, 1990), these elemental culture structures are not always available to us at the level of practical consciousness (see Garfinkel, 1967; Goffman, 1974; Bourdieu, 1977). Consequently, the deep meanings that cultural sociologists seek to bring out may not be "immediately obvious to the investigator or to the investigator's subjects" (Reed, 2011, p 36) even though meaning, like power, is everywhere. What is needed, then, is a method of analysis that allows the investigator to dearticulate the sign (given to us, like embodiment, as a whole) in order to identify its underlying cultural codes that structure the webs of meaning within which the embodied self is suspended. Hermeneutic reconstruction provides such a method.

In the hermeneutic tradition, the part is understood in relation to the whole, and vice versa. In classical hermeneutic philosophy, this relay exemplifies the interpretive work that takes place at the interactional horizon between a text and a reader. But this relation is applicable to any interpretive horizon, be it between the familiar and the unfamiliar, an existing schema and new information, or the local and the global, to name but a few. To approach the body hermeneutically is to conceptualize it as proposing a fusion of interpretive horizons—as constituting a meaning-relation between the physical body and the lived body and, therefore, between the localized embodied self and the social world. Maintaining a deep interest in these points of fusion, a hermeneutical, strong cultural sociology of the body brackets out nonsymbolic structures in order to foreground the cultural codes and interpretive processes that bind individual sense experience, and the material body more generally, to systems of meaning.

This meaning-centered approach stands in stark contrast to materialist and praxeological approaches that either reject interpretation outright (cf Latour, 1996) or reduce meaning to a behavioral relation between objectivities (cf Mead, 1934; Bourdieu, 1984). Hewing too closely to observable effects is like mistaking the movements of a weathervane for the wind itself. People need not observe a weathervane to know windiness, not when they already have stories and metaphors about and an aesthetic sense of the wind. How people handle meanings is not always conspicuous, and sometimes meaning construction happens in our most intimate moments. To access the inconspicuous requires an interpretive lens with an aperture wide enough to isolate meaning structures from within and against their experiential backgrounds. Narrowly pragmatic, action-centered approaches are simply too restrictive to attend to the structures of meaning within which "objective" actions, flows, and displays are, themselves, relationally interpreted and produced. Consequently, they do not permit us appreciable insight into how social actors locate and relocate themselves through sensuous, embodied webs of meaning, which, having both a subjective and an objective component, can prevail even when their objective conditions have changed.

Such is the case with breast cancer-related mastectomy, where the derangement of normative objective relations (ie, breastedness with biological sex) is believed to effectuate a "biographical disruption" necessitating repair (Bury, 1982; Champagne, 2018). Whereas materialist-praxeological perspectives emphasize a need for materially (or mimetically) restoring the taken-for-granted homology between breastedness and female sex (and by association femininity), discursive-constructivist perspectives emphasize a need for narrative (or diegetic) repair (Champagne, 2018). An SPCS hermeneutical approach walks a line between the two, giving us a way to understand how meanings are activated and reactivated through a combination of ritual-like everyday practices, materiality, and narrativity.

Take, for instance, this account of a daily parent–child interaction ritual presented to me (see Champagne, 2018) by Holly, a 40-something, nonreconstructed, Black female breast cancer survivor. As you read it, see if you can identify where the phenomenon of reversibility occurs and how it creates a part-to-whole relationship between the present and the past. Then ask yourself: What sort of meaning is reconvening here?

> With my son, because he was breastfed and he was still co-sleeping with me, and he'd still touch them [my breasts] for comfort, we had conversations constantly in preparation of this drastic change [mastectomy]. To this day [postmastectomy], his hand will still go in my shirt, and he's like, "The skin is still so soft." And that's just like heartwarming—that *that's* not a big deal [to him].

When Holly says "that *that's* not a big deal [to him]," she is referring to the absence of her breasts. What makes this embodied encounter particularly "heartwarming" is that it retains and reinforces, for Holly and her son, the familiarity of a premastectomy bonding ritual and its attendant meanings. That Holly's nonreconstructed chest has retained an element of its original softness creates a sensuous, mimetic, material and therefore durable link between Holly's former healthy breast and her currently mastectomized chest. It therefore permits, under new material conditions, the reconvening of some of the deeper meanings of *wellness* previously articulated by the reversable arrangement held between a soft material surface, the breast, and ideas of feminine wholeness. Here, meaning is restored not by recreating a breast mound but by reconnecting embodied experience (a part) to deeper meanings established over time (a whole). This is a distinctively hermeneutic, interpretive process, one that strictly pragmatic approaches to the body are ill-equipped to explain.

### *Maximal interpretation: theory, description, and explanation*

There is a tendency in the social sciences to equate interpretation with description. It may indeed be the case that social meanings are made visible through experiential contact with descriptively discrete arrangements of form, such as symbols or things (Cassirer, 1957; Alexander, 2008, 2010; cf Champagne, 2018), but that does not mean that description alone is capable of conveying the social significance of those arrangements. Because meaning-making involves a hermeneutic relation between part and whole, one cannot presume to comprehend the proverbial forest by merely mapping out its trees. In *The Interpretation of Cultures*, Clifford Geertz asserts that "cultural analysis is (or should be) guessing at meanings, assessing the guesses, and drawing explanatory conclusions from the better guesses," not charting, like a cartographer, the surface "continent[s] of meaning" (1973, p 20). Geertz dubbed his interpretive method *thick description*, not because it is rife with detailed observation but because every guess, being comprised of interpretations of other people's interpretations, is already thickly layered with meaning. The aim of analysis, then, is not to render empirical observations in exhaustive detail. The goal is to unpack their conceptual worlds—the underlying signifying structures, the symbolic webs (or "fasciae" as I have referred to them elsewhere) that connect parts to wholes—in order to evaluate and explain "their social ground and import" (Geertz, 1973, p 9). Cultural analysis of this type seeks to disclose the insinuated symbolic background within and against which bodies and social action are observed. To do this, to "ferret out" the hidden landscapes of social meaning, requires a combination of thick description and analytical abstraction, a fusion of evidence and theory that cultural sociologist Isaac Ariail Reed (2011) defines as *maximal interpretation*.

According to Reed, building a maximal interpretation involves moving between the signs of fact, which we easily infer from empirical observation, and the signs of theory, which reflect more comprehensive understandings of "the causes and consequences of social action in many times and places" (2011, p 24). The purpose of hermeneutically tacking back and forth between these two sets of signs is to bring a piece of theory to bear upon a piece of evidence in order to excavate the "deeper social force ... or underlying discursive formation" (p 23) it conceals and thereby move beyond an initial minimal interpretation of evidence to develop a new maximal interpretation capable of expressing the cultural-symbolic depths of the empirical facts at hand. To better understand the relationship between evidence and theory and the difference between minimal and maximal interpretations that Reed is proposing, let us examine a brief example from Durkheim's *Elementary Forms* (1915, p 116):

> Among the Arunta, the extraction of teeth is practised only in the clans of the rain and of water; now according to tradition, the object of this operation is to make their faces look like certain black clouds with light borders which are believed to announce the speedy arrival of rain, and which are therefore considered things of the same family.

Durkheim has provided a minimal interpretation of an Arunta bodily practice. With only a basic semantic understanding of terms, one can make connections between the reported events and conclude from the evidence that the mimetic correspondence between tooth extraction and certain black clouds accounts for the observed behavior.

While all interpretation begins with evidence, or signs of fact, which Durkheim has furnished in the quoted example, facts alone do not constitute a maximal interpretation. And although mimetic similarity can both constrain and motivate highly iconic forms of emblematization that are no less rich in constructed meaning than symbols that are devoid of such "natural" correspondence, this particular interpretation of an Arunta rite of passage fails to move beyond explicit knowledge and thin description to reconstruct the deeper collective representations—here, the myths, believed supernatural relations, complexes of meaning with no obvious relation to the signifying form, and so forth—that not only present a unifying external marker of identity to this segment of the Arunta population but also give to them a sense of participating in a shared moral life.[11] In other words, a symbol may be "thick" with significance, but a social scientist's interpretation of that significance is only maximal when it (1) moves beyond description and evidence to unpack and reconstruct the underlying "webs" of meaning that have been condensed and subsumed under the sign-symbol, which may take the form of a ritual or practice, and then (2) disentangle this "webbing" for others by abstracting it through an explanatory theoretical lens (cf Geertz, 1973; Reed, 2011). To move from minimal to maximal interpretation, Durkheim would have to apply theoretical signifiers, such as his notion of the *totemic principle* or *collective consciousness*, in order to illuminate how the feeling of sacred communion (collective consciousness) that the Arunta experienced while gathered together and acting in unison can be given emblematic (totemic) expression, such that the collective sentiment of unity they previously experienced may continually reconvene in the material presence of their missing teeth long after the original extraction event has transpired. This—the application of theoretical signifiers and interpretation to evidence—is maximal interpretation.

Certainly SPCS is not the only cultural approach to bring theory to bear upon empirical facts, but it does so with a meaning-centered understanding of culture and the body. This distinction is important, not in the least because where we locate meaning and thereby define culture affects how we theorize body and embodiment. For SPCS, the meanings that give the lived body its moral depth are not the byproducts of objective structures (Bourdieu, 1977, 1984), uses (Mead, 1934), or tasks (Frank, 1991). Nor are they confined to the cultural and economic capitals or the expressive garb that individuals respectively mobilize or strategically don and doff to differentiate themselves from others (Goffman, 1959; Bourdieu, 1984). This is not to suggest that observable behavior and structures are not riven with meaning but rather that meaning is not reducible to them.

In the same vein as the aphoristic warning that one "[can]not see the forest for the trees," to presume to know the embodied self solely from the performative doings of the physical body—to consider the act everything (cf Butler, 1990)—loses sight of the underlying sentiments that give the lived body and social action their organizing moral, motifactional force. This moral force is not intrinsic to things themselves, but it also does not emerge from the irruption of either material or gestural matter upon the senses (see Mead, 1934; Latour, 2005, p 80). Actions are meaningful only when they find anchorage in a shared symbolic system, such as a common discourse. Meaning, therefore, is neither an "hallucinatory effect" of repetition (Butler, 1990) nor the perceptibility of deviation from a mean (Canguilhem, 1978; Foucault, 1999). As Durkheim reminds us, neither the habitual rising and setting of the sun nor its occasional eclipse can account for the religious feeling of awe or the myths we impute to it (1915, pp 28–29, 84). By way of analogy, it is not the appearance of performative regularity (or irregularity) or the presence of material affordances that account for the body's significance but rather the horizons of meaning within which these perceptual phenomena are embedded and through and out of which the lived body is constructed (Butler, 1993; Champagne, 2018).

The meanings and personalities that the "imagination place[s] behind things" (Durkheim, 1915, p 77) are enabled by the collective representations of culture. These representations allow us to connect "from within the confines of the skin to what lies beyond [as well as within our] bodily frame" (Dewey, 1934, p 13). As both matter and idea, the body comprises a fundamental medium through which we are brought into direct, interpretive contact with the conceptual tissues and material anchors that hold meaning in place. Through the surfaces of the body, we connect culture to sensuous form and sensuous form to culture, not only praxically or through ratiocination alone but, more durably, by way of sense, feeling, emotion, affect, imagination, and symbolization—the very personal means of mind–body connection that undergird our individual and collective representations.

If, as Alexander asserts, "interpreting is a way of positioning, of saying who we are" (2008, p 158), then it may be said that the lived body, in calling out to itself, actively participates in its own meaning-making, and in so doing helps each of us to formulate our own maximal interpretations of the self and society. As the nexus of self and world, body and embodiment are already thick with meaning. So it is the task of the strong cultural sociologist to draw equally thick, maximal interpretations of the culture structures that give body and embodiment their significance.

## Conclusion

In this chapter I advance the possibility of developing a meaning-centered, strong cultural sociology of the body and embodiment, one that approaches body and embodiment as constituting a uniquely hermeneutical situation—a fusion of subject and object, ideality and materiality—structured by cultural codes and dependent upon interpretation for getting itself out into the social world. Tracing the thematization of culture and the body along the modern, postmodern, and neo-modern analytical impulses (or moods) that are still present in contemporary sociological thought, I show how competing understandings regarding the degree to which symbols and meanings comprise a relatively autonomous and ideal (as opposed to dependent and instrumental) resource have shaped how each of these impulses define and locate the cultural dimension of social life. In this manner, I concordantly show the degree to which each analytical mood considers culture a "motifactional" (Black, 1994) force capable of suffusing bodies and materialities with moral significance and thus capable of animating and structuring social action. Situating the Strong Program in cultural sociology within the neo-modern context, I specify its methodological commitments to the relative autonomy of culture, hermeneutic reconstruction, and maximal interpretation, claiming each of these for the development of a strong cultural sociology of the body and embodiment. Such a program is, I argue, uniquely suited to ferreting out the conceptual tissues—the personal and collective representations, senses and sensibilities—through which the physical body comes to embody *self*, *society*, and *world*.

## Notes

[1] For a full discussion of cultural pragmatics as a macro-sociological model of social action *qua* cultural performance, see Alexander (2004).

[2] In this paper I use the term praxeological to distinguish perspectives of subject formation that emphasize the role of practices worked on or through the body (eg, disciplines, displays, doings, performances) from those that emphasize meaning-making or interpretation.

[3] Philosopher David Black argues that motives, which we tend to think of in the value-neutral terms of cause and effect, are mitigated by underlying motifs (narrative patterns, themes, and metaphors) that "not only move[ ] us from one moral place to the next, but also create the moral places we move among" (1994, p 361). In contrast to motivation, which supposes an instrumental, means–ends relationship to action, motifaction refers to a narrativistic orientational power that directs action.

[4] The professionalization of sociology as a nomothetic science directed toward policy is due in part to the pragmatic and statistical traditions of, respectively, the Chicago School and Columbia University (see Calhoun et al, 2009).

[5] See Turner's (1992, p 33) discussion of Weber, Pareto, and Parsons and the interaction between sociology and economics.

[6] Bodies coded male/masculine were associated with the morally elevated Apollonian characteristics of objectivity, rationality, form, and order, whereas bodies coded female/feminine were associated with the morally abased Dionysian characteristics of subjectivity, emotion, formless content, and disorder (see Nietzsche, 1993; Grosz, 1994).

[7] See Alexander and Smith (2010) contra Stoltz (2021). If, as Stoltz argues, representational signs do not derive their meaning in opposition to other signs, then culture may still exercise relative autonomy from other social structures, just not vis-à-vis a system of binary oppositions.

[8] Consider that on a number line there exists between 0 and 1 an infinite number of divisions—divisions that are locatable by their proximity to and distance from the flanking integers. Similarly, the proliferation of identifiable genders in the American context occurs

within a relational and therefore self-referential system—expressly, in reference to the outer male–female representational poles of a binary sex-gender order.

[9] See Bordo's (1998, p 52) reference to the "Doll Test" used in the *Brown v. the Board of Education* court hearings to demonstrate the negative effects of segregation on children's attributions of positive and negative value, which varied according the presented doll's skin color.

[10] According to Barthes (1964, p 47), because a signifier mediates the associative elements—objects, images, and discourses—of a sign, some matter is necessary to it; the signifier is, therefore, always material (eg, a sound, an image, an object).

[11] For further discussion on a variety of related issues, including the distinction between icons and symbols, motivated and unmotivated signs, etc, see Charles S. Peirce (1955), Roland Barthes (1957, especially "Myth as a Semiological System," "The Form and the Concept," and "The Signification"), Ernst Cassirer (1957, in particular Chapter 2 "Concept and Object" and his discussion of intuitive symbolic reality on p 319), Claude Lévi-Strauss (1966, specifically Chapter 1 "The Science of the Concrete"), Mary Douglas (1970), Ferdinand de Saussure (1972), Jeffrey C. Alexander (2010), and Anne Marie Champagne (2018).

## References

Alexander, J.C. (2003) *The Meanings of Social Life: A Cultural Sociology*, Oxford: Oxford University Press.

Alexander, J.C. (2004) 'Cultural pragmatics: social performance between ritual and strategy', *Sociological Theory*, 22(4): 527–573.

Alexander, J.C. (2008) 'Geertz and the Strong Program: the human sciences and cultural sociology', *Cultural Sociology*, 2(2): 157–168.

Alexander, J.C. (2010) 'Iconic consciousness: the material feeling of meaning', *Thesis Eleven*, 103(1): 10–25.

Alexander, J.C. and Smith, P. (2003) 'The Strong Program in cultural sociology: elements of a structural hermeneutics', in J.C. Alexander (auth) *The Meanings of Social Life: A Cultural Sociology*, Oxford: Oxford University Press, pp 11–26.

Alexander, J.C. and Smith, P. (2010) 'The Strong Program: origins, achievements, and prospects', in J.R. Hall, L. Grindstaff and M. Lo (eds) *Handbook of Cultural Sociology*, London: Routledge, pp 13–24.

Barthes, R. (1957) 'Myth today', in R. Barthes (auth) *Mythologies*, translated by R. Howard and A. Lavers, New York: Hill and Wang, 2013, pp 215–274.

Barthes, R. (1964) *Elements of Semiology*, translated by A. Lavers and C. Smith, New York: Hill and Wang, 1977.

Barthes, R. (1977) *Image, Music, Text*, translated by S. Heath, New York: Hill and Wang.

Berger, P.L. and Luckmann, T. (1966) *The Social Construction of Reality: A Treatise in the Sociology of Knowledge*, New York: Anchor Books.

Black, D.W. (1994) 'Rhetoric and the narration of conscience', *Philosophy and Rhetoric*, 27(4): 359–373.

Bordo, S. (1998) '"Material girl": the effacements of postmodern culture', in D. Welton (ed) *Body and Flesh: A Philosophical Reader*, Oxford: Blackwell, pp 45–59.
Bourdieu, P. (1977) *Outline of a Theory of Practice*, Cambridge: Cambridge University Press, 2013.
Bourdieu, P. (1984) *Distinction: A Social Critique of the Judgement of Taste*, London: Routledge, 2010.
Broch, T.B. (2020) *A Performative Feel for the Game: How Meaningful Sports Shape Gender, Bodies, and Social Life*, London: Palgrave Macmillan.
Bury, M. (1982) 'Chronic illness as biographical disruption', *Sociology of Health and Illness*, 4(2): 167–182.
Butler, J. (1990) *Gender Trouble: Feminism and the Subversion of Identity*, New York: Routledge, 2010.
Butler, J. (1993) *Bodies That Matter: On the Discursive Limits of 'Sex'*, New York: Routledge, 2011.
Calhoun, C., Duster, T. and Van Antwerpen, J. (2009) 'The visions and divisions of American sociology', in S. Patel (ed) *The ISA Handbook of Diverse Sociological Traditions*, London: SAGE, pp 114–125.
Canguilhem, G. (1978) *The Normal and the Pathological*, translated by C.R. Fawcett and R.S. Cohen, New York: Zone, 2007.
Cassirer, E. (1957) *The Philosophy of Symbolic Forms, Volume 3: The Phenomenology of Knowledge*, New Haven, CT: Yale University Press.
Champagne, A.M. (2018) 'Beauty and the breast: mastectomy, materiality, and the iconicity of gender identity', paper presented at the American Sociological Association Annual Meeting, August 9, Philadelphia, PA.
Crossley, N. (1995) 'Merleau-Ponty, the elusive body and carnal sociology', *Body and Society*, 1(1): 43–63.
Csordas, T.J. (1994) 'Introduction: the body as representation and being-in-the-world', in T.J. Csordas (ed) *Embodiment and Experience: The Existential Ground of Culture and Self*, Cambridge: Cambridge University Press, 1997, pp 1–24.
De Beauvoir, S. (1949) *The Second Sex*, translated by C. Border and S. Malovany-Chevallier, New York: Vintage Books, 2011.
De Saussure, F. (1972) *Course in General Linguistics*, Chicago, IL: Open Court, 2009.
Deleuze, G. (1992) 'Ethology, Spinoza and us', in J. Crary and S. Kwinter (eds) *Incorporations*, translated by R. Hurley, New York: Zone, pp 625–633.
Dewey, J. (1934) *Art as Experience*, New York: Perigee, 1980.
Dilthey, W. (1976) *Selected Writings*, edited by H.P. Rickman, Cambridge: Cambridge University Press.
Douglas, M. (1970) *Natural Symbols: Explorations in Cosmology*, London: Routledge, 2010.

Durkheim, E. (1915) *The Elementary Forms of the Religious Life*, translated by J.W. Swain, New Orleans, LA: Quid Pro Books, 2012.

Featherstone, M. (1989) 'Towards a sociology of postmodern culture', in H. Haferkamp (ed) *Social Structure and Culture*, New York: Walter de Gruyter, pp 147–172.

Featherstone, M. (2007) *Consumer Culture and Postmodernism* (2nd edn), London: SAGE.

Foucault, M. (1978a) *The History of Sexuality: An Introduction*, translated by R. Hurley, New York: Vintage Books, 1990.

Foucault, M. (1978b) *Discipline and Punish: The Birth of the Prison*, translated by A. Sheridan, New York: Vintage Books, 1995.

Foucault, M. (1999) *Abnormal: Lectures at the Collège de France 1974–1975*, translated by G. Burchell, New York: Picador.

Frank, A.W. (1991) 'For a sociology of the body: an analytical review', in M. Featherstone, M. Hepworth and B.S. Turner (eds) *The Body: Social Process and Cultural Theory*, London: SAGE, pp 36–102.

Frank, A.W. (2012) 'The force of embodiment: violence and altruism in cultures of practice', in J.C. Alexander, R.N. Jacobs and P. Smith (eds) *The Oxford Handbook of Cultural Sociology*, Oxford: Oxford University Press, pp 698–721.

Fraser, M. and Greco, M. (2005) 'Introduction', in M. Fraser and M. Greco (eds) *The Body: A Reader*, New York: Routledge, pp 1–42.

Friedman, A. (2013) *Blind to Sameness: Sexpectations and the Social Construction of Male and Female Bodies*, Chicago, IL: University of Chicago Press.

Garfinkel, H. (1967) *Studies in Ethnomethodology*, Cambridge: Polity Press, 1989.

Geertz, C. (1973) *The Interpretation of Cultures*, New York: Basic Books.

Gimlin, D. (2002). *Body Work: Beauty and Self-Image in American Culture*, Berkeley: University of California Press.

Goffman, E. (1959) *The Presentation of Self in Everyday Life*, New York: Anchor Books.

Goffman, E. (1974) *Frame Analysis: An Essay on the Organization of Experience*, Boston, MA: Northeastern University Press, 1986.

Grosz, E. (1994) *Volatile Bodies: Toward a Corporeal Feminism*, Bloomington: Indiana University Press.

Haraway, D. (1994) 'A manifesto for cyborgs: science, technology, and socialist feminism in the 1980s', in S. Seidman (ed) *The Postmodern Turn: New Perspectives on Social Theory*, Cambridge: Cambridge University Press, pp 82–115.

Howson, A. and Inglis, D. (2001) 'The body in sociology: tensions inside and outside sociological thought', *Sociological Review*, 49(3): 297–317.

Jameson, F. (1991) *Postmodernism, or, the Cultural Logic of Late Capitalism*, Durham, NC: Duke University Press, 2003.

Latour, B. (1996) 'On actor-network theory: a few clarifications', *Soziale Welt*, 47: 369–381.
Latour, B. (2005) *Reassembling the Social: An Introduction to Actor-Network Theory*, Oxford: Oxford University Press.
Leder, D. (1990) *The Absent Body*, Chicago, IL: University of Chicago Press.
Lévi-Strauss, C. (1966) *The Savage Mind*, Chicago, IL: University of Chicago Press.
Lyotard, J.-F. (1984) *The Postmodern Condition: A Report on Knowledge*, Minneapolis: University of Minnesota Press.
Martin, E. (1992) 'The end of the body?', *American Ethnologist*, 19(1): 121–140.
Mead, G.H. (1934) *Mind, Self and Society from the Standpoint of a Social Behaviorist*, Chicago, IL: University of Chicago Press, 2015.
Merleau-Ponty, M. (1945) *Phenomenology of Perception*, London: Routledge, 2014.
Nietzsche, F. (1993) *The Birth of Tragedy*, translated by S. Whiteside, London: Penguin Books, 2003.
O'Neill, J. (1998) 'Parson's Freud', *Cultural Values*, 2(4): 518–532.
Paz, O. (1969) *Conjunctions and Disjunctions*, translated by H.R. Lane, New York: Viking Press.
Peirce, C.S. (1955) 'Logic as semiotic: the theory of signs', in J. Buchler (ed) *Philosophical Writings of Peirce*, New York: Dover Publications, 2014, pp 98–119.
Reed, I.A. (2011) *Interpretation and Social Knowledge: On the Use of Theory in the Human Sciences*, Chicago, IL: University of Chicago Press.
Robertson, R. (1988) 'The sociological significance of culture: some general considerations', *Theory, Culture and Society*, 5(1): 3–23.
Seidman, S. (1994) *Contested Knowledge: Social Theory Today* (6th edn), West Sussex: Wiley-Blackwell, 2017.
Shilling, C. (2012) *The Body and Social Theory* (3rd edn), London: SAGE.
Shilling, C. (2016) 'The rise of body studies and the embodiment of society: a review of the field', *Horizons in Humanities and Social Sciences: An International Refereed Journal*, 2(1): 1–14.
Simko, C. and Olick, J.K. (2021) 'What we talk about when we talk about culture: a multi-facet approach', *American Journal of Cultural Sociology*, 9(4): 431–459.
Simmel, G. (1971) *On Individuality and Social Forms*, Chicago, IL: University of Chicago Press.
Stoltz, D.S. (2021) 'Becoming a dominant misinterpreted source: the case of Ferdinand de Saussure in cultural sociology', *Journal of Classical Sociology*, 21(1): 92–113.
Susen, S. (2015) *The 'Postmodern Turn' in the Social Sciences*, London: Palgrave Macmillan.

Swidler, A. (1986) 'Culture in action: symbols and strategies', *American Sociological Review*, 51(2): 273–286.

Turner, B.S. (1991) 'Recent developments in the theory of the body', in M. Featherstone, M. Hepworth and B.S. Turner (eds) *The Body: Social Process and Cultural Theory*, London: SAGE, pp 1–35.

Turner, B.S. (1992) *Regulating Bodies: Essays in Medical Sociology*, New York: Routledge.

Turner, B.S. (2008) *The Body and Society: Explorations in Social Theory* (3rd edn), London: SAGE.

Turner, T. (1995) 'Social body and embodied subject: bodiliness, subjectivity, and sociality among the Kayapo', *Cultural Anthropology*, 10(2): 143–170.

Waskul, D. and Vannini, P. (2006) *Body/Embodiment: Symbolic Interaction and the Sociology of the Body*, London: Routledge, 2016.

Weber, M. (1930) *The Protestant Ethic and the Spirit of Capitalism*, London: Routledge, 2008.

Williams, S.J. and Bendelow, G. (1998) *The Lived Body: Sociological Themes, Embodied Issues*, London: Routledge.

Woodward, I. (2012) 'Consumption as cultural interpretation: taste, performativity, and navigating the forest of objects', in J.C. Alexander, R.N. Jacobs and P. Smith (eds) *The Oxford Handbook of Cultural Sociology*, Oxford: Oxford University Press, pp 671–697.

Young, I.M. (2005) *On Female Body Experience: "Throwing Like a Girl" and Other Essays*, Oxford: Oxford University Press.

2

# Thinking the Molecular

*Ben Spatz*

> What are you made of? Look at your hands. Draw one palm across the other. Feel the density of your tissues, the bones, musculature, and sinuous ligaments. What gives your tissues substance and form? You have probably been told that your body is composed of trillions of living cells. But what are your cells made of? What is the stuff of life?
>
> — Natasha Myers, *Rendering Life Molecular*

In this chapter, I contest the assumed primacy of technoscientific and biochemical methods in determining what human (and other) bodies are made of. From a perspective grounded in critical race, cultural, and performance studies, as well as embodied artistic research, I offer an expanded molecular theory of identity that foregrounds the radical asymmetry of what are still too often glossed as sociocultural signs or attributes rather than material substances. This argument builds upon and extends my previous theorization of technique as knowledge (Spatz, 2015, 2020a). I begin by surveying a handful of recent critical treatments of "hard"—that is, technoscientifically graspable—physical and chemical molecules that foreground their racial and gendered construction. I then consider the politics implied by a more expansive conception of the molecular, comparing and contrasting this with theories of the molecular that follow Gilles Deleuze and Félix Guattari. The final section begins to imagine the implications of such a conceptual shift for experimental research methods. These include not only a richer way to theorize embodied difference but also a radical reshuffling of the dominant disciplinary hierarchies that attach greater epistemic primacy to more quantitative methods. To understand the radical asymmetry of the molecular, I argue, we must recognize that critical race theory and other politicized new materialisms refer as much to the substance of the world as do the harder sciences.¹

## Hard and soft molecules

As Natasha Myers explains in *Rendering Life Molecular*, the discovery and definition of biochemical molecules as "the stuff of life" has revolutionized the scientific understanding of human embodiment and led, like other technoscientific developments, to the invention and implementation of technologies with far-reaching impact that only continues to grow. "In the twenty-first century," Myers writes, "life and living bodies have been rendered thoroughly molecular" (2015, p x), so that the very word *life* in some contexts becomes almost synonymous with an analysis of the cells, tissues, and molecules that biochemistry, neuroscience, physiology, and other technoscientific disciplines investigate. Yet, as she acknowledges on the same page, the concept of the molecular begins long before the modern scientific map of the body: a "propensity to parse the world into molecular components has a long history that extends back to ancient philosophers who postulated that the worldly stuff we could see and feel had an unseen 'inner constitution'; matter, it was thought, was made up of subvisible atoms or particles." In her ethnographic study of protein crystallographers, Myers continues the important work of social epistemology, revealing how laboratory scientists do not simply discover preexisting material objects but "render" them in ways that are at once material, social, cultural, and aesthetic, as well as embodied and performative. Such studies have been crucial to my own previous attempts to wrest from technoscience the exclusive claim to authoritative knowledge.² However, the cultural construction of technoscientific knowledge is only one side of the coin. In this chapter I explore the other side, which is no less important: the materiality and relative reliability of that which is known and rendered by non-technoscientific experts.

Several recent studies demonstrate that even the most rigorously quantifiable and technoscientifically specified molecules are also thoroughly sociocultural. The most critically astute of these, a handful of which I consider in this section, also highlight the ways in which positing such molecules as purely biochemical objects not only entrenches the power of technoscientific ontologies but also reinscribes the racial and gender hierarchies attached to those ways of knowing. As a first example, the ongoing centrality of DNA in scientific, political, and critical debates is due to its powerful yet still not fully understood relationship to the development of bodies. As Kim TallBear (2013) explains, while DNA is typically formulated as the material foundation of racial and ethnic heritage, the genetic mapping of inherited biochemical links also depends upon prior groupings of populations, which are necessarily social and often racial in nature. DNA thus does not cause or define racial identity any more than it is caused and defined by social processes of racialization. In human genome diversity research, faith in "molecular origins" refers back to "ancestral populations," which are themselves defined via contemporary "reference populations" (TallBear, 2013, pp 5–6). As a result, "each of those constitutive elements operates within a loop of circular reasoning," inasmuch as the categories into which genes are sorted are themselves defined by reference to socially and historically grouped populations. While the rhetoric of DNA assumes that it grounds populations in materiality, the process of genetic analysis is itself also grounded in stories about peoples.

DNA is thus "material-semiotic" insofar as it is both "supported by and threads back into the social-historical fabric to (re)constitute the categories and narratives by which we order life" (TallBear, 2013, p 7). Moreover, "as DNA is increasingly called upon to speak to questions of racialized and exclusionary citizenship and belonging, understanding genetic ancestry as a multivalent political object could not be more important" (Tamarkin, 2020, p 14). Following such analyses, we must conclude that DNA is not simply the "stuff of life," out of which racial, ethnic, national, and citizen identities are constructed; it is also constructed out of racial imaginaries and linked to genetic markers by unmarked but hegemonically white disciplinary histories. What kind of molecule is this, then? On the one hand, DNA is undeniably a *molecule of identity*, a material particle that not only represents but also concretely transmits identity and links individuals together in a way that is not just social. On the other hand, it is also a *molecule of technique*, a socially constructed unit that becomes available only through the enactment of "repeatable pathways" or disciplinary knowledge (Spatz, 2015, p 44), in this case of both social history and technoscientific biochemistry. If my previous work on technique attempted to show how *identity is made of technique*—"what we know becomes who we are" (Spatz, 2015, p 56)—I have since become more aware of the importance of stressing a complementary claim, that *technique is made of identity*—what we know arises out of who we are. In other words, the "loop of circular reasoning" that generates a material-semiotic object like DNA is not a glitch or a flaw in genetic knowledge but an essential feature of knowledge production. A theory of the molecular that emphasizes only the technical, or only the identitarian, is therefore incomplete. What I hope to develop here, drawing upon TallBear and others, is a concept of the molecular that embraces the mutual construction of identity and technique.

Quite similar social and political debates and contestations apply to testosterone, although its molecular structure and its biochemical function are very different. If DNA is commonly understood as constituting race, while in fact also being constituted by race, then testosterone is typically understood as constituting gender, while in fact its substance and workings are also constituted by gender. Paul Preciado's theory-memoir *Testo Junkie* makes this abundantly clear in its investigation and contextualization of testosterone, or "T," within a vast social and political matrix of gender and sexuality. For example, the makers of the Testogel brand of T assume that its user "is a 'man' who isn't producing enough androgen naturally and who, obviously, is heterosexual" (Preciado, 2013, p 60). This "man" is presumed to have his preexisting but insufficient manhood confirmed and consolidated by testosterone, in a similar way as ancestry is presumed to be preexisting but inconclusively established before it is confirmed by DNA testing. Biomedical renderings of transgender identity as a medically approved passage between two preexisting categories further sediment a one-way relationship between testosterone and gender, since "in order to legally obtain a dose of synthetic testosterone, it is necessary to stop defining yourself as a woman." In contrast, what Preciado wants to introduce as gender "piracy" or "hacking" involves a radical destabilization of the relationship between technique/technology (testosterone as biochemical hormone) and identity (testosterone as molecular manhood). This can be effected, he suggests, through a kind of embodied research that embraces "the invention of new techniques of the self and repertoires of practices" (Preciado, 2013, pp 55, 351).[3] The molecule at the heart of such research cannot be simply biochemical, as it is produced through both technoscientific practices of biochemistry and cultural and embodied practices of gender and sexuality. For Preciado, a principle of self-experimentation must be at the heart of gender liberation, so that "anyone wishing to be a political subject will begin by being the lab rat in her or his own laboratory" (p 353). But the counterpart to this claim is the possibility of inventing genuinely and materially new gender identities through experimental practice. After all, the point of experimenting with a molecule like DNA or testosterone—not in the technoscientific laboratory but in the laboratory of everyday life—is not merely to change oneself by changing one's techniques but also to invent new techniques that, because they are made of the "stuff" of identity, may carry a politics of their own.

DNA and testosterone are among the innumerable biochemical molecules that make up human and other living bodies. Tracking the animate journeys of the metals lead and mercury, Mel Y. Chen analogously examines how these two substances, despite occupying "the lowest end of the animacy hierarchy"—even Aristotle considers them "dead" matter, lacking the animating principle of "soul"—can nevertheless become racialized, both constituting and being constituted by racial formations (Chen, 2012, p 4). For Chen, the metal lead is not only the chemical element Pb but also, again, a "material-semiotic" substance that may at times be "animated in novel ways," taking on "new meaning and political character" as it shifts racial identities—for example, from a disabling pollutant raced and classed as black and poor to an invasive asian or chinese toxin endangering the presumed intelligence and innocence of white children (p 166).[4] Going even further to theorize the "biomythography" of racialized molecules, Tiffany Lethabo King explores the relationship between blackness and indigo as portrayed in Julie Dash's film *Daughters of the Dust*.[5] Rejecting the concept of labor as too reductive to capture the relationship between black embodiment and the indigo plant, T.L. King describes "Blackness as coterminous with a series of chemical reactions and as porous bodies that exceed the humanist ontological boundaries that would separate plant, objects, and human flesh from one another" (2019, p 119). In Dash's portrayal of indigo plantation workers as "blue-handed," we find not merely a portrayal of black labor but also a project of artistic research that reveals "a molecular process of a body becoming both flesh and indican" (p 130; indican is a chemical precursor to indigo dye). While the "indigo stain is knowable only at the molecular level"—"slaves are poisoned and die," but the chemical does not really appear as a bluish tint on the skin—it becomes "perceptible to the human eye ... through decolonial art such as Dash's," which makes visible forms of molecular violence that are otherwise hidden by colonial regimes of knowledge (p 130). As with Chen's tracing of lead, toxicity here is racialized in ways that biochemistry cannot explain. It is not only that the biochemical molecule indican helps to construct the meaning of blackness; equally, the indigo dye is blackened through a historical retelling that refuses to exclude slavery and colonialism from the realm of the material.

My claim here is that a racial analysis of molecules, or a molecular analysis of race, does more than reveal how material objects and substances are swept up into social and cultural discourse. This claim could be made while keeping intact an ontological distinction between culture and matter that attends to only one direction of flow between them: the way in which sociocultural forces act upon material substrates. No scientist would deny that this is the case. What critical thought contributes, however, is a further claim: that molecules are themselves materially constituted by sociocultural practices, there being no pure substrate of materiality outside the sociocultural. If this is the case, then no absolutely distinct biochemical model can be separated from the racialized and gendered contexts in which it is mobilized. Instead, what we encounter are relatively distinct yet overlapping disciplines, each with their own methods and onto-epistemologies for storying the material: molecular biology, with its technoscientific quantification of matter; anthropology, with its studies of the work that molecules do in particular situations, including those of the scientific laboratory; cultural studies, analyzing the entanglement of the biochemical with other discourses on a larger scale; and others even farther afield, such as the biomythographics of artistic research. A genuinely interdisciplinary perspective must recognize the legitimacy of all these disciplines—as well as those still excluded from academic recognition—in making claims about what a given molecule means or does. A truly radical interdisciplinarity—one that is also intersectional—would also recognize the differential power dynamics among these fields and critique the prevailing hierarchy of knowledge by which they are accorded differing ontological force. It is, after all, social and political history that determines why some disciplines are understood as defining the most fundamental reality, others as studying the merely cultural, and others, with even less epistemic legitimacy, as merely forms of culture themselves.[6] To approach the question of what is material therefore demands an inquiry into the differential legitimization of diverse forms of knowledge.

I have introduced the molecular through the "hard" molecules of technoscience in order to appropriate it for a range of molecules that are not measurable or localizable in the same ways. To begin with, let us consider the materiality of what I call embodied technique.[7] A gesture, a melody, a joke, a dance, a rhythm, a habit, a gait, an exercise: By what right are such named chunks of embodied technique habitually excluded from the realm of the material? In whose interest is it assumed that aspects of embodiment that cannot be reliably located and measured by technoscientific means are in that sense immaterial? Would it not be more accurate—and more ethical—to name those aspects of material embodiment that are localizable and quantifiable *as such*, appreciating the extent of their reliability, and the technologies this affords, but not for that reason according them greater ontological reality? Taking the primary example developed in my own artistic research practice, a song cannot be extracted from the body (see Spatz, 2015, pp 136–147; Spatz, 2019). One cannot pull a song out of the body and examine its structure independently, using the anatomical and anatomizing method that arguably founds modern science by extracting natural objects from their temporal and geographical contexts (Knorr Cetina, 1992). But this does not mean that we cannot work with songs or that they do not push back against us in their own material ways. A song is materially embodied, even if it cannot be isolated anatomically. What must be rejected is a definition of materiality that is based upon anatomical dissection.[8] Songs are also components or elements of our bodies. They are inside us while also constituting us, like biochemical molecules, even if they cannot be extracted or measured biochemically. The same goes for all kinds of embodied knowledges: the only way to get such phenomena *out of matter* is to actively exclude or dematerialize them through the invention of an immaterial stratum of "mind" or "culture," that which is defined against matter. If we avoid this step, we can affirm the materiality of phenomena that otherwise remain trapped within limiting categories of the social, the cultural, and the cognitive.

What then are bodies made of? We are, of course, made of molecules in the sense developed in biochemistry. We are composed of cells, inhabited by bacteria, orchestrated by hormones, coordinated by neurons, and constituted by many kinds of molecules moving at different speeds, from the slowness of bone to the lighting of electrochemical impulse. But we are also literally, materially, and not just metaphorically made of songs, gestures, memories, ideas, and techniques. There is no strict ontological line to be drawn between technoscientific molecules and other kinds of molecular substances.[9] On the contrary, the former are simply and precisely that: *molecules accessible to technoscientific methods*. This does not make them more real or more material. A wider world of the molecular would include many other relatively reliable patterns—flows of repeatability that subtend, enable, and compose organisms and societies—whether or not these can be physiochemically isolated. Even within the "hard" (quantifiable and quantifying) sciences, the "stuff" of the world is not as symmetrical or epistemologically stable as the folklore of scientific positivism would suggest. It is already not possible to handle or manipulate an atom of hydrogen and an atom of iron in the same way, to say nothing of what it means to "handle" or work with a photon or a quark. My aim here is not to determine what counts as a molecule but to offer a conceptual move through which such a question might be seriously posed in an epistemic context much wider than that normally suggested by the concept of the molecular. To do that, we must first let go of certain assumptions that limit and reduce the concept of the molecular, even in post-structuralist theory, by romanticizing it.

## The romance of the molecular

I cannot go any further without putting the concept of the molecular developed thus far into conversation with that developed by and in response to the work of Deleuze and Guattari. I began this chapter by surveying racialized and gendered instances of the molecular, in which what is salient is the extent to which allegedly purely biochemical molecules such as DNA and testosterone are in fact heavily determined by formations of race and gender, not only in their effects but in their very constitution. A molecule in this sense is always "material-semiotic," as both TallBear and Chen assert, or what Deleuze and Guattari call a "particle-sign," here perhaps imaginable as a glob or chunk of identity-technique that must be analyzed in terms of both knowledge and power, interdisciplinarity and intersectionality.[10] The application of Deleuze and Guattari's work to race and racialization has been undertaken by a number of thinkers who, in the face of the "deontologisation of race" (Saldanha, 2006, p 9), a widely accepted strategy to undercut racism by rejecting racial categories, call instead for an alternative reontologization of such categories. According to Arun Saldanha, race must be conceived as a chain of contingency, in which the connections between its constituent components are not given, but are made viscous through local attractions. Whiteness, for example, is about the sticky connections between property, privilege, and a paler skin. There is no essence of whiteness, but there is a relative fixity that inheres in all the "local pulls" of its many elements in flux. Emergence and viscosity are complementary concepts, the first pertaining to the genesis of distinctions, the second to the modality of that genesis. (p 18)

The dynamics of viscosity and emergence that Saldanha describes are not mere metaphors. These terms aim to describe the actual, material ways in which racial and other identities operate in practice, rematerializing race and revealing the ways in which identities are not merely constituted by knowledge but also subtend every epistemic technique. Drawing on Elizabeth Grosz's Deleuzian feminist analysis of how sex is dichotomized into "the great binary aggregates" of male and female, which Deleuze and Guattari posit might be dismantled and recombined to proliferate "a thousand tiny sexes," Saldanha suggests that "the molecularization of race would consist in its breaking up into *a thousand tiny races*" (2006, p 21, italics original). I would add, however, that the molecularization of race cannot take place purely through desedimentation. Instead it calls for a kind of material experimentation with identity that must not only fracture and dismantle old identities but also generate new ones. Following Saldanha, race might be conceived as "irreducible" (2009, p 9) in a chemical rather than social sense. It is not that an individual's racial identity is unchangeable; on the contrary, a molecular or reontologizing approach to identity troubles the fixed assignment of identities to individuals. In Saldanha's terms: "Nobody 'has' a race, but bodies are racialised" (2006, p 18). How might we begin to think the relations of technique and identity in this way?

The Deleuzo–Guattarian concept of the molecular is defined in opposition to the molar. Both terms have the same root, *moles*, meaning mass or barrier, indexing the heaviness or inertia of forces; "molecule" simply adds the diminutive *cule*.[11] In the extraordinarily generative key passages on the molecular in *A Thousand Plateaus*, what comes through is the latter's power of flight, its capacity for resistance and excess, always in relation to a dominating molar force:

> You become animal only molecularly. You do not become a barking molar dog, but by barking, if it is done with enough feeling, with enough necessity and composition, you emit a molecular dog. ... Yes, all becomings are molecular: the animal, flower, or stone one becomes are molecular collectivities, haecceities, not molar subjects, objects or

form that we know from the outside and recognize from experience, through science, or by habit. If this is true, then we must say the same of things human: there is a becoming-woman, a becoming-child, that do not resemble the woman or the child as clearly distinct molar entities. (Deleuze and Guattari, 1987, p 275)

The opposition between molar and molecular is evocative, but it easily falls into a romance of the latter, or what I would call an (interdisciplinary) knowledge analysis lacking an (intersectional) power analysis. If oppressive power is equated with the molar—that is, the solidly aggregate—then where is the scope for building robust solidarities, let alone alternative societies and more just worlds? By the same token, if the molecular is imagined as inherently ethical, or "radical" in a positive political sense, then we have no way to work practically with violent or dangerous molecules. What shall we do with molecular whiteness or particles of toxic masculinity? What if some molecules form a tumor? Is it good to become a molecular dog? And how can a molecular "woman" or "child" come to be if they bear no relation to the molar entities out of which they have desedimented? Some varieties of current black studies, especially those called afropessimist, vehemently contest the claim that "bastard and mixed-blood are the true names of race" (Deleuze and Guattari, 1987, p 379; Saldanha and Adams, 2013).[12] To dissolve identity categories is not always desirable. Guattari writes: "It seems important to me to destroy such gross categories as 'woman,' 'homosexual' and so on. Nothing is ever as simple as that. When we reduce people to categories—black or white, male or female—it is because of our own preconceptions" (1984, p 235). But what if, in order to avoid reducing people to categories, we need not destroy the categories themselves, as elementary but irreducibly complex substances? What if the categories, molecularized, reveal a diversity of potential and effect that far exceeds the basic formulation of molar and molecular?

From proteins to songs, every kind of molecule works differently and in differing combinations. When the molar is simplistically rejected in favor of a romance of the molecular, we miss the diverse operations that a richer molecular paradigm can reveal. This concern is raised by a handful of incisive critiques of molecular theories that follow Deleuze and Guattari. Christopher Miller's (1993) early critique of *A Thousand Plateaus*, for example, is concerned directly with the politics of identity and with the way in which the anti-identitarian or "nomadological" stance of that volume conceals its profound reliance upon anthropological and indeed colonial sources of knowledge. Of particular relevance here is Miller's critique of what he calls "nomadological immunity" (1993, p 21): the way in which molecularization, understood as the dissolving of molar identities, can be operationalized as an escape from politics and the analysis of power. This leads Miller to ask if there is "not a certain cosmopolitan arrogance at work" (1993, p 21) in Deleuze and Guattari's attempts to sever anthropological knowledge from its origins in particular identities, nations, and cultures. A related point is made by Jodi Byrd, who criticizes those who call "for transformational new worlds of relation and relationship that move us toward a joyously cacophonic multiplicity and away from the lived colonial conditions of indigeneity within the postcolonizing settler society" (2011, p 18). Like Miller, Byrd highlights how the "Indian" or indigenous figure appears in Deleuze and Guattari's work as a "philosophical sign" and a "ghost in the system" that underwrites the radical line of flight into the molecular while itself being erased in that transit (p 19). In such calls, Byrd suggests, indigenous technique (knowledge and ways of being) is exalted and romanticized in the same breath as that in which indigenous identity (a political formation) is erased. An even more sharply worded critique is offered by Jordy Rosenberg, who suggests that the "molecular" posited by some new materialisms may actually be defined by its exclusion of politics, "as particulate matter becomes a kind of sublime miniature and a point at which ontological wonder blooms" (2014). As Rosenberg suggests, the fetishization of technoscientifically produced molecules can be another kind of (white/male) fantasy in which the capacity to redesign bodies at a chemical level allows for the jettisoning of cultural politics with a kind of "vicious, amnesiac joy."

In my view, these important critiques demand not a complete rejection of the molecularization of race and identity but rather the restoration, to the material substance of race, of a certain heaviness (perhaps that of the "molar," but now without any sharp distinction between the two terms). It is not the joy of molecular experimentation that is the problem but the erasure that joy enables. If a focus on molecularization as a process can overemphasize flux and flow and make the transformation of the world appear too easy, this needs to be counterbalanced by a greater awareness of sedimentation and a willingness to look more unflinchingly—although not in structuralist terms—at violence, including racism, antiblackness, and colonial genocide, as part of what is carried in the molecular.[13] This is, again, why I did not begin this chapter with the work of Deleuze and Guattari, as influential as it has been. To think of identity and technique in terms of the molecular should not be an invitation to jettison larger-scale political analysis in favor of a micropolitics imagined as radically freeing. On the contrary, the concept of the molecular should equally serve to remind us that very tiny things can be very dangerous and that molecules too small to see can bring down worlds. After all, there exist molecules of which half a gram or less will kill you on contact, while other molecules are so ubiquitous as to be confused with empty space. In short, there is nothing light or easy about molecules. To restate my earlier claim: *identity is made of technique, but technique is also made of identity*. There is, then, no escape from identity in the molecular. Chemicals are not simple, easy, or light just because they are physically small. Some molecules are indeed common and mundane. Some are inert and barely react or combine with others. But molecules also exist that are deadly, volatile, and explosive, even in small quantities. In their thinking of the molecular, Deleuze and Guattari do not fully account for this radical asymmetry. As much as they attempt to offset such a reading, they stage a series of oppositions between the molar and the molecular in which the latter invariably functions as the hero. As Miller observes, Deleuze and Guattari frequently state that there is nothing superior about the molecular over the molar, but their prose does not read that way and their examples do not bear this out. If Deleuze and Guattari offer a power analysis of the molecular, it is one that does not go very far into the details.

I do not reject the possibility of joy and transformation—or even moments of limited, provisional, and immanently contestable artistic or nomadological "immunity," in which the world and its injustices seem to fall away. It would not be possible to go on living from day to day if such experiences were strictly denied. But I do reject the idea that the process of molecularization works in one direction only, or that molecularization is a good in itself. I would defend a politics of identity by reminding thinkers of molecules that identity does not disappear when it is molecularized. That *identity is made of technique* means that it can never be fully locked down. Even the most heavily sedimented identities will always remain open to change as they travel across times, places, and bodies. But that *technique is made of identity* means that it never fully or finally escapes the sedimented structures of power that produce and sustain it. Hence molecules of technique, in their relatively free circulation, are real and can be dangerous—can have violent effects—particularly when their substance as molecular identity is misunderstood. As Thomas DeFrantz writes:

> Again, and again, dances created in black environments are shared and then later used in contexts that have little reference to breathing black people. You drop the stanky leg or the nae stinky into your contemporary performance project. It's supposed to feel hip and aware or funny and ironic. You vogue or j-sette to demonstrate your of-the-moment ability to get down with the kids. Just stop it. You don't understand what those dances are for or how they operate or what they can do. *It's like playing with fire.* (2007, p 10)

I have added italics to the final sentence to highlight its resonance with the language of chemistry. With DeFrantz's admonition in mind, I would jettison any remaining attachment to the molecular as a good in itself, turning instead to focus on its radical asymmetry.

"Asymmetry" is one of the key concepts proposed by Andrew Culp in seeking to exchange a positive, joyful Deleuze for a negative or "dark" Deleuze. The term, for Culp, "expresses difference as formal inequivalence. Asymmetry works to impede reciprocal relations and prevent reversibility." It establishes a "relationship of incommensurability," in contrast to mere complexity, which more often enacts a "flattening," a "uniformization of diversity," which "can both mobilize and impair forces" (Culp, 2016, pp 33–34). I do not find a negative Deleuze more satisfying or useful than a positive one, but I agree that asymmetry is much more than nondialectical. A molecule of whiteness behaves entirely differently than a molecule of blackness—and neither whiteness nor manhood, nor any other category of hegemonic domination, can be reduced to an abstract concept of the molar. This means, among other things, that we have no business talking about embodiment or materiality without taking seriously the work that has been undertaken in critical race theory, black studies, critical indigenous studies, and other politicized new materialisms to theorize the matter (and not just the sociality) of the world. This is what it means to go into the details. Such fields recognize the twisting of power and knowledge in material-semiotic molecules and are thereby enabled to undertake radically interdisciplinary and intersectional analysis. With regard to "the body," it must then be stated that the body as archive, as memory, as habitus, as sociomaterial formation—the whole messy and excessive nonbiomedical body long theorized by cultural studies—*is the gendered and racialized body*. Racial and gender identities are not added secondarily to a substrate of technoscientifically determined embodiment. They are the very stuff of life, as much as bones and tissues. If we do not recognize this materiality and substantiality of identities, then we misunderstand the body, and indeed society, on a material level. But such recognition requires, as suggested here, a radical overturning of the disciplinary hierarchies that would locate cultural analysis on a more superficial level than quantitative sociology and the even more strictly quantitative fields of technoscience.

## Radical asymmetry

In the first section of this chapter, I argued that racial and other identities are not merely layers of culture, symbol, or discursive meaning added to a more fundamental physical or technoscientific reality but should instead be understood as "material-semiotic" chunks or molecules of *technique-identity*. In the second section, I clarified that the molecular substance of such identities does not automatically become easier to work with when it is rendered in this way. While molecularizing identity can open up new possibilities for experimentation and intervention, the identification of molecules as racialized and gendered rules out any easy escape into molecularity. Conceiving of embodiment and identity in this way—for this is precisely a theory of embodiment that refuses to separate cultural identity from the materiality of the body—opens the door to a world of material complexity and interactive dynamics.

The point is that "white" and "black," for example, are not only mutually constituted principles but also incommensurable and irreducible substances. Perhaps even more importantly, in their irreducibility such identities also establish no larger container, and certainly no grid or axis, onto which other identities could be mapped. Recent critiques of "identity politics" as defined by a static grid (eg, Massumi, 2002; Puar, 2017), often drawing on Deleuze and Guattari, have failed to dislodge prevailing models of race and gender, perhaps in part because they have replaced the grid model with an open field of undefined interactivity that flattens out crucial asymmetries. Reacting against such moves, Frank Wilderson has offered a structuralist, afropessimist mapping, in which the "red" or indigenous being is located halfway between the white and the black—a schematic model that ignores the complex relations of indigeneity to land and citizenship, which trouble the very constitution of the racial (cf Barker, 2005; Wilderson, 2010; T.L. King, 2019; Rifkin, 2019). My own theorization of the molecular began from an engagement with jewishness, another identity that also cannot be mapped onto a black/white spectrum or grid and which may at various times and places be more or less or differently racialized (see Brodkin, 1998; Slabodsky, 2014; Traverso, 2016; Spatz, 2019). From this starting point, I have attempted to think through the politics of identity in a way that avoids both the trap of structuralism, exemplified by Wilderson, and the excesses of some post-structuralism, as described in the previous section. The key to this delicate navigation is the radical asymmetry of molecules.

While we might say that blackness, whiteness, brownness, indigeneity, and jewishness all circulate in practice as molecular substances, these identities are no more functionally symmetrical or equivalent to one another than are water, diamonds, and neurotoxins. Not only are these identities not four "positions" on any kind of grid, they are arguably entirely different kinds of things, radically asymmetrical phenomena, which, in any attempted comparison, must take us far away from any gridded or spectrum-like model of identity, technique, and embodiment. To think identities in this way is to leave behind some of the meta-categories that remain hegemonic and pernicious in social theory: "race," "gender," "sexuality," "class," and so on. It is these categories, apparently so innocent, that lead us toward a false symmetry: as if black and white, or male and female, were two sides of a coin, rather than radically asymmetrical materialities. Even the term "identity" itself must be questioned, although I retain it here as the slower and more inertial counterpart to technique. For the same reason, I cannot fully avoid the term "race"—many of the sources I am working with rely upon it—but I employ it only to summon a series of more powerful molecular substances to displace it. In fact, the same displacement applies to many other meta-categories of identity that might at first seem to be separate from race but which ultimately bleed into it: nation, language, citizenship, gender, ability, and so on. I focus here on the racial because of the vital work being done in critical black and indigenous studies and related fields—work that is more politically trenchant, and more engaged with radical asymmetry, than related theories of gender or class. Whereas theories of gender seem to have moved more easily into a molecularizing or technicizing approach, race—in an ongoingly colonial, capitalist, and white supremacist age—seems to carry a greater inertia, a greater stubbornness, that troubles the line of flight into the molecular. Class analysis, for its part, unless it reontologizes race and nation, cannot avoid the limitingly quantifying assumptions of economic theory. Specific racial identities are then especially powerful and urgent leverage points for rethinking the molecular relations of technique and identity.

Thinking race in apprenticeship to black studies especially compels us to push beyond the idea that certain bodies carry race—that race is a property of racialized bodies—and to recognize instead how race intersects and transects bodies, inheres in the floors and windows, floats in the air, and is atmospheric, palpable, chemical. Yet, in the same breath, race theorized from blackness extends its slippages to other kinds of identities and causes a vast conceptual house of cards to collapse. Blackness may be a gender (Ziyad, 2017; Nyong'o, 2021). Whiteness may be a religion (Carter, 2021). Jewishness may be a gender, a language, a way of thinking (Pellegrini, 1995; Boyarin, 1996; Kraemer, 2020). From the perspective of a critical hermeneutic methodology based in the arts and humanities, sociological categories of race and gender are rough approximations of what is materially experienced in concrete moments, events, and practices. Such a perspective might even take the nation-state, major religious formations, and Marxist formulations of class as subcategories of the racial, where the racial is understood as the molecular materiality of technique/identity. The materialities of blackness—and, indeed, of whiteness, brownness, and other ethnicons beyond the grammar of color—are not limited to "race" as a census category offered by the nation-state.[14] These materialities are transnational, in some cases perhaps planetary, and their recognition is bound up in a call that increasingly exceeds that of antiracism: decolonization (Tuck and Yang, 2012; Mignolo and Walsh, 2018; Gopal, 2021).

In this sense, race refers to a concept of technique/identity that incorporates not only embodiment and culture but also deep histories and materialities of trauma, dissociation, shame, violence, pleasure, and loss. The concept of embodiment, like many others, has been rendered misleadingly uniform by technoscientific methods of measurement. Thinking race anew, even reontologizing it (to ontologize it in a *different* way), reminds us that embodiment is shot through with difference as well as similarity and that colonialism is embodied both as sedimented memory, or "traces of history" (Wolfe, 2016), and as present technique. Colonialism and its racial substances are in the buildings and roads, in the air and water, and in our bodies (Liboiron, 2021). Identity, as much as bones and tissue, is what we are made of. To begin to grasp this, we may have to replace sociological models of identities as labels or axes with an experimentally oriented, historically grounded, politically trenchant, and epistemologically provisional molecular engagement with identities as asymmetrical substances that compose the world. This requires a non-gridded, nonbinary formulation of identity as comprising and comprised of technique but not one that therefore envisions a world of pure flux and flow.

Here again the language of chemistry is instructive: while molecules can be reduced to atoms and subatomic particles, physics on that level reveals little about how actual molecules behave. There will be no "table of elements" for a molecular theory of identity, let alone a set of general laws or principles to govern them. As Philip Ball writes: "The Periodic Table really belongs to that realm where chemistry becomes physics, where we must wheel out the algebra and the cosines to explain why atoms of the elements form the particular unions called molecules" (2002, p 6). The Periodic Table, according to Ball, gives us only atoms, not the molecular: "Many people believe that the nuclear bomb was itself the product of physics, but writing $E=mc^2$ does not give you Hiroshima." On the contrary, creating the atomic bomb required "separating isotopically distinct molecules of uranium compounds" (p 9)—along with, we might add, particular material structures of orientalism, coloniality, whiteness, and fascism, which Ball cannot think alongside uranium. Following Ball's account of chemistry as beginning in the moment when the gridded quantification of the table of elements is exceeded, the molecular upon which I would call to think racial and other identities is a much wilder zone than any table can grid. This molecular, too, is "a craft full of possibilities," of "wonderful, inspiring, inventive possibilities," of "terrible, nightmarish possibilities," and of "mundane but useful things, bizarre things, hard-to-understand things" (p 10). What I hope to approach by thinking identity and embodiment in this way is the possibility of establishing theoretical and practical links between the large-scale analysis of race on sociological and historical levels and the micro analysis of specific moments and events. While much work in cultural and performance studies has aimed to do this, the vocabulary available for theorizing relationships between bodies, identities, and knowledges still often remains constrained by a dominant model in which (material) bodies are, on the one hand, defined and positioned by racial and other (social) identities and, on a completely different level, in possession of (cognitive) knowledge. If, on the other hand, bodies are actually made up of identity-technique molecules, then a very different lexicon of analysis and pragmatics of experimentation might be activated.

We might speak of how racial and other identities operate in particular moments and instances, including on the largest scales: flexible like rubber, flickering like flame, impenetrable like diamond, or any of the properties of bone, ebony, steel, ice, sand, and so on. Such imagery is already present in Sara Ahmed's assertion that "race, like sex, is sticky; it sticks to us, or we become 'us' as an effect of how it sticks, even when we think we are beyond it" (2004, §49). Or, as another writer and poet muses: "I think about identity particles all the time; they hover like bees or clouds depending on my mood" (r. erica doyle, in Rankine et al, 2015, p 253). In such usages, the language of chemistry evokes a materiality of embodied identity that extends further into a world of mess and complexity than any geometrical model can express, but which at the same time avoids leaping or spiraling into an open field of free experimentation—as if the total replacement of the molar by the molecular could offer anything more than a kind of heat death, a dissolution into meaninglessness. Radical asymmetry here is not geometrical asymmetry. Instead, its ontology is more like the chemical.

What, after all, is racial brownness, if not, as José Esteban Muñoz conceives it, the "brown commons":

> I mean "brown" as in brown people in a very immediate way, in this sense, people who are rendered brown by their personal and familial participations in South-to-North migration patterns. I am also thinking of people who are brown by way of accent and linguistic orientations that convey a certain difference. I mean a brownness that is conferred by the ways in which one's spatial coordinates are contested, and the ways in which one's right to residency is challenged by those who make false claims to nativity. Also, I think of brownness in relation to everyday customs and everyday styles of living that connote a sense of illegitimacy. Brown indexes a certain vulnerability to the violence of property, finance, and to capital's overarching mechanisms of domination. (2020, p 3)

The slippage here, from brown commons to brown people to brown customs and styles, like that from black bodies to black thought to black worlds, is not a mistake or a gap in logic. It is an innovation, a challenge, a demand for a kind of poetic thought that can see through the division of knowledge and power, or technique and identity. A similar slippage is found in the yellowness of Anne Anlin Cheng's "yellow woman," which "is not meant to essentialize but to name the processes of racialization" and which therefore "denotes a person but connotes a style" (2019, p 1). It is found again in Jean-François Lyotard's lowercasing of "jews" as a figural position, in principle open to anyone, rather than a particular identity grounded in "real Jews" (Hammerschlag, 2010, p 10). Of course, jewishness is not a color—or is it? Does the same figurality, the same slippage between real people and transferable styles, apply to judaism, to islam, to queerness, to class positions, to nations large and small, to the european, to whiteness? As a slippage between knowledge and power, or identity and technique, we must affirm that, yes, something like this characterizes all identity categories, all ethnicons, including and beyond those indexed by an emerging decolonial grammar of colors: white, black, red, brown, yellow, muslim, jewish, queer, trans, disabled, and so on. But this slippage does not apply in the same way to each. It does not apply symmetrically.

The molecularity of identity is nowhere more evident than in the making and sharing of what is called art. Yet the capitalist framework of art production works incessantly to conceal that molecularity as it unfolds through embodied and artistic research. Perhaps, then, it could be the work of emerging experimental research methods, including those that go by names like "practice (as) research" and "artistic research," to reveal the ways in which the complexities of the world are present in specific moments of encounter. This would be done not in order to resolve those complexities, or even to posit the artistic encounter as an exceptional or utopian space (Miller's "immunity"), but in order to generate new forms of knowledge that might participate in long-overdue reconciliations. Certainly, my own need to theorize identity in relation to technique, and my interest in the molecular as a way of avoiding both the static grids of "identity politics" and the erasures of postidentitarian proposals, arises from my epistemic position at the intersection of performance studies and performance practice, as well as from my racial and gender identities. Artistic and embodied research methods claim to develop new ways to investigate the materiality of life, practice, and worlds. They apply methodological rigor and institutional resources to the study of being and existence through new forms and new structures of knowledge. They could therefore be sites at which racial and other identities are investigated with a combination of critical precision and poetic force. Learning from black studies means acknowledging that one can never separate the meaning of blackness, at least in europe and the americas, from the history of slavery and the ongoing forces of antiblackness and white supremacy, but neither can blackness be reduced to or equated with that history. If black studies research models a trenchant analysis of molecular identity that moves beyond "race" into a poetic and biomythographic ontology that is in some ways aligned with artistic research, then much work remains to be done in the tracking of whiteness, jewishness, queerness, and numerous other materialities beyond the limited ways in which they have thus far been conceived and modeled. In every case, there are heavy histories and ongoing, large-scale power relations to contend with, but also emergent and unfixed relations of experimentation, discovery, and care, all of which might be brought to presence in future methods.

Artistic research—with other experimental methods that reject the onto-epistemic cut separating technique and identity, knowledge and power, instead placing the cut elsewhere to reveal other realities (on this notion of the cut, see "Two Cuts" in Spatz, 2020b)—implements a shift from the register of theoretical account to that of practical experimentation. It calls for experimental research *in*, rather than *on*, both identities as fields of knowledge and knowledges as fields of identity. Such approaches cannot claim to solve or resolve the problem of identity but perhaps can offer a different way into it, taking identities as substantive and asymmetrical research problems rather than barriers to research. What if we took for granted that racial, gender, and other identities are constantly present, in our bodies, in architecture, in places, but that they manifest in different ways, radically asymmetrically? What if we attempted to investigate the phases and states, the reactions and catalysts, the compounds and solutions, through which identities act and interact in particular moments?

This would be both a chemistry of identity and a reframing of chemistry from the perspective of critical decolonial thought. It would be both an expansion of a conceptual framework (the molecular) and a methodological shift in the very forms of knowledge (embodied, artistic, situated, poetic research). Perhaps such a move could allow us to speak of identity as real and present, full, material, active, dynamic, and, at the same time, not static, not individualized, not amenable to any kind of grid. Perhaps a turn away from some of the disciplinary limitations of sociology and law (to say nothing of economics and cognitive science) could enable us to recognize that the being of identities operates not only in the classification of bodies but also as the substances that make up those bodies. This claim is not so much paradoxical as it is experimental. It is not so much anti- or postdisciplinary as radically interdisciplinary, with everything yet remaining to be said and with much more than saying needed.

## Notes

[1] An early form of this argument was advanced in Spatz (2019). That article focuses on an experimental approach to contemporary (jewish) identity developed in my artistic research, whereas this one attempts to establish a wider theoretical framework. Following an orthographic practice that I first implemented in the 2019 article, in this chapter I lowercase all identity terms, even those that are often capitalized (jewish, black, white, chinese, etc.). In quotations, I retain each author's capitalization or lowercasing of such terms.

[2] My previous work (Spatz, 2015, 2020a) has relied especially upon Karin Knorr Cetina's discussion of the unfolding nature of scientific objects, including proteins, and the "libidinal" quality of the relationships scientists develop with them, in Schatzki, Knorr

Cetina and von Savigny (2001); and upon Hans-Jörg Rheinberger's (1997) detailed treatment of the constantly shifting boundary between the known and the unknown through the iteration of experimental systems; see also Pickering (1995). I find these works in some ways more precise and compelling than Karen Barad's better-known but limitingly physicalist concept of "intra-action" (2007).

3   For more on Preciado's work as a model for embodied and artistic research, see Spatz (2020a). On gender as technique, see Spatz, "Gender as Technique" (2015, pp 171–214).

4   Chen's discussion of viruses as "nonliving" yet "closer to life" has become even more relevant in the era of COVID-19, including with regard to the racialization of its chinese origins. On the lowercasing of chinese and other identity terms in this chapter, see note 1.

5   On biomythography as method, see also Chen (2012, p 167) and Rosamond S. King (2019).

6   A call for interdisciplinary intersectionality, or intersectional interdisciplinarity, is the endpoint of my chapter "Thresholds" in *Blue Sky Body* (Spatz, 2020a), as well as a central aspect of the larger project of which this chapter is part.

7   Developing a materialist and epistemic concept of technique is the main goal of *What a Body Can Do* (Spatz, 2015). That book builds upon and extends the work of Mauss, Foucault, Bourdieu, and Butler, arguing that embodied technique is epistemic: It is *knowledge* as much as it may also be repetition, performance, habit, or rules.

8   It might be suggested that, from Mauss and Merleau-Ponty to more recent developments in new and speculative materialisms, the embodiment and materiality of technique is already well established. Perhaps this is true within a certain narrow theoretical register, but there is no sense in which the materiality of song or gesture is broadly understood to rival that of bone or tissue. Moreover, recognizing that a song is materially embodied in the act of singing is very different from treating songs as substantive knowledge, let alone as a kind of material substance. My thinking here begins from the predominantly white thinkers of technique, habitus, and performativity cited in Spatz (2015) and extends further through an engagement with radically new materialist approaches being developed in black studies. Some of the works I have been learning from include those of Weheliye (2014); Sharpe (2016); Moten (2018); Nyong'o (2019); T.L. King (2019); Bey (2020); and McKittrick (2021).

9   This is not to suggest that anything and everything exists in molecular form, as in a "flat" ontology. As I have argued elsewhere (see "Thresholds" in Spatz, 2020a), the problem with a flattening "object-oriented ontology" (eg, Harman, 2018) is that, in its attempt to render everything commensurable, it jettisons any concern for the depths of knowledge. Such an approach is not even interdisciplinary, let alone intersectional.

10  For an application of Deleuze and Guattari's "particle-sign" to the "molecular action of art," see Katve-Kaisa Kontturi, "From Double Navel to Particle-Sign: Toward the A-Signifying Work of Painting" in Barrett and Bolt (2013).

11  Online etymology dictionary: *https://www.etymonline.com/word/molecule*.

12  For an analysis of the antiblackness sometimes carried by calls for multiracialism, see Sexton (2008).

13  The need for an analysis that is unflinching but not structuralist refers to my critique of Frank Wilderson's work, which I develop briefly later in the chapter and more extensively in the larger project of which this chapter is a part.

14  I borrow an expanded sense of the term "ethnicon" from Baker (2017, pp 16–46).

# References

Ahmed, S. (2004) 'Declarations of whiteness: the non-performativity of anti-racism', *Borderlands*, 3(2), available from: https://rbb85.wordpress.com/2014/08/24/declarations-of-whiteness/.

Baker, C.M. (2017) *Jew*, New Brunswick, NJ: Rutgers University Press.
Ball, P. (2002) *Stories of the Invisible: A Guided Tour of Molecules*, Oxford: Oxford University Press.
Barad, K. (2007) *Meeting the Universe Halfway: Quantum Physics and the Entanglement of Matter and Meaning*, Durham, NC: Duke University Press.
Barker, J. (ed) (2005) *Sovereignty Matters: Locations of Contestation and Possibility in Indigenous Struggles for Self-Determination*, Lincoln: University of Nebraska Press.
Barrett, E. and Bolt, B. (eds) (2013) *Carnal Knowledge: Towards a 'New Materialism' through the Arts*, London: I.B. Tauris.
Bey, M. (2020) *The Problem of the Negro as a Problem for Gender*, Minneapolis: University of Minnesota Press.
Boyarin, J. (1996) *Thinking in Jewish*, Chicago, IL: University of Chicago Press.
Brodkin, K. (1998) *How Jews Became White Folks and What That Says about Race in America*, New Brunswick, NJ: Rutgers University Press.
Byrd, J.A. (2011) *The Transit of Empire: Indigenous Critiques of Colonialism*, Minneapolis: University of Minnesota Press.
Carter, J.K. (2021) 'Jews and the religion of whiteness', Katz Center for Advanced Judaic Studies, University of Pennsylvania, February 11, available from: https://www.reconstructingjudaism.org/center-jewish-ethics/jews-race-and-religion/3.
Chen, M.Y. (2012) *Animacies: Biopolitics, Racial Mattering, and Queer Affect*, Durham, NC: Duke University Press.
Cheng, A.A. (2019) *Ornamentalism*, New York: Oxford University Press.
Culp, A. (2016) *Dark Deleuze*, Minneapolis: University of Minnesota Press.
DeFrantz, T.F. (2007) 'I am Black (you have to be willing to not know)', *Theater*, 47(2): 8–21.
Deleuze, G. and Guattari, F. (1987) *A Thousand Plateaus: Capitalism and Schizophrenia*, Minneapolis: University of Minnesota Press.
Gopal, P. (2021) 'On decolonisation and the university', *Textual Practice*, 35(6): 873–899.
Guattari, F. (1984) *Molecular Revolution: Psychiatry and Politics*, Harmondsworth: Penguin Books.
Hammerschlag, S. (2010) *The Figural Jew: Politics and Identity in Postwar French Thought*, Chicago, IL: University of Chicago Press.
Harman, G. (2018) *Object-Oriented Ontology: A New Theory of Everything*, London: Pelican Books.
King, R.S. (2019) 'Radical interdisciplinarity: a new iteration of a woman of color methodology', *Meridians: Feminism, Race, Transnationalism*, 18(2): 445–456.
King, T.L. (2019) *The Black Shoals: Offshore Formations of Black and Native Studies*, Durham, NC: Duke University Press.

Knorr Cetina, K. (1992) 'The couch, the cathedral, and the laboratory: on the relationship between experiment and laboratory in science', in A. Pickering (ed) *Science as Practice and Culture*, Chicago, IL: University of Chicago Press, pp 113–138.

Kraemer, D. (2020) 'Talmud talk and Jewish talk', *Geveb: A Journal of Yiddish Studies*, June, pp 1–16, available from: https://ingeveb.org/articles/talmud-talk-and-jewish-talk.

Liboiron, M. (2021) *Pollution Is Colonialism*, Durham, NC: Duke University Press.

Massumi, B. (2002) *Parables for the Virtual: Movement, Affect, Sensation*, Durham, NC: Duke University.

McKittrick, K. (2021) *Dear Science and Other Stories*, Durham, NC: Duke University Press.

Mignolo, W.D. and Walsh, C.E. (2018) *On Decoloniality: Concepts, Analytics, Praxis*, Durham, NC: Duke University Press.

Miller, C.L. (1993) 'The postidentitarian predicament in the footnotes of *A Thousand Plateaus*: nomadology, anthropology, and authority', *Diacritics*, 23(3): 6–35.

Moten, F. (2018) *The Universal Machine*, Durham, NC: Duke University Press.

Muñoz, J.E. (2020) *The Sense of Brown*, Durham, NC: Duke University Press.

Myers, N. (2015) *Rendering Life Molecular: Models, Modelers, and Excitable Matter*, Durham, NC: Duke University Press.

Nyong'o, T. (2019) *Afro-Fabulations: The Queer Drama of Black Life*, New York: New York University Press.

Nyong'o, T. (2021) 'My gender is Black? The speculative refusals of Black queer/trans/feminism', Oakland, California, March 18, available from: https://performingarts.mills.edu/broadcasts/2021/tavia-nyongo.php.

Pellegrini, A. (1995) 'Jewishness as gender', *Shofar*, 14(1): 138–141.

Pickering, A. (1995) *The Mangle of Practice: Time, Agency, and Science*, Chicago, IL: University of Chicago Press.

Preciado, P.B. (2013) *Testo Junkie: Sex, Drugs, and Biopolitics in the Pharmacopornographic Era*, New York: The Feminist Press at CUNY.

Puar, J.K. (2017) *Terrorist Assemblages: Homonationalism in Queer Times* (2nd edn), Durham, NC: Duke University Press.

Rankine, C., Loffreda, B. and Cap, M.K. (eds) (2015) *The Racial Imaginary: Writers on Race in the Life of the Mind*, Albany, NY: Fence Books.

Rheinberger, H.-J. (1997) *Toward a History of Epistemic Things: Synthesizing Proteins in the Test Tube*, Stanford, CA: Stanford University Press.

Rifkin, M. (2019) *Fictions of Land and Flesh: Blackness, Indigeneity, Speculation*, Durham, NC: Duke University Press.

Rosenberg, J. (2014) 'The molecularization of sexuality: on some primitivisms of the present', *Theory and Event*, 17(2), available from: https://muse.jhu.edu/article/546470.

Saldanha, A. (2006) 'Reontologising race: the machinic geography of phenotype', *Environment and Planning D: Society and Space*, 24: 9–24.

Saldanha, A. (2009) 'So what is race?', *Insights*, working papers of Durham Institute of Advanced Study, 2(12): 2–11.

Saldanha, A. and Adams, J.M. (eds) (2013) *Deleuze and Race*, Edinburgh: Edinburgh University Press.

Schatzki, T.R., Knorr Cetina, K. and von Savigny, E. (eds) (2001) *The Practice Turn in Contemporary Theory*, New York: Routledge.

Sexton, J. (2008) *Amalgamation Schemes: Antiblackness and the Critique of Multiracialism*, Minneapolis: University of Minnesota Press.

Sharpe, C. (2016) *In the Wake: On Blackness and Being*, Durham, NC: Duke University Press.

Slabodsky, S. (2014) *Decolonial Judaism: Triumphal Failures of Barbaric Thinking*, New York: Palgrave Macmillan.

Spatz, B. (2015) *What a Body Can Do: Technique as Knowledge, Practice as Research*, London: Routledge.

Spatz, B. (2019) 'Molecular identities: digital archives and decolonial Judaism in a laboratory of song', *Performance Research*, 24(1): 66–79.

Spatz, B. (2020a) *Blue Sky Body: Thresholds for Embodied Research*, New York: Routledge.

Spatz, B. (2020b) *Making a Laboratory: Dynamic Configurations with Transversal Video*, New York: Punctum Books.

TallBear, K. (2013) *Native American DNA: Tribal Belonging and the False Promise of Genetic Science*, Minneapolis: University of Minnesota Press.

Tamarkin, N. (2020) *Genetic Afterlives: Black Jewish Indigeneity in South Africa*, Durham, NC: Duke University Press.

Traverso, E. (2016) *The End of Jewish Modernity*, London: Pluto Press.

Tuck, E. and Yang, K.W. (2012) 'Decolonization is not a metaphor', *Decolonization: Indigeneity, Education and Society*, 1(1): 1–40.

Weheliye, A.G. (2014) *Habeas Viscus: Racializing Assemblages, Biopolitics, and Black Feminist Theories of the Human*, Durham, NC: Duke University Press.

Wilderson, F.B. (2010) *Red, White and Black: Cinema and the Structure of U.S. Antagonisms*, Durham, NC: Duke University Press.

Wolfe, P. (2016) *Traces of History: Elementary Structures of Race*, London: Verso.

Ziyad, H. (2017) 'My gender is Black', *Afropunk*, available from: https://afropunk.com/2017/07/my-gender-is-black/.

3

# Interpreting Africa's *Seselelãme*: Bodily Ways of Knowing in a Globalized World

*Kathryn Linn Geurts and Sefakor Komabu-Pomeyie*

West Africans enjoy a sensory-emotional, embodied way of knowing that can be summed up with the Anlo-Ewe phrase *seselelãme*. This compelling term, *seselelãme*, comes from the language Sefakor Komabu-Pomeyie grew up speaking in southeastern Ghana, and it forms the basis for decades of work Kathryn Geurts has conducted as an anthropologist and guest among Anlo people. Functionally, *seselelãme* captures a panoply of sensory-emotional experiences, signals, and perceptions, distinguishing it from ontological traditions that emphasize atomization, fragmentation, and categorization. This situates *seselelãme* almost in opposition to longstanding Euro-American ways of being, which have privileged splits among cognition, sensory perception, emotional feeling, and behavioral expressions.[1] Those seeking to challenge the mind/body dichotomy can be found throughout society, from academics such as linguist George Lakoff and philosopher Mark Johnson (1999), as well as neuroscientist Antonio Damasio (2000), to practicing psychotherapists such as Susan Aposhyan (2007) or medical doctors such as James S. Gordon, who founded and directs The Center for Mind-Body Medicine. With Anglo-Americans and other Global North populations fervidly trying to weave or knit together entities that have been epistemologically separated for centuries (such as mind, body, spirit; individual, community, globe; human, animal, planet),[2] *seselelãme* seems to appeal to some as a potential (if small) panacea. This chapter explores its contemporary spread into a globally popular phenomenon appearing in films, workshops, blogs, therapy sessions, and other venues spotlighted on the world wide web.

This early twenty-first century spread of *seselelãme* raises thorny questions. For example, what sorts of interpretations are being made about *seselelãme* by people attempting to deploy it in Euro-American contexts? When claiming that *seselelãme* is a "concept" that "posits that everything is connected" (Jude, 2016), how does this distort and "Westernize" an organically African phenomena? What are the implications of individualizing and commoditizing *seselelãme* in New Age, self-actualization workshops in Global North contexts? In what ways does this perpetuate "symbolic and structural asymmetries underpinning institutional power/violence" (Champagne and Friedman, personal communication, November 5, 2019)? When *seselelãme* is culturally appropriated and then marketed as "an inner realm in which all the world is experienced and felt" (Shepherd, 2017, p 17), how does this compound Global North and Global South discrepancies, tensions, and mistrust? We agree with French anthropologist François Laplantine's assertion that "five centuries of rationalocentrism" succeeded in mistreating, repressing, and forgetting "the sensible, the life of the emotions, the body, and the physical character of thought as it takes shape" (Laplantine, 2015, p 1). But we also submit that *seselelãme* proves Laplantine's assertion to be true for *only some people* on the planet. Despite centuries of Western dominance through enslavement, colonization, neocolonialism, and neoliberalism, Africans have persisted in valuing *bodily ways of knowing*, and recent processes of globalization have allowed others to pick up on this valuable way of knowing that is crystalized (for some) in the Anlo-Ewe word *seselelãme*. Here we work to problematize some of the ways in which *seselelãme* is being used in Global North contexts, and we argue that materially more powerful people (often connected to Global North institutions, geographies, and economies) are culturally distorting, culturally appropriating, and culturally stripping *seselelãme* of its organic meanings and biotic qualities.

## *Seselelãme* in African everyday terms and in academic parlance

In the spring of 2020 Komabu-Pomeyie put out a social media inquiry on WhatsApp to a network of Ghanaians, asking a number of questions about what *seselelãme* means to them. A 32-year-old female teacher we call Sena answered with the following discussion:[3]

> *Seselelãme* is a word which implies a lot of personal innate experiences: for example, such experiences that start from the mind [and go] to the heart or any of the senses which can *reflect in the entire body system* of the individual. It can create emotional experiences such as joy, anger, sadness, rejection, acceptance. It can also create sensational experiences such as love, fear, cold, heat, excitement, shock, hatred.

Another respondent, Mawuli, a 40-year-old male attorney, succinctly pointed out:

> *Seselelãme* can mean a lot of things. It can mean intuition, or instinct, or sensation. It depends on the context. That's how Ewe is. For example, the word "whu" ... can mean *move away* or *open* or *blood*; and when doubled it can mean *dust*. So, context is important for Ewe words.

Indeed, context is important. *Seselelãme* emerges from Ewe-language contexts in West Africa, and Anlo-Ewe is typically associated with coastal southeastern Ghana. Over the decades we have variously translated *seselelãme* into the English language using phrases such as bodily ways of knowing; feeling in the body; hearing in the flesh, organs, and skin; and, at the level of the morpheme, perceive-perceive-at-flesh-inside. Our interest in *seselelãme* is rooted in the study of *sensory* aspects of Anlo history and sociocultural orientations (Geurts, 2002a, 2003).[4] However, a subsequent research project (Geurts and Adikah, 2006) led to our assertion that *seselelãme* should be considered a local (Anlo-Ewe) iteration of a broad pan-African—even Black Atlantic—foundational schema or source domain. Following Brad Shore's (1996, p 118) theoretical ideas about analogical transfer underpinning "the creative life of cultural models," we suggested that *seselelãme* operates as an out-of-awareness or "usually unconscious schematizing process" resulting in a globally reaching "family of related cultural models" threading together Black Atlantic sensibilities and worlds.

Shore's theoretical approach belongs within psychological anthropology's efforts to embed cognition and problems of meaning within culturally deep contexts and webs (building from Geertz, 1973). This framework supports our earlier claims that *seselelãme* functioned in Black Atlantic worlds as a kind of interpretive "template, a common underlying form that links superficially diverse cultural models" while simultaneously contributing to a "sometimes ineffable sense of 'style' or 'ethos'" characteristic of a particular social group (Shore, 1996, p 117). As examples, we pointed to such cultural models as signifyin(g), doing the do, an aesthetic of the cool, spirit work, conjuring, and so forth (described in Geurts and Adikah, 2006). These interpretations sit at the far psychological and cognitive pole of our interpretive work. Gradually we realized a model and schema approach (utilized by a number of psychological anthropologists, such as D'Andrade and Strauss, 1992) was overly mentalistic for our purposes. *Seselelãme* demanded that we move beyond psychology's often disembodied approaches and also beyond what Howes (2006, p 115) identified as "the verbocentrism of the linguistic model, the ocularcentrism of the visual culture model, and the holism of both the corporeal and material culture models." *Seselelãme* was very clearly rooted in relationality, not only of individuals and their cultural communities but also of minds and bodies as well as of perceiving people and "sensible objects." We found promising theoretical frameworks in some of the early work of anthropologist Thomas Csordas.

Csordas developed a cultural phenomenology approach in his early work on embodiment, experience, and the self (see Csordas, 1994), and we borrowed his phrase "somatic modes of attention" (Csordas, 1993) as we described the significance of *seselelãme* (or *bodily ways of knowing*) in Anlo everyday life (Geurts, 2002a). Csordas (1990) drew heavily on Merleau-Ponty and Bourdieu, so, taking his cue, we explored (Geurts, 2002a, p 233) ways in which *seselelãme* was akin to *habitus*—especially when conceptualized as "history turned into nature" or a "durably installed generative principle of regulated improvisations" (Bourdieu, 1977, p 78). A weakness in Bourdieu's theory lay in his failure to explain how one develops or internalizes *habitus*, so we paid special attention to child socialization practices in Anlo settings and documented ways in which certain sensory orientations were reinforced (Geurts, 2002a, pp 73–107). We demonstrated that *seselelãme* is most certainly *durably installed* in Anlo-Ewe people, but generational changes, cultural conflicts, globalization, and additional forces also lead to *improvisations*. For example, certain classical religious orientations persist, such as perceiving a rock at a threshold as a *legba*, or spiritual guardian, even though modernity's rationality enables Anlo people to improvise by cognitively acknowledging it is a stone while physically avoiding any encounter or confrontation with the entity (for a longer exploration of this ethnographic point, see Geurts, 2002b). A person's "nature," sedimented and cultivated through socialization experiences, bumps up against global cultural forces that spur human adaptation "instincts" and call forth improvisational responses. By this we are not suggesting that there is a singular Anlo-Ewe "history-nature" but rather a multiplicity—variations in class, gender, age, ability, religious orientation, and so forth—and therefore *habitus* has been a useful theoretical tool in exploring the extent to which *seselelãme* undergirds Anlo identity formation and relationality.

Most significantly, however, our work on *seselelãme* has been influenced by the sensory anthropology of David Howes (1991, 2003) and the cultural histories of Constance Classen (1993, 1997). Howes and Classen have long argued that the "ways we use our senses, and the ways we create and understand the sensory world, are shaped by culture. Perception is informed not only by the *personal meaning* a particular sensation has for us but also by the *social values* it carries" (2014, p 1, emphasis added). Historically, studies of sensation in Euro-American scholarship were the purview of the discipline of psychology, so anthropological and cultural-historical treatments of the senses (emerging in the late 1980s and early 1990s) helped pave the way for our own excavation of an Indigenous Anlo sensorium (see Geurts, 2002a, pp 37–69; Geurts and Adikah, 2006). These initial projects brought *seselelãme* to the foreground as we investigated not only the personal meanings of sensory experiences but also the cultural grounding of *bodily ways of knowing* and child socialization practices that inculcated such implicitly relational selves (Geurts, 2002a, pp 73–165). Our approach to "the body" therefore aligned well with an emerging interdisciplinary approach called "sensory studies," which in part aimed "to help problematize the increasingly homogenized notion of 'the body' in contemporary scholarship by advocating a modal and intermodal or relational approach to the study of our corporeal faculties" (Bull et al, 2006, p 6).[5] Indicating clearly that "the senses mediate the relationship between self and society, mind and body, idea and object," the authors of "Introducing Sensory Studies" took the following stance on the body:

> This relational focus will disrupt the presumption of the unity of the body (which has simply taken over from the modernist presumption of the unity of the subject) by highlighting the differential elaboration of the senses in diverse times and places, and underscoring the multiple forms of human sensuousness. (Bull et al, 2006, p 6)

Our own excavations of an Indigenous Anlo sensorium, and our explorations of *seselelãme*, further disrupted assumptions about the supposed universality of a five-senses model of the body and the privileging of categorical ways of thinking and knowing the world.

When Howes then brought to the English-speaking world French anthropologist and philosopher François Laplantine's *Life of the Senses*, this profoundly underscored the work we had already done on Anlo experiences and epistemologies. Laplantine's exposé helped to breathe new life into *seselelãme*. Howes provided us with a snapshot of Laplantine's insight by explaining that "categorical thought ... attributes properties to those things it isolates from the flux of existence and cleaves to the logic of the excluded middle," whereas modal thinking encourages us "to focus on duration, modulation, and rhythm instead of essence and identity" and is "sensitive to the slightest gradations and movements and affects" (Howes, 2015, pp ix–x). As mentioned earlier, Komabu-Pomeyie reached out on social media to a network of Ghanaians, asking them to share experiences and musings about *seselelãme*. We will now turn to one of the responses to illustrate modal thinking. The following is an unedited communication from Kodzo, a Ghanaian medical doctor. What we want to draw particular attention to is how his meditation on *seselelãme* captures a rhythm about his life, a movement looping his professional focus and intensity into his feelings of delight, elation, disappointment, frustration, and shame. His dedication to learning and academic achievement does not occur at the expense of being alert to his sense of happiness, joy, and worthiness. Kodzo wrote:

> I am an Ewe who hails from Dodome in the Ho West District of the Volta Region of Ghana. I learnt Twi as a second African language due to my professional work in Twi or Akan speaking communities. The nearest word I learnt in Twi similar to *seselelãme* or feelings is *atinka*. I experienced happiness, joy, delight and elation especially when I excelled academically. E.g. As best pupil in basic school, first to qualify to enter secondary school form 3; best biology student in sixth form; graduation with first degree in medicine and surgery; and Master's degree with distinction.

He then goes on to list a series of events and accomplishments that have given him "a feeling of self-satisfaction and fulfillment (*dzidzeme kporkpor* – Ewe)"; for example:

> Professionally, when I had a successful cervical cerclage at the first attempt. The product of that salvaged pregnancy is now a lecturer in University of Ghana. Also a successful first tracheostomy to save a child's life and received a commendation from my former Teaching Hospital. I also diagnosed and treated a lady who suffered 14 years from Sheehan's Syndrome (dysfunction of pituitary gland) with only a good clinical history taken without the aid of laboratory tests. And recently the detection of a rare congenital abnormality of Dextrocardia/situs inversus in a 4 month old [sic] baby referred to the Cardiologist. In all these cases and other similar cases, I experienced a sense of worthiness or usefulness (*nudzedze/vevinyenye* – Ewe). I have also felt a sense of disappointment, frustration, shame when I lost some of my patients I thought I could have saved, if I had acted differently, or more swiftly. E.g. my first attempt at hysterectomy, a snake bite, and a road traffic accident case.
>
> I also experienced a sense and feeling of being very useful/worthy/important to my home community when I undertook free health screening and treatment in my traditional area on 2 occasions after which the chiefs and elders came to express their gratitude with the donation of foodstuffs and fruits to my team. The same was when I rehabilitated a bore-hole to supply potable water to one community under the IFP Alumni Award in 2015. These are a few of the instances that readily come to mind talking of my feelings or *seselelãme*. I hope you will find them useful.

Kodzo's reflection is striking in the way it tacks back and forth from achievement (successfully performing a cervical stitch on his first attempt) to heartfelt sentiment (the baby delivered through that procedure is now a professor); the way it moves from palpably sensible activities (performing a tracheotomy on a child, rehabilitating a bore-hole to bring forth clean water) to a wide range of emotions (gratitude, happiness, disappointment, and shame). We can feel an alertness and intensity as the doctor recollects what *seselelãme* calls to mind. Another response from Komabu-Pomeyie's network of Ghanaians came from Akpene, a 40-year-old nurse, and we present it here unedited:

> To me *seselelãme* means feeling … this feeling comes at different levels. It could be very strong or very low. It could be an expression of joy or sadness. When it is extreme, one feels he or she is dreaming. I had this experience when I lost hope of getting admission to the university. At the final stage, I (out of the blue) received my admission letter. On my way from my station back to Accra, I had to constantly touch some passengers or ask them to pinch me in order to confirm that I was not dreaming. The second one was when I lost my elder brother. I lost the use of my limbs for some minutes because of how I was extremely shocked.

Reference to dreaming is very telling here, as it connotes an alternate state of consciousness. Feelings are so strong (extreme) that Akpene shifts into a qualitatively different mode of being (a dream-like state) and requests pinching of her skin to transform her orientation back toward the surrounding passengers. Laplantine (2015) stresses how modal thinking dwells on forming, deforming, and transforming rather than concerning itself with fixity and stability. Categorical thinking, by contrast, dwells on *drawing* but never *withdrawing* traits, since withdrawal would dissolve the category's fixity (Laplantine, 2015). Dreaming, however, perpetually draws and withdraws. It revels in processes of forming, deforming, and transforming, so likening an experience of extreme *seselelãme* to dreaming illustrates its modal nature. Another striking feature of this recollection is the mixture of emotions and physicality: joy, sadness, loss of hope, shock, dream state, touching, pinching, and paralysis of limbs. Another response, from a university lecturer named Nunanan, exhibits these same features:

> *Seselelãme* is an emotional expression of the self on seeing or hearing anything that depicts a situation of sorrow, regret, fear or pity at an event. It may lead to goose bumps where your bodily hair may stand on edge with a thrilling sensation running through you. This feeling varies in degrees depending on the event. It may be mild when the event depicts sorrow. But intense when it depicts fear.

We are initially told of emotional dimensions of *seselelãme*—sorrow, pity, fear—but then encounter *body hair standing on edge*. This physical manifestation, the goosebumps (piloerection), evoke an energy, a palpable change that is also indicative of modal thinking. We would suggest that these Ghanaian accounts of *seselelãme* are organic and vital: they are "without additives"; they are "free from pollutants" and exude an alive, sentient, breathing quality. We now turn to instances of its globalization and examine efforts to fix, stabilize, and commoditize *seselelãme*.

## *Seselelãme* and globalization

A rapid migration of *seselelãme* into Global North contexts (primarily via the world wide web) has led to some peculiar and occasionally simplistic interpretations. For example, a fitness coach declared on her website that *seselelãme* better categorized—compared to a range of English language descriptors—the kinds of classes she taught. She indicated that on the gym schedule her classes were typically listed under Body Mind Classes, as opposed to Group Exercise Classes, but she found "the arbitrary distinction sometimes hilarious, sometimes exasperating" and asked: "What Body Pump or High Intensity Interval Training (HIIT) class isn't using both body and mind and what yoga or Nia class isn't group exercise?" (McCulley, 2019). She indicated that if she had to describe or categorize what she taught, she would "call it movement, not exercise or dance or martial arts" and she would "say it is systemic, whole-body and sensory-centered … it is about presence, awareness and responsiveness … it creates health through integration and is as much about what we do outside the studio as it is what we do in it" (McCulley, 2019). Finally, McCulley indicated: "I might call it *Seselelame*."[6]

Though we are completely in favor of fitness students and mainstream Americans moving their bodies more regularly and pursuing greater attention to their feelings, we are not convinced that these practices or experiences automatically translate to *seselelãme*, and we are dubious about its cultural borrowing or appropriation.

Linguist George Lakoff and philosopher Mark Johnson open their 600-page book *Philosophy in the Flesh* with three short sentences: "The mind is inherently embodied. Thought is mostly unconscious. Abstract concepts are largely metaphorical" (1999, p 3). It was bold and provocative for them to assert the basic premise of our brains and cognitive processes as being somatically embedded or corporeal. Several implications of their assertion will help to shed light on our concerns about a globalization of *seselelãme*. They contend, "since reason is shaped by the body, it is not radically free, because the possible human conceptual systems and the possible forms of reason are limited" (Lakoff and Johnson, 1999, p 5). As a species, humans evolutionarily share basic body morphology, and it is through this limited body morphology that human reason has grown (Lakoff and Johnson, 1999). However, cultural diversity in language and experience creates at least some variation. In fact, they explain, "once we have learned a conceptual system, it is neurally instantiated in our brains and we are not free to think just anything" (p 5). If conceptual systems are neurally instantiated, resulting in our not being free to think outside or beyond them, then what about the instantiation of "bodily ways of knowing" or something like *seselelãme*? If a fitness coach in the United States declares what she teaches to be *seselelãme*, will students in her Body Pump or High Intensity Interval Training class be able to then experience *seselelãme*? Lakoff and Johnson (1999, p 6) hedge by suggesting that "our conceptual systems are not totally relative and not merely a matter of historical contingency, even though a degree of conceptual relativity does exist and even though historical contingency does matter a great deal." A degree of relativity does exist; historical contingency does matter. Here, as the term moves "out of Africa" and circulates around "the web," we wonder to what degree historical contingencies surrounding *seselelãme* matter and what happens as it is reinterpreted in new contexts.

The whimsical phrase "focus pocus now dot com" is used by McCulley, the fitness coach, to designate one of the sites where she imparts her wisdom. As indicated, she thinks that *seselelãme* aptly captures what she teaches, and she provides the following background:

> *Seselelame* is a West African word that a genius coach friend taught me not long ago. She learned it from Philip Shepherd's book *Radical Wholeness* in which seselelame is described as "an inner realm in which all the world is felt." I haven't read Shepherd's book but this term captures my imagination. (McCulley, 2019)

*Seselelãme* as "an inner realm in which all the world is felt" sounds like the end goal of a spiritual quest; it has the ring of New Age promises of enlightenment, or attainment of a godlike overview. To be able to *feel all of the world*—from Asia to Europe to Africa to the Americas—inside of yourself, in your inner realm, once you have engaged in a workout at the gym is, needless to say, a tall order. Some would say this is simply hyperbole and not meant to be taken literally. But a second claim found on focus pocus now dot com is that "*seselelame* ... recognizes that the entire human experience is felt in our bodies" (McCulley, 2019). In comparison with what Ghanaians say about *seselelãme*, this is a rather preposterous claim. To suggest a workout at a gym can lead to feeling *the entire human experience* in one's body is simply *not sensible*; it is abstract and categorical. Through recourse to measurement (entire, not just partial), it makes an attempt at prestige. What we want to ask is, how did *seselelãme* become linked to such a claim? What was "picked up" from Geurts' writings that then led people in Global North contexts to embellish, exaggerate, or distort *seselelãme* in this way?

Anthropology has rightfully been criticized for advancing the European Enlightenment project of "differencing" and "othering" peoples all over the world. Princeton University professor of music Kofi Agawu, who grew up in the northern Ewe-speaking area of Ghana, has argued eloquently about the disingenuousness of supposedly comparing cultural practices when the people live in drastically different *economic* spheres (2012, p 123). He calls out those of us ethnographers who have been too wedded to "a persistent strategy of 'differencing'" and too slow to "embrace sameness" (p 120). While Geurts' work resisted "essentializing" Anlo-speaking people and made great effort to account for processes by which the so-called "knowledge" reported in publications was arrived at, in the end some of the renderings of *seselelãme* may very well have downplayed "residual similarities" among Anlo-Ewe people and other human groups, and some of the descriptions of *seselelãme* may have given an "edge to strangeness and novelty" (pp 119, 123). But a perceived "edge" of difference has been amplified through the globalization of *seselelãme*.

Interpretations of *seselelãme* as novel and exotic are apparent in Phil Shepherd's use of this Ewe term. On his website, Shepherd describes himself as an "international authority on embodiment," and the autobiographical opening of his book *Radical Wholeness* portrays a longstanding interest in "cultures radically different from [his] own" (2017, p 7). In fact, his first chapter title—"Feel-Feel-at-Flesh-Inside"—seems aimed at demonstrating such global cultural awareness. He devotes at least ten pages to explaining what he learned about Anlo-Ewe sensory philosophy from reading *Culture and the Senses* (Geurts, 2002a), and as a jumping off point for explaining his own journey "into greater embodiment," he borrows our morpheme-by-morpheme account of what *seselelãme* can be understood to index. Shepherd's enthusiasm is palpable. Writing for a lay rather than scholarly audience, his book blends genres of memoir and self-help guide. He asserts that relative to "our culture" in which "we live in our heads" and "deem the body to be without intelligence," in some "radically different cultures" (such as Anlo-Ewe), people are attentive to their bodies (Shepherd, 2017, p 43). For purposes of *interpreting the body*, Shepherd's view is a provocative hypothesis, but it is unproven (which will be discussed later) and by no means representative of what we think the existence of *seselelãme* means.

Othering, exoticizing, and cultural appropriation are, of course, completely entangled. Making "other cultures" appear exotic or at least "non-Western" evolved alongside the discipline and profession of anthropology, a religious zeal for missionizing, and a political agenda of expansion and colonization. Negative (racialized) stereotyping has been transmogrified, to some extent, into lucrative cultural appropriation (eg, see Greene, 2008), so that trafficking in things (formerly marked as) "primitive" can now be profitable. It is not surprising, therefore, that Shepherd has trademarked (for profit) a practice by means of which people can appropriate/acquire such a different and desired way of being. On his website we find options to pay-to-engage in training workshops on The Embodied Present Process™ (TEPP), "a series of practices that were developed by Philip Shepherd to help people gently undo the stress and imbalances that are caused by living in the head, and find instead what it means to rest in the deeper, connected intelligence of the body." Categorical thinking is on clear display here with the head and the body understood as separate, divided, and distinct. Various societies are also categorized and distinct, which comes through in the following text from Shepherd's website where he accentuates distinctions between "our culture" and those that are "radically different":

> The Anlo-Ewe don't just hear sounds; they feel them through the body. They don't just see sights; they feel them in the body. So while we have only the Chosen Five—each an exteroceptor that imputes a boundary around the self—the Anlo-Ewe have seselelame, an inner realm in which all the world is felt. ... Seselelame is an umbrella or "uber" sense that feels reality reverberate through "the cavern." (Shepherd, 2017, pp 17, 23)

The phrase "an inner realm in which all the world is felt" is what McCulley, the fitness instructor, mentioned in relation to how her classes at the gym are unique. One of the problems here is that *seselelãme* has nothing to do with feeling "all the world." We are also not aware of any *bodily way of knowing* (nor an organ or "an inner realm") that makes such an experience possible. These distortions of *seselelãme* remind us of one of Agawu's points in his essay "Contesting Difference": "While Africans deserve full recognition for whatever is unique about their critical and cultural practices, they do not need *fake or facile attributions*" (2012, p 120, emphasis added), and "what I am arguing for ... is not sameness but the hypostatized presumption of sameness" (p 126). Imagining Anlo-Ewe people possessing an "uber sense" and an ability to *feel the whole world* creates a caricature, not simply a difference.

Julia Jude is a systemic psychotherapist who vacillates between equating *seselelãme* with AOTI (an acronym she uses for African Oral Traditional Ideas [2016, p 555]), passing it off as "my inventive approach [sic] Seselelame" (2013, p 194) and elevating it to an analytic perspective on the same plane as phenomenology, feminism, and systemic constructivism (p 136).[7] When conducting a Google search query about *seselelãme*, Jude's *Journal of Family Therapy* article (2016) comes up as the first search engine response page, which is disappointing since *seselelãme* does not coincide with any of the ways she deploys it. What are we to make of this? Similar to McCulley and Shepherd, Jude both distorts *seselelãme* and treats it pragmatically—zeroing in on its potential for commoditization. At the end of her dissertation she explains that she plans on "applying the Seselelame approach within a clinic-based setting" and "facilitating workshops ... as a way of introducing the Seselelame frame" and "establishing a training placement, creating opportunities for trainee family therapists to experience the Seselelame approach" (2013, p 225). She also indicates engagement in "publication of a Seselelame tool kit" and "a Seselelame performative arts project for working with young people" (p 226). Barely attributing *seselelãme* to the Ewe language or Anlo-Ewe people, Jude explains: "I came to take on knowledge from my ancestry that promotes a feeling in the body perspective" (2016 p 556), and "the description of ideas from AOTI provides an understanding of the themes that I found helpful which led to transforming some of the main principles of AOTI resulting in the invention of Seselelame" (2013, p 108). Other than a passing comment about how "I was encouraged by my supervisor to become curious with my inventive approach Seselelame" (p 194), we can find no reason for the word to even appear in her dissertation; she uses it incorrectly, and in nearly every instance it could be replaced by the English word "feeling." On the other hand, *seselelãme* has an exotic, catchy quality; it could yield good market appeal and merchandizing power, which seems to be the motivation behind Jude's claims to have established these trademark-worthy expressions: The Seselelame Tool Kit book (p 94); The Seselelame Approach (p 98); The Seselelame Model (p 197). Making *seselelãme* itself into products and services is a manifestation of categorical-rationalist thinking in the extreme and the antithesis of the modal thinking so beautifully exhibited by *seselelãme*. It isolates, fixes, and stabilizes *seselelãme's* properties into three categories of services. Mirroring Shepherd's description of *seselelãme* as "an inner realm in which all the world is felt" (2017, p 17), Jude ultimately concludes that "seselelame posits that everything is connected" (2016, p 563).

The distortions and exaggerations we see in the claims of Shepherd, McCulley, and Jude play to Global North cultural trends centering on personal transformation, mindfulness training, and the human potential movement. The Esalen Institute in California, for example, describes itself as "a global network of seekers devoted to the belief that we are all capable of the extraordinary," so a *seselelãme* workshop teaching people to find their *inner realm*, where they will be able to *connect everything* and *feel the whole world*, could certainly appeal to those desiring extraordinary capabilities and be quite lucrative as well. At this point we return to more organic renderings of *seselelãme* as a means of probing why the reification and commoditization of *seselelãme* is problematic.

## Ewe speakers interpret *seselelãme*

As Ghanaians wrote text messages to Komabu-Pomeyie in the spring of 2020, reflecting on situations when they considered *seselelãme* to be at play, they used English words such as intuition, instinct, emotion, and feeling; they provided examples that included spiritual experiences, emotional reactions, sexual encounters, and more. A teacher named Akosiwa communicated: "The semantic field (meaning) of the Ewe word *seselelãme* is very wide and subjective. *Seselelãme* could have English equivalents like sensation, ecstasy, feelings, emotions, excitement, agitation, etc." Another person, named Mensah, who is a typical traditional farmer from Dzodze, reflected that if he used the English language to describe *seselelãme* he would say: "Feelings, like attitudes, are predispositions to behavior. They run deep inside our bodies and are in fact the basis of our emotions, like anger and joy. They may not necessarily be logical but yet influence and sometimes determine our behavior." Predispositions to behavior running deep inside our bodies is close to Bourdieu's *habitus* as "history turned into nature" or "durably installed generative principles" (1977, p 78). What follows is Mensah's example of experiencing *seselelãme* (punctuation and phrasing edited lightly):

> For instance, yesterday I hired some three women to help me harvest my corn and the agreement was that at the end of everything they would take a bowlful of corn as payment. They were to work from 8 am to 3 pm. They came around 10 am and closed at 1:30 pm without harvesting all the corn on the farm. However, they insisted they wanted a bowlful each of corn, per the agreement. Remember, these are visibly poor village women. Now, here is the feeling: I felt pity for them and at the same time felt bad about their not fulfilling their side of the bargain. And so (even though out of the feeling of pity for them) I agreed they should fetch their bowl each of corn. But, when they started filling their bowls, I had a very bad feeling that they were cheating me, and so I became restless but had to control myself not to stop them. That feeling that they cheated me got the better part of me for the rest of yesterday. I felt pity for the poor guys [sic] so I agreed they should take the corn, but at the same time I had another feeling that nearly made me stop them.

In Mensah's recollection we find neither an epiphany nor a claim that "all the world is felt." Instead we hear a somewhat complex account of corporeal stirring, visceral provocations, intuitions, even conflicted emotions. We are reminded of Howes' observation (2015, p x) that modal thinking encourages us "to focus on duration, modulation, and rhythm instead of essence and identity" and it is "sensitive to the slightest gradations and movements and affects." While Mensah made a passing reference to an identity marker ("visibly poor village women"), it does not dominate the reflection. Instead, there is an emphasis on deeply embodied feelings that are predispositions to behavior, and then the account of fluctuations from a sense of pity and charity to resentment (at being cheated) and then even honor (at fulfilling the bargain). He made an agreement, then felt restless and conflicted, yet mustered (self-)control to refrain from reneging on the deal. We get a clear sense of modulations and gradations, movements and affects in the account. Thinking, analysis, and conclusions (cognitive processes) were also involved in his working through the experience, but we think he used this as an example of *seselelãme* because he wanted us to appreciate how his body's visceral, palpable sensations were vital. There was no clear and easy way to categorize the situation (cheating and fraud? pity? charity and justice?) and his body provided signals that marshaled a history (upbringing, training, parenting, enculturation) that called forth those "durably installed generative principles." For Anlo-Ewe and other African people, this *bodily way of knowing* or *seselelãme* is deeply valued.

Reflecting on recent experiences she could recall that would also help to illustrate what Anlo-Ewe people mean when they use the term *seselelãme*, Komabu-Pomeyie wrote (personal communication, January 20, 2020):

> A lady and I were carrying the setup communion table to the front of the congregation during a communion service at church last Sunday. Then, suddenly, I felt "the glass communion cup will fall and break" because I was in [a] wheelchair. I smiled it off because I thought it was a strange thought. After we had put the table down, the lady, in an attempt to lift up the lace covering the table, caused the communion cup to tilt, fall, and break. Instantly, I felt, "Oh! God was speaking to me through that feeling before. Why didn't I take it seriously and forewarn the lady to be careful?" I consider *seselelãme* the appropriate word to convey this experience because I had heard and perceived (within me) the consciousness that something was going to happen.

Premonition, clairvoyance, and intuition are English words that seem appropriate here. So why do we want to consider this an instance of *seselelãme*? Komabu-Pomeyie drew attention to herself in the wheelchair: this dimension of her embodiment was at the forefront of her premonition that the communion cup was going to break. Concluding it was a strange thought (probably questioning why she herself would think that a person with disability was not capable of setting up communion), she then *smiled it off*. She dismissed the thought, or put it aside, and in recollecting what she did, she referred to it as *smiling it off*. This is a brilliant way of capturing how a human smile can have the effect of melting, soothing, or calming feelings in the body, flesh, or skin. It also demonstrates the high value that Komabu-Pomeyie and Anlo-Ewe people place on being attentive to visceral dimensions of knowing. In this example we also see that *seselelãme* does not always result in *bodily ways of knowing* that lead to triumph or positive outcomes. Sometimes knowledge is off or wrong, no matter how we arrive at it, and so this also contrasts sharply with Global North appropriations of *seselelãme* that fixate on how it supposedly brings power or extraordinary capabilities.

## Psychology, possessive individualism, and *seselelãme*'s intersubjectivity

Academic psychology has also shown an interest in interpreting *seselelãme*, and here we will discuss two studies. The first of these aimed at bringing into social and cultural psychology a historically underrepresented group, Africans, and sought to explore "differences in the importance of the internal body in the experience and expression of emotions in two cultural contexts: Ghanaian and Euro American" (Dzokoto, 2010, p 69). These are laudable goals, and our discussion of the study is not meant to imply any condescension. The experiment involved 70 undergraduate students from two different social science departments at a Ghanaian university and compared them to 100 Euro-American students from a large midwestern university. It drew on two different tests: the Body Awareness Questionnaire (BAQ) and the Trait Meta-Mood Scale Attention to Emotion subscale (TMMS). Dzokoto found that "Ghanaians were significantly lower on the attention to emotion subscale," and her hypothesis was confirmed that "Ghanaian subjects would score significantly higher on a measure of somatic-focused awareness" (2010, p 72). She then explained, "According to these results, the concept of 'feel-feel-at-flesh-inside' was successfully demonstrated numerically through the concept of somatic-focused awareness as measured by the Body Awareness Questionnaire." Interestingly, Dzokoto points out that the Ghanaian participants in the study were English-speaking university students, which brings in two factors we might expect to cause them to exhibit more "Western influence" in their mode of thinking and being. But even though they were from the more, relatively speaking, "Westernized sector" of their own African society, they still exhibited the difference that Dzokoto hypothesized.

Several subsequent studies have referenced Dzokoto's work as they have taken up what is often called "the mind–body problem."[8] One particular study featured Anlo-Ewe people and *seselelãme* quite prominently and raised questions about distinctions between "interoceptive awareness and interoceptive accuracy" (Chentsova-Dutton and Dzokoto, 2014). The researchers reviewed a range of qualitative studies that demonstrated cultural elaboration of somatic attentiveness and they wanted to explore whether experimental psychology could verify such differences. Interoception included both proprioception and visceroception, the processing of signals from the skin, muscles, joints, and inner organs (2014, p 667). Awareness was defined as the "self-reported tendency to attend to actual or perceived internal changes," and accuracy meant a "degree of precision in estimating actual physiological signals, such as heart rate" (p 667). Participants in the experiments included 61 West Africans in Accra, Ghana, and 61 Euro-Americans in Washington, DC. In a nutshell, the experiment involved participants viewing two different film clips (one neutral and one fear-provoking) while their heart and respiratory rates were measured, and they continuously recorded perceived changes to their heart rates. The study's conclusions reported:

> West Africans were more likely than European Americans to endorse beliefs about being able to accurately monitor their bodily signals. Yet the measure of interoceptive accuracy, as captured by the coherence between in-the-moment perceived and actual heart rate in response to a scary film clip, told a different story. Although participants across cultural groups had little success in accurately perceiving changes in their heart rates, *West Africans fared worse*, not better, than European Americans in this task. (Chentsova-Dutton and Dzokoto, 2014, p 674, emphasis added)

The authors were surprised that participants who engaged in the study in Accra were not able to demonstrate greater accuracy at perceiving their heart rates. They asked: "How can we explain the fact that West Africans, who think of themselves as highly attuned to their bodies, are actually less able than European Americans to detect bodily changes" (Chentsova-Dutton and Dzokoto, 2014, p 674)? Several possible explanations were explored. The discipline of psychology shows that people who report more somatic symptoms (relative to other people) are often not good at accurately detecting actual physiological changes in their bodies. Certain situational circumstances can activate their somatic schemata, and this seems to interfere with accuracy, or seems to have a disruptive effect. It is possible that asking participants to track their heart rates caused the activation of their "schemata for the types of heart rate changes that are associated with fear," which include an expectation of spikes. But anticipating the fear-induced spikes could inadvertently cause them to overlook "actual, typically more gradual, increases and drops in heartbeat over the course of the film" (p 675).

Unlike the uses of *seselelãme* discussed previously, which aim to appeal to popular audiences and enhance commercial activities, these psychological studies were conducted by academic researchers and described for a scholarly audience. We are not trying to suggest, therefore, that all of the cases presented in this chapter are alike, and we are not trying to blanketly call into question the value of psychological studies. We are, however, concerned that even the treatment of *seselelãme* by well-meaning psychologists diverges quite a bit from how it functions in its organic context. Ghanaians and Ewe-speakers consulted for this project by and large provided examples in which *relationality* was of primary importance as they considered how *seselelãme* functioned in their everyday lives. In the psychology settings there is a kind of artificially constructed individualism: subjects are treated in isolation of each other and asked to fixate on something that has little or no intersubjectivity. Among the responses Komabu-Pomeyie received, Ama related the following (edited lightly for grammatical purposes) as instances when *seselelãme* captures what she has experienced:

> I hear how a dear one passes on and tears begin rolling down my cheeks, just because my receptive heart told me that's a loss. I hear that someone dear or close to me has won a visa lottery and quickly I jump up in excitement, all because my receptive heart tells me that's good news and so my emotions follow and are exposed publicly or openly because of that piece of news. This indicates that I experience emotional changes based on what I receive into myself as information—good and bad, positive and negative—as well as what my senses receive.

The emphasis here is on how sensory and bodily ways of knowing influence social-emotional relationships, rather than serve as a microscope for individualized and self-contained physiological measures. This latter fixation links up with Global North trends in individualized medicine and fitness regimes, which are often cast in a positive light, but it also "pollutes" *seselelãme* (to extend our organic metaphor). Connectedness to other people, or sociality, consistently emerged as we asked Ghanaians to offer examples of *seselelãme*. Kwame wrote:

> What does *seselelãme* mean? It means what I feel after an occurrence. The emotions that fill my heart after an experience. How do you translate *seselelãme* into the English language? Emotional rapture; emotional meltdown. There was a time when someone insulted me—*Eku gbagbawo* (boy with a damaged eye). All through my childhood as a boy with partial disability with regards to my eyes, countless people looked down on me and teased me and it really affected my self-esteem growing up. So I can relate to *seselelãme* as a growing-up boy.

Kwame initially offered feelings of his individualized self, so we might anticipate reflections or comments on interior sensations. But immediately after suggesting the creative translation of "emotional rapture, emotional meltdown," his grounded example of *seselelãme* reflected an intersubjective consciousness. His deflated self-esteem, or his feelings of emotional meltdown, came about because of teasing, insults, people looking down on him. *Seselelãme* nearly always conjures intersubjectivity rather than an individualized psycho-physiology fixated on counting or measurement (of something such as heartbeat).

While this difference in understanding and investigating *seselelãme* is certainly reflective of differences in disciplinary methods (eg, psychology versus anthropology and sociology) and the approaches taken by various scholars, we would suggest that the schism extends beyond academic fields. It also highlights a fundamental difference in what is valued and what is believed to be real. In the psychological studies of *seselelãme* that we discussed earlier, the social is absent; *seselelãme* is stripped of its cultural context, for who lives in a psychological experiment?[9] Imposing onto *seselelãme* the question of interoceptive awareness compared to interoceptive *accuracy* introduces a value system that has little connection to the lived reality of *seselelãme*. Whether or not a person can accurately measure their own heart rate is a question emerging from a cultural world valuing atomization, categorization, calculation, measurement, and power—as well as reality as that which can be perceived in data. This cultural world also privileges possessive individualism, whereas *seselelãme* comes from a cultural world in which fluidity, movement, synesthesia, and intersubjectivity are valued.

## Concluding remarks

This chapter has presented a handful of ways in which *seselelãme* has been culturally appropriated, commoditized, distorted, removed from its organic context, and adulterated. Why should this matter? What is at stake here and why should we care? In the first instance, if *seselelãme* attracts people (especially in the Global North) because it offers an alternative to mind–body dualism or "five centuries of rationalocentrism," then it behooves us to listen closely to those who organically live with *seselelãme* and align our own interpretations of *seselelãme* with theirs rather than distort—or pollute it with our own. Only then might we actually learn from *seselelãme* and maximize our potential to cross over into a more rhythmic, sensible, transformative (noncategorical) mode of being and knowing. We repeat Kofi Agawu's claim that "While Africans deserve full recognition for whatever is unique about their critical and cultural practices, they do not need fake or facile attributions" (2012, p 120). Fake and facile representations lead to stereotypes and racialized misunderstanding; so does theft of natural resources, which leads to our second point.

Commoditization of *seselelãme* perpetuates an age-old symbolic and structural asymmetry rooted in the violence of the transatlantic slave trade, the looting of Africa for gold, timber, oil, coltan, and more, and the institutionalized power-hold Global North entities and people have over people of African descent. At this point it is doubtful that more than a few hundred or few thousand dollars have as yet been earned in the Global North through *seselelãme*, but that is beside the point. What is at issue is a persistent pattern of extractive practices, when it comes to Africa, by those who are more economically powerful. In his essay "Interrogating Piracy," South African scholar Adam Haupt (2014) discusses how things African have been consistently appropriated and "reworked" as if they are simply "raw material" without any attempt being made to engage the actual cultural context in which the thing originates.[10] His use of "raw material" strikes a chord because it links historical extractions from the ground with contemporary appropriations of aesthetic, symbolic, and bodily material—all of which can be "reworked" in ways not unlike what we observed in gyms, workshops, and therapy strategies.

Finally, from the vantage point of Euro-American Enlightenment-inspired academic and scientific perspectives, *seselelãme* does, in technical ways, "belong" to a person; however, in its organic context it is much less about individualism than intersubjectivity. For centuries, Anglo-American tendencies have favored "one body, one self" and "one person, one vote,"[11] while Anlo-Ewe tendencies have privileged socio-centrism, porosity of selves, and intersubjectivity. As we have seen with Laplantine's distinctions of categorical and modal thinking, these alternate ontologies and epistemologies amount to almost a civilizational difference. When the discipline of psychology attempts to insert an ancient (and "non-Western") phenomenon into its experiments it ends up distorted and even polluted. To extend our metaphor, this bourgeois and possessive individualist approach to humanity, animality, and the planet has resulted in catastrophe. Until Global North entities and the individuals who populate these institutions change deeply, something as organic and biotic as *seselelãme* will remain beyond their grasp.

## Notes

[1] For an extended discussion of these categories and how *seselelãme* poses alternative pathways to processing experiences and ways of knowing, see Geurts' (2002b) piece that deals with "cultural categories."

[2] For yet another three-way division, see Laplantine's (2015, p 59) discussion of "the impossibility or at least the difficulty that is still often ours today, of perceiving a continuity between the different dimensions of the living: organic life (reduced in Descartes to the mechanical), psychological life, life in society."

3   Participants in the survey have all been given pseudonyms and composite identities.
4   A plural "we" and "our" is used in this chapter to refer historically to Geurts and numerous Anlo people involved in this research, as well as specifically to Komabu-Pomeyie and Geurts as coauthors. For background on how we met see Geurts and Komabu-Pomeyie (2016).
5   For a more current overview of sensory studies, also see Howes (2019).
6   Variations in the spelling, accenting, italicization, and capitalization of the term *seselelãme* reflect its usage among the Western institutions and persons discussed in this chapter.
7   Here we might point out that *seselelãme* could very well be or become such an analytic perspective or ideology. It is not difficult to try a thought experiment in which Africa colonized Europe (in history) and therefore nowdays in school instead of studying Cartesianism or phenomenology we would be studying *ubuntu* or *seselelãme*. But that did not happen, so it is only in a thought experiment that *seselelãme* presently holds such stature.
8   The "mind–body problem" takes up the relationship between mental entities and physical/material phenomena, or the problem of consciousness and the brain (see Feigl, 1967; Kim, 2010). Within the field of psychology, a particular programmatic orientation has recast the mind–body problem in terms of "visceral perception" or the mind's ability to detect shifts, changes, or movement within internal organs of the body.
9   By critiquing specific studies that touch on *seselelãme* we do not mean to suggest that all psychology research absents the social (see especially Markus and Kitayama, 2010). And while psychology may not center the social, social-psychology and cognitive cultural sociology certainly do (see Turner, 2008).
10  In this specific instance Haupt is referring to the Solomon Linda case of his song "Mbube," which was appropriated numerous times over and eventually used by Disney Corporation in its film *The Lion King*, but the point is more generalized throughout the piece.
11  See our critique of Antonio Damasio's neuro-biologically based psychology in Geurts (2005).

## References

Agawu, K. (2012) 'Contesting difference: a critique of Africanist ethnomusicology', in M. Clayton, T. Herbert and R. Middleton (eds) *The Cultural Study of Music* (2nd edn), New York: Routledge, pp 117–126.

Aposhyan, S. (2007) *Natural Intelligence: Body-Mind Integration and Human Development*, Norwell, MA: Now Press.

Bourdieu, P. (1977) *Outline of a Theory of Practice*, Cambridge: Cambridge University Press.

Bull, M., Gilroy, P., Howes, D. and Kahn D. (2006) 'Introducing sensory studies', *The Senses and Society*, 1(1): 5–7.

Chentsova-Dutton, Y.E. and Dzokoto, V. (2014) 'Listen to your heart: the cultural shaping of interoceptive awareness and accuracy', *Emotion*, 14(4): 666–678.

Classen, C. (1993) *Worlds of Sense: Exploring the Senses in History and across Cultures*, London: Routledge.

Classen, C. (1997) 'Foundations for an anthropology of the senses', *International Social Science Journal*, 49(153): 401–412.

Csordas, T. (1990) 'Embodiment as a paradigm for anthropology', *Ethos*, 18(1): 5–47.

Csordas, T. (1993) 'Somatic modes of attention', *Cultural Anthropology*, 8(2): 135–156.

Csordas, T. (1994) *The Sacred Self: A Cultural Phenomenology of Sacred Healing*, Berkeley: University of California Press.

Damasio, A. (2000) *The Feeling of What Happens: Body and Emotion in the Making of Consciousness*, Boston, MA: Mariner Books.

D'Andrade, R. and Strauss, C. (eds) (1992) *Human Motives and Cultural Models*, Cambridge: Cambridge University Press.

Dzokoto, V. (2010) 'Different ways of feeling', *Journal of Social, Evolutionary, and Cultural Psychology*, 4(2): 68–78.

Feigl, H. (1967) *The Mental and the Physical: The Essay and a Postscript*, Minneapolis: University of Minnesota Press.

Geertz, C. (1973) *The Interpretation of Cultures*, New York: Basic Books.

Geurts, K.L. (2002a) *Culture and the Senses: Bodily Ways of Knowing in an African Community*, Berkeley: University of California Press.

Geurts, K.L. (2002b) 'On rocks, walks and talks: cultural categories and an anthropology of the senses', *Ethos: Journal of the Society for Psychological Anthropology*, 30(3): 178–198.

Geurts, K.L. (2003) 'On embodied consciousness in Anlo-Ewe worlds: a cultural phenomenology of the fetal position', *Ethnography*, 4(3): 363–396.

Geurts, K.L. (2005) 'Consciousness as "feeling in the body": a West African theory of embodiment, emotion and the making of mind', in D. Howes (ed) *Empire of the Senses*, Oxford: Berg, pp 164–178.

Geurts, K.L. and Adikah, E.G. (2006). 'Enduring and endearing feelings and the transformation of material culture in West Africa', in E. Edwards, C. Gosden and R.B. Phillips (eds) *Sensible Objects: Colonialism, Museums and Material Culture*, Oxford: Berg, pp 35–60.

Geurts, K.L. and Komabu-Pomeyie, S. (2016) 'From "sensing disability" to seselelame: non-dualistic activist orientations in twenty-first-century Accra', in S. Grech and K. Soldatic (eds) *Disability in the Global South*, Cham: Springer International Publishing, pp 85–98.

Greene, K.J. (2008) 'Intellectual property at the intersection of race and gender: lady sings the blues', *Journal of Gender, Social Policy and the Law*, 16(3): 365–385.

Haupt, A. (2014) 'Interrogating piracy: race, colonialism and ownership', in L. Eckstein and A. Schwarz (eds) *Postcolonial Piracy: Media Distribution and Cultural Production in the Global South*, London: Bloomsbury Academic, pp 179–192.

Howes, D. (ed) (1991) *The Varieties of Sensory Experience*, Toronto: University of Toronto Press.

Howes D. (2003) *Sensual Relations: Engaging the Senses in Culture and Social Theory*, Ann Arbor: University of Michigan Press.

Howes, D. (2006) 'Charting the sensorial revolution', *Senses and Society*, 1(1): 113–128.

Howes, D. (2015) 'The extended sensorium: introduction to the sensory and social thought of François Laplantine', in F. Laplantine (auth) *The Life of the Senses: Introduction to a Modal Anthropology*, translated by J. Furniss, London: Bloomsbury, pp vii–xiv.

Howes, D. (2019) 'Multisensory anthropology', *Annual Review of Anthropology*, 48: 17–28.

Howes, D. and Classen, C. (2014) *Ways of Sensing: Understanding the Senses in Society*, London: Routledge.

Jude, J. (2013) 'Family systemic therapy in the home: reigniting the fire', unpublished dissertation, University of Bedfordshire, UK.

Jude, J. (2016) '*Seselelame*: feelings in the body: working alongside systemic ideas', *Journal of Family Therapy*, 38: 555–571.

Kim, J. (2010) *Essays in the Metaphysics of Mind*, Oxford: Oxford University Press.

Lakoff, G. and Johnson, M. (1999) *Philosophy in the Flesh: The Embodied Mind and Its Challenge to Western Thought*, New York: Basic Books.

Laplantine, F. (2015) *The Life of the Senses: Introduction to a Modal Anthropology*, translated by J. Furniss, London: Bloomsbury.

Markus, H.R. and Kitayama, S. (2010) 'Cultures and selves: a cycle of mutual constitution', *Perspectives on Psychological Science*, 5(4): 420–430.

McCulley, S. (2019) 'Seselelame: holistic integrated interoceptive training' [Blog], May 19, available from: https://web.archive.org/web/20201101015846/https://focuspocusnow.com/2019/05/19/seselelame-holistic-integrated-interoceptive-training/.

Shepherd, P. (2017) *Radical Wholeness*, Berkeley, CA: North Atlantic Books.

Shore, B. (1996) *Culture in Mind: Cognition, Culture, and the Problem of Meaning*, New York: Oxford University Press.

Turner, B.S. (2008) *The Body and Society: Explorations in Social Theory* (3rd edn), London: SAGE.

4

# Gender on the Post-Colony: Phenomenology, Race, and the Body in *Nervous Conditions*

*Sweta Rajan-Rankin and Mrinalini Greedharry*

What is the body and what can it do? How does the lived body experience itself and what are the structural and historical vectors that mediate its emergence and disappearance? The intermittent appearance of the racialized body in and out of theory, history, and politics compels us to ask the questions that have dominated body and embodiment studies (Douglas, 1966; Elias, 1978; Turner, 1984, 2012; Featherstone et al, 1991; Butler, 1993; Shilling, 2003) in a new way. This chapter was written in a moment when Black and racialized bodies have once again gained prominence because of the brutal murder of George Floyd in the United States, suffocated under a white policeman's knee. And yet, we have been here before and found that just as suddenly as the racialized body appears in our critiques and analyses, it disappears.

Critical approaches to the body, from social constructionism (Weinberg, 2012) to feminism (Mohanty, 1991; Crenshaw, 1994) to critical race studies (Weheliye, 2014), have attempted to respond to the disappearance of the racialized body with varying levels of success. Feminism, as a unifying arc and promise of gender justice, has needed to reckon with its own racializing imaginaries, working through white feminisms' uncomfortable relationship with Black women's class and race subordination (Olufemi, 2020). Epistemological claims advanced within white feminism and the European philosophical tradition—about gender as a category and gender equality as a social process—have failed to consider how colonial histories perpetuate unequal subject locations for people of color and, in particular, women located in the Global South. While there have been movements toward integrated analysis (intersectional theory presents one example [Crenshaw, 1994]), the basic crux of the argument has not been addressed. The bodies, stories, narratives, and embodied histories of Black, Indigenous, and other women of color have been noticeably absent in both white feminist scholarship and race scholarship.

We contend that gender is a colonial formation, insofar as the concept and constructs of gender have been derived from Western epistemologies that underpin social orders and norms typical of Western societies. Due to the mainstreaming of concepts concerning gender, patriarchy, and sexual and reproductive control, the multifarious representations through which women's identities and embodied belongings emerge—for example, within African countries—are read or interpreted through lenses of oppression and victimhood. Similarly, while there have been powerful theoretical interventions that have explored the phenomenology of Blackness and racialized bodies, they have tended to focus on the Black man's struggle within colonialism, and Black women's experiences are again sidelined. The solution is not further expansion of representation and identity politics. Rather, it is a full force challenge to the conceptualization of gender and race as distinct but parallel categories; it is a reinterpretation of the multiple axes within which gendered and racialized bodies are constructed and eroded in different and uneven ways in the development of colonial histories.

In order for this reinterpretation to be successful, however, meaning and materiality associated with bodies must be spoken *from* as well as *through* an engagement with Black feminist writers—for such an engagement is both the interpretative (theoretical) device and the method by which the Black woman's body appears and stays visible in our theories and our research. It is in this spirit that we explore the formation of "gender on the post-colony" through a close reading of Tsitsi Dangarembga's (1988) award-winning novel *Nervous Conditions*, which advances and speaks to the limitations of Frantz Fanon's (1986) phenomenology of Blackness.

The phenomenological tradition of body studies has been slow to understand how the corporeal schema of racialized subjects develops in a racist or colonial world, but postcolonial novelists have theorized this through their representations of the colonial architectures of power. Dangarembga's *Nervous Conditions*, for instance, theorizes the potentialities and limits of Zimbabwean girlhood through the eyes of two African girls, Tambu and Nyasha. The use of dual protagonists, similar but not identical, allows us to see the intersecting interpretive frames that link colonial actors with their material and biographical environments through, for example, ruralism, the homestead, and colonial patriarchy; religion, sexuality, and the regulation of women's bodies in the missionary school; modernity, purity and danger, and embodied erasures; pleasure and self-awareness; disease and sickness; starvation and longing; colonial mimicry, ambivalence, and arrival. We argue that our textual analysis allows for a nuanced understanding of how African womanhood is negotiated and how girls' bodies are made available for, and find ways to resist, colonial architectures of power.

## Phenomenology of Blackness

The phenomenological tradition of body studies emerges from the writings of Husserl (1990), Heidegger (1962), and Merleau-Ponty (1962), who each in their own way sought to challenge Descartes' famous proposition "cogito, ergo sum" (I think, therefore I am), which, situating the seat of the self in the reasoning faculty of the mind, set up a dualism between mind and body. Phenomenology did not offer a method for solving this mind–body dichotomy so much as it presented a new analytical lens through which to interrogate it (Crossley, 2012). According to Descartes, the search for the truth required a quest for rationality outside the fleshy self: "in Cartesianism, the human mind is viewed as an island of awareness afloat in the vast sea of insensate matter" (Leder, 1990, p 8). Descartes' proposition sets up a split between rationality and sensuous experience, with the seat of the self (the thinking/rational mind) capable of existing in spite of—and thus independent from—bodily senses.

The premise of mind–body dualism has been debunked by numerous theories of the self, most notably the social constructionist tradition, which relocates bodies within social contexts, histories, cultures, and institutions. Social constructionists such as Mauss (1973) refer to techniques of the body as specific ways in which the bodily practices of everyday life are products of enculturated experience, arguments that are also found in Foucauldian and Bourdieusian perspectives on social life (see Foucault, 1979; Bourdieu, 1984). The most profound challenge of social constructionists to Cartesian dualism has been their dismantling of biologically essentialist ideas of the naturalized body to explain social differences, particularly gender, race, and sexuality. Constructionists consider instead how institutional structures create conditions for these inequalities. As Weinberg (2012, p 144) notes, the social constructionist tradition provides a rigorous epistemic basis from which to challenge essentialist thought, which "seeks to reduce historical and cultural difference to biology" and thus "runs the risk of reifying and indeed promoting inequality and injustice."

While Cartesian dualism locates the mind (and hence the reflective rational self) *outside the body*, Husserl (1990) considers that perception is a sensuous experience and that knowing the self is a relational exercise involving an embodied disposition—a way of seeing and interpreting experience. Drawing on Husserl and influenced by Heidegger (1962), Merleau-Ponty (1962) expands the interpretive process by which bodies can know themselves through intersubjectivities and relational engagements with social and cultural life. He maintains that locating bodies is the central process through which we become "beings-in-the-world." He suggests in the *Phenomenology of Perception* (Merleau-Ponty, 1962) that the body cannot know itself without engaging with the external world, a process that can be achieved only through the senses. "The corporeal schema is a sense of itself that the body arrives at through the meditation of its involvement with the world" (Crossley, 2012, p 137).[1]

It is precisely this corporeal schema that Frantz Fanon (1986), in his groundbreaking book *Black Skin, White Masks*, suggests is an unachievable task for Black bodies who cannot know themselves under the weight of colonial oppression. The freedoms and agencies that Merleau-Ponty alludes to—of becoming a self-knowing, rational, agentic self—are ultimately denied to Black bodies, who under colonial capture are stripped of their humanity and relegated to objecthood. Locked in colonial struggle, the white man is overidentified as subject and the Black man as object (Rajan-Rankin, 2018). In response to the colonial problematic, Fanon reveals not how it feels to be Black but how it feels to be made to feel one's Blackness in a world that reviles it. The method that Fanon develops for this account combines psychoanalytic theory and phenomenology of racism with what he calls "sociogeny," a term he coins to convey that, notwithstanding the way it is lived in body and mind, racism is rooted in socially, rather than biologically, produced phenomena. The term sociogeny thus allows him to do several things at once, including: prioritizing a genealogical account of racism itself; critiquing the insufficient explanations of racism found in psychoanalysis, psychology, and psychiatry (Mannoni, 1956; Adler, 1964; Lacan, 1977); and challenging the phenomenological schemas of European philosophy that fail to account for the struggle of the colonized subject to attain their humanity as anything but the belated entry of racialized men and women into a universal existential drama (Sartre, 1976). What Fanon wants to assert, by contrast, is that "Black consciousness is immanent in its own eyes" (1986, p 135). He writes, "I am not a potentiality of something else; I am wholly what I am. I do not have to look for the universal" (p 135). The phenomenology of the racialized body that Fanon gives us, then, is rooted in an account of how colonial societies produce Black bodies.

However, Fanonist phenomenologies of Blackness are centered on the Black man's body, which raises questions about how Fanon's work can be used to theorize the lives of colonized women. Fanon recognizes both gender and sexuality as vital parts of the colonial machine and questions whether there can be authentic human relationships in a society structured by colonial inequalities. He knows that the experience of women of color differs from that of men of color in the colony, but his discussion of Black women is confined to his chapter on sexuality, specifically Black women's relationships with white men (and their referred impacts on Black men's psyche) rather than gendered experiences of colonialism per se. As feminist critics have argued, the theoretical scope of Fanon's methodology is too limited to help us understand the gendering of the colonial body. While he observes the difference that gender makes in people's lived experiences of colonialism, he cannot assemble a theoretical space in which gender and race are both crucial factors of subject formation (Doane, 1991; Bergner, 1995; Greedharry, 2008).

Since Fanon's study of the existential and psychoanalytic dimensions of race, postcolonial critics have articulated structural formulations of the phenomenology of Blackness. Achille Mbembe's (2001) theorization of "becoming blackness" explores the vertiginous assemblage of human bodies as commodity orders of modernity and capitalism. Thus, cemented by modernity and class power, colonial power simultaneously creates hierarchies of gender, race, and sexuality. Colonial architectures of power then create "structuring processes" by which racialized bodies are placed within hierarchies of difference. As we will discuss in our textual analysis of Dangarembga's *Nervous Conditions*, Black male power, while subordinate to colonial power, nonetheless asserts its privilege through the control of gendered and sexualized bodies. These structural frames become absorbed into narratives of everyday life, and gendered and racial identity formulations become internalized by Black bodies. These structures are not static but self-reinforcing; even in the absence of coloniality, they persist as separate heuristic devices that position gendered power and racial power in ambivalent relationship to each other.

## Gendering the colonial body

The limitations of Fanon's phenomenology and psychoanalysis of race call for us to supplement his work with an understanding of how gender is inscribed onto the native body as a consolidation of colonial power. Our aim here is to demonstrate how gendering, as much as racialization, is a product of colonial ambitions to categorize, tame, discipline, and shape the colonized body. This may seem a counterintuitive proposition, since the racialization of bodies can be readily understood as a strategy of colonial power while gender does not tend to be understood in these terms. However, building on the work of postcolonial feminists and gender historians (Nandy, 1988; McClintock, 1995; Sinha, 1995; Stoler, 1995, 2002; Oyewùmí, 1997; Puar, 2008), we argue that gendering operates in parallel ways to racialization. For example, sexist discourses commonly ascribe irrationality to women in order to render them inferior, just as racist discourses commonly cast people of color as inferior to whites both biologically and mentally. Nevertheless, such ascriptions may also work in divergent ways; for example, where white women's bodies are understood to be delicate and physically fragile, Black women's bodies are thought to be robust and able to endure significant physical stress. In this case, the effect is to naturalize the deployment of Black women's bodies for the labor that keeps the colony functioning and profitable. The colonial order of things produces this differential gendering of the body in order to reinforce colonial relations of power, confining white women to the business of producing and reproducing the colonial home and Black women to the business of physically maintaining the colonizers and building the colony.

Certain practices and processes of gendering are thus effects of the colonial machine, rather than a reflection of natural, universal differences between genders. The historical process by which gendering was used to colonize has only been further entrenched by Western feminist thought, which has the authority to delimit the range of meanings of the word "woman" as well as the embodied experiences that correspond to it (Jayawardena, 1986; Trinh, 1989; Mohanty, 1991, 2003; Spivak, 1993, 2010; Oyewùmí, 1997). Oyewùmí (1997) argues it was British colonialism that first brought particular forms of gendered thinking to precolonial Nigeria. She particularly disputes the Western gender analysis that Yoruba women were already oppressed as women in their culture, and then additionally oppressed as Africans—a commonplace reading of colonized women's oppression. Instead, she argues it was the colonization of Africa that brought gender thinking to Yorubaland at the same time as it produced racial difference, thus colonizing the women "as Africans together with African men and then separately inferiorized and marginalized as African women" (Oyewùmí, 1997, p 122). As a result of both historical processes and epistemic dominance, Western scholarship does not recognize the importance of colonialism in forming the gender categories to begin with, and yet it offers feminist analyses based on those ostensibly universal categories as an emancipatory solution for colonized women.

None of this is to suggest that colonies were free from gender-based oppression before colonialism, especially since different gender orders with their own dynamics of power and resistance were in place before contact with Western Europeans. However, it is to draw attention to the fact that in former colonies the emancipatory trajectories available to women, which Western feminist analyses had advanced (eg, access to Western education), bound them ever more closely to the structures and discourses of modernity. As subaltern studies and decolonial scholars have noted, modernity, like the Enlightenment, turns out to be another incarnation of provincial European values presented as universal ones (Chakrabarty, 2000; Mignolo, 2011). The colonized woman's journey into modernity frequently demands that she abandon embodied practices that give her meaning and presence (such as non-Western clothing, cultural rituals, foods), thereby, in effect, recolonizing what remains of her already colonized body.

The key problematic, then, remains the disappearance and erasure of the colonized woman's body precisely because in feminist analyses the bodies central to the analysis are white women's bodies and in colonial analyses they are Black or Brown men's bodies. Which theoretical approach will allow us to make visible a body that has been colonized through both racialization and gendering? It seems clear that we must begin with the colonized woman's own account of her body and its experiences. It is for this reason we propose to turn to literary texts as a source of theory about the lived experience of the colonized woman. Literature produced by colonized or formerly colonized women themselves offers us not a simple transcription of what these women experience but an interpretation of how their bodies live, move, and shape themselves in a world that does not see them. It signals a return, and an intention, to reclaim the telling of their own stories, without they themselves or their stories being filtered through gendered or racialized hierarchies that have historically silenced their voices.

## Literature as organic theory

Given their unequal access to academia and other sites of intellectual influence, colonized women have frequently used literature and life-writing as modes in which to build theories. Since available academic theories neither visibilize nor allow colonized women to imagine their bodies, literary forms offer them the freedom to describe worlds that would be almost impossible to capture through the methods and practices of academic research and theory. In this chapter, we read the novel *Nervous Conditions* by contemporary Zimbabwean author Tsitsi Dangarembga (1988) as an instance of what we might call an organic theory of the native woman's body. Part of the justification for our interpretation lies in the author's own explicit intention to create a set of maps that might allow Black Zimbabwean women to navigate their particular terrain. As Dangarembga notes in an interview published in the novel: "I think mapping the ground helps in making choices. Such maps, written in an engaging way, are part of what I perceive some of my responsibility as a novelist to be" (1988, p 211).

The author also signals an intention to respond to the limits of Fanon's phenomenology of racism and colonialism. The title itself provides an intertextual clue to its connection with Fanon's work, taking a line from Jean-Paul Sartre's introduction to Fanon's final book, *The Wretched of the Earth*: "the status of 'native' is a nervous condition introduced and maintained by the settler among colonized people with their consent" (Sartre, 1968, p 20). For Sartre, as much as for Fanon, the nervous condition is one induced by the violent effects of living under colonial rule, but Fanon rarely discusses the nervous conditions found in colonized women. In taking her title from Fanon for a narrative that is consistently and clearly focused on the lives of women, Dangarembga turns the text into an explicit challenge to both Fanon's and Sartre's theories of colonialism, which see colonialism as a pathology lived primarily in men's minds and bodies. Sartre's reference to "consent" in the creation and perpetuation of the nervous condition also speaks to the structural machineries of colonized memory that persist in locating racialized bodies as being out of place (Douglas, 1966). The embodied task of Black presencing is, then, to examine how Black bodies are not just bluntly thrust into emergence or erasure but are agentic actors who pivot, navigate, resist, and recover within an unequal plane of power.

Finally, a central aspect of our interest in the novel lies in the close, defamiliarized attention that Dangarembga gives to embodied experiences. Defamiliarization is a literary technique whereby close, phenomenological, attention to ordinary everyday experiences renders them new to the reader, enabling them to experience familiar situations and sensations as if for the first time (Shklovsky, 1965). In this way the text grants us entry to a landscape wherein the vitalism and enchanted materialism of everyday life can come to the fore (Bennett, 2001). *Nervous Conditions* is replete with moments in which adolescent girls discover what is possible in a native, female body. It thus offers an immediate account of how gender *makes* their bodies available to colonialism even as they offer resistance through subtle and overt forms of refusal.

## Setting the scene: Tsitsi Dangarembga's *Nervous Conditions*

*Nervous Conditions* is the first novel in a trilogy about the life of Tambudzai, a young woman who grew up on a rural homestead in Southern Rhodesia in the late 1960s. Tambu is coming of age at the same time as the nation. Rhodesia, then under minority white government rule, entered a period of civil war in 1965, which led to the formation of the independent nation of Zimbabwe in 1980. Tambu's world consists of the dynamics of life within an extended Shona family. Her mother, Ma'Shingayi, and father, Jeremiah, rely on the patriarch of the family, Jeremiah's oldest brother, Babamukuru, who takes his patriarchal responsibilities very seriously. Babamukuru is married to Maiguru, who, like him, is a college graduate and works as a teacher. Together they have a son, Chido, and a daughter, Nyasha. Soon after the novel opens, Babamukuru has just returned from studying in England to take up the post of headmaster at a Christian mission school. Tambu's older brother, Nhamo, seems destined to continue in his uncle's footsteps, going to live and study at the mission school until a sudden illness takes his life and it is decided by the patriarch that Tambu will be given his educational opportunities instead. Against her mother's will, Tambu leaves the homestead to go and live in Babamukuru's house and begins to experience colonial education for herself. The action of the novel shifts back and forth between the homestead and the mission school, which allows us to see how both Tambu and Nyasha struggle to shape themselves into "good native girls."

Though deeply attached to each other, the girls have different understandings of what is possible, and they choose different strategies for navigating their lives. By the end of the novel, we see two versions of African girlhood struggling with modernity and Black identity. Nyasha's Western education brings a restless consciousness that sits in deep conflict with her traditional roles and is manifest in her "nervous condition" of disordered eating. Tambu has won a scholarship to the prestigious Sacred Heart convent school and is about to leave her uncle's home for further trials in colonial education. She has learned to survive "under the radar," navigating the classed expectations of being a poor relative and learning to capitalize on her uncle's benevolence, only to find herself in an ambivalent relationship with her emerging self. Unable to go back and uncertain about what lies ahead, both girls are locked in a vertiginous assembly of becoming and disappearing: the nervous condition.

## A colonial education

Dangarembga's foregrounding of the problem of education is commonplace in postcolonial literature, where education is the apparatus through which colonial subjects acquire worth and mobility. However, as Nair (1995) notes, the many fictional representations and critical discussions of colonial education do "not address the anonymous female subjects who were not allowed an education in the first place" (p 130). When we first meet her, Tambu's body is valued as one that may be exchanged for material value to her family, in the future, as a wife and mother. An education does not appear to increase the value of Tambu's body within this economy and so she is not allotted one. Through much of her early life in the homestead, Tambu is almost invisible: Babamukuru has sent money for her school fees, but her father has misappropriated those funds. She works hard growing her own crops to sell and obtain money for her fees, and her brother thwarts her efforts. However, when her brother dies unexpectedly, she takes his place at the missionary school. The death of her brother gives her a new life within the colonial patriarchy. It is a reality that she states matter-of-factly: "I am not sorry my brother died. ... [T]he event of my brother's passing and the events of my story cannot be separated, my story is not after all about death, but about my escape" (Dangarembga, 1988, p 1). It is only the absence of other colonized boys in the family that makes Tambu's body available for education. Access to the school is a crucial turning point in her life, since education gives her female body license to move around the world as the men do, off the homestead and into the mission school.

Thus far, the story conforms to an understanding that education is what liberates colonized women from their oppressed situation within traditional family and kinship structures. Dangarembga's narrative, however, is equally scrupulous in its reflection of how education that moves Black women in new directions simultaneously shuts off the other paths along which they traveled easily before and which are important to them. When Tambu arrives at the mission, she has a sense of herself as a peasant body in her "tight, faded frock that immodestly defined [her] budding breasts, and in [her] broad-toed feet that had grown thick-skinned … the way the keratin had reacted by thickening and, having thickened had hardened and cracked" (Dangarembga, 1988, p 58). Arriving at her uncle's luxurious house, Tambu acutely feels her class inferiority and seeks familiar markers of home. She is consoled by the idea that she might be sleeping with the live-in servant, Anna. Tambu's speculations are disproved, as Anna begins to adopt new behavior such as "kneeling down to talk to [her] and not looking at [her] as she talked but at a spot on the floor a few inches in front of [her]. The worst thing was that she hardly talked at all, said no more than the few words necessary to convey her message" (p 86). Tambu is discomforted by this change. A body still so like hers, familiar to her, suddenly becomes unreachable. She appears to hold out hope that she will remain a person with whom Anna can talk, since her education "was not to be such a radical transformation that people would have to behave differently towards [her]. It was to be an extension and improvement of what *[she] really was*. Anna's behavior made [her] feel uncomfortably strange and unfamiliar with [her]self" (pp 86–87).

The strange feeling Tambu has about herself is an early signal to the reader that education not only improves lives but can also bring a sense of loss and nonbelonging. It is a mark of her misunderstanding of colonial education-as-liberation that Tambu did not understand that these changes would happen to her, too. Before his death, her brother Nhamo also slowly disconnected from the homestead, avoiding the rural women who "smelt of unhealthy reproductive odours" (Dangarembga, 1988, p 1) and the rural men who "gave off strong aromas of productive labour" (p 1). Tambu's cousin, Nyasha, and her older brother, Chido, are similarly alienated from the homestead when they return to it after a period of living in England. They no longer speak Shona and cannot take their place easily in the family life of the homestead.

By contrast, returning to the homestead is a notably happy occasion for Babamukuru, because it redoubles his sense of agency. On the homestead he is a hero, celebrated and able to see his own accomplishment. He is even allowed to pick up a hoe and join in as if he was still a homestead boy (Dangarembga, 1988, p 6). For an educated woman, such as Babamukuru's wife, Maiguru, returning to the homestead is more ambiguous because she cannot comfortably occupy the spaces of both the traditional homestead and school. The agency that Maiguru has on the homestead is at the same time overdetermined and curtailed. Her role as the patriarch's wife means that greater demands for certain kinds of reproductive labor fall upon her—cooking, laundry, management of food—so she appears to be in charge. At the same time, however, the women on the homestead do not trust or valorize her accomplishment as an educated woman and merely defer to her as custom requires. Maiguru experiences her education as a burden that forces her to work harder and harder for a home and family in which her labor goes unrecognized. Tambu does not experience her return to the homestead as a celebration either, which contrasts strongly with her account of the triumphal homecoming given to her brother.

## Regulating "good native girls"

The degree to which education both gives women access to mobility and changes the way they relate to other bodies is closely tied in the novel with sexuality, and how the women experience and use their own bodies. Dangarembga establishes, at several points, that the "puritanical" colonial norms Babamukuru seeks to impose on his daughter, niece, wife, and sisters-in-law are derived from the Christian morality he has learned at school. Tambu's relatives neither express shame nor use euphemism on the homestead when discussing the young women's sexual development. We see this, for example, when family members discuss the near future in which Nyasha will become sexually active: "'The breasts are already quite large,' [Mainini] declared, pinching one and causing Maiguru to wince with embarrassment. 'When do we expect our *mukwambo*,' my mother teased her niece" (Dangarembga, 1988, p 133). Sexuality on the homestead is regulated, but according to different norms. Babamukuru's incorporation of Christian norms into his role as the patriarch of the family enables him to extend his authority further, even into the girls' pleasures and experiences of their own bodies.

Tambu and Nyasha are both aware that bodily pleasures are structured by social relations. Tambu experiences pleasure in her body's sensations and capacities, but she is acutely sensitive to how others perceive her. She enjoyed dancing with her family as a child, "music and movement pulsing through the night to make your skin crawl and tingle, your armpits prickle, your body impatient to be up and concerned with the beat" (Dangarembga, 1988, p 42). The dancing she describes here is at the same time a communal practice and an individual sensation. The sensation she feels in her own body develops further as she pays more attention to the music: "My movements had grown stronger, more rhythmical and luxuriant; but people had not found it amusing anymore" (p 42). She does not refer to any sexual feelings. This sensation is purely something she enjoys within herself, but the failure to elicit amusement from others leads her to conclude that "there were bad implications in the way I enjoyed the rhythm" (p 42) and, accordingly, her "dancing compressed itself into rigid, tentative gestures" (p 42). What Tambu expresses here is not a conscious attempt at self-discipline ("I danced") but rather something the "dancing" does to itself. She does not stop dancing, since dance is a communal activity in her family and, as evidenced by reactions to Nyasha's and Chido's failure to dance at the homestead (p 43), it would be abnormal to avoid it. But Tambu no longer takes the same pleasure in her body for herself for some time afterward.

Tambu's decision to continue dancing, albeit in "rigid, tentative gestures," is characteristic of her strategy for resolving the conflicts of being a female body in the post-colony. She perceives that there are contexts and social relations that she must attend to if she is to survive: "I was always aware of my surroundings. When the surroundings were new and unfamiliar, the awareness was painful and made me behave very strangely. At times like that I wanted so badly to disappear that for practical purposes I ceased to exist" (Dangarembga, 1988, p 112). As she learns what is expected of her, she finds the easiest way to negotiate those expectations is to make herself smaller—like the compression of her dancing—so that she can participate normally without drawing attention to her own feelings or desires. Tambu's desire to make herself disappear is a poignant reflection of how the problem of being a colonized woman, constantly under erasure between gender and race, becomes embodied. She literally experiences her body as one that must disappear in order to resolve the tensions of colonized womanhood. In so doing, Tambu's disappearance from her knowing self might suggest a Cartesian split, a mind–body dualism, where the mind confronts a reality where her native body cannot be in its natural state. Considered in the light of the distinction that Leder (1990) makes between the "ecstatic" and "recessive" body, whereby pleasure and pain respectively expand or contract the body's capacity for self-recognition, it is far more likely that Tambu's "dys-appearing body" is keenly aware of pain and pleasure and bends to accommodate the environment it inhabits. Leder writes, "As ecstatic [pleasure], the body projects outside itself into the world. As recessive [pain], the body falls back from its conscious perception and control" (1990, p 169). Tambu's innocent pleasure as she dances for herself can be seen as the ecstatic body expanding its sense of freedom with each rhythmic movement. As she becomes aware of the disapproving gaze of her family members, the ecstatic body recedes—she becomes more self-conscious and the recessive body intrudes, bringing her movements in line with the expectations of social control.

The contrast between Tambu's and Nyasha's negotiation of pleasure is one of the most marked differences between them. If at times they are almost twins, at other times their embodied experience demonstrates both different understandings of the limits and possibilities of their bodies and the different strategies for surviving colonialism that these generate. At a school dance, Nyasha dances with Andy, a wealthy white Rhodesian boy, and lingers with him in the driveway when they return home. The innocent circumstance becomes a trigger for a violent showdown between father and daughter, in which he beats her mercilessly and she, refusing to be docile, fights back. Babamukuru's concerns about how it might seem if a daughter of his is seen or thought to behave in sexually inappropriate ways are heavily tied to his sense of himself as a model colonial subject. Nyasha, who intuits the absurdity of her father's investment in colonial norms, is more acutely aware than Tambu that the requirement placed upon her to discipline her own body's sensations and needs is demanded of her in the name of colonial patriarchy. It is an awareness she has gained through her education. It is, however, a demand she utterly rejects.

As the fight between father and daughter subsides, however, Babamukuru warns that Nyasha's audacity in fighting back will lead to her death because "we cannot have two men in this house" (Dangarembga, 1988, p 117). The colonial Christianity that has structured Babamukuru's existence turns into a grave for the colonized woman: if she tries to inhabit the same space as the colonized man, she risks death. A phenomenological reading of Nyasha's conflict suggests that while colonial Christianity has structured her education and liberation, it also has produced in her a dissident body with modernizing notions of female selfhood that threaten African patriarchy and must be subject to control.

## Sick bodies: hunger, longing, and wasting away

Under the constant pressure of gendered and racialized colonial discipline, the colonized woman develops a nervous condition of her own. Although some critics have argued that the women's hysteria portrayed in the novel is a manifestation of the impossibility of women articulating their critiques (Thomas, 1992), we agree instead with Patchay (2003, p 152), who contends that "when women's voices are silenced, their bodies can speak" (see also Bahri, 1994). Nyasha, Tambu, and Ma'Shingayi, the three women in the novel who experience sickness, each use their bodies to refuse the incursions of colonial modernity into their lives. Yet, in their lines of refusal, each deploys different tactics consonant with their varying positions within the colony. In Nyasha's case, the line is what she is allowed to be in her own body. For Tambu, the line is what relationship she can have to her community. And for Ma'Shingayi, the line is what form of life is left to her.

Early in the novel we see that Nyasha has a difficult relationship to eating, not because of a biological or psychological condition but as a response to an environment in which patriarchal control is repeatedly played out through the preparation and consumption of food. Tambu's first visit to the mission home includes an elaborate dinner in which Babamukuru and Maiguru enact gender hierarchies—one in which men are served first, for example, and women and children make do with what is leftover. Babamukuru insists that everyone act in accordance with his rules, and even though Nyasha's capacity to question, if not defy, his rules is evident, she is not as divested from his rules as she seems. Her disordered eating intensifies when she is under pressure to succeed in her studies, an internal conflict that occurs at least partly because she senses that her success satisfies Babamukuru's colonial ideals. Her academic success vindicates his strategy of colonial obedience, but it also means that her intellect, the very thing that allows her to challenge Babamukuru's thinking, is compromised. She undertakes a strategy of overcompliance with his authority, as Tambu witnesses on one of her visits back to the mission.

> She sat down very quietly and that was the beginning of a horribly weird and sinister drama. Babamukuru dished out a large helping of food for his daughter and set it before her, watching her surreptitiously as he picked casually at his own meal to persuade us he was calm. Nyasha regarded her plate malevolently, darting anguished glances at her father, drained two glasses of water, then picked up her fork and shovelled food into her mouth, swallowing without chewing. (Dangarembga, 1988, p 202)

Having disciplined her body to swallow what the social order demands, she immediately retreats to the bathroom to throw up everything she has eaten, refusing to absorb or digest it. Despite the spectacle of compliance, she loses weight, becomes frail, and passes out at the dinner table one evening, but this still does not drive her parents to consult a doctor. As with Tambu's desire to disappear, the fact that Nyasha is apparently ever more compliant and literally takes up less and less space is not in itself a problem in the body of a colonized woman. It is, instead, her expression of both violent rage and despair that finally pierces the family's denial:

> Nyasha was beside herself with fury. She rampaged, shredding her history book between her teeth ("Their history. Fucking liars. Their bloody lies"), breaking mirrors, her clay pots, anything she could lay her hands on and jabbing the fragments viciously into her flesh. ... "They've trapped us. They've trapped us. But I won't be trapped. I'm not a good girl. I won't be trapped." Then as suddenly as it came, the rage passed. "I don't hate you Daddy," she said softly. "They want me to, but I won't." She lay down on her bed. "I'm very tired," she said in a voice that was recognisably hers. "But I can't sleep. Mummy will you hold me?" She curled up in Maiguru's lap looking no more than five years old. "Look what they've done to us," she said softly, "I'm not

one of them but I'm not one of you." She fell asleep. (Dangarembga, 1988, p 205)

The scene is heartbreaking—a colonial subject who is exhausted by the effort simply to find a way to be herself, to be in a body that must consume the colonial order of things but never take up more space within it. The speed with which she vacillates from wanting to efface and destroy herself to then deeply desiring reconciliation with those she loves gives the reader a sense of the pain Nyasha feels—the pain of being colonized not only by those in authority (Nyasha's "they") but those most intimate with you. Even in the depth of her anguish, Nyasha recognizes that Babamukuru is not really the one to blame and that hating him would only be to complete the cycle of self-colonization.

Perhaps because of her proximity to the patriarch, Nyasha's embodied howl against what the colonizing natives are doing to themselves is the most spectacular and prolonged. Tambu's conflict with Babamukuru is more episodic and occurs when he insists on a Christian solemnization of the marriage in which her parents have been living for several years. Babamukuru "solves" the problem of Tambu's father's multiple sexual relationships by insisting on a Christian wedding to reinforce both a European and Christian model of monogamous relationship. As soon as the prospective wedding is discussed, Tambu experiences it as disease in her body: "I suffered a horrible crawling over my skin, my chest contracted to a breathless tension and even my bowels threatened to let me know their opinion" (Dangarembga, 1988, p 151). All of these might be considered classic symptoms of anxiety, but Tambu herself understands it as the product of a conflict in her understanding of Babamukuru's authority, which expresses itself through her body. Fully inculcated into the mission's teachings about sinfulness, she sees the moral rightness of Babamukuru's idea that her parents should be married, but the wedding also "made a mockery of the people [she] belonged to and placed doubt on [her] legitimate experience in this world" (p 165). The conflict between what she feels about herself, in herself, and the demands of the (post)colonial Christian order leads her to an even more intense embodied experience in which she does not know, once again, *how* she can exist. Now she is not merely compressing herself and her movements, she is losing a sense of her own coherence and solidity. The conflict brings her to the realization that she has lost a part of herself that she had before she settled into mission life: "My reverence for my uncle, what he was, what he had achieved, what he represented and therefore what he wanted, had stunted the growth of my faculty of criticism, sapped the energy that in childhood I had used to define my own position" (p 167). It is a reminder that the homestead is not inevitably the site of silence, oppression, or incapacity for the colonized woman. Contact with colonial education dissolves some capacities even as it develops others.

At first, only Tambu's body is able to manifest this understanding: "I found I could not get out of bed. I tried several times but my muscles simply refused the half-hearted commands I was issuing to them" (Dangarembga, 1988, p 168). There is even a suggestion that she knows she is only pretending, a remnant of the part of Tambu that desperately tries to govern her body according to her uncle's rules, but the appearance of Babamukuru himself at her bedside does not result in any change. Tambu, now narrating the experience as if she were outside her body, notices that "the body on the bed did not twitch" (p 168). Nevertheless, she continues: "Meanwhile, the mobile me, the alert me, the one at the foot of the bed, smiled smugly, thinking I had gone somewhere he could not reach me, and I congratulated myself for being so clever" (p 168). At last, instead of disappearing as a response to colonial gendering, Tambu takes herself elsewhere, leaving her body behind to deceive others. The splitting of her body continues while Maiguru and Babamukuru discuss her condition, but she cannot sustain this displacement: "I slipped back into my body. I found I could speak again" (p 169). Finding herself back in her body, Tambu asserts, for the first time, that she does not want to go to the wedding. As with his reaction to Nyasha's supposed indecency, Babamukuru responds to this challenge to his authority with physical punishment. Yet Tambu is able to endure it. Unlike her mother and her cousin, she redoubles her control over her body "with a deep and grateful masochistic delight" (p 171). She explains: "To me that punishment was the price of my newly acquired identity" (p 171). Tambu does not destroy herself but instead cultivates a capacity to enjoy the pain. Although, like Nyasha, her bodily refusal does not help her to recover what she has lost, she learns a different way of surviving in the colony, and it is this strategy that carries her toward the conclusion of the novel—it indicates Tambu's agency in being able to pass between the recessive and ecstatic body state and negotiate between "presence" and "dys-appearance" (Leder, 1990).

## Ambivalence and arrival

If the point of Tambu's journey has been to acquire the same colonial education as Babamukuru and Maiguru, then the novel comes to an ambiguous conclusion. Tambu accomplishes her goal and the final chapter begins in a triumphal tone: "All the things that I wanted were tying themselves up into a neat package which presented itself to me with a flourish" (Dangarembga, 1988, p 195). The sting comes, however, as soon as Babamukuru, Maiguru, and Nyasha deliver Tambu to the school. At a moment when she hopes to be "seen" for her individual accomplishments, the force of erasure redoubles. Having made it through the trial of Babamukuru's colonial discipline, the signs are all around Tambu that she has not arrived at the better place she had imagined and that others who have tried to acquire a colonial education before her have not fared any better. Nyasha, as we saw in detail earlier, suffers a breakdown, causing Tambu to wonder: "If Nyasha who had everything could not make it, where could I expect to go?" (p 206). Indeed, whether or not Nyasha will survive remains unclear at the conclusion of the novel. Ma'Shingayi diagnoses the "Englishness" Tambu is learning as the ultimate threat, the thing that is killing Nyasha and might kill Tambu, too, if she is not careful. The last page of the novel is crystallized by Ma'Shingayi's diagnosis, which Tambu finally acknowledges as an important and real understanding of colonialism's effects on the lives of the women she loves. The triumph that began the chapter dissolves into a genuine moment of postcolonial awareness: "Although I was not aware of it then, no longer could I accept Sacred Heart and what it represented as a sunrise on my horizon" (p 208). Tambu has arrived at her goal, but she is also beginning to understand that within the colonial order of things, the goal itself might be the trap.

## An end to nervous conditions?

The nervous condition is not only a state of flux, a liminal space between modernity and tradition, a form of entrapment, but also an awakening. Postcolonial modernity presents a key dilemma for racialized subjects: How can a body just *be* without being devoured by disappearance? We began our chapter by noting that the racialized body becomes visible only intermittently, sometimes sharply when movements such as Black Lives Matter focus our eyes on what has always been before us. At other times, however, our vision is weakened, obscured by the narratives of emancipation and education we have cultivated in order to believe that the "body" really could mean the Black woman's body as much as the Black man's body or the white woman's body. Our reading of *Nervous Conditions* highlights a phenomenology of Blackness that is as relevant to the colony as it is to the metropole. It makes visible the silent and sometimes violent ways in which agency erupts in the patterns of appearance and disappearance of the girls through the text, in ways that mirror the larger patterns of appearance and disappearance of the Black woman's body in our theories and politics.

Tambu's body appears on the scene of education, enrolled in the trajectory of modernity and emancipation postcolonial society proffers, only when no men are left. She works her way through the structuring process of colonial education and learns to make her girl's body appear and disappear at will in order to survive and make progress. This is a subtle art because it is highly contextual and socially structured but also agentic and negotiated within the limited choices available to her.

Nyasha has an intuition, perhaps from her earlier contact with the postcolonial metropole, that she must not tolerate any attempts to make her disappear. Instead, she experiments with her body in a chaotic but determined way, sometimes complying with the demand to be a "good native girl" in a way that also damages her body. Like her cousin Tambu, she recognizes the colonial demand to appear and disappear as a young woman whenever it is asked of her, but she refuses to understand that demand as a reasonable one. In Nyasha's analysis, colonial education might still hold out the possibility of escape from colonialization if it also allows her to remake the contours of trajectories that have been shaped to fit the bodies of men like Babamukuru, Nhamo, and Chido.

To argue, as we have, that gender is a colonial construct is to draw attention to the multiple ways in which the colonial architecture is built for and imagines racialized male bodies, just as the feminist response to colonial power has been built for and imagines gendered white bodies. Living in such a world has brought young women like the fictional Tambu and Nyasha to experience a nervous condition of their own, in which they try to understand how they could enjoy, make use of, exceed, and care for their unimagined bodies, bodies that neither the colonial nor postcolonial worlds have yet been shaped to hold. We all live in nervous conditions: caught between consciousness and the limits of our immediate realities. The difference is that some of us cannot describe our realities in a way that is understood as real, material, and consequential because gender and race are continually separated out as separate threads of a deeply interwoven fabric. It is in this wakeful state that we recognize gender on the post-colony as an ambivalent, constantly negotiated, reinterpretative activity of being, becoming, existing, surviving. By resurfacing the phenomenology of the Black female body, we are able to witness these artful forms of resistance.

### Note
1   We do not have space here to provide a more detailed comparison of social constructionism and phenomenology (nor is it opportune, since this would detract from the emphasis on Black feminist voices), but the contrasts between the two approaches to the body and theories of self are important when we consider how histories are interpreted, how stories of self are told, and by whom they are told.

### References
Adler, A. (1964) *The Individual Psychology of Alfred Adler*, New York: Harper Torchbooks.
Bahri, D. (1994) 'Disembodying the corpus: postcolonial pathology in Tsitsi Dangarembga's *Nervous Conditions*', *Postmodern Culture*, 5(1), available from: https://www.pomoculture.org/2013/09/24/disembodying-the-corpus-postcolonial-pathology-in-tsitsi-dangarembgas-nervous-conditions/.

Bennett, J. (2001) *The Enchantment of Modern Life: Attachment, Crossings and Ethics*, Princeton, NJ: Princeton University Press.

Bergner, G. (1995) 'Who is that masked woman? Or, the role of gender in Fanon's *Black Skins White Masks*', *PMLA*, 110(1): 75–88.

Bourdieu, P. (1984) *Distinction: A Social Critique of the Judgement of Taste*, London: Routledge, 2010.

Butler, J. (1993) *Bodies that Matter: On the Discursive Limits of 'Sex'*, New York: Routledge, 2011.

Chakrabarty, D. (2000) *Provincializing Europe: Postcolonial Thought and Historical Difference*, Princeton, NJ: Princeton University Press.

Crenshaw, K.W. (1994) 'Mapping the margins: intersectionality, identity politics, and violence against women of color', in M.A. Fineman and R. Mykitiuk (eds) *The Public Nature of Private Violence*, New York: Routledge, pp 93–118.

Crossley, N. (2012) 'The phenomenology of the body', in B.S. Turner (ed) *The Routledge Handbook of Body Studies*, London: Routledge, pp 130–143.

Dangarembga, T. (1988) *Nervous Conditions*, London: The Women's Press.

Doane, M.-A. (1991) 'Dark continents: epistemologies of racial and sexual difference in psychoanalysis and the cinema', in M.-A. Doane (ed) *Femmes Fatales: Feminism, Film Theory, Psychoanalysis*, New York: Routledge, pp 209–248.

Douglas, M. (1966) *Purity and Danger: An Analysis of Concepts of Pollution and Taboo*, London: Routledge.

Elias, N. (1978) *The Civilizing Process*, translated by E. Jephcott, Oxford: Basil Blackwell.

Fanon, F. (1986) *Black Skin, White Masks*, London: Pluto Press.

Featherstone, M., Hepworth, M. and Turner, B.S. (eds) (1991) *The Body, Social Process and Cultural Theory*, London: SAGE.

Foucault, M. (1979) *The History of Sexuality: An Introduction*, translated by R. Hurley, London: Allen Lane.

Greedharry, M. (2008) *Postcolonial Theory and Psychoanalysis*, Basingstoke: Palgrave Macmillan.

Heidegger, M. (1962) *Being and Time*, Oxford: Blackwell.

Husserl, E. (1990) *Cartesian Meditations*, Dordrecht: Kluwer.

Jayawardena, K. (1986) *Feminism and Nationalism in the Third World*, London: Zed Books.

Lacan, J. (1977) *Ecrits*, New York: Norton.

Leder, D. (1990) *The Absent Body*, Chicago, IL: University of Chicago Press.

Mannoni, O. (1956) *Prospero and Caliban: The Psychology of Colonization*, New York: Methuen.

Mauss, M. (1973) 'Techniques of the body', *Economy and society*, 2(1): 70–88.

Mbembe, A. (2001) *On the Postcolony*, Berkeley: University of California Press.

McClintock, A. (1995) *Imperial Leather: Race, Gender, and Sexuality in the Colonial Contest*, London: Routledge.

Merleau-Ponty, M. (1962) *Phenomenology of Perception*, London: Routledge.

Mignolo, W.D. (2011) *The Darker Side of Western Modernity: Global Futures, Decolonial Options*, Durham, NC: Duke University Press.

Mohanty, C.T. (1991) 'Under Western eyes: feminist scholarship and colonial discourses', in C.T. Mohanty, A. Russo and L. Torres (eds) *Third World Women and the Politics of Feminism*, Bloomington: Indiana University Press, pp 51–80.

Mohanty, C.T. (2003) *Feminism without Borders: Decolonizing Theory, Practicing Solidarity*, Durham, NC: Duke University Press.

Nair, S. (1995) 'Melancholic women: the intellectual hysteric(s) in *Nervous Conditions*', *Research in African Literatures*, 26(2): 130–139.

Nandy, A. (1988) *The Intimate Enemy: Loss and Recovery of Self under Colonialism*, New Delhi: Oxford University Press.

Olufemi, L. (2020) *Feminism Interrupted: Disrupting Power*, London: Pluto Press.

Oyewùmí, O. (1997) *The Invention of Women: Making an African Sense of Western Gender Discourses*, Minneapolis: University of Minnesota Press.

Patchay, S. (2003) 'Transgressing boundaries: marginality, complicity and subversion in *Nervous Conditions*', *English in Africa*, 30(1): 145–155.

Puar, J.K. (2008) *Terrorist Assemblages: Homonationalism in Queer Times*, Durham, NC: Duke University Press.

Rajan-Rankin, S. (2018) 'Race, embodiment and later life: re-animating aging bodies of color', *Journal of Aging Studies*, 45: 32–38.

Sartre, J-P. (1968) 'Preface', in F. Fanon (auth) *The Wretched of the Earth*, New York: Grove Press, pp 7–23.

Sartre, J.-P. (1976) *Black Orpheus*, Paris: Présence Africaine.

Shilling, C. (2003) *The Body and Social Theory* (2nd edn), London: SAGE.

Shklovsky, V. (1965) 'Art as technique', in L.T. Lemon and M.J. Reis (eds) *Russian Formalist Criticism: Four Essays*, Lincoln: University of Nebraska Press, 2012, pp 3–24.

Sinha, M. (1995) *Colonial Masculinity: The 'Manly Englishman' and the 'Effeminate Bengali' in the Late Nineteenth Century*, Manchester: Manchester University Press.

Spivak, G.C. (1993) 'Echo', *Culture and Everyday Life*, 24(1): 17–43.

Spivak, G.C. (2010) 'Can the subaltern speak?', in R.C. Morris (ed) *Can the Subaltern Speak? Reflections on the History of an Idea*, New York: Columbia University Press, pp 21–78.

Stoler, A.L. (1995) *Race and the Education of Desire: Foucault's 'History of Sexuality' and the Colonial Order of Things*, Durham, NC: Duke University Press.

Stoler, A.L. (2002) *Carnal Knowledge and Imperial Power: Race and the Intimate in Colonial Rule*, Berkeley: University of California Press.

Thomas, S. (1992) 'Killing the hysteric in the colonized's house: Tsitsi Dangarembga's *Nervous Conditions*', *The Journal of Commonwealth Literature*, 27(1): 26–36.

Trinh, T.M. (1989) *Woman, Native, Other: Writing Postcoloniality and Feminism*, Bloomington: Indiana University Press.

Turner, B.S. (1984) *The Body and Society: Explorations in Social Theory*, Oxford: Blackwell.

Turner, B.S. (ed) (2012) *The Routledge Handbook of Body Studies*, London: Routledge.

Weheliye, A.G. (2014). *Habeas Viscus: Racializing Assemblages, Biopolitics, and Black Feminist Theories of the Human*, Durham, NC: Duke University Press.

Weinberg, D. (2012) 'Social constructionism and the body', in B.S. Turner (ed) *The Routledge Handbook of Body Studies*, London: Routledge, pp 144–156.

5

# Reinterpreting Male Bodies and Health in Crisis Times: From "Obesity" to Bigger Matters

*Lee F. Monaghan*

In the context of an ongoing, highly contentious "war on obesity" (O'Hara and Taylor, 2018), bodies categorized as "too heavy" or "fat" are routinely positioned as targets for "helpful" interventions. Simplistic calls to eat less and move more, incorporating "pedagogies of disgust" (Lupton, 2015) that are amplified by dramatizing and moralizing mass media (Raisborough, 2016), routinely incite populations to get trim and "win the battle of the bulge." Bodies medically deemed to be overweight or obese (read: most people) are, after all, "known" to be a "big problem" not only for individuals but also health systems and economies that can ill afford to be further burdened. "The end of the obesity epidemic," as suggested by Gard (2011), has not materialized. Rather, rhetoric about this putative problem has been reinvigorated amid entangled and cascading crises (notably economic and fiscal concerns following the 2008 Great Financial Crisis) and, most recently, the urgency evoked by a "dual COVID-19/obesity crisis frame" (Monaghan et al, 2022). Amid the fear, panic, moralizing action, and intense stigmatization that typically accompany the outbreak of a novel infectious disease (Strong, 1990), populations have been warned that "excess" weight/ fatness increases the risks of SARS-CoV-2 (the virus that causes COVID-19), notably hospitalization and death. It was in this context that the United Kingdom's (now former) Conservative prime minister Boris Johnson reiterated the virtues of weight loss for himself and fellow citizens after contracting COVID-19 and being admitted to intensive care (O'Connell et al, 2021).

As per Johnson's publicly expressed concerns about his physicality and fitness, male bodies and health are thoroughly implicated in a biomedical gaze that would seek to render us all conscientious weight watchers. A central premise of this chapter is that there is a need to reinterpret this gendered "body project" (Shilling, 2012), especially amid pathologizing medicalized calls that seemingly provide an incontestable basis for state-sanctioned interventions. Such a proposition is made in view of numerous problems and questions. For instance, what prejudices are expressed when health promoters repeatedly target "idle fat blokes" and urge them to get off the couch and lose weight (Monaghan, 2008)? What about the ethics of such calls given that most people are unable to lose weight and keep it off (Rothblum, 2018) and suggestions that the "fight against fat" is a form of communicated or "symbolic violence" (Bourdieu, 2001; see also Warin, 2020)? Arguably, such issues tend to be ignored as part of a more general problem. As explored by Monaghan and Atkinson (2014), with reference to a range of discredited masculinities, whether the targets are "fat blokes" or other "deviant groups" (eg, drug-using bodybuilders, nightclub security staff, boys who "fail" to participate in physical education), the problem is reduced to certain types of male bodies. These types must be targeted and corrected, whether via therapeutic interventions or regimes of discipline and punishment.

In qualifying what follows, I am not trivializing real problems enacted and experienced by groups of men and boys or the gendering of institutions that are observably toxic in their effects. As explained by Scott-Samuel (2014), patriarchy and neoliberalism might be viewed as two intertwined venomous snakes that have proven disastrous in contexts such as the politics of warmongering and health promotion (see also Scott-Samuel et al [2009] on problematizing masculinity as an ideology). Rather than trivialize such concerns, I will offer the sociological argument that the war on obesity risks obfuscating social structures and processes that demand critical interpretation. When advancing this argument, I will first discuss the putative "problem" of weight/fatness, including reference to some of my previously published research on male bodies. Rather than detract from feminist scholarship on women's and girls' corporeal concerns, my aim is to complement a profeminist agenda by interpreting the war on obesity as a bellicose expression of masculine domination (Monaghan, 2008). Second, I will offer a critical lens on the broader context that impacts people's life chances, health, and well-being. In particular, connections are made with calls within medical sociology and critical studies on men's health to scrutinize embodied social structures and broader material conditions of existence (Lohan, 2010; Robertson and Williams, 2010). Such thinking, comprising efforts to theorize rising inequalities, serves as a point of contrast to a "narrowly logical" focus on "deficient" male bodies and behaviors.

## The "problem" of men's and boys' weight/fatness: things are not what they seem

Populations have reportedly been facing a public health catastrophe since the late 1990s—an obesity crisis or "global epidemic" (World Health Organization, 1998, 2021)—caused by an excess of calories ingested relative to those expended, otherwise interpreted as gluttony and sloth (UK Parliament, 2004). People are allegedly storing up problems for the future not only in terms of unnecessary illnesses and early mortality but also by burdening health services, whether publicly funded, through taxation, or privately funded, with higher insurance premiums (The Report of the National Taskforce on Obesity, 2005). In short, the obesity epidemic has been constructed as "modernity's scourge" requiring "a 'war on obesity'" (Gard and Wright, 2005, p 69). We are told that "excess" weight/fatness must be combated, with US surgeon generals making statements such as obesity is "the terror within" and is more threatening than "weapons of mass destruction" (Monaghan, 2008, p 1). In Britain, successive chief medical officers have described obesity as "'a health time bomb' that must be defused" (UK Parliament, 2004, p 8) and a threat that is in the same league as "terrorism, war, flooding and disease pandemics" (Borland, 2015). Such alarmism persists. "The problematisation of fatness in COVID-19" (Pausé et al, 2021) is the most recent manifestation of this crisis frame, comprising signature elements that divert attention away from political and structural factors (eg, rising inequalities) that incontrovertibly undermine health.

The authoritative framing of weight/fat as a public health crisis (Kwan and Graves, 2013) is symbolically and materially significant. It adds gravitas to what might otherwise be dismissed as the superficial (yet oftentimes oppressive) preoccupations of the fashion-beauty complex, a web of meanings and practices that have long been critiqued by feminist scholars (Chernin, 1981; Bordo, 1993). Feminist writings on the vicissitudes of weight-loss culture retain their relevance and bite, though "obesity discourse" (Evans et al, 2008) also exceeds gendered concerns about normative discontent and the tyranny of slenderness among women and girls. Within the anti-obesity terrain everybody is a potential target for corrective or preventative action, in the interests of promoting healthy bodies and a healthy, productive nation (Academy of Medical Royal Colleges, 2013). Furthermore, given the social construction of childhood as a crucial stage in the lifecourse, with young people defined as the future lifeblood of the nation, anti-obesity interventions often target schoolchildren whose "vulnerability" warrants urgent action (Rich et al, 2020). Interventions include the monitoring of children's body mass index (BMI) and lunchboxes or even being made to run "fat laps" during physical education (Gard and Wright, 2005, p 185). As seen in my ethnographic research in a college in England, efforts to tackle childhood obesity proceeded even when boys' bodies appeared underweight. Here "health" served as a thin rationale for interventions that were in practice geared toward promoting middle-class ideals of social fitness—the civilizing of recalcitrant male bodies (Monaghan, 2014a).

The framing of "excess" weight/fat as a massive public health crisis also means that men are extolled to work on their bodies as part of a responsible effort to overcome their exposure to (self-imposed) risk (eg, in terms of diabetes and heart disease; for a recent critical review of obesity science and epidemiology, see Monaghan et al, 2022, pp 45–54). The advancement of this "body project" (Shilling, 2012), which ostensibly seeks to "empower" men but discredits many as deficient or deviant, has attracted the attention of scholars who critique the absence of the "fat man" within feminist writings. "So widely is the net of deviance and its attendant gaze being cast," write Bell and McNaughton (2007, p 126), "that it is impossible to continue to deny or downplay the impact of the war on fat on both women *and* men" (emphasis in original). Those studying men's health have subsequently critiqued discourses that target men for corrective body work. For example, Gough (2010, p 128) states that much attention is being directed at "the particular vulnerability of 'fat blokes' in an age of media inspired male objectification." This observation emerges in Gough's critique of a men's "obesity reduction manual," which prioritized hegemonic masculinity more so than health—for instance, the value of the rational mind over the emotional body or the construction of male bodies as machines that require maintenance and fixing much akin to cars that must be given the "correct fuel" and technical servicing. Hence, Gough urges caution when reading popular media that "recycle a restricted range of masculinised symbols and practices—and which focus mainly on individual rather than societal changes" (2010, p 138) that could improve health.

While obesity discourse, or the Weight-Centered Health Paradigm (WCHP) (O'Hara and Taylor, 2018), has considerable traction in body-oriented consumer cultures and masculinity scholars are rightly addressing this (similarly, see Lozano-Sufrategui et al, 2016), concerns about male fatness or corpulence are not new (Gilman, 2004). Whether referring to Falstaff in Shakespeare's *Henry IV*, whose flesh signified frailty (reproduced on the cover of a report on obesity by the United Kingdom's National Audit Office, 2001), or concerns about "tubby" Canadian men during the Cold War (McPhail, 2009), men's fatness has been discredited in various times and places. Similarly, Monaghan and Hardey (2011, p 64) note how in Britain "the social, scientific and political concerns of the Enlightenment gave rise to" such figures as George Cheyne (1673–1743) and William Banting (1796–1878)—men who "suffered" from corpulence, with Banting writing the first recognizably modern diet book in the late 1800s. However, contemporary obesity epidemic rhetoric has, especially since 2000 and most recently following the outbreak of COVID-19, rendered the fight against fat (or simply *weight*, given that the BMI does not actually measure fatness) ubiquitous in its manufacturing of deficient or risky (male) bodies. "Surveillance medicine" holds sway here via "attempts to bring *everyone* within its network of visibility" (Armstrong, 1995, p 139, emphasis added).

Medicalized calls to fight fat/weight are expressed in myriad contexts. These contexts not only include popular manuals wherein male bodies are commodified as objects for aesthetic evaluation and scrupulous body work (Gough, 2010). They also include mass media, which mockingly claim that most men are "denting their seats" (BBC Online, 2007) or trumpet ministerial exhortations, as seen when Boris Johnson asserted that his weight-loss efforts were worthy of emulation in order to "save" the health service "time and money" (Sky News, 2020). One might also note less abrasive or moralizing statements within masculinities scholarship, which, though generally valuable, takes medicine's epistemic authority for granted when discussing "overweight" as one of those "risk factors" where "men as a group really are worse off" (Connell, 2000, p 193). The medicalization of men's bodies as "overweight," to draw from Conrad and Schneider (1992), might help to reframe putative deviance as an issue deserving of compassion and care (badness becomes sickness). But an "obvious" problem here is that millions of people are socially constructed as pathological (unhealthy or potentially so) and in need of correction, often via behavioral prescriptions. This medicalization, which has shaded into medical imperialism and even iatrocracy (rule by the medically qualified) in the COVID-19 era (Dingwall, 2022), is also highly dubious on scientific grounds. Epidemiological evidence would suggest that "overweight" may generally be associated with a mortality advantage at the population level (Flegal et al, 2013), and even moderate obesity may protect health in certain instances—what has been termed "the obesity-survival paradox" (for a recent review, see Monaghan et al, 2022, pp 51–54).

Critical literature on "the obesity epidemic" systematically challenges the conventional narrative, echoing earlier feminist and fat activist writings on the body, health, and medicine. As suggested within critical weight and fat studies (eg, Rothblum and Solovay, 2009; Cooper, 2010; Rich et al, 2011; Monaghan et al, 2013; Monaghan, 2014b; Pausé et al, 2021), things are not what they seem. Indeed, the science, ethics, and ideology of obesity discourse and the WCHP have come under increasing scrutiny (Gard and Wright, 2005; Campos, 2011; Lupton, 2018). It is not my intention to review this literature or its calls for a paradigm shift; I lack the space and others have done a useful job in that regard (eg, Bombak, 2014; O'Hara and Taylor, 2018). Rather, in what remains of this section of the chapter, I will highlight (1) some core themes, (2) principles associated with an alternative approach, and (3) resistances to critical thinking before (4) noting aspects of my research on men and the war on obesity. By covering these points, I aim to further the broader editorial remit of this volume to interpret human bodies, with reference to a specific field of health (practice). In so doing, and as will be elaborated upon in the remainder of the chapter, I seek to advance an embodied sociological approach that scrutinizes social structures and processes that exceed, while affecting, fleshy bodies.

Critics of the war on obesity acknowledge that there are weight extremes, at both ends of the light–heavy continuum, wherein certain health risks are amplified (eg, Campos, 2004, 2011; Campos et al, 2006). However, their general argument is that this fight is "off target" and the "cure" may be worse than the "condition." An important lesson from this literature is that an ostensibly well-meaning project to slim down the population not only is ineffective but has many unintended negative consequences. Problems include reinforcing the idea that certain body shapes and sizes are unacceptable, fueling disordered eating and other harmful weight-loss practices, and promoting individualistic rather than social-structural interventions that may amplify health inequalities (Evans et al, 2008). Accordingly, critics argue that obesity discourse must be challenged and even rejected in favor of a more holistic and socially just approach that prioritizes *health and well-being* rather than *weight* (Bombak et al, 2019; Aphramor, 2020).

Body materiality and biomedical concerns are not necessarily rejected by those who challenge the war on obesity. Indeed, conscientious objectors in the health professions include critical dieticians who advocate Health-At-Every-Size (HAES®), a weight-neutral approach that aims to measurably improve metabolic health and well-being through behavioral change. HAES® is by no means perfect. For example, practitioners have been urged to avoid reproducing nutritionism and "healthism" (Crawford, 1980) where food and lifestyle "choices" become a panacea for problems that are beyond individual control (Brady et al, 2013). However, rather than becoming "administrators" in the weight-loss business, a subtype of "obesity epidemic entrepreneur" (Monaghan et al, 2010), HAES® practitioners reject the WCHP in favor of what they consider to be a more ethical, inclusive, and effective approach (Aphramor and Gingras, 2011; Bacon and Aphramor, 2011, 2014). HAES® principles include intuitive eating, taking joy in bodily movement, and respecting one's body and its treatment. Those supporting HAES® also encourage an understanding of and resistance to size-ism, or stigma and other forms of discrimination directed at "fat people." More radically, with their Well Now project, Aphramor (2020), a former HAES® advocate, seeks to challenge the architecture of an individualizing lifestyle-oriented or behavioral approach to health. Their challenge is articulated via a focus on structural issues, including white supremacy and the embodied consequences of trauma in oppressive societies. When questioning the public health focus on obesity, other critics have recently attempted to integrate weight-inclusive paradigms with Indigenous knowledges. Cyr and Riediger (2021), for instance, foreground histories of colonial violence and theft of land in Canada, exposing the inadequacies (likely offensiveness and strategic ignorance) of public health advice to Indigenous communities to eat "traditional, land-based food" (pp 494–495) to redress "health disparities" (for further discussion, see Monaghan et al, 2022).

These critical responses might be difficult for some readers to swallow, given the evil view of obesity and the authoritative legitimization of fat fighting by the state and medical–industrial complex. Furthermore, there are emotional as well as cognitive constraints (as embodied by those charged with administering the war on weight/fat) rendering reflexivity difficult, if not painful. Aphramor and Gingras (2011), for example, discuss how middle-class women working as dieticians may have to come to grips with the shame of unintentionally harming larger people who are under their care. Grappling with shame sits alongside the fear of institutional repercussions, such as charges of professional irresponsibility when going against the party line. And there are obvious difficulties for advocates of men's health and well-being. After all, claiming that most men are overweight or obese and that their physiology renders them especially at-risk concords with "the new public health" wherein men are deemed "weaker and more physically vulnerable than women" (Petersen and Lupton, 1996, p 87). The idea that something should be done to combat obesity is thus promoted in the name of a "gender equitable" approach—a seemingly laudable call that nonetheless reproduces stigma or even "civilized oppression" (see Rogge et al, 2004). Reports of men's greater susceptibility to COVID-19, especially if obese, are also marshalled in the ongoing war on obesity. The aforementioned "dual crisis frame" has been widely circulated by the mass media despite uncertain and contradictory scientific knowledge (Hartmann-Boyce, 2021; Monaghan et al, 2022; on disconfirming evidence among men, see Taylor et al, 2021).

There are additional constraints on advancing critical perspectives, at least among Western populations who do not share the same appreciation of fatness as observed in other cultures (Popenoe, 2004). For example, there is a quasi-religious and highly profitable fervor to eradicate fatness amid pervasive sociocultural anxieties about national fitness, degeneracy, and, as with declining US hegemony (Wallerstein, 2004), increasing redundancy and military impotence. It is not unusual for cultural anxieties to be projected onto minority ethnic groups or "the darker races" as a covert form of racism (Campos, 2004; Campos et al, 2006), as well as onto women's bodies amid changing gender relations and familial obligations. However, sociocultural anxieties are also transposed onto white male bodies qua embodied subjects who risk failing as presumed guardians and agents of social progress (White, 2013). Obesity warmongering is executed on well-established gendered terrain, which also means that "collateral damage" (Herndon, 2005), such as body dissatisfaction, is unevenly distributed (Monaghan and Malson, 2013). This fight not only potentially discredits larger male bodies, it also impacts many females in a cultural context wherein fatness is feminized and women are more likely than men to embrace popular weight-loss methods—what Germov and Williams (1999) term "the sexual division of dieting." Indeed, there is a case for arguing that the war against female and feminizing fat reproduces masculine domination at a macro-social level while, paradoxically, both threatening it and promising to recoup it at an individual and microinteractional level (Monaghan, 2008). Aspects of this process are intimated by Gough (2010), noted earlier, though I will further ground this argument by outlining some insights from my previously published research on men and weight-related issues.

Monaghan (2007, 2008) draws from an ethnography undertaken at a commercial weight-loss club in Northeast England and in-depth interviews with 37 men. Participants were predominantly white and working class, the mean age was 43, and most would have been medically classed as overweight or obese based upon self-reported weight and height. Data were generated between 2004 and 2006 against the backdrop of a highly publicized war on obesity. Particularly large men, who might be medically defined as "morbidly obese" (sic), talked about their experiences of stigma (eg, being called a "fat pig" in the street), with some also mentioning how their children were discredited by association, something Goffman (1968) refers to as "courtesy stigma." These men's sense of masculinity—a relational identity entwined with a publicly expressed ethic to care for oneself and significant others—was spoiled in these contexts. While it was anticipated that most of the men from the weight-loss group would endorse the BMI, insofar as "health" and longevity provided an acceptable account for publicly seeking to lose weight (medicalization helped to masculinize dieting and efforts to recoup a more gender-appropriate body), many rejected this "gold standard" (Ruppel Shell, 2003, p 33) measure of "excess" weight/fat. In fact, the BMI was consistently referred to as ridiculous. Only two men sought to comply with the BMI; both were retired middle-class members of the weight-loss club who had recently been told by a nurse that they were (almost) obese (Monaghan, 2007).

Interestingly, most men sought to lose weight (sometimes a considerable amount), but they refused to achieve what medicine deems a "healthy weight" (BMI 20 to 24.9 kg/m$^2$). This "secondary adjustment" to—or, more precisely, "expressed distance" (Goffman, 1961) from—the gendered culture of slenderness was compatible with the social construction of masculinities. After all, manhood is associated with having a physical presence, of occupying space in the social world, and everyday perceptions of "bodily bigness" (incorporating a certain degree of fatness as well as lean body mass) are more accommodating for men. For instance, Campos

(2004) writes that while Brad Pitt would be deemed overweight on the BMI, Jennifer Aniston would have to gain approximately 55 pounds in order to have the same BMI (implying she would likely be perceived as "fat," or at least "too big" or "heavy" and thus unattractive according to normative ideals of femininity). Other actors, such as Russell Crowe, would be classed as obese. In short, everyday perceptions of overweight/obesity are gendered in ways that typically enable men to accommodate "larger" bodies and be viewed by others as acceptable, if not desirable (similarly, see Bergman, 2009). This gendered inequality in body norms has long been challenged by feminist scholars when arguing that "societal disapproval of fatness" mainly hurts women (Wiles, 1994, p 33).

Yet, as suggested earlier, men do not necessarily escape weight-related harms. While normative male embodiment may incorporate a range of acceptable shapes and sizes, "big fellas" (Monaghan, 2008) are not immune from fat oppression. Indeed, respondents in my research shared hurtful insights on forms of surveillance, domination, and symbolic violence. Large male bodies were, metaphorically speaking, "shot at" from numerous directions, for example, clinicians who labeled them "obese" (itself an offensive term to laity), wives who "nagged" them and refused to have sex until they lost weight, abrasive remarks from parents, and so forth. Most men understandably wanted to become smaller targets, even if that meant entering a traditionally woman-centered weight-loss group. Certainly, there were culturally circumscribed limits to their weight-loss efforts, noted earlier with reference to their expressed distance from the BMI. Such responses might irk health promoters. However, rather than correcting laymen who dismissed medicalized weight-for-height measures, Monaghan (2007) reported and honored their justifications for levels of body mass that medicine labels too heavy (implicitly or explicitly too fat). Justifications included the compatibility of heaviness, healthiness, and physical fitness (eg, some elite sportsmen, such as world-class rugby players, are technically obese); looking and feeling ill at a supposedly "healthy" BMI; and resisting irrational standardization amid bodily diversity. One conclusion from this research is that while men often seek accommodation within a symbolic system of masculine domination wherein feminine and feminizing fat must be combated, there remains a broader politicized need to challenge the war on obesity wherein women and children are typically less able to shield themselves. For instance, women and girls with a BMI $\geq 25$ kg/m$^2$ (ie, what medicine calls overweight) cannot justify their size with appeals to robust models of masculine physicality. Arguably, important life events may help mitigate societal disapproval of women's fatness, such as pregnancy (Wiles, 1994), though the increasing degree to which medicine defines maternal weight as risky for the unborn also needs to be reckoned with here (Bombak et al, 2016).

In sum, medicine and public health define weight/fatness as modernity's scourge, necessitating a war on obesity. The expressed rationale for this metaphorical war is to promote health and mitigate or avoid the risks commonly attributed to people's increasing girth, a "pathologizing frame" that was further amplified early in the COVID-19 pandemic (Monaghan et al, 2022). Men are deemed especially vulnerable in the new public health, and there are well publicized efforts to shame male bodies into joining the collective fight against fat, a movement that has long irked feminists and fat activists. Echoing and expanding upon earlier politicized critiques, various parties have systematically challenged the science, morality, and ideology of obesity discourse or the WCHP (O'Hara and Taylor, 2018). In line with such reasoning, I have argued that the war on obesity may be interpreted sociologically as a corrosive body project that unfolds on an uneven field of power. In such a context, social divisions mediate the fallout from obesity warmongering, with masculinity providing a status shield for male body-subjects seeking to deflect opprobrium and construct moral worth. Yet, there are limits. Men and boys also risk getting hurt in the war on obesity (Monaghan, 2008; 2014a).

I will now turn my attention toward a broader macro-social canvas and offer a sociological reading of "the bigger picture," wherein health is a matter that extends beyond fleshy male bodies and the putative poor lifestyle choices of people deemed overweight/obese/fat. In qualifying what follows, the intention is not to "throw the baby out with the bathwater" and claim behaviors and human agency are irrelevant when promoting health (as noted earlier with critical reference to HAES®). Rather, drawing from medical sociology and other literature on (growing) health inequalities, my intention is to underscore how individual behaviors—and/or bodyweight as a crude proxy for such behaviors—are much less significant for health than is commonly assumed.

## Structured health inequalities: insights from medical sociology and men's health

Medical sociologists, along with colleagues in epidemiology and public health, have done an important job in documenting health inequalities and the growth in inequity in recent decades (Scambler, 2012, 2018; Scott-Samuel et al, 2014). The consistent observation in this literature is that there is a social gradient for most causes of death and measures of morbidity, with those in lower socioeconomic groups being far more likely to die younger and experience more illness and disability than more privileged groups. Moreover, much of this gradient cannot be explained in terms of individual "poor behaviors" such as diet, physical inactivity, drinking alcohol above recommended levels, or smoking tobacco (Marmot, 2004). Rather, health inequalities reflect socioeconomic inequalities, a point similarly articulated in fat studies when contributors discuss linkages between lower socioeconomic status (SES) and health problems attributed to adiposity. After stating that "known risk factors accounted for only a small proportion of the mortality risk of low SES," Ernsberger (2009, p 27) adds: "Nonetheless, many experts persist in the assumption that poor people are often unhealthy because they are fat. Instead, fat people might be often unhealthy because they are often poor."

In line with such reasoning, critical literature directs attention "upstream" toward powerful societal determinants, or the fundamental causes of health inequalities (McCartney et al, 2021). Factors include, for instance, living in impoverished neighborhoods and, significantly in the US context, the obstacles faced by many people seeking to access formal medical care for diseases such as cancer and diabetes. One might add to this the consequences of structural racism and the attendant risk of lethal force, which young Black men disproportionately face when confronted by police officers and which has resulted in mass protests and reinvigorated calls for justice and civil rights, as per the recent Black Lives Matter movement. Such arguments regarding the structures and injurious processes of a divided society, incorporating a repressive state apparatus, resonate with high-profile, social-scientific literature on health inequity. For Wilkinson and Pickett (2009), if a society is highly unequal (think of the United States compared to Sweden), there tends to be a greater burden of public health and social problems such as homicide and incarceration. This is an important argument, albeit one that should be qualified when "obesity" is simply taken as a valid biomedical construct rather than an imprecise marker for health problems and behaviors that can be traced to the structures and processes of neoliberal capitalist societies (Monaghan et al, 2022).

Macro-social factors impacting health include the political economy, modes of social organization, and policies that repeatedly seek to resuscitate a highly unstable and crisis-prone world capitalist system (eg, off-shoring labor to more easily exploited populations and bailing out private banks at the expense of a nation's public finances and democratic representation). An expansive literature underscores the salience of neoliberalism and reinvigorated class relations when explaining social and health inequality within and between nation states (see Coburn, 2004; Scambler, 2012, 2018; Scott-Samuel et al, 2014). Such literature maintains that it is no coincidence that there has been a stark increase in inequality since the 1980s, for this is when elites in nations such as Britain and the United States enthusiastically embraced neoliberalism and its attendant ideologies of market fundamentalism, financial deregulation, privatization, and individual responsibility (ideologies that are, of course, contradicted in practice when capital needs to be saved from itself). To take one particularly toxic aspect of this class project, high finance, Scott-Samuel et al (2014, p 53) note how the "big bang" financial deregulation of 1986 led to "substantial increases in socioeconomic and health inequalities [that] were effectively marginalized and ignored by [Thatcher's] government."

Other aspects, such as the depoliticizing emphasis upon the individual and the rolling back of the welfare state, have also had a notable impact on UK health policy. Such policy, following US-based psychological models of behavioral intervention, is blinkered insofar as it neglects social context. Ong et al (2014, p 227) trace such policy making from the 1990s, adding that from 2010 the economic rationale for the "self-management" of patients gained momentum "against the backdrop of financial austerity and reductions in public sector funding." Under such conditions, politicized concerns to address macrostructural factors affecting public health tend to be sidelined by a myopic focus on irresponsible (overweight) neoliberal subjects who are allegedly culpable for their own ills. This is an instance of scapegoating, a blame game directed at multiple "soft" targets such as single mothers, the unemployed, immigrants, and public sector workers who purportedly cost too much for the system (O'Flynn et al, 2014). Such maneuvers have been dissected within critical public health scholarship with reference to a "stigma system," wherein scapegoating works as a "divide-and-rule" strategy for the powerful (Friedman et al, 2022).

In short, individual level approaches have ideological appeal and currency under historically transmitted social conditions, with health policy typically emphasizing behavioral change as an antidote to people's presumptively "maladaptive" activities (Ong et al, 2014, p 229), bodies, and "lack of preparedness" for infectious pandemics. However, in siding with the Black Report (DHSS, 1980), medical sociologists have explained health inequalities largely in terms of people's material conditions of existence (for cogent analytical work that melds materialist concerns with a multidimensional focus on the lived body, see Williams, 2003). The materialist approach draws attention to working environments and labor markets (eg, job insecurity, low pay, reduced pension provision, and unemployment), housing, healthcare, social infrastructure, and related concerns such as affordable transportation that facilitates networks of interdependency and connection. For medical sociologists such as Scambler (2018), it is crucial to recognize the fundamental contradictions of capitalism and antagonistic class relations when offering a materialist explanation for health inequity. If behaviors are to be accorded any weight, then there is a case for arguing that attention should be directed upward. That is, rather than focusing on the behaviors of people in poorer socioeconomic circumstances (as often happens in state-funded research), attention needs to be directed toward the illness behaviors of the rich and powerful whose search for profits largely takes priority over public health and well-being. Here critics acknowledge that common cultural/behavioral factors contribute to health inequalities, for instance, higher rates of smoking among lower socioeconomic groups. However, the crucial point is that such behaviors are indebted to social structures; "personal choices" are shaped and constrained by material circumstances. As observed in Graham's (1994) research on women and smoking, and in Williams et al's (1995) study on health beliefs in a deprived English inner city, feelings of segregation, poverty, exclusion, hopelessness, and powerlessness influence people's health behaviors and outcomes.

While debates about health tend to be moralized and conflated with individualized concerns (eg, personal failure, shame, blame, and correction), it is clear from the foregoing discussion that hegemonic narratives are also subject to considerable contestation and reframing. In line with the "social justice frame" (Kwan and Graves, 2013), which is politicized and challenges inequity, I will finish this section by making further connections with critical perspectives on men, masculinities, and health. Scholars in this field have, over the past two decades, made inroads on a complex and contested terrain (Scott-Samuel et al, 2009; Gough and Robertson, 2010; Gottzén et al, 2019). Relevant themes include the differential effects of unemployment on men's and women's mortality, especially for men in their early- to mid-career, and dramatic increases in male suicide during the latter part of the twentieth century, which has been linked to growing income inequality and instability in heterosexual relationships (for a review, see Robertson and Monaghan, 2012). Disability, embodiment, and masculinity also constitute a complex matrix of investigation, with attention recently paid to themes such as technology and neoliberal logics that render many bodies and lives dispensable (ie, the impaired and chronically ill who are systemically disadvantaged by a competitive work-orientated system) (Robertson et al, 2019). However, rather than detail this burgeoning literature I will limit myself to two insightful contributions that promote critical thinking about the material/structural conditions that shape and constrain life chances and health. In keeping with my preceding arguments, I will flag literature that challenges the sort of alarmism that would have us believe that individual "laymen" are their own worst enemies and are endangering or burdening others when, for instance, their actions result in poor health outcomes that (purportedly) drain already overstretched health services. More specifically, I will draw from Lohan's (2010) and Robertson and Williams' (2010) insights on men's health. These writings are noteworthy because they integrate diverse theorization and connect health problems to social structures and processes more so than men's individual attitudes, behaviors, or psychological predispositions.

Lohan (2010) explains that the "critical studies on men" (CSM) literature often prompts health service providers to simply focus on the goal of modifying service delivery and education in an effort to change men's attitudes, lifestyles, their uptake of such services, and their health outcomes. Unfortunately, this means that health service providers often lack an "awareness of the relational power context of gender relations" and an appreciation of "the embeddedness of men's gendered health practices in broader sets of structured inequalities in society" (pp 14–15). For Lohan, "[i]t is precisely this embeddedness" that necessitates CSM to engage "the broader inequalities in health literature" (p 15). Consequently, she moves the spotlight onto power, outlining how theories that explain material inequalities (alongside other theories, such as cultural/behavioral and lifecourse approaches) might be integrated into CSM in future research. For instance, while structural explanations have been underutilized in studies on men's health, Lohan makes a good case for redressing that issue, not only when considering health differences between groups of men but also when considering how materialist relations between men and women exert their effects. Accordingly, the goal is to "tease out the interactions between class and gender in men and women's health" (p 17). I would also add "children" to Lohan's proposition in order to overcome possible accusations of an adult-centric bias, alongside other intersecting axes of power (eg, ethnicity and sexuality) that pattern population health (see Part 1 of Monaghan and Gabe, 2022). Furthermore, when interrogating broader structures and their effects on health, critical attention should be directed at forms of exploitation, oppression, and domination as emergent properties of a historically unfolding world-system. Whether theorized in terms of the inherent contradictions of capitalism (Scambler, 2018) and/or masculine domination (Bourdieu, 2001; for Bourdieu's neglect of feminism here, see Connell, 2007), a key message is this: real social structures matter and their effects should not be misrecognized as individual pathology (bad behavior, fatness).

Robertson and Williams (2010) similarly advance critical knowledge of social structures as part of an explicitly embodied approach to men's health and health promotion. Revisiting some of their previous qualitative research, they challenge the media-fueled myth that "all men are irresponsible when it comes to self-care and promoting their health" (Robertson and Williams, 2010, p 48). Refuting essentialist constructions that locate men's health problems within their biology or "the male psyche" (p 49), these authors challenge health promotion ideologies that all too easily reiterate the centrality of individual responsibility and the need for behavioral change. Flagging the limitations of public health and health promotion, their contribution unpicks "normative conceptualisations of 'health' and 'healthy lifestyle'" with reference to men's own accounts. Importantly, they retain an eye on "issues of social justice and social determinants [of health] without denying the importance of men's agency" (p 49). After outlining dominant biomedical constructions of health—and the salience of "risk," "behaviors," and "lifestyles" within epidemiologically inspired discourses—Robertson and Williams urge readers to regard men's departures from healthist prescriptions as not necessarily acts of resistance (in the Foucauldian sense) but pragmatic enactments that make sense within given social contexts (eg, smoking among stressed workers as a release from an extremely hectic schedule). These authors, drawing from Bourdieu and other theorists (eg, Lupton and Crawford), conceptualize men's enactments in terms of "a logic of practice" that is embedded within specific "social locations." Empirically, respondents juggled notions concerning "good citizenship" and hegemonic masculine discourses wherein men "cannot be seen to be too concerned about 'health' (feminine) issues" (Robertson and Williams, 2010, pp 54–55). One conclusion here is that both compliance and noncompliance to "lifestyle advice" do not occur in a social vacuum. Accordingly, such action must be understood in terms of men's intersubjective meanings and, more broadly, socially structured requirements wherein control and release are basic "requirements of contemporary capitalism" (p 57). Attentive to the physicality of the lived body, Robertson and Williams also underscore men's embodiment, taking the materiality of social structures plus human corporeality into account. And, the dialectics of such processes are underscored in context: social agents are "corporeal, physical bodies, which are affected within the inequitable social arrangements generated and fostered through neo-liberal politics" (p 58).

In sum, health is affected by many factors. However, within medicalized Western culture, there is a common emphasis on lifestyles/behaviors as inferred from the size, shape, and weight of the physical body. While there is no suggestion within critical weight studies that behaviors are unimportant and all "fat people" are necessarily healthy, there is, as per some of the medical sociology and men's health studies literature cited earlier, recognition of the larger context that patterns health outcomes. At a minimum, what may be taken from such writings is that social justice (and, by implication, gender justice), alongside embodied human agency, matters when seeking to promote healthier societies. This realization, in turn, means grappling with the social collectivity, co-constituted by real flesh and blood bodies that are never merely "targets" of medicalization, surveillance, correction, and control. By extension, policies could be formulated in a manner that connects with everyday meanings while also seeking to redress growing inequalities (especially accelerating inequalities in wealth). Here, overriding emphasis could be given to respectfully advancing health equity and shared well-being regardless of the contingencies of an individual's size, age, ethnicity, sex, or gender.

## Concluding reflections

As explained by Robertson and Williams (2010), much about contemporary masculinity remains anecdotal or misunderstood based on stereotypes. Indeed, it is all too easy to reproduce myths of masculinity (Monaghan and Atkinson, 2014), which include, among other things, the view that men and boys are a homogenous "toxic" class rather than a diverse body politic that incorporates intersecting relations of power tied to economic status, ethnicity, and other divisions. Hegemonic fabrications, including the latest round of obesity alarmism, tend to construct male bodies as essentially problematic and in need of targeting for health promotion or, more disturbingly, potentially lethal forms of discipline and punishment. Taking as its point of departure various representations of male bodies as inadequate, pathological, and risky, this chapter sought to encourage a broader community of scholars and health researchers/workers to reinterpret the field and those bodies of knowledge that may inform debate and action.

To avoid potential misrecognition or misunderstanding, the basic rationale I am offering when reinterpreting male bodies is not to celebrate men's and boys' lives and practices, or, as with reactionary men's studies, tell men that they are OK (Lohan, 2010). In many circumstances, male bodies are clearly under assault (Kehler and Atkinson, 2010). This, it should be stressed, is within a gender order that is irreducible to individuals and which typically rewards aggressive competitiveness, toughness, and one-upmanship (Scott-Samuel et al, 2009). It is also a gender order wherein forms of public health promotion, as seen in the war on obesity, threaten embodied masculinity while simultaneously promising to recoup it—for example, the emasculated idle fat man who is "targeted" within a militarized discourse but who may "save" himself by "battling the bulge" (Monaghan, 2008). Rather than naively reassure men and boys that all is well, my intention has been somewhat different. My aim has been to challenge cultural clichés, stereotypes, and one-dimensional accounts that fail to capture the complexity, messiness, and embeddedness of people's lives in a world where gender and intersecting axes of power are embodied and exert their effects. Arguably, such a task is vital given the urgency often ascribed to the problem of men's and boys' health (behaviors), with images of issues (obesity, among others) offering a seemingly solid rationale for well-intentioned—if often misguided, empirically uninformed, and ethically suspect—interventions (Monaghan and Atkinson, 2014).

In addition to reviewing research on weight-related issues, the chapter aimed to think "big" (systemically) when advancing critical perspectives on male bodies and health. Such an approach should remain attentive to microlevel concerns and agency, although, as illustrated by Robertson and Williams (2010), Lohan (2010), and others (eg, Scott-Samuel et al, 2009), attention should also be directed at broader structures of power and inequality. At a time when capitalism has proven itself to be highly unstable, inequitable, exploitative, and oppressive, calls from men's health researchers to interrogate the material conditions of existence and the politics of neoliberalism should be heeded. In so doing, we better situate ourselves to connect with and help expand other bodies of literature, such as sociological writings on health inequalities that offer challenging explanations for observed social gradients and the repeated failure of governments to address them (Scambler, 2012, 2018). Of course, certain audiences will remain unreceptive, especially in these crisis times. Obesity discourse, after all, fits well with a culture of "healthism" (Crawford, 1980) and other mechanisms that scapegoat people (O'Flynn et al, 2014; Friedman et al, 2022). Yet it is possible to challenge such mechanisms and to do so without writing out the materiality of the body. For instance, biomedical health may be promoted through HAES® or through more radical approaches that are highly reflexive, topical, and sociologically imaginative (namely, Well Now; see Aphramor, 2020; Monaghan et al, 2022).

In closing this chapter, all that remains to be added is that significant progress is being made in the critical study of masculinities and health, and there is an important literature that advances calls for greater gender/social justice (Connell, 2000; Robertson et al, 2019). Such writing is attuned to the body and bodily practices within hierarchies of hegemony and subordination. At the same time, progress always implies that current understandings are open to improvement, refinement, and even rejection. Our collective knowledge remains an ongoing project. As part of that task, let us work to advance critical thinking about the bigger context and the fundamental causes of health inequalities (such as the strategic behaviors of elites, especially today amid financialization, iatrocracy, and authoritarian calls for biosecurity and pandemic preparedness). This is vital, I would argue, at a time when it is all too easy to champion individualized bodily interventions that are entangled with (and help to fuel) prejudice, political expediency, and various other processes that demand sociological critique (eg, cultural anxieties about emasculation, corrosive pandemic psychologies, the search for class distinction, and the vested interests of the multibillion-dollar health industrial complex that hypes "quick" technical "fixes"). Once placed in the context of a broader gender order and capitalist world-system in structural crisis, we may be better situated to subject hegemonic understandings and practices to critique and ask more penetrating questions about the sort of society we wish to live in. Such questioning will encounter resistances and misrecognition, itself a form of violence that reproduces class privilege, masculine domination, and so on. The personal stakes may also be high for some, especially in contexts such as the health services and government scientific advisory boards. However, to renege on such a commitment in formal pedagogical settings, which are explicitly oriented to developing critical perspectives, is irresponsible scholarship. Rather, there is a need to collectively reinterpret the putative problems that surround our bodies and lives and to debate, based upon what we learn, alternative visions for macro-social change. These times of crisis demand nothing less. I therefore call upon the community of body scholars, health researchers, and workers more generally to help advance this politicized task by "rethinking obesity" as well as the social conditions under which the war on weight/fat has emerged and continues apace.

**Acknowledgments**

This chapter is a thoroughly revised and updated version of a previously published article: Monaghan, L.F. (2015) 'Critiquing masculinity myths: rethinking male bodies, obesity and health in context', *International Journal of Men's Health*, 14(3): 250–266. Monaghan would also like to thank the book's editors for their invitation and helpful suggestions when revising the chapter.

**References**

Academy of Medical Royal Colleges (2013) *Measuring Up: The Medical Profession's Prescription for the Nation's Obesity Crisis* [Report], available from: https://www.aomrc.org.uk/reports-guidance/measuring-up-0213/.

Aphramor, L. (2020) 'Eight signs of white supremacy in HAES (Health at Every Size) and ideas for action', *Medium*, June 9, available from: https://medium.com/@lucy.aphramor/eight-signs-of-supremacy-in-haes-health-at-every-size-and-ideas-for-action-e04b7f5c86fb.

Aphramor, L. and Gingras, J. (2011) 'Helping people change: promoting politicised practice in the health care professions', in E. Rich, L.F. Monaghan and L. Aphramor (eds) *Debating Obesity: Critical Perspectives*, Basingstoke: Palgrave Macmillan, pp 192–218.

Armstrong, D. (1995) 'The rise of surveillance medicine', *Sociology of Health and Illness*, 17(3): 393–404.

Bacon, L. and Aphramor, L. (2011) 'Weight science: evaluating the evidence for a paradigm shift', *Nutrition Journal*, 10(9), available from: https://doi.org/10.1186/1475-2891-10-9.

Bacon, L. and Aphramor, L. (2014) *Body Respect*, Dallas, TX: Bennella.

BBC Online (2007) *Health, Obesity by Dr Rob Hicks*, available from: http://www.bbc.co.uk/health/mens/_health/issues_obesity.shtml.

Bell, K. and McNaughton, D. (2007) 'Feminism and the invisible fat man', *Body and Society*, 13(1): 107–131.

Bergman, S.B. (2009) 'Part-time fatso', in E. Rothblum and S. Solovay (eds) *The Fat Studies Reader*, New York: New York University Press, pp 139–142.

Bombak, A.E. (2014) 'The "obesity epidemic": evolving science, unchanging etiology', *Sociology Compass*, 8(5): 509–524.

Bombak, A.E., McPhail, D. and Ward, P. (2016) 'Reproducing stigma: interpreting "overweight" and "obese" women's experiences of weight-based discrimination in reproductive healthcare', *Social Science and Medicine*, 166: 94–101.

Bombak, A.E., Monaghan, L.F. and Rich, E. (2019) 'Dietary approaches to weight-loss, Health-At-Every-Size® and beyond: rethinking the war on obesity', *Social Theory and Health*, 17(1): 89–108.

Bordo, S. (1993) *Unbearable Weight: Feminism, Western Culture, and the Body*, Berkeley: University of California Press.

Borland, S. (2015) 'Obesity in women as dangerous as "terror threat"', *Mail Online*, December 11, available from: http://www.dailymail.co.uk/news/article-3355256/Obesity-women-dangerous-terror-threat-Extraordinary-claim-health-chief-uses-speech-demand-condition-added-list-public-health-threats.html.

Bourdieu, P. (2001) *Masculine Domination*, Cambridge: Polity Press.

Brady, J., Gingras, J. and Aphramor, L. (2013) 'Theorizing Health at Every Size as a relational cultural endeavour', *Critical Public Health*, 23(3): 345–355.

Campos, P. (2004) *The Obesity Myth: Why America's Obsession with Weight Is Hazardous to Your Health*, New York: Gotham Books.

Campos, P. (2011) 'Does fat kill? A review of the epidemiological evidence', in E. Rich, L.F. Monaghan and L. Aphramor (eds) *Debating Obesity: Critical Perspectives*, Basingstoke: Palgrave Macmillan, pp 36–59.

Campos, P., Saguy, A., Ernsberger, P., Oliver, E. and Gaessar, G. (2006) 'The epidemiology of overweight and obesity: public health crisis or moral panic?', *International Journal of Epidemiology*, 35(1): 55–60.

Chernin, K. (1981) *The Obsession: Reflections on the Tyranny of Slenderness*, New York: Harper.

Coburn, D. (2004) 'Beyond the income inequality hypothesis: class, neo-liberalism, and health inequalities', *Social Science and Medicine*, 58(1): 41–56.

Connell, R.W. (2000) *The Men and the Boys*, Cambridge: Polity Press.

Connell, R.W. (2007) *Southern Theory: The Global Dynamics of Knowledge in Social Science*, London: Routledge.

Conrad, P. and Schneider, J.W. (1992) *Deviance and Medicalization. From Badness to Sickness* (3rd edn), Philadelphia, PA: Temple University Press.

Cooper, C. (2010) 'Fat studies: mapping the field', *Sociology Compass*, 4(12): 1020–1034.

Crawford, R. (1980) 'Healthism and the medicalization of everyday life', *International Journal of Health Services*, 10(3): 365–388.

Cyr, M. and Riediger, N. (2021) '(Re)claiming our bodies using a two-eyed seeing approach: Health-At-Every-Size (HAES®) and Indigenous knowledge', *Canadian Journal of Public Health*, 112: 493–497.

DHSS (1980) *Inequalities in Health: Report of a Working Group (The Black Report)*, London: HMSO.

Dingwall, R. (2022) 'Pandemics and epidemics', in L.F. Monaghan and J. Gabe (eds) *Key Concepts in Medical Sociology* (3rd edn), London: SAGE, pp 3–9.

Ernsberger, P. (2009) 'Does social class explain the connection between weight and health?', in E. Rothblum and S. Solovay (eds) *The Fat Studies Reader*, New York: New York University Press, pp 25–36.

Evans, J., Rich, E., Davies, B. and Allwood, R. (2008) *Education, Disordered Eating and Obesity Discourse: Fat Fabrications*, New York: Routledge.

Flegal, K.M., Kit, B.K., Orpana, H. and Graubard, B.I. (2013) 'Association of all-cause mortality with overweight and obesity using standard Body Mass Index categories: a systematic review and meta-analysis', *The Journal of the American Medical Association*, 309(1): 71–82.

Friedman, S.R., Williams, L.D., Guarino, H. et al (2022) 'The stigma system: how sociopolitical domination, scapegoating, and stigma shape public health', *Journal of Community Psychology*, 50(1): 385–408.

Gard, M. (2011) *The End of the Obesity Epidemic*, New York: Routledge.

Gard, M. and Wright, J. (2005) *The Obesity Epidemic: Science, Morality and Ideology*, London: Routledge.

Germov, J. and Williams, L. (1999) 'Dieting women: self-surveillance and the body panopticon', in J. Sobal and D. Maurer (eds) *Weighty Issues: Fatness and Thinness as Social Problems*, New York: Aldine de Gruyter, pp 117–132.

Gilman, S. (2004) *Fat Boys: A Slim Book*, Lincoln: University of Nebraska Press.

Goffman, E. (1961) *Asylums: Essays on the Social Situation of Mental Patients and Other Inmates*, Harmondsworth: Penguin Books.

Goffman, E. (1968) *Stigma: Notes on the Management of Spoiled Identity*, Middlesex: Penguin Books.

Gottzén, U., Mellström and T. Shefer (eds) (2019) *Routledge International Handbook of Masculinity Studies*, London: Routledge.

Gough, B. (2010) 'Promoting "masculinity" over health: a critical analysis of men's health promotion with particular reference to an obesity reduction "manual"', in B. Gough and S. Robertson (eds) *Men, Masculinities and Health*, Basingstoke: Palgrave Macmillan, pp 125–142.

Gough, B. and Robertson, S. (eds) (2010) *Men, Masculinities and Health*, Basingstoke: Palgrave Macmillan.

Graham, H. (1994) 'Surviving by smoking', in S. Wilkinson and C. Kitzinger (eds) *Women and Health: Feminist Perspectives*, London: Taylor and Francis, pp 102–123.

Hartmann-Boyce, J. (2021) 'COVID-19: is obesity really more of a risk factor for men than women?', *The Conversation*, May 12, available from: https://theconversation.com/covid-19-is-obesity-really-more-of-a-risk-factor-for-men-than-women-160567.

Herndon, A.M. (2005) 'Collateral damage from friendly fire? Race, nation, class and the "war against obesity"', *Social Semiotics*, 15(2): 127–141.

Kehler, M. and Atkinson, M. (2010) *Boys' Bodies*, New York: Peter Lang.

Kwan, S. and Graves, J. (2013) *Framing Fat: Competing Constructions in Contemporary Culture*, New Brunswick, NJ: Rutgers University Press.

Lohan, M. (2010) 'Developing a critical men's health debate in academic scholarship', in B. Gough and S. Robertson (eds) *Men, Masculinities and Health: Critical Perspectives*, Basingstoke: Palgrave Macmillan, pp 11–29.

Lozano-Sufrategui, L., Carless, D., Pringle, A. and Sparkes, A.C. (2016) '"Sorry mate, you're probably a bit too fat to be able to do any of these": men's experiences of weight stigma', *International Journal of Men's Health*, 15(1): 4–23.

Lupton, D. (2015) 'The pedagogy of disgust: the ethical, moral and political implications of using disgust in public health campaigns', *Critical Public Health*, 25(1): 4–14.

Lupton, D. (2018) *Fat* (2nd edn), New York: Routledge.

Marmot, M. (2004) *The Status Syndrome: How Your Social Standing Directly Affects Your Health*, London: Bloomsbury.

McCartney, G., Dickie, E., Escobar, O. and Collins, C. (2021) 'Health inequalities, fundamental causes and power: towards the practice of good theory', *Sociology of Health and Illness*, 43(1): 20–39.

McPhail, D. (2009) 'What to do with the "tubby hubby"? "Obesity," the crisis of masculinity, and the nuclear family in early Cold War Canada', *Antipode*, 41(5): 1021–1050.

Monaghan, L.F. (2007) 'Body Mass Index, masculinities and moral worth: men's critical talk about "appropriate" weight-for-height', *Sociology of Health and Illness*, 29(4): 584–609.

Monaghan, L.F (2008) *Men and the War on Obesity: A Sociological Study*, New York: Routledge.

Monaghan, L.F. (2014a) 'Civilising recalcitrant boys' bodies: promoting social fitness through the anti-obesity offensive', *Sport, Education and Society*, 19(6): 691–711.

Monaghan, L.F. (2014b) 'Debating, theorising and researching "obesity" in challenging times', *Social Theory and Health: Inaugural Virtual Special Issue on Obesity*, available from: https://link.springer.com/article/10.1057/sth.2014.10.

Monaghan, L.F. and Hardey, M. (2011) 'Bodily sensibility: vocabularies of the discredited male body', in E. Rich, L.F. Monaghan and L. Aphramor (eds) *Debating Obesity: Critical Perspectives*, New York: Palgrave Macmillan, pp 60–89.

Monaghan, L.F. and Malson, H. (2013) '"It's worse for women and girls": negotiating embodied masculinities through weight-related talk', *Critical Public Health*, 23(3): 3014–3019.

Monaghan, L.F. and Atkinson, M. (2014) *Challenging Myths of Masculinity: Understanding Physical Cultures*, Farnham: Ashgate.

Monaghan, L.F. and Gabe, J. (eds) (2022) *Key Concepts in Medical Sociology* (3rd edn), London: SAGE.

Monaghan, L.F., Hollands, R. and Pritchard, G. (2010) 'Obesity epidemic entrepreneurs: types, practices and interests', *Body and Society*, 16(2): 37–71.

Monaghan, L.F., Colls, R. and Evans, B. (2013) 'Obesity discourse and fat politics: research, critique and interventions', *Critical Public Health*, 23(3): 249–262.

Monaghan, L.F., Rich, E. and Bombak, A.E. (2022) *Rethinking Obesity: Critical Perspectives in Crisis Times*, Oxon: Routledge.

National Audit Office (2001) *Tackling Obesity in England*, London: The Stationary Office.

O'Connell, L., Quigley, F., Williams, O., West, H., Metolli, S. and Pitham, H. (2021) '"It's all right for you thinnies": "obesity", eating disorders, and COVID-19', in P. Beresford, M. Farr, G. Hickey, M. Kaur, J. Ocloo, D. Tembo and O. Williams (eds) *COVID-19 and Co-production in Health and Social Care Research, Policy and Practice, Volume 1: The Challenges and Necessity of Co-production*, Bristol: Policy Press.

O'Flynn, M., Monaghan, L.F. and Power, M.J. (2014) 'Scapegoating during a time of crisis: a critique of post "Celtic Tiger" Ireland', *Sociology*, 48(5): 921–937.

O'Hara, L. and Taylor, J. (2018) 'What's wrong with the "war on obesity?" A narrative review of the weight-centered health paradigm and the development of the 3C framework to build critical competency for a paradigm shift', *SAGE Open*, 8(2), available from: https://doi.org/10.1177/2158244018772888.

Ong, B.N., Roges, A., Kennedy, A. et al (2014) 'Behaviour change and social blinkers? The role of sociology in trials of self-management behaviour in chronic conditions', *Sociology of Health and Illness*, 36(2): 226–238.

Pausé, C., Parker, G. and Gray, L. (2021) 'Resisting the problematisation of fatness in COVID-19: in pursuit of health justice', *International Journal of Disaster Risk Reduction*, 54: 102021.

Petersen, A. and Lupton, D. (1996) *The New Public Health and Self in the Age of Risk*, London: SAGE.

Popenoe, R. (2004) *Feeding Desire: Fatness, Beauty and Sexuality among a Saharan People*, Abingdon: Routledge.

Raisborough, J. (2016) *Fat Bodies, Health and the Media*, London: Palgrave Macmillan.

Rich, E., Monaghan, L.F. and Aphramor, L. (eds) (2011) *Debating Obesity: Critical Perspectives*, Basingstoke: Palgrave Macmillan.

Rich, E., Monaghan, L.F. and Bombak, A.E. (2020) 'A discourse analysis of schoolgirls engagement with fat pedagogy and critical health education: rethinking the childhood "obesity scandal"', *Sport, Education and Society*, 25(2): 127–142.

Robertson, S. and Williams, R. (2010) 'Men, public health and health promotion: towards a critically structural and embodied understanding', in B. Gough and S. Robertson (eds) *Men, Masculinities and Health: Critical Perspectives*, Basingstoke: Palgrave Macmillan, pp 48–66.

Robertson, S. and Monaghan, L.F. (2012) 'Embodied heterosexual masculinities, part 2: foregrounding men's health and emotions', *Sociology Compass*, 6(2): 151–165.

Robertson, S., Monaghan, L. and Southby, K. (2019) 'Disability, embodiment and masculinities: a complex matrix', in L. Gottzén, U. Mellström and T. Shefer (eds) *Routledge International Handbook of Masculinity Studies*, London: Routledge, pp 154–164.

Rogge, M.M., Greenwald, M. and Golden, A. (2004) 'Obesity, stigma and civilized oppression', *Advanced Nursing Studies*, 27(4): 301–315.

Rothblum, E. (2018) 'Slim chance for permanent weight loss', *Archives of Scientific Psychology*, 6: 63–69.

Rothblum, E. and Solovay, S. (eds) (2009) *The Fat Studies Reader*, NY: New York University Press.

Ruppel Shell, E. (2003) *Fat Wars: The Inside Story of the Obesity Industry*, London: Atlantic Books.

Scambler, G. (2012) 'Health inequalities', *Sociology of Health and Illness*, 34(1): 130–146.

Scambler, G. (2018) *Sociology, Health and the Fractured Society: A Critical Realist Account*, New York: Routledge.

Scott-Samuel, A. (2014) '"Men behaving badly": patriarchy, public policy and health inequalities', paper presented at the *Men, Health and Wellbeing: Critical Insights Conference*, Leeds Metropolitan University, July 8.

Scott-Samuel, A., Stanistreet, D. and Crawshaw, P. (2009) 'Hegemonic masculinity, structural violence and health inequalities', *Critical Public Health*, 19(3): 287–292.

Scott-Samuel, A., Bambra, C., Collins, C., Hunter, D., McCartney, G. and Smith, K. (2014) 'The impact of Thatcherism on health and well-being in Britain', *International Journal of Health Services*, 44(1): 53–71.

Shilling, C. (2012) *The Body and Social Theory* (3rd edn), London: SAGE.

Sky News (2020) 'Coronavirus: Boris Johnson says he was "too fat" as he launches obesity crackdown', July 27, available from: https://news.sky.com/story/pm-targets-checkout-sweets-and-buy-one-get-one-free-deals-in-national-obesity-plan-12037000.

Strong, P. (1990) 'Epidemic psychology: a model', *Sociology of Health and Illness*, 12(3): 249–259.

Taylor, E.H., Marson, J., Elhadi, M. et al (2021) 'Factors associated with mortality in patients with COVID-19 admitted to intensive care: a systematic review and meta-analysis', *Anaesthesia*, 76(9): 1224–1232.

The Report of the National Taskforce on Obesity (2005) *Obesity: The Policy Challenges*, available from: www.healthpromotion.ie.

UK Parliament (2004) *House of Commons Health Committee: Obesity*, third report of Session 2003–2004, volume 1, ordered by The House of Commons, May 10, 2004, available from: https://www.publications.parliament.uk/pa/cm200304/cmselect/cmhealth/23/2302.htm.

Wallerstein, I. (2004) *World-Systems Analysis: An Introduction*, Durham, NC: Duke University Press.

Warin, M. (2020) 'The "gentle and invisible" violence of obesity prevention', *American Anthropologist*, 122(3): 672–673.

White, F.R. (2013) '"We're kind of devolving": visual tropes of evolution in obesity discourse', *Critical Public Health*, 23(3): 320–330.

Wiles, R. (1994) '"I'm not fat, I'm pregnant": the impact of pregnancy on fat women's body image', in S. Wilkinson and C. Kitzinger (eds) *Women and Health: Feminist Perspectives*, London: Taylor and Francis, pp 33–48.

Wilkinson, R. and Pickett, K. (2009) *The Spirit Level*, London: Allen Lane.

Williams, G.H., Popay, J. and Bissell, P. (1995) 'Public health risks in the material world: barriers to social movements in health', in J. Gabe (ed) *Medicine, Health and Risk*, Oxford: Blackwell, pp 113–132.

Williams, S.J. (2003) *Medicine and the Body*, London: SAGE.

World Health Organization (1998) *Obesity: Preventing and Managing the Global Epidemic*, Geneva: WHO Press.

World Health Organization (2021) *Controlling the Global Obesity Epidemic*, available from: https://www.who.int/activities/controlling-the-global-obesity-epidemic.

6

# Beauty, Breasts, and Meaning after Mastectomy

*Piper Sledge*

Breast cancer is an ugly disease, visible on the surface of the body in garish display. Yet the images we regularly see in the media are remarkably sanitized, feminized, and beautified. In the standard imaginary, breast cancer is a lump that you might feel but not see, an illustration of internal processes, a highly edited image of tiny and uniform scars, or maybe an image from a pathologist's slide. Rarely depicted are the long (stretching from the middle of the chest to under the armpit), jagged, or raised scars that are often the reality of mastectomies.

The relative invisibility of mastectomy scars is part of what Dorothy Broom (2001) refers to as the imperative of concealment. At the center of the cultural framing of breast cancer is the notion that the disease fundamentally disrupts femininity and ideals of feminine beauty through disfigurement of the breasts (Potts, 2000; Broom, 2001; Crompvoets, 2003, 2006a, 2006b; Ericksen, 2008; Sulik, 2011; Champagne, 2018). Repairing this disruption to body and identity via attention to feminine beauty is infused in discourse concerning breast cancer treatment, healing, and activism. Recovery becomes linked to concealing the physical reality of breast cancer treatment through beauty practices, including breast reconstruction. Mainstream government programs,[1] nonprofit programs, and organizations of medical professionals provide resources and support to cisgender women as they recover from breast cancer, with the sole focus of restoring a conventionally feminine appearance centered on normative standards of beauty. Programs such as the American Cancer Society's "Reach to Recovery Program," the "Look Good Feel Better Program," and BRA-Day International seek to improve "self-image and appearance through … beauty sessions that create a sense of support, confidence, courage, and community" (Look Good Feel

Better Foundation, nd) or to promote the idea that breast reconstruction can help "women feel whole again" after breast cancer, according to singer/songwriter and BRA-Day spokesperson Jewel (2012). These programs align with medical research and commentary, suggesting that breast cancer recovery is most psychosocially successful when a woman's body regains a normative physical appearance (Dean et al, 1983; Cunningham, 2000; Wilkins et al, 2000; Parker, 2004; Stavrou et al, 2009; Rabinowitz, 2013; Nahabedian, 2015).

In the mainstream discourse of breast cancer activism and recovery, breast cancer disrupts normative femininity by attacking one of the most visible physical markers of female embodiment and beauty, the breasts (Clarke, 2004). The appearance of beautiful breasts after breast cancer can be a powerful semiotic means by which to mend this disruption. Beauty can be achieved via various technologies and practices (plastic surgery, makeup, prosthetics, etc) but necessitates presenting a particular embodiment to the world. In the remainder of this chapter, I will show how women who choose to live flat after mastectomies draw on this conventional system of beliefs and reinterpret the meaning of beauty in order to make sense of their breast cancer experiences and embodiment.[2] While other studies consider the importance of an online community of experience in shifting these interpretations of the body (Pitts-Taylor, 2001, 2004; Doh and Pompper, 2015; La et al, 2017), the women's stories highlighted here suggest that the basis for acts of reinterpretation of bodies and beauty in the context of breast cancer may also be facilitated by supportive interactions in daily life and by life experiences prior to cancer diagnosis that situate a person on the periphery in relation to existing discourses for understanding gender and breast cancer. As these and other studies suggest, the influence of ideologies of femininity is particularly powerful in the experience of breast cancer, and largely unavoidable since patients and providers must work within the institutional norms of the medical profession and in the context of the gender structure. What remains to be understood are the ways that women may reinterpret the meaning of beauty in the service of recovery. The narratives discussed here represent an interpretive shift through which women who live flat postmastectomy understand their breastless bodies as beautiful in ways that disrupt and reimagine the predominant narrative of feminine beauty and breast cancer recovery.

## The meaning of beauty in breast cancer recovery

The relationship between mainstream conceptions of feminine beauty, identity, and breast cancer is well established in feminist scholarship (Potts, 2000; Ericksen, 2008; Doh and Pompper, 2015). The centrality of beautiful breasted bodies to cancer recovery highlights the relationship between individual agency and the structure of gender that have played out in feminist debates about beauty and cosmetic surgery (Davis, 1995, 2009; Gagné and McGaughey, 2002; Gimlin, 2002, 2013; Felski, 2006; Furnham and Swami, 2007; Bordo, 2009; Stuart and Donaghue, 2011). In Bordo's (2009) assessment, all women are under a cultural imperative to be beautiful, yet they also retain considerable agency and choice. She points out the contradiction of the dual imperatives women experience to, on the one hand, embrace "triumphant individualism" and, on the other hand, conform to the normative ideologies of gender (Bordo, 2009, p 27). Even as women who live flat insist that they make this choice in contradiction of conventional beauty norms, these norms nevertheless remain integral to their self-narratives.

The meaning and pursuit of beauty are at the heart of this deceptively simplistic debate between social structures and individual agency, particularly with respect to gender.[3] The pursuit of beauty via surgery becomes a sign of either individual autonomy or conformity to social pressure. Rita Felski intervenes in this false dichotomy, arguing that there has been an evolution in feminist understandings of beauty from "the rhetoric of victimization and oppression to an alternative language of empowerment and resistance" (2006, p 280). Beauty thus becomes a powerful discursive tool that can be deployed in the construction of self-identity regardless of whether that identity conforms to normative expectations or not. More specifically, attention to beauty can make clear the complex relationship between individual agency and the imperatives of gendered expectations. Rather than reifying a binary debate between structure and agency where beauty can only be repressive, the interpretation of beauty can be the path out of the dichotomy. Jennifer Millard posits that beauty is achieved via the "manipulation of semiotic resources, such as hair or skin to achieve desired ends" (2009, p 150). Beauty, in this configuration, refers to practices that are informed by cultural ideologies, a range of material resources and attributes, and personal choices bounded by normative expectations of gender. Situating beauty at the nexus of ideology, personal choice, and performance creates space for beauty to encapsulate the empowerment and resistance that Felski describes.

As a dominant ideology and a discursive tool for resistance, beauty must be decoded and reinterpreted, becoming a site for "disidentification" (Muñoz, 1999). José Esteban Muñoz defines disidentification as "descriptive of the survival strategies" of those who do not conform to cultural norms (1999, p 4). Importantly, he argues that disidentification "neither opts to assimilate within such a structure nor strictly oppose it; rather, disidentification is a strategy that works on and against dominant ideology" (p 11). Through processes of disidentification, women who live flat are able to reinterpret beauty in the service of resisting the pressures of cultural ideologies as well as medical providers who may strongly promote breast reconstruction. In the narratives presented by women who live flat, breasts and their removal become a semiotic resource for reinterpreting beauty. This reinterpretation is achieved not only via relationships with other women who live flat but also through interactions with supportive family and friends who bolster women's understandings of their mastectomized bodies as beautiful.

## Methods

Data for this chapter come from the narratives of 19 mastectomized cisgender women: 15 who chose contralateral mastectomies after a single breast cancer diagnosis and flat closure, 1 participant who had a single mastectomy after a breast cancer diagnosis with flat closure, and 3 women who had bilateral mastectomies and flat closure after testing positive for one of the BReast CAncer (BRCA) gene variants. The narrative data discussed in this chapter are part of a larger study of the ways in which normative expectations of gendered bodies shape the experience of breast and gynecological cancer care (Sledge, 2019, 2021).[4] The women whose stories are presented here ranged in age from 32 to 70 at the time of the interviews (age at diagnosis ranged from 24 to 63). Some received their diagnosis decades before the interviews took place while others had been diagnosed within the previous year (interviews took place between 2012 and 2015). Three women were single, and the rest were married (some married to men and others to women). Nearly all women had some college education, and most were white. This was a group of people with relative social privilege and resources. These women occupy social locations from which normative standards of beauty have been historically derived (Strings, 2019).

Participants largely learned about my project through the filter of online communities designed to support women who live flat. Victoria Pitts-Taylor (2001, 2004) posits that because the internet represents a disembodied space, individuals may have greater freedom to perform their identities, thus opening space for resistance to the common narratives of breast cancer presented by the media and breast cancer activism. Although Pitts-Taylor recognizes that cyberspace is not free of gender norms, the prominence of online communities for breast cancer survivors helps to create new discursive spaces for positively interpreting one's body, gender, and sexuality after mastectomy (Crompvoets, 2003; Doh and Pompper, 2015; La et al, 2017).

I began the interviews by asking women to imagine that they were writing a story (ie, a novel or a memoir), a movie script, or a theater script about their experience of breast cancer and then to describe the opening scene. Interviews unfolded from this point at the direction of the women sharing their experiences. My questions consisted of clarifying questions about timelines, relationships to people mentioned, or for specific examples/details. I did not specifically ask women about their ideas about beauty. Rather, the exploration of this topic emerged as a pattern directed by women themselves. After transcribing the interviews and identifying patterns in the way they spoke about beauty and aesthetics, I turned back to feminist scholarship on beauty and cosmetic surgery, as well as to symbolic interactionist literature, to situate these narratives in ongoing feminist debates and begin to understand the various contexts that appear to support women's reinterpretations of their bodies outside of the normative frames of "accountability" (West and Zimmerman, 1987) that typically shape behaviors (Hsieh and Shannon, 2005).

## Reinterpreting beauty

The stories in this chapter question taken-for-granted assumptions that underpin breast cancer care—namely the imperative of concealment and the belief that a singular understanding of beauty is the pinnacle of recovery. Furthermore, these stories question our cultural conflation of normative feminine beauty with health (Litva et al, 2001; Berlant, 2010; Klein, 2010) and indicate that beauty has the potential for much greater complexity and multiplicity than our rigid, gendered norms allow. Women who live flat described two linked premises that emerged organically in their narratives, and which represent the interpretive filters that facilitate women's reinterpretations of their bodies and redefinitions of beauty. First, they rejected the predominant discourse of disfigurement. As Kate (age 46, PhD, straight, married) stated, "I don't go around thinking that I am deformed. But I am not formed the way other women are, and I do not choose what to wear or what not to wear based on trying to hide the fact that I don't have breasts." Second, they rejected the notion that reconstructed breasts were beautiful and the most appropriate pathway to psychosocial healing. The statement of another participant, Edie (age 50, bachelor's degree, straight, married), is representative of the sentiment of many women I spoke with:

> The first thing I did was to go look for reconstructed boobs on the internet. ... I started looking at these things [images of postmastectomy breast reconstruction] and I'm like, holy shit, because, to my way of thinking, this stuff looked horrific. I mean, we cancer ladies, we like to call them "Frankenboobies."

As they rejected discourses of disfigurement and that reconstructed breasts are beautiful, interview participants catalyzed three key interpretive lenses that women used to make sense of living flat: functional bodies as beautiful, the aesthetics of symmetry, and scars as beautiful. These lenses are key to the process of disidentifying with dominant narratives of breast cancer via the reinterpretation of scarred, flat bodies as beautiful.

## Form and function

The narrative put forth by mainstream breast cancer activism and plastic surgeons suggests that reconstruction will make a woman "whole again" (Jewel, 2012). Yet the women I interviewed who live flat see reconstruction as "horrific." This is a complete inversion of normative understandings of cancer as a disease that makes "the body unclean and unruly" and thus subject to "unrelenting potential degradation" that threatens "the accomplishment and maintenance of dignified selfhood" (Waskul and van der Riet, 2002, pp 487–488). Furthermore, cancer leads to "bodily anomie and loss" (Steinberg, 2015, p 117). Women who live flat invert this narrative; they frame reconstructed breasts as deformed and horrific, as that which leads to what Kristeva (1982) calls an "abject body." In the mainstream cultural imagination, recovery from cancer occurs through a return to a visibly whole and embodied self. This imagined pre-cancer form is normatively feminine with visible, presumably desired, breasts. This reflects the imperative of concealment identified by Broom (2001). By choosing to live flat, female breast cancer survivors reject the imperative of concealment. Moreover, the reinterpretation of reconstruction as something that is visually horrific and poses an obstacle to physical recovery from cancer (understood in terms of function) forms a basis from which women who live flat reinterpret the meaning and importance of beauty to their recovery process.

Maggie (age 43, PhD, queer, married) could not understand the appeal of reconstruction in order to have a breasted body and specifically addressed the issue of muscle function.

> You know, the sheer number of women who go through four, five, and six surgeries, and we're not talking minor things, just to have boobs. It's hard for me to relate to that. … This one friend of mine had a meter of incisions so that she could have reconstruction from her own body tissue. A meter! A meter of incisions. I find that unfathomable.

Maggie and Edie each commented on autologous reconstruction in which skin, muscle, and fat are removed from one area of the body (typically the back, abdomen, thighs, or buttocks) and used to create breast-like shapes. These surgeries can have long recovery times, significant side effects, and result in a loss in functionality of various muscle groups.

The loss of muscle function was as repugnant a thought for some as the image of reconstructed breasts. Many of the women were artists, athletes, or performers who relied on their range of motion and strength for their professions. Others lived alone or were primary caregivers for young children and felt that it was imperative to physically recover from breast cancer as quickly as possible in order to resume normal daily activities. This focus on function was a key counter to recovery narratives prioritizing the appearance of breasts through reconstruction. For the former group of women, the movement of their bodies and the physical aspects of their daily lives were the facts of beauty. For many in the latter group, the surgeries needed to create breast shapes were more disfiguring than mastectomy scars. I understand this reinterpretation of breast reconstruction as an affront or disruption to the body similar to breast cancer in the dominant narrative. In this reinterpretation, the resulting breasts themselves are ugly both in a visual sense and in a sense of ugliness permeating beneath the skin in an inverse of the way we might understand beauty to be more than skin deep. Edie had an emphatic reaction to the idea of silicone implants.

> I remember thinking, not on my fucking life. ... I mean, the idea of having foreign material under my skin is a hideous thought to me. And then when I realized that, for the surgery, they actually disconnect your pectoral muscle to stick the silicone under the muscle, I was like, are they fucking kidding me? I mean, women do report that not only does it hurt like hell, but they have diminished function.

Edie's story here is instructive. Ideals of femininity do not typically involve physical strength and the integrity of muscles,[5] so form is prioritized over function. Like Edie, Sandy (age 59, bachelor's degree, straight, married) was deeply concerned about the impact of various surgeries on her muscles.

> I just like my muscles the way they are. Actually, that's a huge piece of my body image. ... I am a competitive athlete. ... I am scrawny enough that the only reconstruction they could have done would've been the expanders. And do not mess with my pecs, thank you very much. You know, alternatively, if I had had the body fat, I wouldn't have wanted my core disturbed for a TRAM.[6] I would not have wanted someone to play with my lats. And breasts are so much less important to me than having the integrity of my muscles.

Sandy's comment suggests that it is more than function that is beautiful. It is the sense of integrity that comes from returning to physical activity and using the body in ways that integrate a person's physical experiences before cancer diagnosis with those following cancer treatment.

Dominant narratives of recovery from breast cancer focus on returning to a normative appearance rather than returning to a pre-cancer state of physical function, since breast reconstruction cannot repair loss of sensation or lactation (Doh and Pompper, 2015).[7] A common pattern among women who live flat was an interest in retaining muscle function and a rejection of the notion that reconstructed breasts serve a function beyond conforming to normative expectations for female embodiment and concealing the embodied realities of breast cancer. Linda (age 63, some college education, straight, single) felt that reconstructed breasts simply do not live up to the expectation that they will look like natural breasts. "The thing is," she said, "these are not breasts. They do not make breasts. They make things that kind of look like them, but they are not breasts. They are dead lumps." The word "lump" was also used dismissively by Sadie (age 64, master's degree, straight, single). These women emphasized that reconstructed breasts are just lumps of material, whether synthetic or transplanted from other parts of the body. Edie spoke clearly about the usefulness of breast reconstruction.

> If you have an amputated leg you want a prosthetic, so that you can walk. It's not a question of trying to appear as if you have a leg. … I do think breasts have a functionality, but it's a different kind of functionality. … If it's simply a question of appearing as if you still have boobs, they serve that purpose. And that's really the only purpose they serve.

Evident in these comments is the notion that form without function, or form only for the visual comfort of others, is not beautiful and may even be interpreted as disfiguring. Here, function is beautiful if it encompasses more than an aesthetic appeal to normative, cisgender, feminine beauty norms. The point women who live flat make is that the relationship between function and beauty must be more expansive than that normative definition allows.

### Symmetry: beauty or vanity?

While function, not form, figured prominently in how women who live flat think about recovery, appearance also mattered to them. This interpretive frame is not entirely distinct from those used by women who choose breast reconstruction, with symmetry being an important factor (Sledge, 2019, 2021). The difference is that women who live flat interpret the symmetry of their flat chests as an end in itself, not as a means to a more symmetrical and thus more beautiful breast reconstruction, as is often the assumption by medical professionals for why women choose bilateral mastectomy (Hawley et al, 2014).

Catherine (age 36, bachelor's degree, bisexual, married) was unequivocal about her decision to choose bilateral mastectomy and to have flat closure. She explained:

> Much of my decision to go bilaterally flat had to do with symmetry. My breasts were DD size. I mean, my chest size is a 34 and my breast

size was DD—and I'm 5'2.'' And, as an artist, I can say without qualm that symmetry is important to me. ... I would love to see the shape of breasts on my body, but, no, I am unwilling to do what it takes to have that. ... I'm unwilling to move tissue from this place to that in order to, I don't know, conform. And I do feel that it is an issue of conformity.

As Catherine decided how she wanted to proceed after her breast cancer diagnosis, symmetry was the main consideration. This was bolstered by her fervent resistance to undergoing lengthy surgeries to reconstruct via autologous tissue reconstruction. Edie also rooted her aesthetic concerns in an artistic sensibility:

I come from a long line of artisans and artists and architects. So, I'm not an artist myself, but I am very visual. I like to draw and knit and sew and paint and whatever. And how things look is important to me—and not from a vanity point of view. It's different from just vanity, okay. You know, I don't wear makeup. I don't care that I have wrinkles, for example, but certain things, especially shapes.

Ellen (age 56, bachelor's degree, straight, married) also referenced vanity in expressing her personal disdain for reconstructed breasts. She explains, "There's no feeling. They're ugly. You don't get your nipple, you know, so what's the point of having boobs for vanity purposes?" Ellen's statement highlights reconstructed breasts' lack of functionality. Holding onto an understanding of beauty that is outside the standard narrative, she refuses the narrative that reconstruction is beautiful and suggests that adhering to this narrative is a matter of vanity.

For Ellen and Edie, vanity means accountability to normative standards of female beauty and to the imperative of concealment. Having aesthetic concerns or a desire to be beautiful is understood as separate from these norms and pressures. The distinction that these women are making centers on their understanding that reconstruction signifies vanity and capitulation to the normative pressures of cultural expectations (what West and Zimmerman [1987] would attribute to "accountability"). The women who live flat emphasize instead a commitment to matters of integrity and authenticity, states of embodied honesty, wholeness, symmetry, and the restoration of an embodied sense of self that could not be achieved had they undergone breast reconstruction (see Throsby, 2008; Shildrick, 2010). These are the characteristics that serve as the foundation for beauty in the context of living flat. It is important to note that symmetry here is not achieved through additive means (ie, breast reconstruction or the use of prosthetics). Rather, women who live flat describe symmetry as inextricably linked to bodily integrity and authenticity that would be further disrupted via breast reconstruction.

Beauty is symmetry, it tells a story, it is visible. By describing their choices in terms of aesthetics, women are creating terminology that resists and rewrites standard narratives of beauty and recovery. It is important to note that symmetry can be specific to a single scar, as was the case for Suzy (age 54, PhD, straight, single) who had a single mastectomy and lives flat on one side. The focus in this instance is on the symmetry of that single scar. After listening to the stories told by women in this study, I contend that symmetry is useful (though not sufficient) for redefining beauty. It is a step in the disidentification process through which women who live flat can maneuver existing discursive tools and cultural frames to expand the interpretive context for what kinds of bodies can be seen as beautiful.

The use of, and separation from, vanity must also be understood not as a judgment of women who choose reconstruction but instead as a rejection of coercive accountability to the normative expectations of female embodiment that dominate our cultural narratives. The dominant narrative of breast cancer is that the disease and its treatment lead to a gender nonconforming body and social stigma (Slatman, Halsema, and Meershoek, 2016). At a time when transgender and gender nonconforming people are becoming increasingly visible and the proliferation of online communities allows people who may be experiencing similar embodiment issues to find one another, women who live flat can draw on a wider array of cultural frames with which to revise the dominant narrative regarding the restoration of normative, feminine beauty. In this way, beauty can be reinterpreted to include a broader set of physical characteristics.

## Scars as beautiful

The in/visibility of mastectomy scars was a crucial embodied experience for women in this study. Within breast cancer activism culture, scars may be emblematic of survival or may be difficult reminders of disease and mortality (Lorde, 1997; Jain, 2007). These framings of scars are not unique to breast cancer. Rose Weitz, for example, conceptualizes scars as a mark of bodily vulnerability and resilience and argues that in constructing narratives about scars, people "'perform' a new self" and, in so doing, "turn first to culturally available frames even as they may use their new embodied knowledge to challenge or broaden those frames" (2011, pp 192–193). In this study, women who live flat engage in precisely this type of narrative work to reinterpret their scars and their bodies after mastectomy. As previously described, beauty as a proxy for the restoration of femininity is a key narrative frame for breast cancer recovery. Women who live flat adopt this frame but shift its meanings in order to include flat, scarred chests.

Samantha (age 57, bachelor's degree, lesbian, married) was clear about the aesthetics of her bilateral mastectomy:

> I have beautiful scars—absolutely beautiful scars, which I think also added to my ability to accept the surgeries better. Because I've looked at pictures on the internet of other bilateral mastectomies and went, holy crap! If I had to deal with those kinds of scars, I don't think I would have adapted as well. ... How many things can be done to show that, although we have these scars, there's an incredible amount of beauty inside of us, and that we can portray it in various ways?

Although Samantha did not elaborate on the specific characteristics of the scars that she saw on the internet, a simple search produces a wealth of images, most of which portray a thick, jagged, asymmetrical scar across the chest. These are scars that surgeons expect women to hide through breast reconstruction or to cover with clothing. The internet likewise provides women opting to live flat access to images of transgender men after top surgery. Although top surgery and mastectomy are different surgeries in the degree of tissue removed, some of the women I interviewed reported seeing surgical results from surgeons who carefully placed scars and made incisions with the knowledge that these scars would be seen in all kinds of situations.

Additionally, new visual resources for interpreting postmastectomy bodies were becoming available through social media groups such as "Flat and Fabulous" and online awareness-raising campaigns such as "The Scar Project," which showcases a series of photographic portraits of topless breast cancer survivors taken by fashion photographer David Jay. These were resources that many women referenced as they described their experiences. Many participants in this research study learned about my project and volunteered their stories after seeing calls posted on a range of social media pages and Twitter feeds created to build community among women who live flat. If, according to Weitz (2011), people draw on available cultural frames to interpret their scars, these types of internet resources are contributing to the creation of new cultural frames from which to build recovery narratives and envision scarred bodies as beautiful.

Catherine was clear that beautiful scars were central to her recovery narrative.

> My scars are absolutely beautiful. There's nothing wrong with them. And my thing is, how do we make this [a flat, scarred chest] beautiful? Do you know? I would love to see a bust that just comes slightly out and away from the body and sort of just gives it a little gentle peek of the scars. Like there is nothing to hide here. It's only beautiful.

She went on to distinguish the beauty of her scarred body from the image popularized in the media and by physicians.

> It feels to me like the breast cancer engine is really just profiting on the shape, on breasts as objects, and really taking away the ability to really connect with self as a human, as the beautiful beings that we are. Do you know? It sucks that I got breast cancer. It sucks. But that doesn't negate my beauty. ... For me to put on the prosthesis and to carry on as if nothing had happened would negate my beauty. It would be saying I am not enough; this is not enough. I am not conforming to an expectation.

The repetition here of the word "enough" suggests that in Catherine's estimation, the pressure to undergo reconstruction is not simply about beauty but also about worth. Over and over, women who live flat indicated that no matter how interested they were in the aesthetic outcome of their breast surgeries, their self-worth comprised more than the degree to which their bodies conformed to standards of feminine beauty or acts of concealment. Kate explained the appeal of this act of conformity and her distance from it: "You can go back to the fact that nobody who doesn't know you can tell that you've had cancer. That's pretty important to a lot of people. It's not of interest to me." The way the body appears to the self may be instrumental to moving from a place of disruption from cancer to a place of normalcy and recovery, but that process is not reliant upon recreating breasts as a symbol of female value. Instead, women who live flat refuse the symbolic prominence of breasts as central to femininity, beauty, sexiness, and self-worth.

## Supports for reinterpreting beauty

Women spoke candidly about their personal sensibilities with respect to flat closure versus breast reconstruction and the role of internet resources/community in shaping their bodily interpretations. Still, the body and its state of breasted or breastlessness has a mediating role in social interactions, particularly with intimate partners. Shifting the frame for women who live flat could not be achieved alone or only in community with other women who live flat. Because the social framework for understanding breast cancer incorporates normative expectations of women as heterosexual partners and mothers, family supports and proximity to queerness/queer communities are prominent interactive filters through which beauty can be reinterpreted and the overall frame shifted.

### Family interactions

The importance of family expectations, relationships, and support structures is a central feature of women's narratives. In this section, I focus specifically on relationships to children and to intimate partners (husbands, wives, partners, etc), as these were the relationships most commonly described in women's narratives. Early in her breast cancer diagnosis, Fran (age 70, PhD, straight, married) considered the way that her decisions about mastectomy and recovery were situated within her family context.

> A friend of a friend was saying how she hadn't told her kids [about her mastectomy] and was having to wear this thing [a prosthetic] all the time so that they wouldn't notice a difference, and I thought, that's not our family. [laughs] You know, that's kind of silly.

For Fran, flat closure was an obvious choice because of her personal feelings about her body, and because she knew that she did not need to conceal the reality of her surgeries from her husband and son. After deciding on bilateral mastectomy and flat closure, Fran told her husband and son (who was 12 at the time). Her husband, Fran explains, "just decided whatever was my decision, that's what it should be. [And if] that would make me full of happiness, because I would not worry any longer, then that's what I should do. So, it was great [laughs]." For Fran, this reaction was perfectly in character for her family members and was exactly the kind of support she needed to live flat. In fact, her son often asked questions that further supported her flatness. In one example, Fran described getting dressed for a wedding and wearing prosthetic breasts to help fill out her dress. As she was getting dressed her son asked why she was wearing the prosthetics and she explained that it would make the dress look better. Her son responded, "Well, it's kind of, like, fake." In this example, it's evident the ways that Fran's family aligned with her refusal to conceal the fact of her surgery and even, in the case of her son, encouraged her to avoid appearing "fake" through the use of prosthetic breasts.

Judy (age 50, degree status unknown, straight, married) also found support in her teenage daughter. "[My daughter] accepted it [her flatness], and now ... I'll ask her opinion: 'How do I look in this? ... Can you tell I have no boobs?' [Her daughter replies,] 'Mom, would you quit obsessing about your boobs?'" Here, the imperative of concealment is apparent, but by answering her mother's question indirectly, Judy's daughter not only puts the imperative of concealment into perspective, she also dismisses it out of hand.

What is striking about the preceding parent–child exchanges is the way that the acceptance of teenage children, as well as the ways that they interact with parents who live flat, helps to normalize women's postmastectomy bodies. The support of preteen and teenage children was unique and important. Other women who live flat described some of the difficulty younger children had in understanding not just living flat but the realities of breast cancer treatment. Teenagers not only have different developmental capacities for understanding this context, they also have a cultural reputation for being a bit critical of parents and very attuned to matters of bodily conformity. Against this backdrop, supportive interactions with older children can be a powerful reinforcing context for women's interpretations of their bodies as beautiful.

Women who live flat described their intimate partners in similar ways. While women were careful to point out that they did not ask permission or advice about closure decisions from their partners, the ways that partners accepted women's decisions mattered to the reinterpretation of bodies and beauty after mastectomy. Edie was particularly explicit about waiting to discuss her decision with her husband until she was certain of what she wanted. She said:

> I told him at one point, after researching, that I had more or less decided that I probably would never get reconstruction. I asked him if it bothered him in any way. And he said, "Oh, for God's sakes!" And then he said, "Look, I would prefer you don't have reconstruction." He's shit-scared of anesthesia; he doesn't like me put under.

This experience of making an individual decision and then sharing it with an intimate partner with the expectation of support was repeated across several women's stories. When talking about her experience with cancer and living flat, Kate described an incredible support network of her husband, friends, local family members, and graduate students. Describing her husband, she said, "I don't have an asshole husband who is saying to me that I need to … get breasts, and do all these things for sexuality. … I feel like I sort of lucked out in feeling like a healthy, sexual, active human being, whether or not I have breasts." This experience directly contrasts discourses promulgated in medical research and in the narratives of women in my larger study who chose reconstruction and also expressed that the form of breasts was important to having successful intimate relationships (Sledge, 2021). Kate's comment highlights the dominance and contours of assumed heterosexuality that women who live flat face. Namely, it underscores the assumption that the presence of breasts is the defining feature of whether a woman will have a healthy and satisfying sexual life with a man after mastectomy. The women I interviewed suggested that this is not as stark, or as absolute, as the medical literature suggests. Rejecting the medical narrative can be aided by interactions with intimate partners who support this rejection and who participate in recasting sexuality and sexual attractiveness in the woman's everyday life.

### Proximity to queerness

Catherine attributed her approach to her husband and to her body after mastectomy to her experiences dating women before meeting and marrying her husband.

> I love being a woman. I love being female. I have always wanted to be flat-chested. Prior to meeting my husband, I dated women. ... I think that the gay, lesbian, bisexual community are just more open and willing to accept difference. Perhaps my ease in making this decision [to live flat] ... was influenced by my experience in relationships with women.

In Catherine's statement are two important factors: the experience of having dated women and her desire to have a flat chest prior to cancer. I understand both of these factors as part of an overall orientation to queerness that allows some women who live flat to couch their decision in a unique frame not shared by women who are more accountable to normative expectations of cisgender heterosexuality. Sally (age 35, master's degree, straight, married), a participant in a group for "previvors" (women who tested positive for one of the BRCA genes), was particularly thoughtful about what allows some people to "be at peace" with their diagnosis and treatment options compared to those who struggle and try to conceal the experience. Sally wondered if some of the difference was attributable to being a lesbian.

> The only other lesbian I know who had a prophylactic surgery also did not have reconstruction. ... [S]o many women feel, like, the loss of [feminine] identity when they lose their breasts. And I don't know if that has as much to do with them or, like, the people that they are with—if, you know, so many women talk about being a disappointment to their husband.

The experience of intimate relationships with women provides a foundation from which to reinterpret sexual attractiveness beyond the bounds of normative heterosexuality. Women who have had these kinds of relationships with women and who choose to live flat may be less bound by the conventions of heterosexuality embedded in mainstream frameworks of breast cancer culture.

Intimate relationships with women were not the only queer experience in these narratives. Many women who chose flat closure expressed either an interest in being flat chested or explained the ways that having breasts may disrupt their relationship to their bodies. Maggie, who identified as queer, never liked her breasts and found them to be discordant with her identity. As soon as she received a breast cancer diagnosis, Maggie knew she wanted to remove both breasts and to live flat. She told me, "The second [the doctors] told me that there would be a surgical plan, I said, 'Well, then I'm going to do a bilateral mastectomy.' And to be 100 percent honest, I never really liked my boobs anyway. Never liked having boobs, and I had *boobs*!" Sally described her breasts as "just obnoxious. They were huge!" As an athlete, Sally found her breasts constantly in the way and removing them via bilateral mastectomy allowed her to regain a freedom of movement she had long missed. Linda also spoke emphatically about her frustrations with large breasts.

> I was extremely large-breasted before this. [laughs] You're going to think I'm lying, but the thing is, I was wearing a 40M bra, as in Mary, and falling out of it. I had girls everywhere. ... I hated these huge breasts. ... I thought about reduction every single solitary day of my life.

Neither Sally nor Linda identified as LGBT or queer; however, their experience of breasts and their sense of breasts being out of place and/or disruptive give them a "queered" perspective on their bodies. These were not women who felt a disruption in their identity at the prospect of mastectomy. Instead, like Maggie, the experience of bilateral mastectomy and flat closure opened a path to embodied freedom and authenticity that had not been possible before.

Samantha wondered outright about the link between women who live flat and the LGBTQ community. Although she does not identify as LGBT or queer, Samantha was connected to an LGBTQ group through a friend who was an artist. This friend asked her to participate in an art installation centered on body image and to join in some of the meetings of the LGBTQ group.

> I've seen that there's similarities going on [between living flat and being LGBT]. ... At one point I was asked [by a friend], after having both breasts removed, if I would have my body painted in front of an LGBT group because they have—that group had problems with self-image. ... [I] was there to show people that regardless of what your body is going through you can still be whole. There was one [person] who is going through all the processes to become a woman—so, [this person] is transgender and was intrigued by looking at somebody with no breasts and no nipples at all. And [she] said to me, "Wow! You know, I thought being a woman really identified with breasts." And I said, "No, not in my case it doesn't."

It is important to consider what a woman's relationship or proximity to queerness might mean in the context of choosing flat closure. This proximity is not just a product of intimate relationships with women; it can also include connections to LGBT people and organizations, as well as what I consider to be a queer orientation to the body (eg, a desire to be flat prior to a breast cancer diagnosis).

Media and medical discourses portray breast cancer as a disruption of normative femininity and women who live flat as gender nonconforming. Whereas these portrayals may once have created a strong market for breast reconstruction, the growing visibility of transgender, gender nonconforming, and queer people suggests that there is an increasing population of people for whom flat closure not only aids in the breast cancer recovery process but does so in ways that affirm an embodied identity that had been disrupted prior to breast cancer (Brown and McElroy, 2018). Several women in this study indicated that even before receiving a breast cancer diagnosis, having breasts felt out of place. In these instances, mastectomy had the effect of bringing bodies into greater alignment with identity in a social context that allowed for a queering of beauty.

## Conclusion

In this chapter, I contend that beauty is a site of disidentification through which women who live flat can understand their mastectomized bodies in ways that resist expectations that women should have breasted bodies, that beauty requires breasts, and that bodies without breasts cannot be beautiful. What these narratives leave intact is the notion that beauty is an important part of recovering from breast cancer, although the meaning of beauty may be subject to change.

In her review of feminist scholarship on beauty, Felski notes the common pattern of exposing the constraining aspects of beauty, but asks, "Is there a place in feminist thought for what we might call a positive aesthetic, an affirmation, however conditional, of the value of beauty and aesthetic pleasure?" (2006, pp 273–274). Beauty and aesthetics matter and can be pleasurable but cannot only be born of individual experience. Rather, as the women in this study indicate, new interpretations of beauty require communities of experience and supportive daily interactions that create pathways for new interpretations of beauty. When these lived experiences counter normative social frameworks, new interpretations can and must emerge through social interactions to make sense of them.

Women who live flat signal a potential expansion in the boundaries of female embodiment and thus a possible interpretive shift for understanding breast cancer experiences. But this shift is only as effective as it is visible. Beauty still matters in breast cancer recovery, but its meaning is expanding. Beauty can come through function, an embrace of bodily imperfection (ie, scars), symmetry, and a sense of authentic embodied experience. This expanded definition is supported not just in the minds of individual women but also by their family members. In a cultural landscape where normative and nonnormative genders visibly coexist, and movements to embrace bodies and embodiments that resist hegemonic norms are on the ascendancy, breast cancer culture must shift too. At the forefront of this shift are people like the women in this study who refuse the normative discourse of breast cancer recovery and recast beauty in more expansive terms.

## Notes

1. The Women's Health and Cancer Rights Act, passed in 1998, codified women's right to and material support for breast reconstruction and prosthetics following mastectomy.
2. Living flat refers to the decision not to undergo breast reconstruction following mastectomy.
3. The relationship between structure and agency often appears to be about a powerful set of ideologies and institutions (structure) that an individual can either conform or not with associated social privileges and sanctions (Garfinkel, 1967; Goffman, 1977; West and Zimmerman, 1987, 2009). These structural constraints severely limit the possibility of emergence and novelty in relating to ideologies of gender. Processes of creative resistance have more traction in the tradition of symbolic interactionists who focus on actions, embodiments, and interpersonal interactions (Waskul and Vannini, 2006; Noland, 2009). Creative resistance through embodied action and interaction represents a path beyond the somewhat intractable debate between structure and agency.
4. In the larger project, I focus on the experiences of 57 transgender men, cisgender men, and cisgender women who challenge the standards of care for breast and gynecological cancers and normative expectations for gendered bodies. I specifically looked at "female specific cancers" because normative feminine embodiment is so deeply embedded within breast cancer culture.
5. Shilling and Bunsell argue that through development of extreme musculature, female body builders are "gender outlaws" who transgress and threaten the "gendered foundations of social interaction itself" (2009, p 142). Although body building is, perhaps, an extreme attention to female muscle and strength, this notion is reflected in other studies of women athletes (Krane et al, 2004). Additionally, women with muscles are racially signified, and physical strength is used to distance Black women from the normative ideals of white femininity that are central to the gender order (Beaubouf-Lafontante, 2003, 2009; Strings, 2019).
6. The TRAM (transverse rectus abdominus muscle) flap procedure is an autologous breast reconstruction using muscle from the lower abdomen.
7. It is also relevant that the perceived imperative for breast reconstruction after mastectomy is a relatively recent development, gaining popularity after the adoption of silicone implants in the 1970s (Jacobson, 1998).

## References

Beaubouf-Lafontante, T. (2003) 'Strong and large Black women? Exploring relationships between deviant womanhood and weight', *Gender and Society*, 17(1): 111–121.

Beaubouf-Lafontante, T. (2009) *Behind the Mask of the Strong Black Woman: Voice and the Embodiment of a Costly Performance*, Philadelphia, PA: Temple University Press.

Berlant, L. (2010) 'Risky bigness: on obesity, eating, and the ambiguity of "health"', in J. Metzl, A. Kirkland and A.R. Kirkland (eds) *Against Health: How Health Became the New Morality*, New York: New York University Press, pp 26–39.

Bordo, S. (2009) 'Twenty years in the twilight zone', in C. Heyes and M. Jones (eds) *Cosmetic Surgery: A Feminist Primer*, Aldershot: Ashgate, pp 21–34.

Broom, D. (2001) 'Reading breast cancer: reflections on a dangerous intersection', *Health,* 5(2): 249–268.

Brown, M.T. and McElroy, J.A. (2018) 'Sexual and gender minority breast cancer patients choosing bilateral mastectomy without reconstruction: "I now have a body that fits me"', *Women and Health,* 58(4): 403–418.

Champagne, A.M. (2018) 'Beauty and the breast: mastectomy, materiality, and the iconicity of gender identity', paper presented at the American Sociological Association Annual Meeting, August 9, Philadelphia, PA.

Clarke, J.N. (2004) 'A comparison of breast, testicular and prostate cancer in mass print media (1996–2001)', *Social Science and Medicine,* 59(3): 547–553.

Crompvoets, S. (2003) 'Reconstructing the self: breast cancer and the post-surgical body', *Health Sociology Review,* 12(2): 137–145.

Crompvoets, S. (2006a) 'Comfort, control, or conformity: women who choose breast reconstruction following mastectomy', *Health Care for Women International,* 27: 75–93.

Crompvoets, S. (2006b) *Breast Cancer and the Post-Surgical Body: Recovering the Self,* New York: Palgrave Macmillan.

Cunningham, B. (2000) 'Discussion', *Plastic and Reconstructive Surgery,* 106(5): 1026–1027.

Davis, K. (1995) *Reshaping the Female Body: The Dilemma of Cosmetic Surgery,* New York: Routledge.

Davis, K. (2009) 'Revisiting feminist debates on cosmetic surgery: some reflections on suffering, agency, and embodied difference', in C. Heyes and M. Jones (eds) *Cosmetic Surgery: A Feminist Primer,* Surrey: Ashgate, pp 35–48.

Dean, C., Chetty, U. and Forrest, A.P.M. (1983) 'Effects of immediate breast reconstruction on psychosocial morbidity after mastectomy', *The Lancet,* 321(8322): 459–462.

Doh, H. and Pompper, D. (2015) 'Beyond the wounds: *The Scar Project* as space for examining breast cancer and mastectomy experiences', *Social Semiotics,* 25(5): 597–613.

Ericksen, J.A. (2008) *Taking Charge of Breast Cancer,* Berkeley: University of California Press.

Felski, R. (2006) '"Because it is beautiful": new feminist perspectives on beauty', *Feminist Theory,* 7(2): 273–282.

Furnham, A. and Swami, V. (2007) 'Perceptions of female buttocks and breast size in profile', *Social Behavior and Personality,* 35(1): 1–8.

Gagné, P. and McGaughey, D. (2002) 'Designing women: cultural hegemony and the exercise of power among women who have undergone elective mammoplasty', *Gender and Society,* 16(6): 814–838.

Garfinkel, H. (1967) *Studies in Ethnomethodology,* Englewood Cliffs, NJ: Prentice Hall.

Gimlin, D. (2002) *Body Work: Beauty and Self-Image in American Culture*, Berkeley: University of California Press.

Gimlin, D. (2013) '"Too good to be real": the obviously augmented breast in women's narratives of cosmetic surgery', *Gender and Society*, 27(6): 913–934.

Goffman, E. (1977) 'The arrangement between the sexes', *Theory and Society*, 4(3): 301–333.

Hawley, S.T., Jagsi, R. and Marrow, M. (2014) 'Social and clinical determinants of contralateral prophylactic mastectomy', *Journal of the American Medical Association Surgery*, 149(6): 582–589.

Hsieh, H. and Shannon, S.E. (2005) 'Three approaches to qualitative content analysis', *Qualitative Health Research*, 15(9): 1277–1288.

Jacobson, N. (1998) 'The socially constructed breast: breast implants and the medical construction of need', *American Journal of Public Health*, 88(8): 1254–1261.

Jain, S.L. (2007) 'Cancer butch', *Cultural Anthropology*, 22(4): 501–538.

Jewel (2012) 'Whole again', PSA for BRA-Day USA, available from: http://www.bradayusa.org/video-gallery/jewel-psa-whole-again.html.

Klein, R. (2010) 'What is health and how do you get it?', in J. Metzl, A. Kirkland and A.R. Kirkland (eds) *Against Health: How Health Became the New Morality*, NY: New York University Press, pp 15–25.

Krane, V., Choi, P.Y.L., Baird, S.M., Aimar, C.M. and Kauer, K.J. (2004) 'Living the paradox: female athletes negotiate femininity and muscularity', *Sex Roles*, 50(5/6): 315–329.

Kristeva, J. (1982) *The Powers of Horror: An Essay on Abjection*, New York: Columbia University Press.

La, J., Jackson, S. and Shaw, R. (2017) '"Flat and fabulous": women's breast reconstruction refusals post-mastectomy and the negotiation of normative femininity', *Journal of Gender Studies*, 28(5): 603–616.

Litva, A., Peggs, K. and Moon, G. (2001) 'The beauty of health: locating young women's health and appearance', in I. Dyck, N. Davis Lewis and S. McLafferty (eds) *Women: Geographies of Women's Health*, London: Routledge, pp 248–264.

Look Good Feel Better Foundation (nd) 'Our Mission' [About], available from: https://lookgoodfeelbetter.org/about/.

Lorde, A. (1997) *The Cancer Journals*, San Francisco, CA: Aunt Lute Books.

Millard, J. (2009) 'Performing beauty: Dove's "real beauty" campaign', *Symbolic Interaction*, 32(2): 146–168.

Muñoz, J.E. (1999) *Disidentifications: Queers of Color and the Performance of Politics*, Minneapolis: University of Minnesota Press.

Nahabedian, M. (2015) 'Overview of breast reconstruction', *Up to Date*, available from: http://www.uptodate.com/contents/overview-of-breast-reconstruction.

Noland, C. (2009) *Agency and Embodiment: Performing Gestures/Producing Culture*, Cambridge, MA: Harvard University Press.

Parker, P.A. (2004) 'Breast reconstruction and psychosocial adjustment: what have we learned and where do we go from here?', *Seminars in Plastic Surgery*, 18(2): 131–138.

Pitts-Taylor, V. (2001) 'Popular pedagogies, illness, and the gendered body: reading breast cancer discourse in cyberspace', *Popular Culture Review*, 12(2): 21–36.

Pitts-Taylor, V. (2004) 'Illness and internet empowerment: writing and reading breast cancer in cyberspace', *Health*, 8(1): 33–59.

Potts, L.K. (2000) 'Publishing the personal: autobiographical narratives of breast cancer and the self', in L.K. Potts (ed) *Ideologies of Breast Cancer*, New York: St. Martin's Press, pp 98–130.

Rabinowitz, B. (2013) 'Psychological aspects of breast reconstruction', in C. Urban and M. Rietjens (eds) *Oncoplastic and Reconstructive Breast Surgery*, Milan: Springer-Verlag Italia, pp 423–429.

Shildrick, M. (2010) 'Some reflections on the socio-cultural and bioscientific limits of bodily integrity', *Body and Society*, 16(3): 11–22.

Shilling, C. and Bunsell, T. (2009) 'The female body builder as gender outlaw', *Qualitative Research in Sport and Exercise*, 1(2): 141–159.

Slatman, J., Halsema, A. and Meershoek, A. (2016) 'Responding to scars after breast surgery', *Qualitative Health Research*, 26(12): 1614–1626.

Sledge, P. (2019) 'From decision to incision: ideologies of gender in surgical cancer care', *Social Science and Medicine*, 239: 112550.

Sledge, P. (2021) *Bodies Unbound: Gender-Specific Cancer and Biolegitimacy*, New Brunswick, NJ: Rutgers University Press.

Stavrou, D., Weissman, O., Polyniki, A. et al (2009) 'Quality of life after breast cancer surgery with or without reconstruction', *Eplasty*, 9: e18.

Steinberg, D.L. (2015) 'The bad patient: estranged subjects of the cancer culture', *Body and Society*, 21(3): 115–143.

Strings, S. (2019) *Fearing the Black Body: The Racial Origins of Fat Phobia*, New York: New York University Press.

Stuart, A. and Donaghue, N. (2011) 'Choosing to conform: the discursive complexities of choice in relation to feminine beauty practices', *Feminism and Psychology*, 22(1): 98–121.

Sulik, G. (2011) *Pink Ribbon Blues: How Breast Cancer Culture Undermines Women's Health*, New York: Oxford University Press.

Throsby, K. (2008) 'Happy re-birthday: weight loss surgery and the "new me"', *Body and Society*, 14(1): 117–132.

Waskul, D. and van der Riet, P. (2002) 'The abject embodiment of cancer patients: dignity, selfhood, and the grotesque body', *Symbolic Interaction*, 25(4): 487–513.

Waskul, D. and Vannini, P. (2006) 'Introduction: the body in symbolic interaction', in D. Waskul and P. Vannini (eds) *Body/Embodiment: Symbolic Interaction and the Sociology of the Body*, Aldershot: Ashgate, pp 1–18.

Weitz, R. (2011) 'Gender and degendering in autobiographical narratives of physical scars' *Gender Issues*, 28(4): 192–208.

West, C. and Zimmerman, D. (1987) 'Doing gender', *Gender and Society*, 1(2): 125–151.

West, C. and Zimmerman, D. (2009) 'Accounting for doing gender', *Gender and Society*, 23(1): 112–122.

Wilkins, E.G., Cederna, P.S., C. Lower, J.C., et al (2000) 'Prospective analysis of psychosocial outcomes in breast reconstruction: one-year postoperative results from the Michigan breast reconstruction outcome study', *Plastic and Reconstructive Surgery*, 106(5): 1014–1025.

7

# "You Are Not the Body": (Re)Interpreting the Body in and through Integral Yoga

*Erin F. Johnston*

From my field notes, Integral Yoga Institute, May–June 2012, lightly edited for meaning:[1]

On the first Saturday of the Integral Yoga Institute's (IYI) teacher training program, the teacher trainees (TTs), myself included, sat on yoga mats arranged around the edges of Ron's living room, which had been cleared of almost all its furniture to make room for the eight TTs and two teachers. Ron and Aadesh,[2] the program's instructors, sat at the front of the room beside a customary Integral Yoga altar: a small rectangular table draped with a burgundy cloth, which held a lit candle in a lotus flower shaped holder and two framed pictures, one of Swami Satchidananda, the founder of Integral Yoga, and one of his guru, Swami Sivananda. The TTs were told that we would spend most of the day's class on the "Sun Salutation Drill," and there was nervous chitchat and laughter among the students as we looked over the handout explaining what we were about to do. The Sun Salutation drill is a method, designed by Aadesh, to help TTs learn as quickly as possible the verbal instructions for teaching Surya Namaskar (the sun salutation): a series of twelve postures that the practitioner moves through in sequence, flowing smoothly from one posture into the next (see Figure 7.1).

Aadesh began, however, by talking about the body and our (ideal) relationship to it. "We are not the body," he remarked, "even though

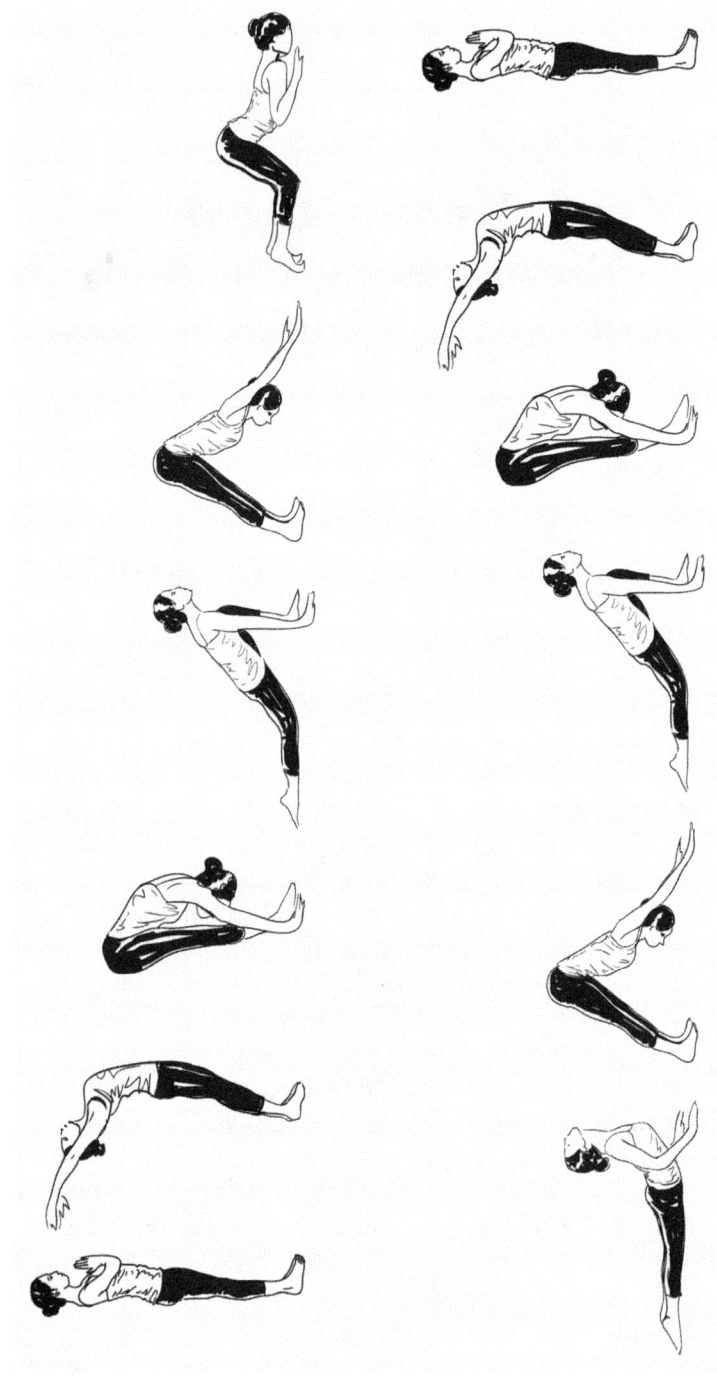

**Figure 7.1:** Surya Namaskar (sun salutation)

Source: Illustration by Ivaskes. Image courtesy of Shutterstock.

we tend to identify with it." During an IY (Integral Yoga) class, he elaborated, we want to help students "feel a little free of that [identification] … so we use the word 'the' in place of 'you' or 'your' when referring to students' bodies." Rather than say to a student "lift *your* arms," the TTs are taught to instruct the student to "lift *the* arms." Part of the goal of an Integral Yoga Hatha class, Aadesh continued, is "to get people to become aware of their Eternal Self, their soul; to let go of their engagement with the body, the mind, and become lucidly aware of this Self." Ron shook his head in agreement, adding that this shift in language really does help students get "into that mindset," and ultimately will help them move closer to achieving yoga (i.e., a sense of union with the divine).

With this objective in mind, we moved into the sun salutation drill. Ron rolled out his mat at the center of the room. The trainees took turns instructing each posture in the sequence. There were a lot of pauses and do-overs as we—the fumbling novice teachers—tried to recall and articulate the verbal instructions necessary to guide Ron effectively and efficiently through the sequence. Laughter erupted whenever Ron became stuck in an awkward pretzel-like shape after taking one of the TT's inaccurate and sometimes physically impossible instructions literally. Aadesh gave corrections and suggestions, offering key phrases and helpful hints on how to instruct the movements more clearly. Getting the instructions right was difficult for all of us, especially at first. Each posture requires several distinct verbal cues and the sequence moves fairly quickly. Though trainees often forgot the order of the postures or used an incorrect cue, they were most frequently corrected for using the word "your" instead of "the" when referencing parts of the body. It was difficult for trainees to overcome what seemed like a deeply ingrained habit in talking about bodies.

We returned to this drill on several occasions over the next few weeks. With each passing session, Aadesh's and Ron's patience with trainees' use of the words "you" and "your" waned; the exasperation in their voices became clearer. In mid-June, about four weeks into the 10-week program, Aadesh reiterated the importance of using this language. He told us, "There are some things we are very demanding about you [not] saying, including 'your.' If you say it every once in a while, that's fine. But we are trying to help people move past their identification with the body. It's not terrible to say it once. But if you keep saying it, that is terrible."

I start with this field note in order to highlight two points that are important to the arguments I will be making in this chapter. First, this field note provides a brief introduction to Integral Yoga's "theology of the body" (Griffith, 2004; Radermacher, 2013)—in other words, how this community interprets the body and its relationship to the transcendent. Most simply, Integral Yoga is rooted in a dualistic conception of the body-mind (conceived as a single unit) and soul, where the two are said to be wholly distinct. Integral Yoga practitioners (including the TTs) are taught that while they *have* a body, they are "not the body." Rather, from the Integral Yoga perspective, the "True Self," what students really are, *transcends* the body. The goal of yoga practice, then, is to become aware of, experience, and ultimately inhabit this "True Self." Doing so, as Aadesh argued, requires that practitioners "let go of their engagement with the body." In this way, practitioners' interpretations of and relationships to their bodies are linked to a broader process of personal spiritual formation. More specifically, "attachment" to or identification with the body is constructed as a *barrier* to spiritual progress, while "detachment" from the body is constructed as both a goal of practice and a marker of spiritual progress.

Second, this field note makes evident the centrality and salience of talk and discourse as a means for cultivating bodily detachment. We see this most explicitly in the assumed power of language—in this case, the teacher's verbal instructions and cues—to shape how students *experience* their bodies. The correct language (ie, "*the* body"), Aadesh tells the TTs, can aid in the cultivation of detachment, while the incorrect language (ie, *your* body) can promote identification with the body, thus impeding spiritual progress. Along these same lines, this field note illustrates how talk interpretively links the practice of yoga to the Integral Yoga community's broader symbolic world. Using the sun salutation drill as an opportunity to do interpretive work, Aadesh frames the Integral Yoga practice as a means to cultivate bodily detachment, which in turn facilitates students' spiritual formation and transformation.

When I initially entered the field for this project, I imagined myself, like Loïc Wacquant (2004) did in his study of becoming a boxer, as someone participating in a kind of "apprenticeship ethnography" (Lizardo et al, 2016)—one involving the acquisition of (largely) practical and embodied knowledge through repeated physical practice. I was surprised to find, however, that the majority of my time in the teacher training program was spent seated on my yoga mat, with a notebook in my lap, *talking* about yoga with the other TTs and the program's three main instructors: Aadesh, Ron, and Ambika. This emphasis on didactic instruction and discussion was not something I expected to encounter; it therefore became a useful puzzle (Timmermans and Tavory, 2012), one that helped me to better understand the process of "becoming" an Integral Yogi by forcing me to attend more closely to the *interplay* between the symbolic and the somatic in the process of enculturation. In this chapter, I build on the work of scholars who have argued for the value of maintaining an analytic distinction between the practical and discursive, experiential and symbolic, in order to examine the dynamic relationship between them (Pagis, 2010; McIlwain and Sutton, 2014; Griera, 2017; Vaisey and Frye, 2019; Winchester and Green, 2019; Winchester and Pagis, 2021; Winchester, 2022).

In the findings, I use empirical examples from my time in the field to illustrate this symbolic–somatic interplay and its role in the transmission and cultivation of bodily "detachment." As my opening field note suggests, I found that "becoming" an Integral Yoga practitioner was intimately bound up with a cognitive and perceptual reframing of the body. This reframing occurred across key areas of practice intended to transmit and cultivate bodily detachment (ie, disidentification). I discuss each of these key areas of practice in this chapter.

First, I consider *vocabularies of motive* (Mills, 1940)—accounts that explain and justify individual actions and behaviors—and show how immersion in the Integral Yoga community exposes newcomers to discourses and narratives that downplay physical goals (eg, bodily appearance or skill) while simultaneously emphasizing spiritual ones (eg, personal formation, enlightenment). In doing so, vocabularies of motive reorient practitioners' attention away from the body and toward the transcendent while interpretively linking the practice of yoga to a broader project of personal spiritual formation. Second, I highlight the metaphors and analogies through which the body is constructed as an object of care and maintenance (separate from the "True Self") as well as the key practices through which this interpretation is *enacted*. Finally, returning to a focus on the verbal instructions given by teachers during Integral Yoga classes, I consider the role that these cues play in facilitating and enabling certain kinds of embodied experiences and, with them, the transmission of shared interpretive frameworks for making sense of these experiences. In particular, I focus on the practice of *yoga nidra*, or "deep relaxation," which I found to be most closely linked to the experience and cultivation of bodily detachment. Throughout my discussion of these three key areas of practice, I foreground the role that talk in situ—talk as it occurs in the context of training and practice (McIlwain and Sutton, 2014)—plays in linking embodied experience to a broader, shared "theology of the body" and, consequently, in facilitating practitioners' shifting interpretations. In this way, I highlight how discourses and narratives enable reinterpretation while also remaining attentive to the ways in which bodily practices activate and reinforce it.

## Making sense of embodied religious practices

The last two decades have been characterized by a broad turn within the academic study of religion toward practice, the body, and embodiment (Griffith, 2004; Shilling and Mellor, 2007; McGuire, 2008, 2016; Ammerman, 2016, 2020; Wuthnow, 2020). There is, however, considerable variation within this broad turn in how scholars have studied or "interpreted" embodied forms of religious practice. These different analytical or interpretive lenses draw our attention to different aspects of religious practices—their contexts, meanings, and consequences. Early work, exemplified in the writings of Mary Douglas (2003) and Clifford Geertz (2010), interpreted religious practices *symbolically*, as texts to read and decipher. Practices were said to *convey* or *express* religious meanings (and identities), which could only be understood by the analyst in reference to the broader symbolic universe within which the practices were situated. The task of the analyst, then, was to decode the rituals and explicate their meaning. These scholars asked: What can we learn about the symbolic worlds of different communities by observing their ritual practice?

More recent research, however, examines what religious practices *do* to the people who perform them, interpreting religious ritual as practices to be undergone rather than merely observed (Winchester, 2022). Some of these scholars focus squarely on phenomenological *experience*, describing and analyzing the sensations, emotions, smells, and sights that characterize different forms of practice (McGuire, 2003, 2008, 2016). These scholars ask: How does religious ritual shape perception, affect, and sensation? Some have shown, for instance, how religious practices such as meditation and fasting involve a kind of somatic inversion in which the body and embodied experience are brought to the forefront of one's attention (Pagis, 2009, 2019; Winchester and Pagis, 2021). Others have focused on the feelings and emotions elicited through collective worship, highlighting the role of music and synchronized movement in shaping the emotional experience of participants (Nelson, 1996, 2005). Much of this work draws attention to the role of physical copresence and interaction in the production of embodied religious experiences (Heider and Warner, 2010; Collins, 2011; Pagis, 2015).

Other scholars, building on the work of Mauss (1973) and Bourdieu (1977), interpret religious practice as akin to "techniques of the body." Countering the perspective put forward by Geertz, these scholars argue that religious practices help form and constitute, rather than merely signal, religious habits, dispositions, beliefs, and values. Practices such as wearing the hijab, for example, do not merely *express* humility, they help cultivate it (Winchester, 2008). From this analytic perspective, religious practices are intimately bound up with identity and subjectivity and are equally important in both joining (Winchester, 2008; Tavory and Winchester, 2012) and leaving

(Davidman, 2015) religious communities. This work draws attention to the lingering effects of practice beyond those that occur in-the-moment; which is to say, it draws attention to the formation of a religious habitus (Mellor and Shilling, 2010).

Finally, some scholars have focused on embodied practices and/or bodies themselves as sites of explicit symbolism and discursive interpretation: people not only perform religious practices, they also *talk* about them (Leledaki, 2014; Winchester, 2016, 2022; Johnston, 2017; Winchester and Green, 2019). Likewise, bodies are not only a means for engaging in religious practice, nor are they merely the sites of practice's effect. They also are the subject of reflection, discussion, and interpretation. Scholars have shown, for example, how different traditions offer distinct "theologies of the body" (Griffith, 2004; Morley, 2008; Radermacher, 2013, 2017; Leledaki, 2014) and how seemingly mundane practices, such as eating or exercise, are (re)interpreted as acts of religious devotion, as a "vehicle for developing close, satisfying relationships with a beloved whom they aim to please through obedient self-discipline" (Griffith, 2004, p 5; see also Johnston et al, 2022). While emphasizing the symbolic, this line of work takes an "emic" (internal) versus "etic" (external) perspective: it seeks to understand how *practitioners* give meaning to bodies and embodied practices.

Each approach tends to foreground *either* the somatic or the symbolic, the experiential or the discursive. There is also, however, a growing body of work that seeks to theorize the *interplay* between the discursive and the practical. This line of research asks: How do embodied practices and experiences become linked to religious discourses and broader systems of meaning? And how do religious beliefs and theologies become embodied or experientially persuasive? Scholars focused on the interplay between the somatic and symbolic "take talk seriously" (Wuthnow, 2011), seeing it as both socially patterned and consequential, linked to experience and action.[3] Recent work, for example, has demonstrated how narratives and discourses work to interpretively link practice to more transcendent goals and to self-identity (Johnston, 2016; Winchester and Green, 2019) and, in doing so, how they help motivate the continuation of practice in the face of struggle and failure (Johnston, 2017). Researchers have also argued that embodied practices and experiences "call out for interpretation" (Winchester, 2022) and thus become metaphors and analogical windows through which abstract concepts are understood and made personally meaningful (Ignatow, 2009; Pagis, 2010; Winchester, 2016, 2022). In this chapter, I build on these insights to "investigate the reciprocal influences of embodiment and thought" (McIlwain and Sutton, 2014; Griera, 2017; Winchester, 2022) in the cultivation of bodily detachment in and through Integral Yoga.

## Data and methods

The findings outlined in this chapter are based on fieldwork and interviews I conducted at an Integral Yoga studio in the New York City metropolitan area between January 2012 and May 2013. Integral Yoga was founded by Swami Satchidananda, a disciple of Swami Sivananda and an internationally recognized spiritual leader who came to the United States from India in the 1960s. Satchidananda describes Integral Yoga as a synthesis of various branches of yoga into a comprehensive system aimed at the cultivation of "an easeful body, a peaceful mind, and a useful life."[4] Integral Yoga is a relatively gentle and explicitly spiritual form of yogic practice. *Yoga Journal*, the most widely read international yoga magazine, classifies Integral Yoga under the "Ease into Enlightenment" category of styles alongside Sivananda, Ananda, and Kundalini Yoga. These styles, which tend to be less physically demanding and place greater emphasis on meditation and breathwork, are for "those who aspire to loftier goals than simply building a hard body" (Cook, 2007).

The studio where I conducted my fieldwork, the Integral Yoga Institute (IYI), was founded and managed by Aadesh, a practitioner and certified teacher who trained under Swami Satchidananda at Yogaville, the Integral Yoga community's ashram (monastic community) in Virginia. According to its website, the IYI's primary goals are (1) to share and provide spiritual support in living the teachings of Integral Yoga as taught by Sri Swami Satchidananda Maharaj and (2) to provide a supportive environment for those interested in spiritual development. The institute's explicit emphasis on spirituality and spiritual development distinguishes it from other yoga studios in the area (Johnston, 2020).

In addition to attending Hatha Yoga classes, workshops, and special programs offered at the IYI during this period, I also participated in a Level 1 (200-hour) teacher training program between May and August 2012. My ethnographic approach was similar to what others have variously called "carnal sociology" (Crossley, 1995; Wacquant, 2004; Martin, 2019), "enactive ethnography" (Winchester, 2022), or "apprenticeship ethnography" (Lizardo et al, 2016). I practiced alongside those I studied and attempted to maintain a daily personal practice of Integral Yoga and meditation while participating in the teacher training program. I completed all program requirements and achieved certification. I kept a detailed journal reflecting on my personal practice and experiences during this time. This approach—of "doing it" (Winchester, 2022)—has interpretive benefits. In taking on the religious practices of a given community, the ethnographer becomes subject to the same corporeal effects of practice *and* to the interpretive processes that surround it (Winchester and Green, 2019; Winchester, 2022).[5]

That being said, I was not, nor am I now, an active member of this community or a practitioner of Integral Yoga. To understand and situate my experiences, I interviewed all eight participants of the teacher training program on three separate occasions: before the training began, immediately after it ended, and one year after training. I also conducted in-depth, semi-structured interviews with fifteen Integral Yoga practitioners and teachers (including Aadesh and Ron, the lead instructors for the teacher training program). All interviews were recorded and transcribed for analysis. All class meetings of the yoga teacher training program were audio-recorded with the permission of the attendees.

Most of the data used in this chapter come from my time in the teacher training program. This program offered a unique perspective on Integral Yoga and how it is taught. As a program designed for aspiring instructors, the usually implicit rules and norms of Integral Yoga practice and pedagogy were made explicit. During class meetings and in assigned readings, the history, meaning, and logic behind the class structure, specific postures and practices, and verbal cues were the topic of discussion. Designed as a program to deepen the TTs' *personal* practice (as a foundation for successful teaching), it also served as a site in which to observe practitioners' ongoing apprenticeship and formation. As a condition of participation, TTs were required to commit to regular attendance at IYI classes and to the maintenance of a suite of daily personal practices. As a result, the TTs occupied the dual position of being in the midst of a personal apprenticeship while also learning how to guide others through the same process.

## Downplaying the physical: vocabularies of motive and transcendent goals

One evening in July, toward the end of the teacher training program, the TTs along with other Integral Yoga students were gathered for a *satsang* (or "spiritual dialogue") with Aadesh. His talk, titled "A New World Order through Yoga," began by addressing a foundational question: "Really, what is yoga?" Aadesh asked, rhetorically. He continued, "In this country ... Hatha Yoga is mostly just asanas [physical postures] and most of the people doing it are not awakened to their spiritual path." Inferring the motivations and intentions of the "average" yoga practitioner, Aadesh told the gathered students, "People get into it because they want to look good, lose weight, [or] their friends are doing it." He added, "Those of you that are *Integral Yogis* know that this is only a small part of yoga." Aadesh went on to explain that yoga puts "you on a spiritual path" even "without any awareness that it does." However, *awareness*, he noted, "pumps up the volume," enabling growth and development to happen "much more quickly." The ticket, he told us, is in knowing that you are on a spiritual path.[6]

This field note highlights the role that vocabularies of motive play in reinterpreting and reexperiencing the body. Aadesh first describes the motivations of the "average" yoga practitioner and then places these motivations in opposition to those of "Integral Yogis." *Integral Yogis*, he argues, are seeking spiritual formation. Implied in this opposition is that Integral Yoga practitioners are *not* motivated by the more mundane bodily goals that drive exercise-oriented yogis (Johnston, 2020). In this way, Aadesh interpretively links the Integral yoga practice and the Integral Yogi identity to a shared set of explicitly *spiritual* aspirations (see Johnston, 2016).

Aadesh is not wrong in his assessment of yoga practitioners' motivations. Many people, including the students I met at the IYI, initially take up the practice of yoga with decidedly physical goals—for example, to lose weight, to become stronger or more flexible, to counter the effects of aging, or to manage anxiety and stress (Yoga Alliance, 2016). Teachers at the IYI, however, offered alternative accounts of the effects of the practice and its ultimate ends. Through immersion in the IYI community, newcomers are repeatedly exposed to discourses—including narratives, personal accounts, and verbal instruction—that interpretively decouple practical ability from spiritual progress by emphasizing the spiritual nature and motivations for practice while simultaneously downplaying the importance of physical appearance and bodily skill. Becoming an Integral Yogi, then, involves a reorientation of motivation and aspiration, one that (re)directs attention away from the body and toward the "soul."

Vocabularies of motive, I found, were transmitted and enacted in a number of different spaces, including Integral Yoga Hatha classes. In a typical class, teachers start by asking students to sit cross-legged with their eyes closed. The instructor then leads students in several rounds of deep breathing (*deergha swasam*). These opening minutes were used to "set intentions" for the practice, and teachers played an active role in guiding students toward establishing the "correct" attitude and set of motivations. While each teacher had a unique style, nearly all took this time to remind students of why they came and how they should approach the practice. The goals were related to connecting to "what matters": leaving behind the concerns of the mundane world (of work, family, etc) and focusing on personal spiritual formation.

This vocabulary of motive was also evident in the biographical accounts of Integral Yoga instructors. Unlike comparable studios in the area, instructors at the IYI were not pictured performing difficult asanas in their online bios. Rather, the studio preferred to use standard headshots, effectively cutting off the instructors' bodies from display. The biographical text that accompanied these pictures explicitly highlighted the spiritual nature of yoga and downplayed physical goals. One bio read: "Although originally seeking yoga as a means to maintain and improve optimal physical health, she [the instructor] has since realized that yoga is so much more than physical postures." And another read: "What initiated as a fitness practice has evolved into a way of being." By downplaying physical aspirations, teacher bios modeled for students the ideal motivations for practice. Through their narrative emphasis on personal evolution, they also described this new perspective as the "logical endpoint on a continuum" of identity development (Brekhus, 2003, p 126), interpretively linking it to ideas of "progress" and "maturity" on a longer journey of spiritual formation.

I heard similar narratives in my interviews with the TTs. Julia, a teacher trainee in her mid-30s, told me that she started practicing yoga at age 16 as "part of an exercise program" primarily aimed at improving her physical health. It was only after taking her first formal yoga class eight years later that she "really started to understand more about the *other side* of yoga; that it wasn't just postures and asanas and breathing and sweating." Julia told me that, over time, yoga "turned from a purely physical practice to, now, what [she] think[s] has become a deeply spiritual practice." Lynn, a 61-year-old TT and practicing Catholic, had been doing yoga for more than 20 years when we spoke at the start of the teacher training program. She told me that she practiced in order to maintain flexibility, strength, and physical health as she aged. By the end of her teacher training, however, Lynn had experienced an important shift in her orientation toward practice. Though she was initially embarrassed to admit it, Lynn confided that she used to leave classes at the IYI after the asanas, skipping the second half of the class, which included the deep relaxation, breathing exercises, and meditation. She recalled,

> Some of that stuff just felt like, "Okay, we're just filling time here." But now, I feel like it's a good practice. I have a different appreciation for it now, so I enjoy it. It just helps to, like, go inward a little bit more. … I think I get that now. Where before, when we did *yoga nidra*, I felt a little agitated: I'm like, "Okay, like, let's go." You know? Where, now, this is like, "I'm relaxed, so we can do whatever." That's helped.

After the training, Lynn told me that she always stays for and enjoys the entire class, viewing the practices she used to skip as equally, if not more, important.

These examples make clear that talk about motives and intentions can have real consequences. Discourses and narrative accounts serve as "hermeneutic hooks that interpretively link [social] actors' present actions with elements of their more temporally extended self-narratives, conjoining their practices in the here and now with a motivational project of identity exploration and development that extends far beyond the boundaries of the present moment" (Winchester and Green, 2019, p 258) into the longer durée. Discourses that link practice to other, less tangible, goals provide a way for practitioners and teachers to encourage adherents to persist in the face of feelings of failure (Johnston, 2017). Adherents often experience plateaus in their practical progress: physically, in their asana practice (eg, an inability to perform a specific posture), or mentally and emotionally, in their meditation practice (eg, an inability to quiet the mind).

We can see evidence of this "hermeneutic hooking" in both Julia's and Lynn's accounts. The dominant narrative template at the IYI becomes a useful tool for interpreting their own past experience and charting their personal progress and development. Notably, this interpretive work also changes their *experience* of the practice. Lynn, for example, reports that she used to find the less physically intensive parts of the Integral Yoga classes frustrating because she *interpreted* them as "a waste of time." Since completing/beginning the teacher training program, however, Lynn now *interprets* these practices as important and impactful, and this new interpretation shapes her experience of the practice (eg, now feeling "relaxed" rather than "agitated" during *yoga nidra*). Importantly, this interpretive framework positions the bodily effects of practice as a means to an end, effectively backgrounding the body while foregrounding the spiritual. As Anthony, a teacher trainee and former high school teacher in his early 60s, described it in the post-training interview:

> It [yoga] is inherently a spiritual practice, so the *only reason* why we do Hatha Yoga is to make our body ready ... so it [the body] can stop thinking about or be led by the imperfections. Then, once your body is in [a] slightly better, fitter, healthier place and all those distractions fall away, that then takes you to the next level.

## The body as object: metaphor, analogy, and practical enactment

> Just because you aspire to these high aspirations [i.e., Enlightenment], don't begin to ignore the physical body. You must tend to it ... even though "I am not this body," you can't disregard it and not eat healthy or worry about it. [Two former students] came up with this: "The body is the Tupperware of the soul." It carries around your little piece of this oneness. Make sure that it is healthy and well-maintained. (Ron, Integral Yoga teacher)

While Integral Yoga practitioners learn to emphasize and prioritize *spiritual* motivations and aspirations, they also learn, as the quote from Ron above makes clear, that they should not ignore the body completely. Practices aimed at managing and caring for the body, such as the asanas (physical postures) and pranayama (breath work), were described as a necessary part of the broader spiritual journey. Beyond these, the TTs were also encouraged to perform and maintain two additional forms of practice—the *shat kriyas*, or six cleansing processes, and a "yogic diet"—as part of a comprehensive routine of bodily maintenance. These practices reflected and constituted an understanding of the body as both a potential impediment to and a vehicle for spiritual progress. Cleansing and purifying the body was thought to help to prepare the practitioner for extended periods of meditation. As Aadesh told the TTs, "Until the body is cleaned, the kriyas are a top priority. You should do them regularly until you get cleaned up. Then, your asana, meditation, and pranayama are improved. Your consciousness is heightened."

When talking about the body, teachers frequently used metaphors and analogies, like the "Tupperware of the Soul," that constructed the body as an *object* requiring attention, care, and management. During the *satsang* described earlier, Aadesh offered another analogy for understanding bodies and illustrating how practitioners should treat them. Scanning the group with his piercing blue eyes, Aadesh asked the audience, "So, we have this body-mind, how should we view it?" Answering his own question, he responded: "I view it as a pet. And you see how I treat pets." His dog, Patty, was present at the time, and he gently stroked her head as he continued, "So I treat myself that way, too. I get lots of treats. I get disciplined sometimes but not too much. Loved a lot and played with." These metaphors and analogies help facilitate the cultivation of detachment by constructing the body as separate from the Self and by framing practice as a form of care aimed at broader goals. It is in and through "work" on the body that this interpretation—of the body as an object separate from the Self—is then reinforced and enacted (Winchester, 2008; Johnston, 2016). I will use the example of the kriyas to further illustrate this interplay between talk and experience.

A few weeks into the teacher training program, Ramdas, an Integral Yoga practitioner and certified instructor, led an introductory workshop on the kriyas for the TTs. He described each of the six areas that require cleansing, including the stomach, colon, and lungs, and reviewed the range of techniques available for doing so. In framing these practices, Ramdas explained that the *shat kriyas* not only purify the body but also help alter our view of and relationship to it. We would, he argued, "come to see the body in a different way. It is an organic piece of machinery. [The kriyas] open up your conception of what this body is—you become less attached to or identified with it while simultaneously taking care of it and respecting it."

During the class, Ramdas demonstrated several techniques, including *sutra neti*, or nasal flossing, walking the TTs through the steps required to successfully perform the practice.[7] *Sutra neti* requires inserting a piece of "floss," usually made of cotton or rubber, up the nose through the throat and out the mouth. The practitioner then "flosses" the nasal cavity by moving the sutra back and forth. Ramdas began by dipping his sutra into a bowl of water and then attempted to thread it through his nasal cavity as the TTs watched in a mix of anticipation and horror. On the first three attempts, Ramdas triggered his gag reflex and had to pull the sutra out, coughing and spitting into the water bowl at his side. Finally, on the fourth attempt, he was able to get the sutra through and grab the threaded end with his fingers. After doing so, he advised the TTs that it can be helpful to flick the sutra forward with the tongue in order to grab it with your fingers—to avoid stimulating the gag reflex.

The need for detachment from the body was evident in watching Ramdas perform these practices but even more evident in *doing* them. Successfully threading the floss through one's nasal passage and "flossing" requires the practitioners to overcome automatic bodily responses including the gag reflex. Other *shat kriyas* required similar mastering and management of bodily responses. In another practice, the practitioner drinks water until they vomit in an effort to cleanse the stomach. More often than not, this practice involved considerable discomfort. To complete the practice, the individual must continue in the face of considerable resistance from the body. The tension between the individual's intentions and desires (to do the practice) and the body's response (of rejecting the attempt) provides a tangible experience of the disconnect between the Self and body. In this way, the discourse "you are not the body" is felt, experienced, and reinforced.

A similar interpretive logic was applied to the practice of maintaining "a yogic diet." Regarding diet, the *Integral Yoga Basic Teacher's Manual* (1983, p 255) specifies:

> Our main object is to keep the mind and body in a tranquil condition. Therefore, our food must be taken into serious consideration. ... The quality of the food, the quantity, the way of eating it, all should be considered in order to get the maximum benefit.

Once again, we see body-focused yoga practices interpreted as preparatory work. In this case, eating in line with yogic guidelines was said to produce the "tranquil condition" necessary for more advanced spiritual work. This perspective was reinforced at a three-hour workshop on yoga and diet held at the IYI as part of the teacher training program. The workshop was led by Manu, an Integral Yoga practitioner, master teacher, and a Certified Yoga Nutrition Therapist. Manu described the basic principles behind the yogic diet: it is primarily *satvic* (light), easy to digest, and full of good prana (energy). Practically speaking, the yogic diet translates into a series of prohibitions: avoiding chemicals and sugar as well as most processed, refined, and packaged foods. It also prescribes a particular way of eating: chewing slowly and carefully, and eating moderately, in small quantities and only when truly hungry. Practitioners are told to avoid watching TV, reading, and talking while eating, and they are encouraged to direct their attention fully to the act of eating. Adhering to these dietary rules transforms the mundane practice of eating into an act of bodily care oriented toward spiritual formation (Griffith, 2004; Radermacher, 2017). Similar to the interpretation of the *shat kriyas* offered by Ramdas, the yogic diet was said to have more than physical effects; it would also transform how practitioners understand and experience their bodies. Practitioners were encouraged to view the act of eating as a means to nourish the body and maintain their "machinery," cultivating a sense of detachment from the body by treating it as an object, one wholly distinct from the Self, that requires maintenance.

In each of these cases, whether performing the *shat kriyas* or adhering to the yogic diet, practitioners must work against their bodies, managing and controlling the automatic or habitual responses of the body. When taught to observe these responses from the detached position of a disinterested observer, physical sensations of resistance and emotional experiences such as frustration or anger are allowed to bubble up and pass through the body. Rather than becoming attached to the body (its feelings, sensations, or abilities) or letting it fade into the background (à la corporeal absence [Leder, 1990]), practitioners learn to observe and manage their bodies. In doing so, the Self *qua* witness and caretaker is *enacted* as distinct from the body *qua* container or pet, resulting in a reinterpretation of the body accomplished through an interplay between discourse and practice.

## Facilitating embodied experiences: verbal instruction in practice

The field note that appears at the beginning of this chapter highlights the belief that language plays an important role in the cultivation of detachment among students of Integral Yoga. TTs were taught that the language they use to talk about and reference the body has real consequences—it could help promote or, alternatively, hinder bodily disidentification. This was not the only time the importance of verbal instruction was emphasized. During my time in the field, I was repeatedly struck by how much weight instructors placed on the precise wording of verbal cues. In fact, learning to teach an Integral Hatha Yoga class often felt like memorizing a script. TTs were provided with direct transcripts and audio recordings of several classes taught by seasoned instructors. They also were given a teacher training manual, which included sample language for instructing each posture and practice. TTs were repeatedly encouraged to use this exact language. They were corrected when they failed to do so and rewarded when they stuck to the script.

Looking closely at the class transcripts and suggested instructions, it is clear that verbal instructions do more than help practitioners move their bodies into different positions. They also aim to facilitate and shape students' embodied experience in class. Instructions for where and how to move the body are, perhaps not surprisingly, the most common form of instruction: for example, "stretch the arms toward the ceiling, take hold of one wrist, and pull up." Alongside these, however, are three other forms of instruction. First, there are instructions that direct students' *attention*: "notice how the breath takes shape as you position the body and work with it"; "focus awareness on the small of the back region, between the small of the back and the abdomen"; "note how the energy is flowing at this point ... just take a look." Second, there are instructions that describe and specify the (ideal-typical) content of experience at different points of the practice: "you'll find that as you do that, the body becomes light and energized [and] the mind becomes still and centered—*relaxed*"; "you'll notice the heart rate has picked up"; "you feel a very powerful surge of energy." And finally, there are instructions that interpretively link practices to the longer-term effects and outcomes of practice: "the eye movements tone up the muscles and nerves of the eyes ... they also help to develop the mind's ability to focus and concentrate very effectively"; "you're squeezing the thyroid gland at the base of the throat, giving the body an efficient, balance[d] metabolism." All four instructional forms—instructions directed toward bodily movement, attention, experience, and longer-term effects—were considered essential components of successful teaching.

While the content of verbal instruction was considered important in all postures, there were a few places in which it was considered particularly impactful, even crucial, that teachers use the "correct" language. *Yoga nidra*, or the "deep relaxation" (also "yogic sleep"), was one such place. The practice of *yoga nidra* begins with students in savasana (or corpse pose, see Figure 7.2). Students are then guided by the instructor through a process of "physical relaxation" involving the tensing and releasing of different parts of the body, beginning one limb at a time, followed by the pelvis, chest, neck, shoulders, and face. Students are then guided through a process of "mental relaxation" in which they are instructed to bring their attention to different parts of their body in sequence, from their toes to their heads, and

**Figure 7.2:** Savasana (corpse pose)

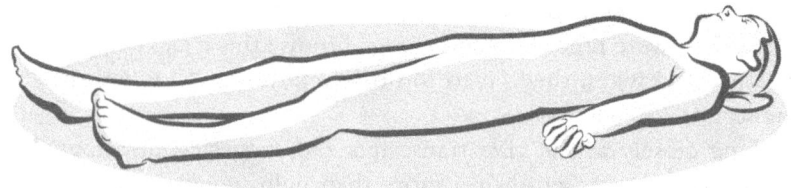

Source: Illustration by HEB Streits. Image courtesy of Shutterstock.

to imagine their bodies filling with "a beautiful relaxation." In the *Integral Yoga Basic Teacher's Manual*, instructors are advised that "release, relax and soften are key words" and to "use them over and over again" (1983, p 84).

Next, the teacher instructs students to "witness," first, the body, then the breath, and then the mind. Finally, the student is told to notice and "witness" the "peace within." Written instructions for this part of the practice were provided to all trainees:

> As you witness the body, you see it is totally at ease. [10-second pause] The breath is flowing easefully as well—relaxed, not requiring any effort at all. Just observe the breath. [1-minute pause] You can even let go of the mind and just watch it—just witness the mind. The mind too has become quite calm and still. It's becoming more and more placid. Sure, you may notice some movement, some thoughts, but you don't have to be involved in them. Just let them roll on and let them go ... just let the mind be. [30-second pause] Focus all of your awareness now at this place from which you're witnessing—the knower, the seer—this is the seat of your True Self. Notice how peaceful it is here. This is your true nature—this peace that's unlimited and ever-present. You're never apart from this. This is your very nature. ... Allow yourself to experience without any reservation at all, without any restrictions, the fullness of your being. Total peace, total bliss. Total love.

Students are left in this position, in complete silence for five minutes, to "observe the peace within" (*Integral Yoga Basic Teacher's Manual*, 1983, p 85). At the end of this period, teachers are instructed to "bring students back" to their minds and bodies with an "om" or by ringing a small gong. Students are then directed to bring attention back to the body—to breathe and then slowly bring movement back to their bodies—before coming to a seated position for the remainder of the class.

According to authoritative sources (eg, teachers, texts), the practice of *yoga nidra* is intended to provide students with an *embodied experience* of their True, Eternal Self and to help cultivate the disposition of "detachment" (Johnston, 2016). By asking students to let go of physical movement and effort and then move into the act of "witnessing," *yoga nidra* encourages practitioners to dissociate from their bodies and minds and to view the mind-body as an object from the perspective of an external observer. The training manual (1983, p 86) offers a list of phrases teachers can use to help students cultivate this sense of detachment during *yoga nidra*, including, among others:

- "Begin to witness the body and just see, like a vapor pouring out of the body, all the tension being completely released and the body becoming

clear and open. Just free floating. ... Let the head be centered as you witness the body."
- "Watch your mind as though it belonged to someone else. Regard any thoughts as apart from who you really are."
- "What is in your mind now?" And again, a few moments later, "And now, what has changed, what thoughts are there? Separate yourself from your thoughts."

While it was suggested that the *practice* of *yoga nidra* itself enables this experience and transmits *practical* (experiential, embodied) knowledge of the "True Self," it was also clear from the training program and the manual that the teacher's verbal instructions are an important *component* of the practice. The teacher's verbal instructions direct students' attention to specific parts of their bodies and particular embodied experiences. In doing so, the verbal instructions facilitate a particular embodied experience *and* provide a shared interpretive lens through which to interpret its meaning. Through the practice of *yoga nidra*, the embodied experience of relaxation is interpretively linked to the practitioner's "true nature" and "True Self." This talk is itself a social practice, one that TTs are required to master in order to graduate. In order to become a certified Integral Yoga instructor, a TT also had to successfully lead a full Hatha Yoga class under the observation of an Integral Yoga instructor who would evaluate the aspiring teacher's performance. Of the many requirements that determined an aspiring teacher's "success," similar to the use of "the" rather than "your" in referring to students' bodies (see introductory fieldnote at the beginning of this chapter), proper instruction during *yoga nidra* was given particular importance. As models of shared practices, *including* discursive practices, Integral Yoga teachers were required to use proper cues.

## Reflections and conclusions

On my very first visit to the IYI in January 2012, I took a Mixed-Level Integral Yoga Hatha class with Aadesh. Afterward, I waited to thank him for allowing me to join the upcoming teacher training program. "Did you enjoy the class?" he asked as I approached the front of the room, cutting my way across yoga mats, blankets, and blocks that were still scattered across the floor. I told him that I had, commenting on how it differed from other yoga classes I had taken. He agreed, with an air of pride in his voice. This practice, he told me, was designed by "a great yogi" and a "truly enlightened being" (referring to Swami Satchidananda, the founder of Integral Yoga). "Did you feel it?" he asked. I was caught off guard. I had no idea what he was referring to. What was the "it" I was supposed to have felt? I stammered and managed to say something about how relaxed

I felt, but I could tell from Aadesh's body language and facial expression that I was not quite getting *it*.[8]

It was only after spending more time in the field that I realized the error I had made. The "it" that Aadesh was referring to was not a bodily sensation (relaxation) or state of mind (calmness) per se but rather a spiritual experience: *it* was "cosmic consciousness," "Samadhi," or "enlightenment," the taste of my "true nature" or "True Self" that the practice was said to provide.

Looking back now, I think I did feel "it" during that initial class—in the sense that I had an embodied experience I would later come to suspect was similar to what others at the IYI labeled experiences of the "True Self." However, I was not equipped at the time to use the correct language to describe that experience—to articulate it in and through the interpretive frameworks of the Integral Yoga community. I felt immersed in the practice and fully present that day—an experience similar to what Mihaly Csikszentmihalyi (2009) has called "flow." I also felt a deep sense of peace and calm during *yoga nidra*. I have had these kinds of experiences both before and since my time at the IYI. It was only during my time there, however, that I would find myself making sense of those embodied experiences through the community's interpretive frameworks—for example, framing absorption in practice as a "moving meditation" or interpreting the relaxed state experienced in yoga *nidra* as evidence of my "true nature."

These frameworks provided a language with which I could articulate to myself and others what these experiences are, what they *mean*, and how they relate to the practices of yoga and meditation and to a broader trajectory of spiritual and personal formation (Konecki, 2016; Griera, 2017). During that first class, however, my inability to describe my embodied experience in ways that made sense to Aadesh marked me as an outsider, or at least as a novice practitioner with much to learn. Like Howard Becker's analysis of becoming a marijuana user, I found that for Integral Yoga practice and discourse to become personally meaningful (and for the individual to become invested in the practice), they must first learn to notice the effects of practice on the body, interpret those effects as enjoyable and beneficial, and connect those effects to the practice (Becker, 1953). The verbal instructions of teachers model and facilitate these interpretive links between practice, experience, and spiritual progress.

In this chapter, I have tried to show how those interpretive frameworks are transmitted and to highlight the role they play in facilitating the cultivation of bodily detachment (or disidentification). More broadly, this chapter suggests that religious subjectivities and identities cannot be located clearly in either the mind (explicit, discursive knowledge) or the body (implicit, practical knowledge). Rather, lived experience and self-understanding are emergent phenomena constituted through the complex interrelations of the somatic and the symbolic. It is for this reason that a study of the lived, embodied character of religious life must be just as attentive to the textual, conceptual, and symbolic aspects of religious life as it is to the practical, experiential, and performative dimensions. This chapter highlights the importance, in particular, of looking at talk and discourse in situ if we want to better understand how religious practices and discourses become personally meaningful.

## Notes

1. All meetings of the 200-hour teacher training program were audio recorded with permission from attendees. Quotes included are direct quotes transcribed from the audio recording with light editing. This example combines material from field notes and audio recordings across several meetings held between May and June 2012.
2. All individual names are pseudonyms to protect confidentiality, except where participants requested to have their real names used.
3. Some scholars in cultural sociology have interpreted narratives and accounts as epiphenomenal—post-hoc justifications for action driven by unconscious habit and deeply ingrained dispositions (Vaisey, 2009; Swidler, 2013). In this chapter, I align myself with scholars who "take talk seriously" (Wuthnow, 2011)—those who interpret the symbolic as an important means through which religious practices and discourses become personally meaningful and persuasive (Winchester and Green, 2019; Winchester, 2022).
4. Integral Yoga Fact Sheet (https://integralyoga.org/wp-content/uploads/2016/02/IY-Fact-Sheet.pdf).
5. Researchers have shown that the corporeal effects of practice may change over time as practices become routine and habitual (Tavory and Winchester, 2012). As a result, this approach is best suited to understanding the experience of novices—as both novices and the researcher are new to the practice and social world.
6. This summary description is based on the author's audio recordings and field notes from July 2012.
7. For more information on the practice of Sutra Neti, see https://www.yogicwayoflife.com/sutra-neti-nasal-cleaning-in-hatha-yoga/.
8. Author's field notes, January 2012.

## References

Ammerman, N.T. (2016) 'Lived religion as an emerging field: an assessment of its contours and frontiers', *Nordic Journal of Religion and Society*, 29: 83–99.

Ammerman, N.T. (2020) 'Rethinking religion: toward a practice approach', *American Journal of Sociology*, 126(1): 6–51.

Becker, H.S. (1953) 'Becoming a marihuana user', *American Journal of Sociology*, 59(3): 235–242.

Bourdieu, P. (1977) *Outline of a Theory of Practice*, Cambridge: Cambridge University Press, 2013.

Brekhus, W. (2003) *Peacocks, Chameleons, Centaurs: Gay Suburbia and the Grammar of Social Identity*, Chicago, IL: University of Chicago Press.

Collins, R. (2011) *The Micro-sociology of Religion: Religious Practices, Collective and Individual*, University Park, PA: Association of Religion Data Archives.

Cook, J. (2007) 'Find your match among the many types of yoga', *Yoga Journal*, August 28, available from: www.yogajournal.com/practice/yoga-sequences/not-all-yoga-is-created-equal/.

Crossley, N. (1995) 'Merleau-Ponty, the elusive body and carnal sociology', *Body and Society*, 1(1): 43–63.

Csikszentmihalyi, M. (2009) *Flow: The Psychology of Optimal Experience*, New York: Harper Perennial Modern Classics.

Davidman, L. (2015) *Becoming Un-orthodox: Stories of Ex-Hasidic Jews*, Oxford: Oxford University Press.

Douglas, M. (2003) *Purity and Danger: An Analysis of Concepts of Pollution and Taboo*, London: Routledge.

Geertz, C. (2010) 'Religion as a cultural system', in M. Banton (ed) *Anthropological Approaches to the Study of Religion*, London: Routledge, pp 87–125.

Griera, M. (2017) 'Yoga in penitentiary settings: transcendence, spirituality, and self-improvement', *Humanistic Studies*, 40: 77–100.

Griffith, R.M. (2004) *Born Again Bodies: Flesh and Spirit in American Christianity*, Berkeley: University of California Press.

Heider, A. and Warner, R.S. (2010) 'Bodies in sync: interaction ritual theory applied to sacred harp singing', *Sociology of Religion*, 71(1): 76–97.

Ignatow, G. (2009) 'Culture and embodied cognition: moral discourses in internet support groups for overeaters', *Social Forces*, 88(2): 643–669.

*Integral Yoga Basic Teacher's Manual* (1983) Buckingham, VA: Yogaville–Satchidananda Ashram, 2011.

Johnston, E. (2016) 'The enlightened self: identity and aspiration in two communities of practice', *Religions*, 7(7): 92.

Johnston, E.F. (2017) 'Failing to learn, or learning to fail? Accounting for persistence in the acquisition of spiritual disciplines', *Qualitative Sociology*, 40(1): 353–372.

Johnston, E.F. (2020) 'Yoga as a way of life: authenticity through identity management', in J.P. Williams and K.C. Schwarz (eds) *Studies on the Social Construction of Identity and Authenticity*, Abingdon: Routledge, pp 27–42.

Johnston, E.F., Eagle, D.E., Perry, B., Corneli, A. and Proeschold-Bell, R.J. (2022) 'Seminary students and physical health: beliefs, behaviors and barriers', *Journal of Religious Health*, 61(2): 1207–1225.

Konecki, K.T. (2016) 'The process of becoming a hatha-yoga practitioner', *Qualitative Sociology Review*, 12(1): 6–40.

Leder, D. (1990) *The Absent Body*, Chicago, IL: University of Chicago Press.

Leledaki, A. (2014) 'Body-selves and health-related narratives in modern yoga and meditation methods', *Qualitative Research in Sport, Exercise and Health*, 6(2): 278–300.

Lizardo, O., Mowry, R., Sepulvado, B. et al (2016) 'What are dual process models? Implications for cultural analysis in sociology', *Sociological Theory*, 34(4): 287–310.

Martin, J.L. (2019) 'Can carnal sociology bring together body and soul?', in W. Brekhus and G. Ignatow (eds) *Oxford Handbook of Cognitive Sociology*, New York: Oxford University Press, pp 115–136.

Mauss, M. (1973) 'Techniques of the body', *Economy and Society*, 2(1): 70–88.

McGuire, M.B. (2003) 'Why bodies matter: a sociological reflection on spirituality and materiality', *Spiritus: A Journal of Christian Spirituality*, 3(1): 1–18.

McGuire, M.B. (2008) *Lived Religion: Faith and Practice in Everyday Life*, Oxford: Oxford University Press.

McGuire, M.B. (2016) 'Individual sensory experiences, socialized senses, and everyday lived religion in practice', *Sociological Compass*, 63(2): 152–162.

McIlwain, D. and Sutton, J. (2014) 'Yoga from the mat up: how words alight on bodies', *Educational Philosophy and Theory*, 46(6): 655–673.

Mellor, P.A. and Shilling, C. (2010) 'Body pedagogics and the religious habitus: A new direction for the sociological study of religion', *Religion*, 40(1): 27–38.

Mills, C.W. (1940) 'Situated actions and vocabularies of motive', *American Sociological Review*, 5(6): 904–913.

Morley, J. (2008) 'Embodied consciousness in tantric yoga and the phenomenology of Merleau-Ponty', *Religion and the Arts*, 12(1–3): 144–163.

Nelson, T.J. (1996) 'Sacrifice of praise: emotion and collective participation in an African-American worship service', *Sociology of Religion*, 57(4): 379–396.

Nelson, T.J. (2005) *Every Time I Feel the Spirit: Religious Experience and Ritual in an African American Church*, NY: New York University Press.

Pagis, M. (2009) 'Embodied self-reflexivity', *Social Psychology Quarterly*, 72(3): 265–283.

Pagis, M. (2010) 'From abstract concepts to experiential knowledge: embodying enlightenment in a meditation center', *Qualitative Sociology*, 33(4): 469–489.

Pagis, M. (2015) 'Evoking equanimity: silent interaction rituals in Vipassana meditation retreats', *Qualitative Sociology*, 38(1): 39–56.

Pagis, M. (2019) *Inward: Vipassana Meditation and the Embodiment of the Self*, Chicago, IL: University of Chicago Press.

Radermacher, M. (2013) '"Theologies of the body": devotional fitness in US evangelicalism', in P. Jonkers and M. Sarot (eds) *Embodied Religion: Proceedings of the 2012 Conference for the European Society for Philosophy of Religion,* Utrecht: Ars Disputandi, pp 265–277.

Radermacher, M. (2017) 'Devotional fitness as discourse and embodied practice', in M. Radermacher (ed) *Devotional Fitness: An Analysis of Contemporary Christian Dieting and Fitness Programs, Popular Culture, Religion and Society: A Social-Scientific Approach*, Cham: Springer International Publishing, pp 127–206.

Shilling, C. and Mellor, P.A. (2007) 'Cultures of embodied experience: technology, religion and body pedagogics', *The Sociological Review*, 55(3): 531–549.

Swidler, A. (2013) *Talk of Love: How Culture Matters*, Chicago, IL: University of Chicago Press.

Tavory, I. and Winchester, D. (2012) 'Experiential careers: The routinization and de-routinization of religious life', *Theory and Society*, 41(4): 351–373.

Timmermans, S. and Tavory, I. (2012) 'Theory construction in qualitative research: from grounded theory to abductive analysis', *Sociological Theory*, 30(3): 167–186.

Vaisey, S. (2009) 'Motivation and justification: a dual-process model of culture in action', *American Journal of Sociology*, 114(6): 1675–1715.

Vaisey, S. and Frye, M. (2019) 'The old one-two', in W. Brekhus and G. Ignatow (eds) *Oxford Handbook of Cognitive Sociology*, New York: Oxford University Press, pp 101–114.

Wacquant, L.J.D. (2004) *Body and Soul: Notebooks of an Apprentice Boxer*, Oxford: Oxford University Press.

Winchester, D. (2008) 'Embodying the faith: religious practice and the making of a Muslim moral habitus', *Social Forces*, 86(4): 1753–1780.

Winchester, D. (2016) 'A hunger for God: embodied metaphor as cultural cognition in action', *Social Forces*, 95(2): 585–606.

Winchester, D. (2022) 'Doing it: ethnography, embodiment, and the interpretation of religion', in E.F. Johnston and V. Singh (eds) *Interpreting Religion*, Bristol: Bristol University Press.

Winchester, D. and Green, K.D. (2019) 'Talking your self into it: how and when accounts shape motivation for action', *Sociological Theory*, 37(3): 257–281.

Winchester, D. and Pagis, M. (2021) 'Sensing the sacred: religious experience, somatic inversions, and the religious education of attention', *Sociology of Religion*, 83(1): 12–35.

Wuthnow, R. (2020) *What Happens When We Practice Religion?: Textures of Devotion in Everyday Life*, Princeton, NJ: Princeton University Press.

Wuthnow, R.J. (2011) 'Taking talk seriously: religious discourse as social practice', *Journal for the Scientific Study of Religion*, 50(1): 1–21.

Yoga Alliance (2016) 'Yoga in America study conducted by Yoga Journal and Yoga Alliance', *Yoga Alliance* [online], January 13, available from: https://www.yogaalliance.org/2016yogainamericastudy.

# 8

# Black Girls' Bodies and Belonging in the Classroom

*Brittney Miles*

Bodies carry us through the world and influence all our social interactions (Story, 2010). Our experiences are mitigated by the politics surrounding our corporeal form. For example, in the shared space of a train, surrounded by strangers, some bodies are marked as outsiders because of skin color, spoken language, clothing, or smell—characteristics to which passengers may impute abject meanings, such as disgust (Miller, 1997), which then serve as personal moral justifications for avoiding bodily interaction (Ahmed, 2000). Black girls experience a form of this outsider status in classrooms. They are cast in the margins of educational spaces based on multiple factors related to their bodies: Black girls experience subjugation for their race, in their Blackness; for their gender, in their girlness; and for their developmental status, in their youthfulness. Many adults view and treat Black girls as older and more mature than their actual age (Epstein et al, 2017). Relatedly, Black girls receive more referrals, are punished more harshly, and are more likely to be removed from school than their non-Black classmates for the same infractions (Blake et al, 2011; Morris and Perry, 2017; Gibson et al, 2019). What is more, they are disciplined more frequently for subjective actions, such as disobedience, than objective violations, such as drug or alcohol possession (Annamma et al, 2016). The misogynoir of these intersectional subjugations—racism, sexism, and ageism—is linked to racial disparities in how social actors interpret Black girls' bodies.[1] In school settings, this misogynoir carries negative implications for Black girls' sense of belonging, exacerbating disparities in educational equality, widening opportunity gaps, and reinforcing performance variances around race (Gregory et al, 2010). Previous research has found, for instance, that experiences with school discipline and constant surveillance lead Black girls to feel devalued in schools (Wun, 2016a). Beyond broader beliefs about the value of their lives, these embodied intersectional subjugations impede healthy identity development and academic performance among Black girls (Hines-Datiri and Carter Andrews, 2017). They also center Black girls' educational lives around the burden of hypersurveillance, exclusionary notions of femininity, and relationships characterized by antiblackness (Carter Andrews et al, 2019).

Moving beyond conversations that tailor educational policy around macrostructural issues, such as technology gaps or testing outcomes, I propose that the consideration of Black girls' embodied subjectivity in the classroom, and the significance of their microlevel interactions, can help illuminate some of the anti-Black messages shaping their corporeal realities in schools. Specifically, examining and reflecting upon the corporeal politics of how Black girls' bodies are read and misread in the interactional context of school allows us to consider how Black girls' bodily negotiations may be understood differently when interpreted from their own perspective. While it may be the case that all face-to-face interactions between teachers and students constitute a mutual exchange of embodied messages between an initiator and a receiver (Goffman, 1963, p 16),[2] in the context of classrooms, it is also the case that the teacher's interpretation will generally be invested with greater authority. Given that Black girls' bodies are often mis/read through racist and sexist frames (López, 2002; Ridgeway, 2009), to resist these misinterpretations, Black girls must strategically rewrite their bodily form—their aesthetic and performance—to reclaim their bodily narratives in an otherwise disempowering school environment.

In this chapter, I argue that Black girls' bodies are mis/read, disciplined, and othered in school settings by way of microlevel interactions that are structured and interpreted through an inherited, transhistorical macrolevel repertoire of misogynoir and anti-Black discursive frames. Particular to the focus of this chapter, these frames comprise the unconscious "discursive, [interpretive] rules" inherited from history, law, and science that teachers carry into the classroom, and which constitute the "nexus[es] of [interpretive] power" between teacher and student (Foucault, 1970; see Shiner, 1982 p 389). After elucidating how these discursive frames shape the way that people "read" and interact with Black girls, and inform their understandings of what being a Black girl means, I examine some of the discursive reversals that Black girls employ to subvert these racist frames in school. More specifically, I explore how the discursive yet corporeal codification of race, gender, age, and the policing of Black girls' bodies (namely, their talk, volume, and dress) manifests in their school interactions.

To illustrate how Black bodies are mis/read by teachers and school policies through an intersectional lens, I present my analytical argument vis-à-vis a curated selection of ethnographic and other empirical examples drawn from over 20 qualitative social-scientific research articles on Black girls' experiences in schools. I first came across this body of scholarship while reviewing literature for a research project I was conducting on Black girls' experiences of school discipline (Miles, 2020). At that time, I detected an oversight in the literature: most studies focused on academic and disciplinary outcomes regarding how Black girls navigate the education system in the United States rather than the role that corporeal politics and bodily interpretation play in shaping their educational lives. There was a clear need for research, and a standpoint, that engaged with Black girls' embodied realities as the central focus. To address this need, I theorize in this chapter the implications of policing Black girl talk, backtalk and sass, volume, and dress for Black girls' notions of belonging in schools. I additionally highlight how misogynoir uniquely emerges in interactional contexts through Black girls' dress code violations, as they are defined by educators.

## Misogynoir and anti-Black discursive frameworks

Throughout history, the problematic—often violent—frames of anti-Black discourses have shaped how people see, interpret, and interact with Black people. Approaching "[d]iscourse as a system of representation," and understanding language to be one layer of representation within that system, we begin to glean how discursive "knowledge" of Black bodies produced in popular culture, science, and law limits our notions of how and who Black people can and "ought" to be (Hall, 2001, p 72). The use of discursive power in the United States to construct and define citizenship through the inherent othering and exclusion of Black people from American identity is woven into the nation's history (Goodwin, 2003). We see it wielded, for instance, in the word "nigger," which, evoking the painful history of enslavement, lynchings, and subordination, is weaponized against Black people.

Discursive power is by no means restricted to speech alone, however. Negative, racialized constructions of Blackness, the Black body, and Black subjectivity have been propagated and maintained by discursive technologies such as the printing press, racist political leaders maintaining the status quo, and discriminatory policies (Kendi, 2017). Racist tropes such as the "deadbeat dad," found in legal discourses, and the "welfare queen," in political rhetoric, have been used to vilify Black parents in welfare policies (Cassiman, 2008; Cammett, 2014). Distorted and demeaning depictions of Black people in America's first popular entertainment, minstrel shows (Lemons, 1977), were foundational to the formation of Black stereotypes in America. Guided by constructed images of Black people as subhuman and criminal, racist policies and rhetoric were bolstered by racist representations in science, law, and media that equated Black people with apes and thugs (Welch, 2007; Goff et al, 2008; Goff et al, 2014). Historically, casual discourses such as jokes that depicted Black people as primates grew in popularity during times of progress, as they did, for example, during Reconstruction and the Obama era (Apel, 2009). These harmful, racializing representations of Black people were, and continue to be, used to justify their oppression and political exclusion (Addis, 1993). Racialized notions of class, sexuality, and gender differences are also discursively embedded in how we have come to understand Blackness throughout history (Higginbotham, 1992).

With respect to school settings, racialized discourses regarding student progress and achievement, which frame Black students as a problem requiring control, infiltrated educational policy initiatives throughout the supposedly "progressive" desegregation era (Dumas, 2016). Steeped in the "color-blind" neoliberal racism of the post–civil rights era, these discourses continue to perpetuate race-based inequalities. For example, in the context of school discipline, narratives about children who misbehave frame Black children as "problem children" (Howard, 2013) and white children as "children with problems" (Freidus, 2020). In school spaces, white children, especially girls, are afforded a reputational "innocence" on the basis of their whiteness (and white femininity), whereas Black children face "Black culpability" and deficit logics (Freidus, 2020). In educational settings, all students are discursively defined by racial and gender frames, but for Black girls these frames are shaped furthermore by misogynoir.

Misogynoir discourses, in the form of the controlling images of the Mammy, Mule, Sapphire, and Jezebel (images that comprise one of the many remaining holdovers of chattel slavery),[3] and in the linguistic use of the term "bitch," have shaped embodied associations and expectations of Black female identity, femininity, and sexuality in the United States (Bucholtz and Hall, 2016).[4] Simultaneously framing Black women as subhuman and superhuman (Ammons, 1995), the controlling images of the Mammy, Mule, Sapphire, and Jezebel regulate Black women's political maneuverability (Harris-Perry, 2011). Deployed in the law, science, and literature of the antebellum period to justify the rape, abuse, and dehumanization of Black women (Simms, 2001), these stereotypes persist in courts of law today and continue to prevent Black women from getting justice in cases of domestic violence and rape (Ammons, 1995). Additionally, the term "bitch" is uniquely used against Black girls and women via the notions of the "Black bitch" or "nigger bitch" (Gross, 1994; Freeman, 2000). For Black women the dehumanizing "nigger bitch" connotation perpetually disassociates them from the possibility of womanhood and femininity (Goodwin, 2003).

As I will argue in this chapter, Black girls' body work in school settings resists and shifts these discourses, subverting anti-Black representations through a form of embodied reverse discourse that makes conceptual space for the production of discursive counternarratives.[5] Black people have frequently used reverse discourse to positively recast the disparaging collective image of the Black self that is dominant within the public consciousness. Examples of reverse discourse include efforts to redefine social citizenship by reclaiming and giving new meanings to formerly cruel words. The words "nigga" and "bitch," for instance, have risen in popularity both as colloquial and familial words between Black people and in modern popular culture and music. Black people's use of "nigga" establishes in-group membership around who can and cannot say it (only Black people can say it [Goodwin, 2003]).[6] And Black women uniquely use the word "bitch" among themselves as a demeaning comparison to a female dog or as a celebratory proclamation, such as being a "bad bitch" or the "head bitch in charge" (Abrahams, 1976).

In the legal realm, the National Association for the Advancement of Colored People (NAACP) used various legislative strategies to perform discursive reversals (Meier and Bracey, 1993; Watson, 1993). For example, when D.W. Griffith's film *The Birth of a Nation* was released in 1915, the NAACP protested and fought to have it legally censored in response to the problematic depiction of Black people (Weinberger, 2011). The Boston branch of the NAACP described the film as prejudiced, immoral propaganda that assassinated the character of Black people by portraying them as beasts (NAACP, 1915). In popular culture, Black people worked to mitigate some of the stereotypical elements in minstrel shows, such as Sambo yelps (Lemons, 1977). Each of these reclamations reflects a relational reversal in the exercise of discursive power (Weedon, 1987).

Like reverse discourses centered in language use, embodied reverse discourses give new semantic meaning to preexisting representations through bodily modification, or body work. Body work, a term popularized by sociologist Debra Gimlin (2007), "refers to the unpaid work individuals do to modify their own bodies" (Mears, 2014, p 1332). The bodily management and modification work done by Black girls is grounded in the corporal performances and emotional labor they undertake to navigate school settings, which, as sites of institutionalized knowledge managed by disciplinary discourse, (re)produce the misogynoir stereotypes that have shaped them and the interactions that take place within them (Gimlin, 2007; Shange, 2019). If, as Arthur Frank posits, "'the body' is constituted in the intersection of an equilateral triangle, the points of which are institutions, discourses, and corporeality" (1991, p 49), then "[d]iscourses do not just *reveal* corporeality but create it" (Shilling, 2012, p 83), and the body itself learns what it is and means from the institutional, discursive landscapes within which it is relationally embedded. It is within such a landscape that Black girls find themselves navigating the institutionality of schools, the discourses of controlling images about Black women and girls, and the politics of their bodies. What is more, the fraught relational interdependency of this landscape raises two important points of understanding frequently missing from educational studies, which tend to portray this interdependency in terms of interpersonal interactions between people in schools without attending to their macro-sociological dynamics (Dennis and Martin, 2005). First, the tenuous relationship between discourses and reverse discourses impacts how subjects are policed and governed as long as the dominant discourse holds social power and authority (Weedon, 1987). And second, macro frameworks of institutionalized discourses work their way through microlevel interactions, given that the meanings of the body are produced and constituted contextually. Making sense of how macrostructural constraints, such as controlling images, shape the narratives and processes that guide the reading and rewriting of Black girls' bodies provides necessary theoretical grounding for conceptualizing the significance of microlevel interactions occurring within schools.

## Symbolic interactionism and bodies: a discursive-interactionist frame

To the extent that the macrolevel discourses I presented in the previous section inform social actions, expectations, appraisals, and beliefs, they function as frames for experience; that is, they are social frameworks or cognitive schemas developed from past experiences, which, according to Erving Goffman (1974, p 22), "provide background understanding" and "standards" for contextualizing and interpreting events as well as individual actors' actions and bodies. Concerned with the interpretive frames and subjective meanings ascertained from a person's previous experiences in the world, symbolic interactionism offers a method for theorizing the body in terms of both the collective, macrolevel social meanings that attach "to particular bodily forms and performances" and the microlevel social actions through which they "become internalized, shaping an individual's sense of self-identity" (Shilling, 2012, p 86). While acknowledging the framing influence of institutionalized discourses, symbolic interactionism also acknowledges the contingency of individual agency; for example, "Goffman argues that individuals can control and monitor their intercorporeal performances" (Shilling, 2012, p 85).

Bringing in a symbolic interactionist perspective allows us to examine the discursive connections that exist between individualist logics and structural forces. It also shines a light on the interactional maneuverability of Black girls in face-to-face encounters in the classroom and their attempts to reverse dominant discourses through body work. While considering the politics of these interactions and ethnographic accounts, it is important to keep in mind that Black girls' bodies are always in conversation with a broader, historically and socially situated archive of discourses. Black girls may exert agency through their own interactional maneuverability, but since their bodies are "produced by social force" (Shilling, 2012, p 85), their meanings are "determined by shared vocabularies of body idiom that exceed individual control" (Goffman, 1963, in Shilling, 2012, p 85).

In the sections that follow, I analyze discursive excerpts taken from various qualitative studies of, as well as a few news articles on, Black girls' embodied experiences in schools to explore how Black girls' bodies—as expressed and experienced through the relational, corporeal elements of Black talk, backtalk, volume, and Black girl dress aesthetics—are mis/read and policed in school spaces. Throughout my examination of the discursive representations of Black girl students' interactions found in these studies and reports, I define what mis/readings of Black girls' bodies are and explain how, filtered through misogynoir discourse, they structure face-to-face interactions between teacher and student and affect Black girls' experiences of belonging in schools. The empirical examples that follow are not exhaustive. Representing a select assortment of teacher–student interactions drawn from a set of cross-disciplinary studies, they are meant to be taken as an illustrative starting point for further analysis and exploration.

## The mis/reading of Black girls' bodies in schools

Being responsible for leading and guiding daily classroom activities, teachers sustain order and shape the emotional structure of the classroom through the power dynamics of teacher–student and adult–child relationships that call these respective roles to the forefront (Goffman, 1963). The intersectional discursive frames concerning race, gender, and age that teachers and students bring with them into classrooms, and through which Black girls' bodies are mis/read, become especially apparent during teacher–student interactions. In what follows, I explore these interactions and mis/readings of Black girls' bodies as they relate to Black talk, backtalk and sass, volume, and dress.

### *Black talk, backtalk, and sass*

Black talk and Black voice have been associated with white racist constructions of Black speech reified in America's first form of popular culture, minstrel shows. Although Black speech depicted in minstrel shows was a bastardization of what Black people sounded like at one point in time, the co-opted language performed on stage should not cast shame upon the actual spoken language (Mahar, 1985). Rebecca Carroll intentionally used the cultural richness of Black language and talk to depict the realities of Black girlhood with authenticity and reverence. Carroll (2011, p 15) writes:

> Black vernacular has been our rightful voice throughout history, and it has, in many ways, survived our souls when we have needed it most.

It is not slang, and it is not improper use of the English language, it is black vernacular, and we are the only ones who know how to speak it.

Black talk captures the cadences, vernacular, and essence of the diverse ways Black people communicate with one another, and it is irreducible to slang (Smitherman, 1986). (Even the use of slang by a non-Black person will not necessarily make them "sound" Black.) Related to Black talk, Black voice describes what we hear when Black people speak; it is part of the essence of *sounding* Black. According to McWhorter (2017), hearing Blackness involves a racialized understanding of accented speech that is situated in an associative sonic process made up of, independent of language use, "sonic flutters" that are "part of the black American cultural tool kit. Five little frills, one could call them, that immediately say black to an American listener even when someone is speaking standard English" (McWhorter, 2017, p 70). What is problematic about this association is not the identification of a "blaccent" (McWhorter, 2017) but the comparative devaluation of a whole people that accompanies it.

Racialized constructions of Black performances and history have attached an anti-Black stigma to the speech and sound of Black girls using their voice in classrooms. In April Baker-Bell's (2020) ethnographic research on Black high school students in Detroit, a Black girl named Janel described how she felt about teachers policing her use of local Black vernacular: "When I came to school and was speaking like that when I was younger, all my teachers would tell me that's not the right way to talk. I just started crying … it took me down. I thought they were trying to scrutinize me!" (p 39). Baker-Bell theorizes a linguistic double consciousness and explains that the anti-Black linguistic racism in schools generated a conflict in Janel toward Black speech. Janel experienced her teachers' response as criticism and extended policing of how she and other Black children spoke outside of school. For Janel, her teachers' scrutinization of the latter in the classroom felt like a critique of who she was and what she knew. In classrooms, the expected dialect is Standard American English; Black English and slang are marked as inappropriate (Mordaunt, 2011; Wheeler, 2016). In this example, I note how it is not only Black talk and voice that are discursively misread but also what it means for Black people, particularly young Black people, to use their voices.

While racialized sonic associations broadly shape perceptions of what Black talk is and means, the senior–subordinate hierarchical relationship of the teacher to the student, which is reinforced by differences in social position and age, influences how disrespect and disruption are perceived in student–teacher interactions. This is something that carries potentially greater consequences for the policing of Black girls, for whom perceptions of inappropriate talk are intensified as they are interpreted through the lenses of gendered macro-discourses that equate feminine, or "ladylike," behavior with being demure and dependent and therefore silent and invisible (Morris, 2005, 2007; M. Morris, 2016). We see this dynamic at work when Black girl students are considered to be using *backtalk*. As a form of reverse discourse, backtalk, or talking back, involves "speaking as an equal to an authority figure," and it is frequently followed by punishment intended to silence the person talking back (hooks, 1986, pp 123–124). It is within the constraints of this gendered interpretive framework and its consequent policing that Black girls develop bodily communication strategies characterized "by speaking little with the mouth and a great deal with the eyes, the arms and shoulders, the whole set of the body" (Abrahams, 1976, p 70). This is Black girl sass.

By employing Black talk and sass, Black girls proclaim their presence and value in the classroom irrespective of their age and gender, and in so doing confidently affirm their cultural body politic while simultaneously challenging dominant discourses about how Black girls are supposed to act and sound in school spaces. This self-assurance is also a feature of talking with attitude (TWA), another form of sass that Black girls sometimes utilize to resist oppressive situations and respond to feelings of mistreatment and misunderstanding from others (Koonce, 2012). Stephanie, one of several adolescent Black girls interviewed by Jacqueline Koonce at a Midwestern Boys and Girls Club, described how she forgot that instead of saying "Okay, you don't have to get loud with me" (Koonce, 2012, p 42) to teachers who are being disrespectful toward her, she should show them respect. Unfair treatment and disrespect from teachers are just two of the challenges Black girls describe experiencing in schools (Joseph et al, 2016; Wun, 2016b). Framing Stephanie's response as indication of her confusion with her teachers' immature behavior, Koonce (2012) considers TWA to be a type of cultural capital that is knowledge-generating and empowering for Black girls. To this I would add that in the face of deciding whether to tolerate their teachers' disrespect and remain silent or talk back, Black girls risk being read through the controlling image of the "loud Black girl," the assertive, unruly, and thus "unladylike" Sapphire (hooks, 1986; Morris, 2007; Collins, 2009; Joseph et al, 2016; Wun, 2016b). Exacerbating this particular struggle, the confidence and self-esteem that are part of Black girl sass and TWA are often misread as disrespect, even in the context of affectionate play or when speaking little with the mouth (Abrahams, 1976), and consequently are met with disciplinary action (Koonce, 2012).

In a study of Black girls and school disciplinary policies, Connie Wun (2016a) reports that Black girls "most often got into trouble for having attitudes or being disrespectful to their teachers or other staff" (p 191). In another study by Wun (2016b) on Black girls and anti-Black racism in schools, Victoria, a Black Puerto Rican ninth grader, confided that, in addition to rarely treating her with respect, her teachers, especially her white teachers, were "more likely to incessantly police and punish her" (p 744). In response to a teacher disciplining her for what are normally considered innocuous activities, Victoria reported:

> He gets mad for everything like if you're drinking Gatorade he yells, "Put that away!" [I say,] "What do you mean?" "I'm thirsty." You have out ChapStick, he yells, "Put that away!" [I think], "Whatchu mean? You want my lips to be chapped? I'm not gonna be crusty like yours [sic]." (Wun, 2016b, pp 743–744)

Wun (2016b) situates Victoria's account as an example of white teachers policing and disrespecting her in ways that disassociate Black children with innocence. I suggest that this disassociation emerges not only from the teacher's verbal exchange with the student but also from a racially primed interpretation of the student's corporeality. Racial bias in schools and pedagogical practices intended to prepare Black students "for a critical White society" can "reinforce dominant representations" (Morris, 2007, p 509) such as the perception that Black children can rarely do right and will often do wrong. Hemmed in by this double-edged stereotype, Black girls may opt to be loud or sassy in order to alternately "play[ ] to or counter[ ] stereotypes and labels," resist "personal and institutional acts of racism in their schools," and defend themselves against the subordinate positions to which they have been relegated (Joseph et al, 2016, p 19). We can see the strategy of choosing whether to be loud or sassy serving this very purpose in the personal accounts of Monica and Kishana. Monica, who is 15 years old, cares for her younger siblings while her mother works the nightshift, a responsibility that sometimes interferes with her school attendance. As Wun reports (2016a, p 186):

> Although Monica previously explained to her teacher [that] she had extenuating circumstances at home, her teacher offered little sympathy but did give her several tardy referrals. Once during an argument with her teacher over a tardy referral, Monica expressed her resentment and hurt by blurting out, "whatever makes you sleep at night." Retrospectively, she thought that her outburst would have alerted the teacher to her desperate frustrations about school and her life at home.

When Monica yelled "Whatever makes you sleep at night," she was using sassy and loud talk to defend herself. I would argue that she was also using backtalk to loudly call someone out so others could hear the commotion, since speaking loudly about information usually thought of as private can be a way to generate witnesses through testimony (Toliver, 2020). Speaking loudly out of turn can empower a student to control the narrative of their supposed misbehavior. It also can bolster the student's reputation among peers and shield them against unfavorable perceptions (Neal-Jackson, 2020). In refusing silence, Monica employed loud sassiness not only as a method for reversing patriarchal and anti-Black discourses that frame acceptable Black femininity in terms of deference, passivity, and invisibility (hooks, 1986; Morris, 2007, pp 21–22) but also as a means for inducing her teachers to regard her more closely and extend greater consideration (and compassion) for the ways she must adapt and endure (Abrahams, 1976).

In contrast to Monica, Kishana, a high school junior, suppresses her loudness to play against and reverse racial stereotypes. In Nicole Joseph et al's (2016) study of Black female adolescents' experiences and definitions of racism in schools, Kishana reports that teachers in the International Baccalaureate program at her school assume, due to their racially biased lower expectations, that she will not succeed. She explains, "[Just] because I'm Black doesn't mean I can't learn" (Joseph et al, 2016, p 18). To mitigate their misperceptions, helping "the teachers come around and view her as a smart, capable student," Kishana says, "[I'm] not playing into the stereotype of I'm going to be ghetto and loud and disrespectful" (p 18). Joseph et al (2016) frames Kishana's acknowledgement of stereotypes in schools as racism in the form of judgment and disrespect rather than recognizing the violent, insidious, othering discourse of the "loud and angry" Sapphire at work. Further, I consider Kishana's experience as indicative of the legacy of racist discourses popularized in minstrel shows that associate Black people with lower intelligence and smaller brains (Mahar, 1985). Keeping these embodied background discourses in mind, we can see that Kishana suppresses her loudness to avoid being *framed* as a loud, angry, and unintelligent Black girl.

These examples of teacher–student interactions depict Black girls' critical reflections on the discriminatory exchanges they experience at school. Together these experiences and reflections comprise powerful catalysts for responding loudly to unfairness and for transforming misconceptions of Black girls' embodiment and educational potential. To further illuminate how alternation between silence and loudness can forge powerful reverse discourses that subvert negative ideas about Black bodies, in the following sections I draw on examples of Black girls' use of silence and laughter to explore how these forms of resistance and survival unfold in the midst of anti-Black background discourses that frame teachers' perceptions of Black talk.

*Quiet Black girls and silence as resolve*

As Kishana's account (introduced in the previous section) attests, quiet Black girls exist. For some Black girls, quietness is a matter of disposition. For others, like Kishana, it is a matter of strategy. Quiet Black girls in classrooms are often viewed as exhibiting appropriate bodily control and docility, behaviors which, from the teacher's perspective, meet the situational expectations of the school setting and therefore do not warrant policing to maintain notions of how students should behave. Guided by this positive reception, some Black girls view silence—or the absence of extemporaneous conversation and speech—as central to their academic success, and they use it to avoid bringing attention to various aspects of their identity, such as their girlness or Blackness, which may be devalued or come under surveillance in the classroom (Fordham, 1993).

As a chosen performative strategy for navigating and negotiating behavioral expectations during teacher–student interactions, Black girls' quietness serves as an embodied politic of survival. It is at once a communication style that coddles the egos and assuages the potential violence of those in positions of power and a strategic maneuver that protects and sustains Black girls' inner lives (Quashie, 2012). Indeed, as reported by Wun (2016a, p 192), in response to feeling trapped, "misunderstood, and despised as they [and their voices] are subject to constant surveillance and control," Black girl students consider silence a feasible way to protect themselves while performing both Blackness and dignity.

The strategic implementation of quiet empowers Black girls to negotiate their presence in the classroom through the deafening withdrawal of their vocal contribution. In Monique Morris' exploration of the criminalization of Black girls in schools in her book *Pushout*, 18-year-old Leila, who describes herself as "one of the ones that talk too much," explains what happens when she chooses to be quiet: "When I do be quiet, couldn't nobody speak up. The teacher didn't encourage them to speak up. Instead, he took me in the hallway and asked if I was okay, even though he just asked me to be quiet the day before!" (Morris, 2016, p 79). Morris highlights the potential misreading of Leila's expressivity as problematic, but she also offers that Leila's loudness can also be helpful and worthy of celebration. From Leila's example, I glean how opting out of her typical communication style completely changed the classroom environment, prompting the teacher to reframe her quietness as a problem, even though it was a direct result of having been previously censured by her teacher for being loud. What might not be so obvious is that in refusing to be her talkative self, she was in actuality adopting a very "loud," conspicuous, peace-preserving strategy that acknowledged the value of her voice in the classroom, even by the person who regularly silences her—her teacher. In quietness Leila recognized the strength of her voice and, simultaneously, the value and power of its absence, which did, after all, compel the teacher to contradict his prior condemnation. In this way, quietness can become a reclamation of unapologetic Blackness (Allen and Miles, 2020): it challenges the typified, expressively outward and public performance of the Black subject by centering the equally expressive inward Black self (Quashie, 2012).

As a performative strategy, silence is not without its drawbacks. The silence of high-achieving Black girls is sometimes mirrored by the silence of their teachers and school administrators, who neglect to acknowledge the student's achievements (Fordham, 1993). Quietness can also reinforce racialized gendered stereotypes that associate silence with "ladylike" passivity labeled "good" and loudness with "unladylike" assertiveness labeled "bad" (Fordham, 1993; Lei, 2003; Morris, 2007). Nevertheless, Black girls' silence does not guarantee them protection from the potential negative perceptions of their peers and teachers, especially when Black girlhood is read as inherently resistive (Fordham, 1993) and resistance is primarily associated with loudness. Though Black girls recognize the false dichotomy that teachers draw between silence and loudness during their interactions, given the unlikelihood that either response will change the circumstances of their oppression, they do what is necessary to survive as wholly as possible.

The supposed counternarrative to loud Black girls would be quiet girls who are believed to perform well in school, and who are, therefore, exempt from discipline or antagonism because *quietness* is interpreted as antithetical to *Blackness*. Whether loud or quiet, all Black girls suffer the misreading of their bodies in schools. A Black girl who has chosen quiet, or who is quiet, may be rendered invisible because quietness does not fit the "loud Black girl" or Sapphire frame. And yet this damaging invisibility is not always easily perceived by others, since Blackness itself—and thus its hypervisibility and misreading as inherently resistive—is often framed as bold and loud. Hence, to make this plight visible, a student may resort to backtalk, as Monica did when she blurted out to her teacher "Whatever makes you sleep at night" (Wun, 2016a, p 186), while still choosing quiet by not revealing the details of her home life. What is important to keep in mind here is that both quiet and loud strategies of resistance and survival emerge from the tension born out of Black girl students' situated need to, on the one hand, defend and visibilize themselves and their dignity and, on the other hand, preserve the peace, particularly their inner peace and integrity. Black girls are, therefore, positioned between and against loud and quiet performances, where neither is acceptable because both will be misread, policed, and framed as "a problem."

### *Loud, laughing Black girls*

To be loud is to be un-American. It is to be nonnormative (read: non-white), unpleasant, and unprofessional. As part of the National Council of Teachers of English's pledge distributed to students in 1917 to honor National Speech Week, students pledged commitment to nationalistic notions of appropriate language use: "I love the United States of America. I love my country's flag. I love my country's language. I promise ... that I will do my best to improve American speech by avoiding loud rough tones, by enunciating distinctly, and by speaking pleasantly, clearly, and sincerely" (Delpit and Dowdy, 2008, p 29). This historical discursive association of standardized grammar and soft vocal tone with nationalism, belonging, whiteness, and civility situates Black speech and Black volume (or perceptions of it) as being unruly, that is, outside the realm of that which is considered acceptable in school spaces. Combined with the racialized and gendered controlling images of the Sapphire and Jezebel, these associations similarly frame the sonic performances of Black girls as wayward, insofar as they view them as violating social expectations that females and children are to be seen, not heard.

As the teacher–student interactions discussed in this chapter suggest, educators actively police Black girls' loudness, which they interpret as disruptive and unfeminine. Said plainly, Black girls are disciplined for having and manipulating their bodies in ways that are discomforting to whiteness. What is more, these interpretations and disciplinary efforts frame, and thereby influence in turn, Black girls' play and laughter. Comprising a delicate dance between affection and aggression, Black children's play may appear confrontational to teachers. Black play is about performatively being bad, smooth, and provocative—all positive characteristics in Black culture of the dopeness that is part of the performance of Blackness (Abrahams, 1976). Teachers, however, might misread these characteristics as disrespect, especially given that play is also about emulating adults and "asserting self-reliance" (Abrahams, 1976, p 71).[7]

The uninhibited loudness of Black play is also a feature of Black girls' laughter, which teachers may frame as loud, ghetto, or transgressive, violating the gendered norms of quiet "feminine" respectability. Thus, even when Black girls are not breaking any particular rules, many educators will police and discipline them for their laughter. High school educator Diedre Houchen describes a conversation she had with Janissa, a Black high school junior she was disciplining for behaving "unacceptably" and "disruptively" with a male student. In the middle of class, Ms. Houchen asked Janissa to step into the hall, offering her the option to change her behavior and stay or not return. She told Janissa, "You are so capable of doing [well in school], but you waste your time, joking and laughing and being rude in class. That's your choice. But you are not going to waste my time anymore" (Houchen, 2013, p 107). Framed as a barrier to learning, the laughter of a Black girl, but not of the male student with whom she was laughing, is considered unacceptable and grounds for removal from class. Calling out Janissa's, but not her male peer's, laughter conveys the idea that it is specifically Black *girls*' laughter that is not in keeping with the seriousness that classroom learning requires. Yet studies show that student laughter can carry positive educative and social benefits. Tied to physical and emotional relief, and therefore inseparable from pleasure, laughter in classrooms can reduce anxiety, boost psychological well-being, improve student engagement and motivation, and foster close, trusting connections between teachers and students (Lujan and DiCarlo, 2016; Savage et al, 2017). Given this, it is especially important for teachers to think about the implications of how they police Black emotions, particularly Black joy. As a critical praxis against respectability politics, Black girls may employ laughter to subvert the power dynamics of classroom interactions (Waller, 1932), neutralize the teacher's suppressive control, and reclaim learning spaces as sites of pleasure and joy (Garner et al, 2019). Permitting boisterous sonic performances in classes disrupts rigid and anti-Black body policing in schools.

The preceding examples of Black girls' use of backtalk, sass, loudness, quietness, and laughter demonstrate how the macrolevel discourses that shape perceptions of Black talk can produce a combination of racialized age- and gender-based mis/readings that lead to the overpolicing of Black girls in classrooms via their embodiment. The "controlling images" (Collins, 2009), antiblackness, misogynoir, and hegemonic notions of gender and femininity that guide the discursive oppression that Black girls face in classrooms denote the ways they are construed as outsiders on a sonic level. Yet the discourses that frame and filter mis/readings of Black girls' vocal performances are also imposed upon their bodies more tangibly, notably through the policing of their dress.

## *Dress code violations when wearing and styling Black girlhood*

The racialized and gendered tropes of respectability associated with Black girls' volume that mark them as outsiders likewise extend, through the sexualized controlling images of the Sapphire and Jezebel, to negative stereotypes about Black girls' "inappropriate" bodies, sexuality, and dress. Moving beyond the voice and vocal performances, in this section I examine how other corporeal politics of self-presentation are policed through discriminatory policies that disproportionately target aesthetic features, styles, and fashion coded as Black. As a means for making oneself visible (or invisible) in social spaces, clothing, hair, and other beautification practices become focal sites of surveillance and accountability for interpreting appropriate (normative) behavior and belonging in the classroom.

Black girls have long reported differential treatment they receive compared to their non-Black peers in schools, including as it applies to enforcing and policing dress codes (Joseph et al, 2016). Recently, an increasing number of students have spoken out about the ways schools have policed students' naturally occurring and traditionally Afrocentric features. The American Civil Liberties Union of Massachusetts filed a complaint against Malden's Mystic Valley Regional Charter School after two female students reported that the school suspended them for wearing braids (Edwards, 2017), a Black style that helps maintain and protect their hair but violates the dress code.

Stemming from the legacy of slavery and a preference for European beauty aesthetics, "school dress codes that prohibit afros, afro-puffs, dreadlocks, small twisted braids, and other culturally Black styles imply that the Black body is unacceptable, unruly, and unprofessional" (Macon, 2014, p 1281). When educators create and enforce culturally insensitive policies targeting Black hairstyles such as the afro, which educators sometimes interpret as unkempt or indicative of personal neglect (Essien and Wood, 2021), they turn a personal aesthetic preference into anti-Black institutional discrimination against Black bodies in their natural state. Discriminatory policies such as these, which associate naturalness with "laxity of control over the self" (Goffman, 1963, p 27) and thereby devalue and stigmatize Black girls' hair, are one way that schools institutionalize anti-Black discourses of what a "beautiful," "feminine," "tidy," "controlled," "productive" body is supposed to look like. They also embolden the notion that "those in positions of authority at these schools think it is their right to swap one environment for another and pick on Black girls because of their 'unnatural natural hair'" (Burton, 2017). Those with power and authority to write and enforce dress codes are key contributors to the proliferation of anti-Black discourses. The trickle-down impact of anti-Black policies is that Black children are singled out, marked as outsiders via their embodiment, and then gaslit by explanations that contend the policies are neutral or about "professionalism" (Macon, 2014).

In addition to the racialized policing of hairstyles, schools enact discriminatory policies that sexualize the female student body and frame it as a threat. By suggesting that feminine bodies and fashion styles "will distract their male classmates or make male teachers feel uncomfortable," these policies "communicate that girls' bodies are inherently sexual, provocative, dangerous, and that harassment is inevitable" (Harbach, 2015, p 1044). The notion embedded within dress codes of an inherent, potentially uninhibited feminine sexuality uniquely targets Black girls through the controlling image of the Jezebel, which promotes negative assumptions about Black girl students' character and behavior. According to Lisette, a Black high school senior, the teachers and most of the students at her school think of Black girls as "negative, loud-talking, pregnant," wearing ill-fitting bras, and dressed inappropriately regardless of what they are actually wearing (Lei, 2003, p 167). Joy L. Lei (2003) highlights these tensions and the resulting negotiations Black girls are forced to make about whether to play into or against stereotypes. No matter which choice they make, Black girls are constrained by the gendered and racial assumptions and disparaging stereotypes that frame them as hypersexual and unbelonging in schools based on their corporeal politics. In a study by Nia Michelle Nunn (2018) on gendered racism in Black girls' educational experiences, one eighth-grade female student reported that "if you're Black AND a girl, the dress code is different for you … even though our bodies are not all the same … it feels like a dress code for Black girl bodies" (p 252). Nunn's study positions Black girls as experts in their experiences of inequality and violence in schools, while also validating the trauma that results from these experiences. These layers of violence in schools mark Black girls as Sapphires and Jezebels who are loud and sexual, and whose inappropriate embodiment is reinforced in their clothing. The misogynoir in school dress code policies draws on hypersexual and anti-Black discursive frames that institutionalize deficit-oriented ideas about Black girls' bodies, how they should be read, and what their bodies mean in school settings.

Sexist dress code policies enforced by teachers put the onus on female students to police and desexualize their bodies, regardless of how they perceive their own self-presentation. Black girls have to "negotiate between what is acceptable, expected, and attractive and what is seen to go too far" (Raby, 2010, p 349). Yet, as Rebecca Raby (2010) points out, distinguishing between acceptable and unacceptable dress is challenging because the distinction is "constantly in flux, based on specific contexts, changing fashions, girls' own changing ages, and definitions of taste that vary by culture and class" (p 349). The burden of navigating normative ideas about appropriate dress, hair, and style that are determined by adults of a different generation (and possibly different race) alongside school policies that uniquely target Black girls creates a hostile educational experience. The quotes offered from diverse Black girls indicate that they disagree with the stereotypical discursive images teachers and school policies perpetuate—as too sexual or unattended to. What is more, the misreading of Black girls' dress can result in school sanctions such as detention, suspension, or, worse, child welfare investigations of the student's family.

## Conclusion

In their school-based interactions, Black girls navigate discursive stereotypes related to their gender, race, and age. Playing into these narratives and sometimes resisting them, Black girls aim to write their own narratives through their bodies. They recognize the politics surrounding their bodies in schools and actively negotiate the politics of their interactions. They shift their behaviors in response to the interpersonal dynamics at play. Black girls work to assert their presence in classrooms and manipulate their behavior and bodies to challenge rules, change the planned itinerary, and reclaim some bodily power in their interactions. Nonetheless, the negative perceptions held by adults against Black girls are guided by stereotypes of race and femininity, as well as auditory factors in sounding and being Black. When articulating how they are policed differently, Black girls highlight the ways that Black talk, Black sass, Black volume, Black laughter, and Black dress are the target of anti-Black and misogynoir disciplining. Yet, they also use these embodied strategies as tools to reclaim their voice. Teacher–student interactions establish a conceptual space within which Black girls identify and challenge these expectations through embodied reclamation and counternarrative. By utilizing the reverse discourses of backtalk, volume, and dress, Black girl students demand respect, fight to freely display their personalities, and effectively refuse to become passive victims of misogynoir.

Black girls are experts on their educational experiences; they use that expertise to maneuver as part of a politic of survival and belonging, and this tells us a lot about schools as institutions. As Frank (1991, p 49) reminds us, "The point of a sociology of the body is not to theorize institutions prior to bodies, but to theorize institutions from the body up." In the institutional context of the school setting, Black girls' bodies are interpreted through misogynoir discourses. Analyzing Black girls' experience of belonging in this space from the body up contributes to literature on education by prioritizing and identifying the Black body as a notable mechanism for disparate forms of discipline, policing, and resistance. It is from the embodied experiences of Black girls in schools that we can better understand the persistence of antiblackness and misogynoir in school-based interactions. Furthermore, this chapter offers an intersectional interrogation of the relationship between micro–macro and agency–structure in schools, encouraging educators to adopt alternative approaches to student management and student–teacher relationships and to consider more carefully how they empower and recognize the humanity of young people, especially Black girls (Jennings et al, 2006; Gervais, 2011; Khatib et al, 2013).

**Notes**

[1] Misogynoir is the perpetuation of violent compounded sexism and racism that Black women and girls navigate (Bailey, 2010; Bailey and Trudy, 2018).
[2] This is true regardless of whether they speak to one another. All linguistic exchanges feature embodied messages, but not all embodied messages include or necessitate spoken language (Goffman, 1963).
[3] Controlling images are stereotypes and biased depictions used by those in positions of power to oppress and degrade a group of people and rationalize their marginalization (Collins, 2009).
[4] The Mammy is usually depicted as a desexualized, domestic housemaid or caretaker who has left her family to serve a white family. The Jezebel is a hypersexual, promiscuous, and sexually insatiable woman (Simms, 2001; Collins, 2009). The Sapphire is an aggressive, intimidating, matriarchal figure who is usually associated with the angry Black woman stereotype (Stephens and Phillips, 2003).

5   A reverse discourse uses the signifiers of an earlier, usually dominant, discourse but employs these signifiers in a way that gives them an alternate interpretation (Weaver, 2010).
6   It is important to note that the word "[n]igga is not simply nigger pronounced 'blackly'" (McWhorter, 2017, p 164).
7   In Black communities, the mixing of affectionate play, backtalk, cursing, and even fake-hitting (or threatening to hit) are necessary defensive survival tools and performance of street smarts that help Black folks to navigate challenges of inequality and systemic silencing (Abrahams, 1976; Anderson, 1999; Hatt, 2007).

## References

Abrahams, R.D. (1976) *Talking Black*, New York: Newbury House Publishers.

Addis, A. (1993) 'Hell man, they did invent us: the mass media, law, and African Americans', *Buffalo Law Review*, 41(2): 523–626.

Ahmed, S. (2000) *Strange Encounters: Embodied Others in Post-coloniality*, London: Routledge.

Allen, S. and Miles, B. (2020) 'Unapologetic blackness in action: embodied resistance and social movement scenes in Black celebrity activism', *Humanity and Society*, 44(4): 375–402.

Ammons, L.L. (1995) 'Mules, madonnas, babies, bathwater, racial imagery and stereotypes: the African-American woman and the battered woman syndrome', *Wisconsin Law Review*, 1995(5): 1003–1080.

Anderson, E. (1999) *Code of the Street: Decency, Violence, and the Moral Life of the Inner City*, New York: W.W. Norton and Company.

Annamma, S.A., Anyon, Y., Joseph, N.M. et al (2016) 'Black girls and school discipline: the complexities of being overrepresented and understudied', *Urban Education*, 54(2): 211–242.

Apel, D. (2009) 'Just joking? Chimps, Obama and racial stereotype', *Journal of Visual Culture*, 8(2): 134–142.

Bailey, M. (2010) 'They aren't talking about me', *Crunk Feminist Collective*, March 14, available from: http://www.crunkfeministcollective.com/2010/03/14/they-arent-talking-about-me/.

Bailey, M. and Trudy (2018) 'On misogynoir: citation, erasure, and plagiarism', *Feminist Media Studies*, 18(4): 762–768.

Baker-Bell, A. (2020) *Linguistic Justice: Black Language, Literacy, Identity, and Pedagogy*, London: Routledge.

Blake, J.J., Butler, B.R., Lewis, C.W. and Darensbourg, A. (2011) 'Unmasking the inequitable discipline experiences of urban Black girls: implications for urban educational stakeholders', *The Urban Review*, 43(1): 90–106.

Bucholtz, M. and Hall, K. (2016) 'Embodied sociolinguistics', in N. Coupland (ed) *Sociolinguistics: Theoretical Debates*, Cambridge: Cambridge University Press, pp 173–197.

Burton, B. (2017) 'Let go of our hair and let our girls learn', *The Root*, May 17, available from: http://www.theroot.com/let-go-of-our-hair-and-let-our-girls-learn-1795349148.

Cammett, A. (2014) 'Deadbeat dads and welfare queens: how metaphor shapes poverty law', *Boston College Journal of Law and Social Justice*, 34(2): 233–265.

Carroll, R. (2011) *Sugar in the Raw: Voices of Young Black Girls in America*, New York: Three Rivers Press.

Carter Andrews, D.J., Brown, T., Castro, E. and Id-Deen, E. (2019) 'The impossibility of being "perfect and white": Black girls' racialized and gendered schooling experiences', *American Educational Research Journal*, 56(6): 2531–2572.

Cassiman, S.A. (2008) 'Resisting the neo-liberal poverty discourse: on constructing deadbeat dads and welfare queens', *Sociology Compass*, 2(5): 1690–1700.

Collins, P.H. (2009) *Black Feminist Thought: Knowledge, Consciousness, and the Politics of Empowerment*, London: Routledge.

Delpit, L. and Dowdy, J.K. (eds) (2008) *The Skin That We Speak: Thoughts on Language and Culture in the Classroom*, New York: The New Press.

Dennis, A. and Martin, P.J. (2005) 'Symbolic interactionism and the concept of power', *The British Journal of Sociology*, 56(2): 191–213.

Dumas, M.J. (2016) 'Against the dark: antiblackness in education policy and discourse', *Theory into Practice*, 55(1): 11–19.

Edwards, B. (2017) 'Mass. ACLU files complaint against charter school that disciplined students over braids', *The Root*, May 17, available from: http://www.theroot.com/mass-aclu-files-complaint-against-charter-school-that-1795290680.

Epstein, R., Blake, J. and González, T. (2017) 'Girlhood interrupted: the erasure of Black girls' childhood', *Social Science Research Network*, June 27, available from: http://dx.doi.org/10.2139/ssrn.3000695.

Essien, I. and Wood, J.L. (2021) 'I love my hair: the weaponizing of Black girls' hair by educators in early childhood education', *Early Childhood Education Journal*, 49(3): 401–412.

Fordham, S. (1993) '"Those loud Black girls": (Black) women, silence, and gender "passing" in the academy', *Anthropology and Education Quarterly*, 24(1): 3–32.

Foucault, M. (1970) 'The archaeology of knowledge', *Information (International Social Science Council)*, 9(1): 175–185.

Frank, A.W. (1991) 'For a sociology of the body: an analytical review', in M. Featherstone, M. Hepworth and B.S. Turner (eds) *The Body: Social Process and Cultural Theory*, London: SAGE, pp 36–102.

Freeman, J. (2000) 'The bitch manifesto', in B.A. Crow (ed) *Radical Feminism: A Documentary Reader*, New York: New York University Press, pp 226–232.

Freidus, A. (2020) '"Problem children" and "children with problems": discipline and innocence in a gentrifying elementary school', *Harvard Educational Review*, 90(4): 550–572.

Garner, P.R., Hill, D.C., Robinson, J.L. and Callier, D.M. (2019) 'Uncovering Black girlhood(s): Black girl pleasures as anti-respectability methodology', *American Quarterly*, 71(1): 191–197.

Gervais, C. (2011) 'On their own and in their own words: Bolivian adolescent girls' empowerment through non-governmental human rights education', *Journal of Youth Studies*, 14(2): 197–217.

Gibson, P., Haight, W., Cho, M., Nashandi, N.J.C. and Young, J.Y. (2019) 'A mixed methods study of Black girls' vulnerability to out-of-school suspensions: the intersection of race and gender', *Children and Youth Services Review*, 102: 169–176.

Gimlin, D. (2007) 'What is "body work"? A review of the literature', *Sociology Compass*, 1(1): 353–370.

Goff, P.A, Eberhardt, J.L., Williams, M.J. and Jackson, M.C. (2008) 'Not yet human: implicit knowledge, historical dehumanization, and contemporary consequences', *Journal of Personality and Social Psychology*, 94(2): 292–306.

Goff, P.A., Jackson, M.C., Di Leone, B.A.L., Culotta, C.M. and DiTomasso, N.A. (2014) 'The essence of innocence: consequences of dehumanizing Black children', *Journal of Personality and Social Psychology*, 106(4): 526–545.

Goffman, E. (1963) *Behavior in Public Places*, New York: The Free Press.

Goffman, E. (1974) *Frame Analysis: An Essay on the Organization of Experience*, Boston, MA: Northeastern University Press, 1986.

Goodwin, M. (2003) 'Nigger and the construction of citizenship', *Temple Law Review*, 76(2): 129–208.

Gregory, A., Skiba, R.J. and Noguera, P.A. (2010) 'The achievement gap and the discipline gap: two sides of the same coin?', *Educational Researcher*, 39(1): 59–68.

Gross, B. (1994) 'Bitch', *Salmagundi*, 103: 146–156.

Hall, S. (2001) 'Foucault: power, knowledge and discourse', in M. Wetherell, S. Taylor and S.J. Yates (eds) *Discourse Theory and Practice: A Reader*, London: SAGE, pp 72–81.

Harbach, M.J. (2015) 'Sexualization, sex discrimination, and public school dress codes', *University of Richmond Law Review*, 50(3): 1039–1062.

Harris-Perry, M.V. (2011) *Sister Citizen: Shame, Stereotypes, and Black Women in America*, New Haven, CT: Yale University Press.

Hatt, B. (2007) 'Street smarts vs. book smarts: the figured world of smartness in the lives of marginalized, urban youth', *The Urban Review*, 39(2): 145–166.

Higginbotham, E.B. (1992) 'African-American women's history and the metalanguage of race', *Signs: Journal of Women in Culture and Society*, 17(2): 251–274.

Hines-Datiri, D. and Carter Andrews, D.J. (2017) 'The effects of zero tolerance policies on Black girls: using critical race feminism and figured worlds to examine school discipline', *Urban Education*, 55(10): 1–22.

hooks, b. (1986) 'Talking back', *Discourse*, 8: 123–128.
Houchen, D. (2013) '"Stakes is high": culturally relevant practitioner inquiry with African American students struggling to pass secondary reading exit exams', *Urban Education*, 48(1): 92–115.
Howard, T.C. (2013) 'How does it feel to be a problem? Black male students, schools, and learning in enhancing the knowledge base to disrupt deficit frameworks', *Review of Research in Education*, 37(1): 54–86.
Jennings, L.B., Parra-Medina, D.M., Hilfinger-Messias, D.K. and McLoughlin, K. (2006) 'Toward a critical social theory of youth empowerment', *Journal of Community Practice*, 14(1–2): 31–55.
Joseph, N.M., Viesca, K.M. and Bianco, M. (2016) 'Black female adolescents and racism in schools: experiences in a colorblind society', *The High School Journal*, 100(1): 4–25.
Kendi, I.X. (2017) *Stamped from the Beginning: The Definitive History of Racist Ideas in America*, New York: Random House.
Khatib, M., Sarem, S.N. and Hamidi, H. (2013) 'Humanistic education: concerns, implications and applications', *Journal of Language Teaching and Research*, 4(1): 45–51.
Koonce, J.B. (2012) '"Oh, those loud Black girls!": a phenomenological study of Black girls talking with an attitude', *Journal of Language and Literacy Education*, 8(2): 26–46.
Lei, J.L. (2003) '(Un)necessary toughness? Those "loud Black girls" and those "quiet Asian boys"', *Anthropology and Education Quarterly*, 34(2): 158–181.
Lemons, J.S. (1977) 'Black stereotypes as reflected in popular culture, 1880–1920', *American Quarterly*, 29(1): 102–116.
López, N. (2002) 'Race-gender experiences and schooling: second-generation Dominican, West Indian, and Haitian youth in New York City', *Race, Ethnicity, and Education*, 5(1): 67–89.
Lujan, H.L. and DiCarlo, S.E. (2016) 'Humor promotes learning', *Advances in Physiology Education*, 40(4): 433–434.
Macon, A.-L.F. (2014) 'Hair's the thing: trait discrimination and forced performance of race through racially conscious public school hairstyle prohibitions', *University of Pennsylvania Journal of Constitutional Law*, 17(4): 1255–1284.
Mahar, W.J. (1985) 'Black English in early blackface minstrelsy: a new interpretation of the sources of minstrel show dialect', *American Quarterly*, 37(2): 260–285.
McWhorter, J. (2017) *Talking Back, Talking Black: Truths about America's Lingua Franca*, New York: Bellevue Literary Press.
Mears, A. (2014) 'Aesthetic labor of the sociologies of work, gender, and beauty', *Sociology Compass*, 8(12): 1330–1343.

Meier, A. and Bracey, J.H. (1993) 'The NAACP as a reform movement, 1909–1965: to reach the conscience of America', *The Journal of Southern History*, 59(1): 3–30.

Miles, B. (2020) 'Black girls' knowledges and resistance to school discipline', *American Sociological Association's Body and Embodiment Section Blog*, April 8, available from: http://sectionbodyembodiment.weebly.com/blog/black-girls-knowledges-and-resistance-to-school-discipline.

Miller, W.I. (1997) *Anatomy of Disgust*, Cambridge, MA: Harvard University Press.

Mordaunt, O.G. (2011) 'Bidialectalism in the classroom: the case of African-American English', *Language, Culture, and Curriculum*, 24(1): 77–87.

Morris, E.W. (2005) '"Tuck in that shirt!" Race, class, gender, and discipline in an urban school', *Sociological Perspectives*, 48(1): 25–48.

Morris, E.W. (2007) '"Ladies" or "loudies"? Perceptions and experiences of Black girls in classrooms', *Youth and Society*, 38(4): 490–515.

Morris, E.W. and Perry, B.L. (2017) 'Girls behaving badly? Race, gender, and subjective evaluation in the discipline of African American girls', *Sociology of Education*, 90(2): 127–148.

Morris, M. (2016) *Pushout: The Criminalization of Black Girls in Schools*, New York: The New Press.

NAACP, Boston Branch and Daniel Murray Collection (1915) *Fighting a Vicious Film: Protest against 'The Birth of a Nation'*, Boston Branch of the National Association for the Advancement of Colored People, available from: https://www.loc.gov/item/72197440/.

Neal-Jackson, A. (2020) 'Muting Black girls: how office referral forms mask dehumanising disciplinary interactions', *Journal of Educational Administration and History*, 52(3): 295–308.

Nunn, N.M. (2018) 'Super-girl: strength and sadness in Black girlhood', *Gender and Education*, 30(2): 239–258.

Quashie, K. (2012) *The Sovereignty of Quiet: Beyond Resistance in Black Culture*, New Brunswick, NJ: Rutgers University Press.

Raby, R. (2010) '"Tank tops are ok but I don't want to see her thong": girls' engagements with secondary school dress codes', *Youth and Society*, 41(3): 333–356.

Ridgeway, C.L. (2009) 'Framed before we know it: how gender shapes social relations', *Gender and Society*, 23(2): 145–160.

Savage, B.M., Lujan, H.L., Thipparthi, R.R. and DiCarlo, S.E. (2017) 'Humor, laughter, learning, and health! A brief review', *Advances in Physiology Education*, 41(3): 341–347.

Shange, S. (2019) 'Black girl ordinary: flesh, carcerality, and the refusal of ethnography', *Transforming Anthropology*, 27(1): 3–21.

Shilling, C. (2012) *The Body and Social Theory* (3rd edn), London: SAGE.

Shiner, L. (1982) 'Reading Foucault: anti-method and the genealogy of power-knowledge', *History and Theory*, 21(3): 382–398.

Simms, R. (2001) 'Controlling images and the gender construction of enslaved African women', *Gender and Society*, 15(6): 879–897.

Smitherman, G. (1986) *Talkin and Testifyin: The Language of Black America*, Detroit, MI: Wayne State University Press.

Stephens, D.P. and Phillips, L.D. (2003) 'Freaks, gold diggers, divas, and dykes: the sociohistorical development of adolescent African American women's sexual scripts', *Sexuality and Culture*, 7(1): 3–49.

Story, K.A. (2010) 'Racing sex—sexing race', in C.E. Henderson (ed) *Imagining the Black Female Body*, New York: Palgrave Macmillan, pp 23–43.

Toliver, S.R. (2020) 'Can I get a witness? Speculative fiction as testimony and counterstory', *Journal of Literacy Research*, 52(4): 507–529.

Waller, W.W. (1932) *The Sociology of Teaching*, New York: Wiley.

Watson, D.L. (1993) 'Assessing the role of the NAACP in the civil rights movement', *The Historian*, 55(3): 453–468.

Weaver, S. (2010) 'The "other" laughs back: humour and resistance in anti-racist comedy', *Sociology*, 44(1): 31–48.

Weedon, C. (1987) *Feminist Practice and Post-structuralist Theory*, Oxford: Blackwell.

Weinberger, S. (2011) '*The Birth of a Nation* and the making of the NAACP', *Journal of American Studies*, 45(1): 77–93.

Welch, K. (2007) 'Black criminal stereotypes and racial profiling', *Journal of Contemporary Criminal Justice*, 23(3): 276–288.

Wheeler, R. (2016) '"So much research, so little change": teaching standard English in African American classrooms', *Annual Review of Linguistics*, 2: 367–390.

Wun, C. (2016a) 'Against captivity: Black girls and school discipline policies in the afterlife of slavery', *Educational Policy*, 30(1): 171–196.

Wun, C. (2016b) 'Unaccounted foundations: Black girls, anti-Black racism, and punishment in schools', *Critical Sociology*, 42(4–5): 737–750.

9

# Embodied Vulnerability and Sensemaking with Solidarity Activists

*Chandra Russo*

I sit down to write about the embodiment of solidarity activism during the early days of the 2020 coronavirus pandemic. I work from home because the university campus where I work has recently closed, the vast majority of our students sent home for the semester. My toddler squeals in the background; daycares and schools have been shuttered. State leaders beg for more medical infrastructure, and public health experts attempt to explain the rationale for what some are terming "the new normal." For many of us living comfortable lives in the Global North, the human body, with all of its vitality and vulnerability, has not in our lifetimes seemed so central to matters political, social, ethical, and epistemological. Nor, perhaps, has our interdependence as a global community ever been so stark.

For nearly a decade, I have been studying, and at points collaborating with, a cohort of activists whose work foregrounds this fundamental interdependence as well as the shared, if unequally allotted, vulnerability of the human body. These predominately white, middle-class activists from the Christian Left protest the racialized violence of US security policies against Latinx migrants, Muslim detainees, and workers in the Global South. These groups include: (1) School of the Americas Watch, which endeavors to close the military training facility at Fort Benning, Georgia; (2) the Migrant Trail Walk, part of the US/Mexico border justice movement; and (3) Witness Against Torture, a grassroots effort to close the Guantánamo Prison. Through "observant participation" (Vargas, 2006), interviews, and archival analysis, I explore how these groups engage in embodied practices of solidarity with the state's targets while contesting

US policies of militarism, torture, indefinite detention, and immigration enforcement (Russo, 2018).

Through a political practice I term *solidarity witnessing*, these activists work to see violence that dominant perspectives occlude and then reveal such violence to broader audiences. Physically demanding and sometimes high-risk tactics, such as fasting, desert pilgrimage, and civil disobedience, play a central role in these groups' practices of solidarity, allowing them to draw attention to state violence while forging community and long-term commitment to a cause. Their bodily *practices* of solidarity, intended to generate moral outrage among their audiences, also spur a range of powerful embodied *feelings* of solidarity, including a sense of close community among activists, deep empathy with the state's targets, and renewed commitment to a struggle for justice. This interpretive pathway that yokes bodily practices to felt orientations depends upon sense experiences of, as well as sensemaking about, embodied vulnerability.

This chapter points to embodied vulnerability as a multivalent access point for making bodily experience more present in social movement study. Social movement scholars suggest that we know very little about how activists' embodied experiences impact them and the movements they join (Sutton, 2010; Maor, 2013; Van Ness and Summers-Effler, 2018). More broadly across the social sciences, scholars have struggled to identify the "methodological and analytic tools with which to do research about embodied experience" (Chadwick, 2017, p 71). This chapter tacks back and forth between myself as a researcher and the activists I study to demonstrate how embodied vulnerability becomes meaningful both to the task of research and to solidarity activism itself. More broadly, the chapter suggests that social movements might fruitfully be considered as *sensemaking* projects as a way to capture the embodied dynamics shaping activists and their movements as well as the cultural tools movements provide their participants for interpreting and directing felt experiences.

In what follows, I outline my approach for theorizing how embodied vulnerability works for the activists in this study and how social movements serve as sensemaking projects. I then turn to three explorations of how embodied vulnerability worked methodologically and analytically to shape sensemaking over the course of my research. In the first section, I consider how my own experiences of embodied vulnerability, and the meanings I attached to these, fundamentally shaped my methodological considerations. I then pivot to analyze participant accounts, which reveal how affective experiences of embodied vulnerability come to be interpreted as instantiations of solidarity.[1] In the last section, I return to consider the methodological implications of embodied vulnerability by way of an accidental encounter in the field that availed me of unexpected insights into my sociological study. I suggest that our bodies themselves are up for interpretation in ways that have important epistemological stakes.

## Making sense of embodied vulnerability

My approach to theorizing embodied vulnerability draws upon the phenomenology of perception and more recent findings in the science of embodied cognition that emphasize the primacy of embodied experience in shaping consciousness and behavior (Crossley, 1995; Jasper, 2018; Van Ness and Summers-Effler, 2018). Sociological treatments of Merleau-Ponty's phenomenology of perception highlight the interplay between the body's "object side" and its "subject side" (Crossley, 1995, p 47) and how our bodies are inscribed by social forces in ways that impact our life experiences and interpretive horizons (Alcoff, 2005). This is distinct from broad trends in the social sciences, replicated in social movement scholarship, which have often treated the human body as a socially significant object while ignoring how the body is itself the very ground of social experience and consciousness (Lyon, 1997; Chadwick, 2017). Most studies of the body in social movements, for instance, emphasize the protesting body and its behaviors as a conduit of meaning for public consumption (Sasson-Levy and Rapoport, 2003; Hohle, 2009). While a focus on the semiotics of bodily *performance* is important in its own right, few studies examine activists' embodied experiences, their efforts to assign meaning to these experiences, or what such interpretive work means for their movements (for notable exceptions see Sutton, 2010; Adler, 2019; Fiorito, 2019).

A phenomenological account holds the potential to bring this range of insights together in order to examine how social forces operate on and through the human body, how bodily experience shapes human consciousness and agency, and how social movements provide resources for interpreting embodied experiences. While not focused on the body per se, Florence Passy and Marco Giugni (2000) suggest that in the study of social movements "a phenomenological perspective ... looks at the constant work of definition and redefinition of the social world by participants in social movements and at their self-positioning within this world" (p 119). A phenomenological approach to embodied vulnerability in social movements thus examines how participants continually and collectively *make sense* both through and about their embodied experiences, structured as these are by social forces, culture, and history.

My conceptualization of embodied vulnerability is itself multidimensional. I consider embodied vulnerability as an ontological given, an always present condition of the human organism. A number of scholars posit bodily vulnerability as the one human universal across our innumerable differences, a commonality that should obligate us toward forms of care and solidarity across these differences (Butler, 2004; Turner, 2006). Certainly, bodily vulnerability is unequally allotted; reigning power dynamics mean that some bodies are rendered much more vulnerable than others. We are not all alike in the sense of being equally vulnerable. Rather, we hold in common our dependence on others as well as our need for basic supports, such as food, water, and shelter.

In line with this, I would suggest that *awareness* of one's own and others' embodied vulnerability, and its unequal allotment, is also structured in part by dynamics of social power. A number of phenomenological thinkers suggest that the very fact of our embodiment can and often does become invisible to us (Leder, 1990; Bendelow and Williams, 1995). Most people do not think about their eyes as they look out on the world or concentrate on their hand before picking up an object. In the accrual of practical knowledge, one learns by doing, not by cognitive reflection on the fact of one's embodiment (Crossley, 1995). For many, this argument goes, embodiment is not front of mind. This is so until one is confronted with experiences that unsettle or disorient habituated embodiments or, put otherwise, that force an awareness of the *vulnerability* of the body. The discomfort and pain that accompany injury, for instance, generate powerful affect that directs one to pay attention to the fact of one's embodiment in new, if often unwelcome, ways.

Yet to have one's body, and its attendant vulnerabilities, recede from ever-present consciousness is surely also a product of privilege and protection. Arguably the majority of the world's people are in fact forced to pay some regular attention to their bodily vulnerability, whether this be for reasons of hunger and endemic disease or other forms of social stigma, oppression, and violence. *Awareness* of one's own and others' embodied vulnerability, and its unequal allotment, then, can come from many epistemological resources. One's lived experience may be more than sufficient. At the other end of the spectrum, one could hear a news story or learn in a class about a kind of suffering that one has not personally experienced. For the activists I study, who have a great deal of privilege in comparison to the state's targets, *experiences of* bodily vulnerability that accompany physically demanding, high-risk protest tactics amplify other ways of coming to know the US security state, such as reading a book or hearing a speech.

The interpretive mechanisms that we as social beings have for making sense of experiences of embodied vulnerability are multiple, and our manner of making sense often impacts our sense experience. Ample evidence suggests, for example, that different cultural schemas work not just to offer distinct explanations for, but also to shift the felt experience of, bodily pain (Bendelow and Williams, 1995; Norris, 2009). Here, I borrow from movement scholar Deborah Gould's (2009) notion of affect as a kind of sense experience that makes itself apparent to us viscerally, as distinct from "an emotion [which] is one's personal expression of what one is feeling in a given moment, an expression that is structured by convention, by culture" (p 20). Affect exerts a force; it is what gives emotion its sensory intensity. Categories of emotion provide the means for communicating affect, generally through speech or gesture. We might be moved to the physiological response of tears for reasons of pain, joy, anger, or fear. Our bodily experience and display are not always transparent to others, and sometimes not even to ourselves. Emotions provide the systems of signification that allow us to communicate affect. Put otherwise, emotions play an interpretive role for the bodily experience of affect, making something that often feels deeply interior, and possibly ambiguous, available for social communication and action. Yet in this interpretive maneuver, emotions also do something to the affective experience, fixing and delimiting the fluid and often ineffable quality of affect.

Gould (2009) suggests that social beings are disposed toward being able to both interpret and express experiences to others such that "affect can generate a strong desire to make sense of itself" (p 38). Social movement groups often provide their participants with the language to name affect and the tools to direct such emotions toward social systemic change. In this way, social movements might be conceptualized as sensemaking projects, in both aspects of that phrase. Movements generate new encounters, such as protest actions, that both ignite and are mediated by activists' *sense* experiences, the range of embodied, affective, and emotional responses to the social world. Movements also provide the cultural tools to *make sense*, that is to interpret and direct affect and emotion. For the solidarity activists I study, desert pilgrimage, fasting, arrests, and jail time generate unsettling felt experiences, a confrontation with both personal and collective bodily vulnerability. When undertaken intentionally and in communities of protest that maintain rich cultural resources for making *sense* of such *sense* experiences, the affective experiences of embodied vulnerability are interpreted and mobilized toward (re)new(ed) and resistant ways of seeing, knowing, and being.

Since this chapter considers both the theoretical and methodological implications of experiences of embodied vulnerability, a note on my research approach seems in order. I am guided by the insights of Ron Eyerman and Andrew Jamison (1991), later taken up by Dylan Rodriguez (2006), who theorize social movements as knowledge projects. Their assertion is that *social movement* is itself the generation, modification, articulation, indeed *movement*, of new ideas, identities, and modes of praxis within groups and across society. What this means for scholars, as Rodriguez (2006) aptly observes, is that social movements can be learned *from* and *with*; they are not mere social units to be empirically assessed or taken as objects of scholarly knowledge. I have suggested that social movements be conceptualized as sensemaking projects as a way to get at the embodied, affective, and emotional dynamics of social movements that an overly cognitive approach might flatten. I too am interested in learning from and with the movements in my study. I suggest that this learning required co-participation in some aspects of physically demanding protest, paying attention to what my experiences of bodily vulnerability helped me to know.

In order to best learn from and with my research participants, my approach to fieldwork is adopted from João Costa Vargas' (2006) notion of "observant participation." Distinct from the "participant observation" central to most ethnographic endeavors (Emerson et al, 1995), observant participation emphasizes participation as the central method by which the social world is interpreted. Observant participation is not just an ethical or political move but centrally an epistemological one as well. It centers on the premise that there is more to be gleaned from active participation in the social world than from merely watching others do what they do. At the very least, the insights will be different. Had I not approached my research through observant participation, I likely would not have experienced embodied vulnerability and its attendant affect, emotions, and resources for sensemaking in the same way as I did alongside my research participants. I now turn to explore some of the ways in which my experiences of bodily vulnerability during physically demanding solidarity activism motivated and shaped the task of data collection.

## Embodied vulnerability and the shape of research

It is the most threatening hour of the day. At just 10 am, we plod on in 100-degree heat under a vicious sun. Even the desert insects have stopped their rattling below the dry burn. I sip at my water bottle. I find it difficult to quench my thirst without filling my belly to sloshing. My lips are chapped. My joints ache as we continue into our fourth day. About 50 people are making this 75-mile trek over the course of a week through Arizona's borderlands, following the general path taken by so many migrants forced into this remote, brutal desert. We begin in Sasabe, Sonora, Mexico, a mile south of the border, and head north toward Tucson, traveling just east of the Baboquivari range and the Tohono O'odham nation. Despite the discomfort, I recognize the immense beauty of this place, stark peaks, fierce but glorious cacti flowering everywhere. The land is saturated with the rich history of peoples and fragile ecosystems that have made this place home for centuries.

After being out here myself with all the comforts we are afforded as walkers, what is surprising to me is not that people have died. It is that anyone makes it at all. I note this as we pass abandoned backpacks along Route 286, signs of migrants who likely survived many days in the desert to be picked up by vehicles. (Adapted from the author's fieldnotes)

The Migrant Trail Walk is one of a number of collective actions planned by the US–Mexico border justice movement to protest thousands of migrant deaths. These fatalities are the result of a US border enforcement strategy inaugurated in the mid-1990s intended to curb illicit migration from south of the border by pushing migrants into ever more desolate and dangerous crossings (Sheridan and McGuire, 2019). The annual Migrant Trail Walk began in 2004 with about 20 participants from different border justice organizations in and around Tucson, Arizona. After years of setting out water in an attempt to save lives and having recovered far too many human remains, these 20 wanted to experience a piece of the journey and draw public attention to the daily reality facing migrants at the border.

I first learned of the Migrant Trail Walk in 2007 while volunteering with immigrant rights efforts in my home state of Colorado. At the time, I had never been to the US–Mexico border and believed the walk, as daunting as it sounded, would be an important way to learn more about US border policy while connecting with others who had been doing this work for longer than I had. My first time walking and living in close community as a form of political protest overflowed with the ineffable. It provided a set of affective and what I (at the time) termed "spiritual" experiences distinct from much that I had encountered in my daily advocacy work and far removed from my own nonreligious, apolitical, white, bourgeois upbringing. In subsequent years, I returned to the Migrant Trail every May to remember and mourn the dead, reconnect with the border justice movement, and nourish myself for the social justice struggles ahead.

In this section, I consider how experiences of bodily vulnerability on the Migrant Trail shaped the motivation for as well as the task of data collection. While not the first to suggest as much, I appreciate Paaige Turner and Kristen Norwood's (2013) insight that in interpretive inquiry the researcher's embodiment "[serves] as impetus, instrument, and impediment for, in, and to qualitative research" (p 700). My early experiences of embodied vulnerability on the Migrant Trail Walk served as both impetus for and instrument in what would become more formal research. As my project progressed, my bodily history and capacities, both shaped by instances of vulnerability, permitted me access to data I might not otherwise secure, while creating impediments to the research process. I treat these in turn.

During my early years on the Migrant Trail Walk, I did not think of myself as doing research. I was not engaged in what sociologists generally recognize as the methods of proper data collection, such as administering surveys, conducting interviews, and collecting field notes. Yet I had begun to compile an embodied archive, rich with affective and cultural evidence, that would motivate my more formal research pursuits. What began as a profound sense of camaraderie and political conviction ultimately morphed into an intellectual project as well. I wanted to understand why the Migrant Trail Walk felt so much more sustaining and transformative than other kinds of political engagement, at least by my own barometer. In 2011, as a then-early graduate student, I set out to understand the meanings Migrant Trail participants attach to their weeklong journey and the impacts of this kind of activism.

There is a vast literature on the challenges of gaining access to and trust from research participants, the ethics of navigating power differentials between the researcher and researched, and the complex obligations of those doing research with activist groups with whom they are aligned (Geertz, 1974; Naples, 2003; Hale, 2008). Migrant Trail participants tend to be highly educated, with many participants in any given year being students in college and graduate programs, K–12 educators, and college professors. Some border activists are nevertheless skeptical of researchers, journalists, and even politicians who they have seen "parachute" into border communities, pursue their respective projects, and leave without reciprocity or accountability to those from whom they have extracted time and resources. I was well aware of this dynamic when I requested permission from organizers to administer surveys and conduct interviews during the 2011 Migrant Trail Walk, which would be my fourth time doing the walk.

I had likely earned organizers' trust in a number of ways. We had common experiences and memories from prior walks, increasingly overlapping social networks, and I had taken on greater leadership over the years, allowing me to demonstrate competence and care. I would suggest that shared experiences of embodied vulnerability on the walk enhanced a sense of mutual trust. Indeed, one of my central research findings would ultimately point to the role of shared physicality on the Migrant Trail as helping participants to forge a sense of solidarity with each other (Russo, 2014). Having been sweaty and dirty, shared blisters and discomfort in the heat, slept and attended to bodily functions in close proximity with each other swiftly builds a sense of intimacy and close connection. Some participants even pointed to a kind of dissolution of the self as being part and parcel of sharing in the affective experiences of embodied vulnerability in close community over time. As Susan, a longtime Migrant Trail participant observed,

> The desert wears you down and this experience kind of breaks away at those barriers that we hold up in our regular lives. We're able to feel things just being out here in the context of this community; we're having a shared experience. And so we kind of have a little bit of an idea of what we're all experiencing. That creates a space for being open and for those emotional things to happen.

A number of sociological thinkers have found that shared physical duress, especially when undertaken in contexts of common intention, often religious ones, can strengthen social bonds between practitioners (Durkheim, 1912; Glucklich, 2003). Some movement research points to a similar dynamic in situations of high-risk activism, though the role of shared embodiment has not been explicitly addressed (McAdam, 1988; Jasper, 2018). What was ultimately a research finding—that the shared embodiment of protest helps to forge intragroup solidarity—was also methodologically significant as I asked for permission to begin the formal research phase of my work.

The impacts of my bodily vulnerability emerged as both help and hindrance during the first year of data collection on the Migrant Trail, when I administered surveys to nearly all participants and conducted hours of interviews in addition to the modality of observant participation (Vargas, 2006). Though I had earned participants' trust, sheer physical exhaustion limited my ability to pitch in as I had done in previous years. I endeavored to contribute to the daily tasks of the walk, such as setting up camp and helping newer participants, just as I had in previous years. Yet with my new obligations as a researcher, I found my energy taxed in ways that it had not been before. After hours of walking, chatting with participants, and taking field notes during breaks, I often doubted my ability to finish the final portion of each day's walk. When we reached our destination, I would often sit in private silence for an extended time rather than helping to set up shade or dig commodes. After an afternoon of conducting interviews or administering surveys, hours when most participants are napping and recovering from the morning walk, I wanted nothing more than to lie down on my sleeping pad. Attending a group meeting at the end of a long day is rarely appealing, even if it is necessary for group communication and basic logistics planning. Having spent the day both walking and collecting data made our evening gatherings especially challenging. During one meeting, I simply dodged my obligations, settling onto my sleeping bag in the still hot dusk and guiltily drifting into unconsciousness.

The researcher's embodied self is on display and up for scrutiny in ways that shape the task of data collection (Turner and Norwood, 2013). Many remarked on the way my fatigue showed up throughout the week. Participants are instructed to partake in a collective care practice by regularly checking for the early signs of heat fatigue and dehydration that many walkers experience. Those who knew me well from prior years continually asked if I was okay and, once reassured that I was not sick, noted that I seemed to be more distant than usual. My affective display was made socially meaningful in ways that I wished to disguise. I felt disappointed by my limitations as both participant and researcher, worrying that my low energy and frequent absences risked eroding trust among the long-term organizers who had invited me in to do research. I also was aware that my physiological limits narrowed the scope of my daily attention, making it impossible to engage in the range of conversations and spaces for observation that I believed I should. My body, it seemed, constrained my ability to be as fully observant and fully participatory as I had wished (Vargas, 2006).

Such limitations could in some ways be mitigated by the fact that I was able to return to the walk over subsequent years, engaging more fully in observant participation without also conducting interviews and surveys in the desert. The point remains, however, that engaging in physically demanding activities as an observant participant can interrupt the kinds of habituated embodiment, themselves structured by social power, that might allow some researchers to ignore the methodological ramifications of their particular embodiment.

The affective experience of unsettled embodiment forced me to acknowledge my body's role in the research enterprise, even when doing so was not my preference. Yet such affective experiences also motivated me to explore how participants discern meaning from physically demanding protest. I now pivot from methodological considerations to an analysis of just this, exploring how Migrant Trail participants make sense of their affective experiences of embodied vulnerability as instantiations of solidarity.

## Interpreting labors

I began my first Migrant Trail Walk with a head cold. I had been so physically miserable the week prior that I considered foregoing the walk altogether. I was undeniably anxious about spending a week with a group of strangers in an activity intended to be uncomfortable. When the 50 of us walkers arrived at our first campsite on the Buenos Aires National Wildlife Reserve, I struggled alone to erect the tent my friend had lent me, warning that I needed such a thing to guard against scorpions and venomous snakes. It was near sunset and still 90 degrees. Having been up since dawn packing trailers, caravanning to the border, walking through the heat of the day, missing a turn, and taking in everything new and tragic about migrant deaths, I was exhausted, hungry, and disoriented. As it turned out, I also was completely unable to pitch a tent. I struggled with my one-person shelter for several minutes, too embarrassed to admit I did not know how it worked or to seek help. I sat in the shambles of nylon, metal posts, and stakes, facing away from the group, sobbing silently. I hoped, correctly as it turned out, that between my sunglasses and huge hat brim, and the fact that everyone else was too busy setting up their own tents, that no one would notice the new girl weeping at the edge of camp.

By the end of that week, I would feel intense camaraderie with other walk participants, and a deep sense of purpose, reflecting on the absurdity that during my first evening a misbehaving tent had brought me to tears. How did I move from a sense of isolation, focused on my petty discomforts in the desert, to a profound sense of connection with my fellow travelers and a deepened commitment to a cause?

I begin with my tent story to demonstrate that there is nothing inherent in experiences of bodily vulnerability that makes uncomfortable affect somehow destined to blossom into feelings of solidarity. Indeed, at the height of my own experiences of bodily vulnerability on the Migrant Trail Walk, I have sometimes felt isolated, self-conscious, and despairing. This was true when I struggled with a tent and, years later, at the height of data collection. At the same time, those undertaking the solidarity practices I study are not blank slates; the affective experiences of embodied vulnerability that accompany their activism are not "up for interpretive grabs." Most of the activists in my study, myself included, embark on physically demanding and sometimes high-risk practices of solidarity with well-considered intentions rooted in rich cultural systems of meaning. These activists turn to a set of commonly held interpretive resources to make sense of the sense experiences of bodily vulnerability within a practice of solidarity. Yet these frameworks for sensemaking need to be continually and collectively mobilized. In this section, I consider accounts from Migrant Trail participants that demonstrate the interpretive maneuvers by which participants understand the affective experiences of embodied vulnerability as instantiations of solidarity. These accounts are selected for the interpretive labor they reveal, not because they are exemplary of participant accounts, most of which reveal much less of activists' interpretive efforts.

> I think I kind of got it when my feet hurt so badly and knowing that it's like this but just a gazillion times worse is how migrants feel at night when it's dark and hiding out, walking on bare flesh. I'm walking and hurting and I have the words in my head, like Teresa said, "For every step you hurt, think of your brothers and sisters." (Adelheid, first-time Migrant Trail Walk participant)

Adelheid gives a fairly explicit account of how she gets from the sense experiences of embodied vulnerability—"feet hurt so badly," "I'm walking and hurting"—to a *feeling* of solidarity with crossing migrants. Key to Adelheid's interpretive pathway are the words of one of the walk's longtime participants, Teresa. During an Indigenous blessing ceremony at the Migrant Trail's beginning, Teresa unravels a string of hundreds of handmade prayer ties. Each tie symbolizes a life lost in the Arizona desert that year. As Teresa wraps the string of prayer ties around its stick so that we can carry it through the desert, she reminds us to think of our migrant "brothers and sisters" for every step that we hurt.

Across the groups that I study, there is a common acknowledgment that insofar as we are all vulnerable we have a common obligation to protect and care for others across the stratification of such vulnerability. Teresa's language of "brothers and sisters," a familial lexicon that is used across these groups, evinces such an understanding. These groups believe that the US security state's policies violate our obligation to care for one another, predicating the supposed security of some on the annihilation and abandonment of others. In their efforts to bear witness to this violence, these groups use embodied tactics that permit them to better see and feel violence and then expose such injustices to others. When they give up food, physical comfort, and in some cases their own safety, these activists find that unsettling affect can feel like a collective force, a bodily insistence to pay attention to injustice. As one Witness Against Torture participant explained the impact of fasting, "I cannot look away." In this way, embodied vulnerability becomes a mechanism to forge what Asia Friedman (2011) terms, albeit in a very different context, "perceptual communities" (p 188). These activists work collectively in order to perceive and then resist the narrow ways of seeing and knowing that constitute the dominant sociopolitical order. Yet, as Adelheid reveals, each movement context also provides important tools for interpreting bodily discomfort as a way of perceiving state violence and enacting solidarity with the state's targets. For Adelheid, these tools include the collective ritual of an Indigenous blessing ceremony, the symbolism of prayer ties, and Teresa's words, as but three specific examples.

Many participants in these groups, though certainly not all, draw on religious frameworks in assigning value and meaning to solidarity tactics. Various faith traditions pursue bodily mortification as a pathway toward sacred experience (Glucklich, 2003). Where an onlooker might see blisters, headaches, hunger, and jail time as barriers to collective action, participants in these groups find such experiences to be socially and often spiritually empowering. Yet, not all participants found the process of attaching this meaning system to physically demanding solidarity activism to be a seamless one. For instance, longtime Migrant Trail participant Molly noted,

> We're all from different backgrounds and varied levels of faith or spirituality and so it can't be at the forefront. But for me what it's become very personally—I use this word pilgrimage. I used it at first a little strangely, like it didn't fit well. But I now claim that as what I do. I think it's a pilgrimage of sorts for the betterment of humanity and then there's a whole kind of interior spiritual thing that happens for me.

Molly's account of coming to call the Migrant Trail Walk a "pilgrimage" is notable on a few levels. First, Molly reveals the complex interpretive work that happens around religion in movement contexts that maintain interfaith roots and traditions while also endeavoring to be religiously open. None of the groups I studied espouse an official religious orientation, though many have origins in radical Christian traditions. Across these groups, atheists get arrested alongside nuns; Muslims fast and protest next to Jews. Thus, at one level, Molly was reticent to ascribe a religious intent to her desert protest in a movement context that downplays religiosity in an effort to be inclusive. At another level, Molly also seems to give voice to the uneasy work of interpreting affect; she struggles over some years to capture the complex affective experiences of the desert journey with a single term. This seems to mirror Gould's (2009) insight that in the effort to capture that which eludes language, to bring affect into the realm of social meaning, the affect itself is necessarily bounded and turned into something else. On a third level, it is noteworthy that Molly seems to understand her attribution of meaning to the walk as deeply personal, intimate, and interior. This experience is, of course, true in every sense, in that it is what she *feels*. At the same time, her profound sense of this "interior spiritual thing that happens for me" is in fact a common, patterned one for Migrant Trail participants, especially those who have some familiarity with religious practices. In this way we see how the energetic force of affect, and the spiritual meaning attributed to it, *feels* interior and unique even though much of this experience is shared by others in the same movement context.

> The walking itself has taken a profound physical and emotional toll on me. Seeing the climate, the border patrol driving by and just rounding up people, loading them up on buses. Then you just see stuff on the road—a bottle, footprints. You just take a step back and think, "They're probably making this passage right now, in our midst." And they don't have the luxuries that we have. They probably have like a four-liter jug of water or whatever, but it's desperate compared to our situation.
> (Rory, first-time Migrant Trail Walk participant)

Hailing from the much cooler territory of Manitoba, Canada, Rory was one of the walk participants who struggled the most with the desert heat. He also misplaced his eyeglasses on the first night of the walk. During a dinner conversation, Rory admitted that he had, at first, felt sorry for himself when confronted with the walk's discomforts. He noted, however, that in being surrounded by others that shared the intention of enacting solidarity with migrants, he was able to reconsider his own struggle and instead pay attention to those forced into the desert. Sitting, head bowed, recovered glasses smudged with the ubiquitous Sonoran dust, he reflected, "I mean, it's not about me, right?"

Perhaps the most significant interpretive frame for the groups in my study is how participants identify their social privilege. These activists emphasize that their efforts are a mere token or gesture in the face of the incomparable violence faced by the tortured, disappeared, and sequestered. While there is important social diversity in each group, nearly all acknowledge that their choice to bear witness through physically demanding and high-risk tactics is predicated on how their own bodies are protected by race, class, and often able-bodied privilege. These activists understand bodily discomfort and risk as a way to divest from their embodied privileges. By forcing themselves to pay attention to their own and others' embodied vulnerability, they resist the seductions of the dominant order that would have us ignore or be apathetic in the face of the US security state's unequal and racialized exercise of violence (Russo, 2018).[2]

Yet, akin to my experience with erecting my tent, Rory's account reveals how the affect that accompanies embodied vulnerability can engender a sense of self-focus and even self-pity. Having one's physical comforts withdrawn can induce the human organism to pay full and immediate attention to the self. Part of the power of physically demanding, high-risk solidarity activism is that it is part of a communal practice to forge counterhegemonic commitments and interpretations that might otherwise feel counterintuitive. By identifying moments of interpretive labor whereby participants endeavor to make sense of their sense experiences, connecting the affective experiences of embodied vulnerability to the work of solidarity, we glimpse how movements serve as sensemaking projects.

## Interpreting raced and gendered bodies

"I need you to stay right there," the officer announced. My shock quickly dissolved into an understanding of my predicament. My stomach dropped, and I froze in place.

"Wait! Can I explain?" I tried to hide my growing anxiety with a diplomatic measure of calm.

It was November 2013, my first visit to the annual School of the Americas (SOA) Watch vigil, and I had in no way intended to trespass onto the Fort Benning military base.

I knew that the military had erected new fencing after the attacks of September 11, 2001, in order to clearly delineate the permitted space of the vigil from the base. Activists now needed to climb over a fence or go well around it if they wished to engage in civil disobedience by "crossing the line." The cost of crossing had increased significantly as well. First-time crossers now received between three and six months of prison time whereas a mere citation was common in the past. The new procedures sounded ominous, and so I had assumed that the infamous gates of Fort Benning where the protesters had gathered for years would be architecturally obvious. It turns out they are a mere chain link installation at the end of what seems to be a side street. It is quite easy to accidentally end up on military property if coming from another direction.

The well-known chain hotel where I along with many other anti-SOA activists were staying for the weekend is separated from the Fort Benning base by an unmarked road. It is easy to walk across the street. There are no signs, little traffic, grass on either side. I had unintentionally wandered onto the base and approached the two traffic cops to inquire which was the permitted route to meet the protesters.

The two officers, young Black men with the police department of Columbus, Georgia, Fort Benning's adjacent town, did not seem to know what to do with me when I first approached.

"Um, Ma'am? What are you doing here? Are you a protester?"

"I'm trying to meet the protesters," I responded. That's when I had been instructed to stay put.

I tried to speak to the officers, but they showed no interest in engagement, pulling out their radios instead. Less than a minute ensued before another officer in riot gear came roaring up the grassy median on his black ATV, where he stayed seated, engine idling. Another vehicle arrived seconds later, its driver wearing military fatigues and also not exiting the vehicle. By the time the sheriff's department's white sedan pulled up, and this driver, a white middle-aged man, approached me, I was undone.

"Ma'am, what's wrong?" the approaching officer inquired with apparent concern.

I stuttered out what had happened, that I was just a mistaken researcher. "There's just so many of you," I hiccupped through tears. It was a spectacle of police power, and I had been reduced to a terrified, small version of myself.

"We just want to make sure people don't get lost," the officer placated. I did not dare to question the pitiful logic of this explanation. Four vehicles, six officers, and at least three branches of law enforcement deployed to ensure I was not "lost"?

Versed in the legal parameters of a police stop, I gathered myself enough to ask if I was free to leave.

"Yes ma'am," the officer from the sheriff's department nodded.

I hurried back across the road to my hotel, adrenaline pumping, my relief flooding in, wits beginning to return. (Adapted from the author's fieldnotes)

Most ethnographers have moments such as these, though maybe not always so dramatic: experiences that reveal something about the social world into which the researcher has ventured but are not the most exemplary of the phenomena they wish to explore and explain. My encounter with the disproportionate power of the US security state—with the complex identities and tactics of its officers and the dynamics of my own raced and gendered embodiment, which likely protected me from force—seemed potentially trivial and distracting for the purposes of presenting my research. I set out to examine activists that have committed their lives to a certain high-risk practice. Their efforts, in turn, are meant to lift up the realities faced by those who experience the most draconian manifestations of state violence. My initial, thwarted, attempt to make it bodily to the Fort Benning vigil as a lost researcher seemed to distract from both of these projects.

I introduce this story now, however, because it serves as a richly social, affective, and embodied experience that no doubt impacted my understanding of state violence as well as my resistance to it. Previous sections explored how bodily vulnerability shaped my research interest and process as well as how activists attach meanings to their affective experiences. This section foregrounds how our bodies themselves are up for interpretation. Social forces that operate on and through the human body mark us as raced, gendered, and classed, with significant implications for how we will experience bodily vulnerability and what sense we will make of such experiences.

While the social identities into which we will be categorized or choose to belong predate the birth of any individual, our bodies render us legible as certain kinds of social subjects from the moment we are physically constituted. Some critical race feminists have adopted a phenomenological account to demonstrate how this is meaningful for forging consciousness. Linda Martín Alcoff (2005), for instance, explains how the identity categories of race and gender, as they are socially enacted, "are most definitely physical, marked on and through the body, lived as a material experience, visible as surface phenomena, and determinant of economic and political status" (p 102). A particular phenotypic presentation denotes race. A way of dressing, moving, speaking is interpreted as gender. Such categorization, in turn, informs how people, institutions, and policies interact with different bodies.[3] Our lived experiences and the insights they make possible are fundamentally shaped by the way our bodies are socially perceived. When I accidentally trespassed onto the base, I did so as a body that presents as white and as a woman. The situation that ensued and the ways I have come to make sense of it were largely predicated on how raced and gendered, and perhaps also classed, embodiments interacted to shape my sense of embodied vulnerability.

As one example, the privileges that usually accompany my lived experience of whiteness seemed as if they could be withheld, albeit only momentarily. One of these privileges is not having to pay attention to my body's vulnerability in the majority of my lived environments. Building on the work of Frantz Fanon to consider a racial phenomenology, Sara Ahmed (2007) suggests that one way that racism works is through a differential in how bodies access a sense of comfort in their environment. The experience of whiteness, Ahmed suggests, is such that one's body is "so at ease with one's environment that it is hard to distinguish where one's body ends and the world begins" (p 158). A heightened awareness of the body's boundaries, its surface and skin as the site where the self ends and the world begins, is a form of racial consciousness insofar as it is disproportionately borne by people of color. One obvious way that racism works, and reinforces such racial consciousness, is by forcing certain social subjects into a pressing awareness of their embodied vulnerability through "a differential economy of stopping" (Ahmed, 2007, p 161). Ahmed gives the example of Black people disproportionately targeted for police stops. The activists in my research align themselves with the targets of state violence who are similarly racialized through immobility regimes. The policing of human movement looks very different at the US border with Mexico, for example, than it does at other ports of entry where brown bodies are not the assumed border-crosser.

When I was stopped and asked to account for the *why* of my whereabouts, I had a momentary glimpse of what it might mean to be a body "out of place" (Ahmed, 2007) as well as one exposed to the state's frightening display of potential force. My gendered embodiment compounded my sense of vulnerability. I was "caught" as a woman, morphologically smaller than the six men marshalled to interrupt my movement, alone without a witness or a weapon, and confronted by different iterations of masculine armor. The state's paraphernalia of power included guns, batons, and riot gear. It is notable that the only people that presented as not white in this encounter were the two traffic police that appeared to be the least powerful officers at the scene. They ended up playing "bad cops" as juxtaposed to the "good cop" with the sheriff's department. Gender and race intersected in ways that continue to make me uncomfortable upon reflection, though I was grateful at the time to be so easily released. My white womanness, complete with the gendered spectacle of tears, provided a platform for a kind of rescue. Was I merely being saved from my own mistake? Was I somehow being protected, whether consciously or not, from two Black officers following orders who found themselves physically proximate to a frightened, crying white woman? The analysis of social, embodied entanglements here could go on.

The point I wish to highlight is that our bodies themselves are up for interpretation as structured by the legacies of violence and inequality that delineate race, gender, and so on. This shapes our social encounters, and the way we will both experience and attach meaning to moments of embodied vulnerability. My encounter at Fort Benning might not map cleanly onto my research endeavor; it was not purposeful co-engagement with solidarity activists but rather an adjacent accident. Yet this experience, no doubt, gave me certain kinds of insight that helped me to sense and make sense of my object of study. I sensed what it could mean to have my bodily vulnerability exploited, but then I swiftly found my embodied privilege reinstated. I had the affective reaction of bodily shaking and tears, which I interpreted and communicated to others as fear and later also understood to be anger and subsequent relief. All of this was structured by my own race and gender as well as the race and gender of those with whom I interacted. More obliquely, it seems I may have also glimpsed how the agents of state power are themselves caught within systems not of their making. Did I witness legacies of racial inequality showing up in the state's ranks, with white male officers holding more prestigious stations with greater authority and a wider range of permissions than Black male officers? The solidarity activists in my study have complex assessments of the officers of the state, seeking to acknowledge their complex humanity as tied into a larger, venal system.

My own encounter had little in common with the carefully planned civil disobedience that routinely brings the groups I study into contact with arresting officers. In this sense, my encounter evoked an affective experience of embodied vulnerability without the same interpretive resources by which solidarity activists make collective sense of their high-risk activism. Yet my unintentional trespass gave me a sliver of insight into the experience of being rendered vulnerable through state force. This allowed me to see and sense contours of the US security state that figured centrally in my study insofar as this state is the target of the activists I research. Given the fact that I have never engaged in civil disobedience as an act of solidarity with the state's targets, my brief encounter perhaps enhanced my ability not just to report on but also to *feel with* those who tell of their horrifying encounters with state force—both the activists I study and the people for whom they bear witness. This *feeling with*, I suggest, can be an important means of learning both from and with social movements as sensemaking projects.

## Conclusion

This chapter argues for the methodological as well as analytic importance of examining felt, embodied experience in social movement research. Reflecting on ethnographic work with solidarity activists contesting the US security state, I explore how embodied vulnerability shapes the research enterprise and how activists work collectively and continuously to make sense of their embodied vulnerability as instantiations of solidarity. As movement scholars move away from predominately structural and historical explanations for protest to emphasize instead the complexities of human agency (Jasper, 2018; Van Ness and Summers-Effler, 2018), there is an increasing need to consider the experiential, and specifically *embodied,* basis of meaning-making and motivation. By suggesting that social movements might fruitfully be considered as *sensemaking* projects, this chapter proposes a broadly phenomenological approach for capturing the embodied and affective dynamics as well as the interpretive maneuvers shaping activists and their movements.

## Acknowledgments

The author is deeply grateful to the book's editors, Anne Marie Champagne and Asia Friedman, who provided generous and incisive feedback on earlier drafts of this manuscript.

## Notes

1. In line with the definition offered by Deborah Gould (2009), I use the term "affect" to mean the range of "nonconscious and unnamed, but nevertheless registered, experiences of bodily energy and intensity that arise in response to stimuli impinging on the body" (p 19).
2. I want to be careful not to exaggerate the role of embodied privilege in the face of state violence during high-risk activism, or even protest events, that do not intend to be high risk at all. During the writing of this chapter, one of the participants in my study was seriously injured by the Buffalo, NY, police force during a racial justice protest, a story that earned national and ultimately global attention (Vigdor et al, 2020).
3. Alcoff (2005) observes how bodies that are not so easily categorized have long been deeply unsettling to social institutions and liable to draw strong cultural responses of fear and disgust. In US society there are elaborate rules and sometimes medical procedures to reconcile such ambiguity. Consider centuries of legal battles around hypodescent and racial mixing (Harris, 1993) or the assumed necessity of surgery for infants with ambiguous genitalia (see, for example, Fausto-Sterling, 2000).

## References

Adler, Jr, G. (2019) *Empathy beyond US Borders: The Challenges of Transnational Civic Engagement*, New York: Cambridge University Press.

Ahmed, S. (2007) 'A phenomenology of whiteness', *Feminist Theory*, 8(2): 149–168.

Alcoff, L.M. (2005) *Visible Identities: Race, Gender, and the Self*, New York: Oxford University Press.

Bendelow, G.A. and Williams, S.J. (1995) 'Transcending the dualisms: towards a sociology of pain', *Sociology of Health and Illness*, 17(2): 139–165.

Butler, J. (2004) *Precarious Life: The Powers of Mourning and Violence*, New York: Verso.

Chadwick, R. (2017) 'Embodied methodologies: challenges, reflections and strategies', *Qualitative Research*, 17(1): 54–74.

Crossley, N. (1995) 'Merleau-Ponty, the elusive body and carnal sociology', *Body and Society*, 1(1): 43–63.

Durkheim, E. (1912) *The Elementary Forms of Religious Life*, translated by K. E. Fields, New York: Free Press, 1995.

Emerson, R., Fretz, R. and Shaw, L. (1995) *Writing Ethnographic Fieldnotes*, Chicago, IL: University of Chicago Press.

Eyerman, R. and Jamison, A. (1991) *Social Movements: A Cognitive Approach*, University Park: Pennsylvania State University Press.

Fausto-Sterling, A. (2000) *Sexing the Body: Gender Politics and the Construction of Sexuality*, New York: Basic Books.

Fiorito, T. (2019) 'Beyond the Dreamers: collective identity and subjectivity in the undocumented youth movement', *Mobilization: An International Quarterly*, 24(3): 345–363.

Friedman, A. (2011) 'Toward a sociology of perception: sight, sex, and gender', *Cultural Sociology*, 5(2): 187–206.

Geertz, C. (1974) '"From the native's point of view": on the nature of anthropological understanding', *Bulletin of the American Academy of Arts and Sciences*, 28(1): 26–45.

Glucklich, A. (2003) *Sacred Pain: Hurting the Body for the Sake of the Soul*, Oxford: Oxford University Press.

Gould, D. (2009) *Moving Politics: Emotion and ACT UP's Fight against AIDS*, Chicago, IL: University of Chicago Press.

Hale, C. (ed) (2008) *Engaging Contradictions: Theory, Politics, and Methods of Activist Scholarship*, Berkeley: University of California Press.

Harris, C. (1993) 'Whiteness as property', *Harvard Law Review*, 106(8): 1707–1791.

Hohle, R. (2009) 'The body and citizenship in social movement research: embodied performances and the deracialized self in the Black civil rights movement 1961–1965', *The Sociological Quarterly*, 50(2): 283–307.

Jasper, J. (2018) *The Emotions of Protest*, Chicago, IL: University of Chicago Press.

Leder, D. (1990) *The Absent Body*, Chicago, IL: University of Chicago Press.

Lyon, M. (1997) 'The material body, social processes and emotion: "Techniques of the Body" revisited', *Body and Society*, 3(1): 83–101.

Maor, M. (2013) '"Do I still belong here?" The body's boundary work in the Israeli fat acceptance movement', *Social Movement Studies*, 12(3): 280–297.

McAdam, D. (1988) *Freedom Summer*, New York: Oxford University Press.

Naples, N. (2003) *Feminism and Method: Ethnography, Discourse Analysis, and Activist Research*, New York: Routledge.

Norris, R.S. (2009) 'The paradox of healing pain', *Religion*, 39(1): 22–33.

Passy, F. and Giugni, M. (2000) 'Life-spheres, networks, and sustained participation in social movements: a phenomenological approach to political commitment', *Sociological Forum*, 15(1): 117–144.

Rodriguez, D. (2006) *Forced Passages: Imprisoned Radical Intellectuals and the U.S. Prison Regime*, Minneapolis: University of Minnesota Press.

Russo, C. (2014) 'Allies forging collective identity: embodiment and emotions on the migrant trail', *Mobilization: An International Quarterly*, 19(1): 67–82.

Russo, C. (2018) *Solidarity in Practice: Moral Protest and the US Security State*, New York: Cambridge University Press.

Sasson-Levy O. and Rapoport, T. (2003) 'Body, gender, and knowledge in protest movements: the Israeli case', *Gender and Society*, 17(3): 379–403.

Sheridan, T.E. and McGuire, R.H. (eds) (2019) *The Border and Its Bodies: The Embodiment of Risk along the U.S.–México Line*, Tucson: University of Arizona Press.

Sutton, B. (2010) *Bodies in Crisis: Culture, Violence, and Women's Resistance in Neoliberal Argentina*, New Brunswick, NJ: Rutgers University Press.

Turner, B.S. (2006) *Vulnerability and Human Rights*, State College: Pennsylvania State University Press.

Turner, P.K. and Norwood, K.M. (2013) 'Body of research: impetus, instrument, and impediment', *Qualitative Inquiry*, 19(9): 696–711.

Van Ness, J. and Summers-Effler, E. (2018) 'Emotions in social movements', in D.A. Snow, S.A. Soule, H. Kriesi and H.J. McCammon (eds) *The Wiley Blackwell Companion to Social Movements*, Chichester: John Wiley and Sons, Ltd, pp 411–428.

Vargas, J.H.C. (2006) *Catching Hell in the City of Angels: Life and Meanings of Blackness in South Central Los Angeles*, Minneapolis: University of Minnesota Press.

Vigdor, N., Victor, D. and Hauser, C. (2020) 'Buffalo police officers suspended after shoving 75-year-old protester', *The New York Times*, June 5.

10

# Our Bodies, Our Disciplines, Our Selves

*Annemarie Jutel*

Where do our choices of disciplines come from? How do we embody our papers or our papers embody us? Rare is the scholar with no embodied connection to their work. We all look at ourselves when we look at something else; that we should look at our bodies is part and parcel of critical thinking about our worlds.

My contribution to this volume is going to be a reflection on how our bodies (often) take us to our disciplines, both consciously and not. I provide this reflection via a retrospective of my own disciplinary work in the sociology of diagnosis.

The sociology of diagnosis is a relatively recent subdiscipline of sociology. It was first suggested as a point of potential interest by Mildred Blaxter in 1978, and then again by Phil Brown in 1990. It started taking off, not unexpectedly, in the era of diagnosis or about 2010. Just as diagnoses were proliferating in number in the International Classification of Diseases (World Health Organization, 2009), as self-diagnosis and crowdsourcing diagnosis started mesmerizing the masses, sociologists also started acknowledging what Blaxter had brought to their attention two decades earlier: that diagnosis was too glibly taken as a simple label for natural facts of disease.

The sociology of diagnosis explores diagnosis as a reflection of social values, beliefs, and power in relation to the material facts of disease. It focuses on understanding how assigning labels to disorders in particular ways affects our experience of disease. While many scholars had focused on what it was like to have a given diagnosis (say, the stigmatizing effect of HIV, the varying identities associated with cancer [Klawiter, 2004], or the bewildering and marginalizing experience of illness for which no diagnosis seems available [Dumit, 2006]), there was little focus on diagnosis itself, not only as a structure in medicine but also as a place at which power converges and social roles are created. Yet diagnosis had, and continues to have, an important definitional role in medicine as well as in social life. More than *an object* of study, the sociology of diagnosis provides *an approach* to studying matters of medical and sociologic concern.

My last book, *Diagnosis: Truths and Tales* (Jutel, 2019), was written to reflect on diagnosis stories. What is the story we tell ourselves, our patients, and the outside world about a serious diagnosis? "It is through stories of diagnosis that we can both understand our reactions and reclaim them," I wrote, noting that "shifting the balance away from the destructive transformative power of the diagnosis requires re-narration and introspection" (Jutel, 2019, p 139). Among other things, I assembled in *Diagnosis* a bouquet of "intellectual documentaries," papers by scholars reflecting on their own serious diagnoses via the disciplines they had at their disposal: linguistics (Fleischman, 1999), sociology (Blaxter, 2009), philosophy (Carel, 2015), and literary criticism (Stoddard Holmes, 2006). What does a linguist write about when she becomes gravely ill? A philosopher? A sociologist? They turn toward their disciplines to reflect on their bodies, as these authors have (most eloquently).

Fleischman (1999) wrote about the language of diagnosis: how the very utterance of the diagnosis had transformative power to divide life into a "before" and an "after," how different registers (professional vs. lay) made different use of the same terms, and how a "metonymic contamination" transfers characteristics of the disease to the affected individual (p 20). According to Fleischman, language both punctuated and transformed the experience of illness and the ability to discuss it. Carel (2015) offered a phenomenological analysis of her own illness, notably using her writing to underline how one can be well in the presence of disease and also how the notion of finitude shapes, rather than undermines, our life. While the way we live today tends to avoid confronting our own death, diagnosis puts it firmly in view and provides, according to Carel, an opportunity to live reflectively.

Awaiting a diagnosis, Blaxter (2009) pondered the stories she told herself and then her doctors about how she understood her problematic X-ray. Paradoxically, as she exposed, her story would be trumped by that of the MRI, "the nature of 'evidence' in a world where neither the individual doctor nor the patient, but rather the measurement and the image, were increasingly becoming the vehicle of decisions" (Blaxter, 2009, p 774). And finally, Stoddard Holmes discussed how not really knowing where an ovary sat, or what it might look like, other than in a kind of Tinkertoy infogram, meant that she could not even consider the possibility of ovarian cancer in relation to her own abdominal symptoms. The absence of ovarian cancer in popular culture, she mused, constitutes an obstacle to early diagnosis.

Maybe these authors would argue that their discipline never had anything to do with their personal embodiment, but they would have to agree that they used their disciplines to understand their embodied quandaries.

But it can be the other way too. From a particular embodied stance (illness, diagnosis, catharsis), the scholar finds their discipline: locating it as a way of understanding, celebrating, or theorizing their physical existence in the world.

That is where I started. My scholarly direction owes much to my own experience of my body. How does my own discipline start from an embodied experience? Discretely, you might be thinking about turning the page, anticipating an episode of oversharing in which I reveal some intimate detail of my life or some past illness. You may already be worrying about my use of the first person, a sign of anti-scholarship: too personal, too subjective.

Maybe you prefer the passive voice, where the subject is absent. You would have liked the editorial guidelines on good scientific writing in *Nature Immunology* in 2005 (hopefully, now the "old days"), which specified that the passive voice "emphasizes the important 'actor' of the manuscript, namely, biology" ("Good data need good writing," 2005). Donna Haraway (1991) refers to this as "disembodied scientific objectivity" (p 185), a way of writing that infers but in no way ensures the neutral positioning of the observer.

But this chapter is "light touch" embodiment. You will not be subjected to stories of pathology but to stories of how I came to my understanding about the location of power and the social generation of values. And, to be clear, even while I landed in diagnosis, my embodied story of the sociology of diagnosis does not start in disease, it starts in gender.

In 1995, I learned what "gender" meant, as distinct from biological "sex." I had used the word previously. I was 34 years old, and while I had not spent my life under a rock, I did not really know what it was until I went back to university, primed to do a degree in physical education. I had decided to return to study after 15 years of nursing. While I was a nurse, I was also an elite runner, and I was a member of the temple of running. At the time, I thought that everyone could benefit from a bit of a jog.

One might imagine my choice of nursing as one connected to a pious altruism, when it was really a misplaced belief that nursing was a health-oriented profession somehow related to running. I had never been in a hospital, or been ill in my life, so there was little experiential (and I now know, theoretical) evidence to support this connection. Neither nursing nor running is, in fact, health oriented, and yet both would uncritically claim to be so. Running: Sport. Nursing: Sickness. Either one of these analogies would deserve an entire chapter. I will leave that as is, other than to comment on the number of surgeries I have had to keep me running and the number of my running friends who died in middle age. Running was not the cardiovascular panacea we had believed it to be.

When I returned to university to study, I felt certain that I would be able to find ways of encouraging more women to join this cult of running. These "ways," I also was certain, would be anchored in science. The word "women" could have been a clue that my work needed to be about gender, but until then, I understood gender to be the M/F on an application form. It was a label affixed uncritically to dichotomous biological facts. I was to learn more about it from my lecturer in PHSE204: History of Sport.

Starting in the second year of the program, having gotten credit for courses I had taken in nursing school, and amid the long list of required courses, I reluctantly settled in to courses, such as PHSE204: History of Sport, on subjects I presumed totally irrelevant to my missionary project of developing women runners. What I did not realize was that understanding the various ways in which women engaged (or didn't) in physical activity at different points in modern history—as well as how the notion of "woman" was both unitary and not—would shine a very different light on what I had understood to be a scientific problem.

Examining the social roles assigned to women with the critical distance that history can provide revealed an explanation, which science could not have brought to light, for how women engage (or not) in physical activity. My lecturer, Douglas Booth, who would become my doctoral supervisor, assigned a chapter from Patricia Vertinsky's (1994) *The Eternally Wounded Woman* about Victorian attitudes to menstruation in the middle classes. I hastily ordered the book, proudly told Doug that I had bought it and read it cover to cover. I will not embarrass myself or my readers with stories of my own menstruation, other than to say that I had not previously considered how menstruation contributed to anything other than a need to plan and hide: Would anything show when I was running? Did I need to slip a pad in my purse? Understanding menstruation as a contributing factor toward women's nonengagement in physical activity was revelatory in surprising ways.

Vertinsky described a Newtonian approach to menstruation. Since energy could neither be created nor destroyed, each menstrual cycle was seen as an important depletion of women's physical reserves, rendering them feeble and "eternally wounded," a stance aptly captured by the words of the president of the American Gynecological Association in 1900:

> Many a young life is battered and forever crippled in the breakers of puberty; if it cross [sic] these unharmed and is not dashed to pieces on the rock of childbirth, it may still ground on the ever-recurring shallows of menstruation, and, lastly, upon the final bar of the menopause ere protection is found in the unruffled waters of the harbor beyond the reach of the sexual storms. (Engelmann, 1900, pp 9–10)

In learning about gender, I learned about critical reflection: the same critical reflection that I try to instill in my students when they walk in the door at university. Things are not as they seem. Scratch the surface. What is going on? What forces are at play? Where is power located?

Motivated by Vertinsky's interest in the historical construction of female frailty, which I could understand, I decided to expand on Vertinsky's work by exploring menstrual product advertising in historical copies of New Zealand women's magazines. This was my honors research project. I spent the summer in library stacks breathing in the dust of the decades and collecting gems like "Poise at trying times is easily attained through using Santex or Sannette" and "Modess, because …"

So, I had discovered the social construction of gender, but I had not yet understood what theoretical framing was or how to find a theoretical frame. Sure, gender was one, but it was not specific enough. And—as I support students to find their own theoretical frames today—I realize that my problem was that I had not yet read enough. I can remember asking my husband, a film and media studies lecturer, "So how do you find one [a theoretical frame]?"—"It's not like you can just pull one off of the shelf!" I interjected, indignant. As students, our shelves are too bare, and it is only as they progressively become populated (volumated?) that we have theories upon which to draw.

I found my theory when I stumbled across Iris Marion Young's (1980) "Throwing Like a Girl," in which she described a kind of "feminine movement" in line with the constructed frailty that Vertinsky wrote about. Feminine movement, as she described it, included three typical stances: restricting the amount of space available for engagement in the world; fragmenting the body, rather than experiencing it as a transcendent whole; and treating the body like a fragile object. What she brought *en sus* was a philosophical reflection regarding the effects this constructed frailty has on the experience of the subject and her engagement with the world.

The theoretical framework I put together from Young and Vertinsky found additional support in Drew Leder's (1990) arguments on the phenomenon of disappearance: the body of the transcendent subject is not perceived, for it disappears in favor of subjective intentions. Presto!

What this meant to me was that everything that brought the female body forward in the consciousness of the subject also somehow constrained it. How can a young girl engage freely and unreservedly in physical activity if she is always at the same time protecting herself like a fragile object? The "presencing" of the body is a barrier to its fulfilment. These advertisements—advocating a need for extraneous support for normal biological function, referring to menstruation as dangerous or trying, and presenting the woman as always poised and pretty—were all presencing discourses.

I could see this directly in my own experience as a runner. This "feminine movement" was typical of even ferocious cross country runners like myself. Here is one example. At about the same time as I was getting ready to explore this question further, I was also competing on a national stage and coaching the cross country teams at both the Otago Boys' High School (OBHS) and the Otago Girls' High School (OGHS). Both teams were preparing to run the national high school cross country championships. This event, unlike the provincial races to which they were accustomed, required them to jump steeple chase hurdles. So, I had to teach the runners how to "take the hurdles." I invited my husband to give the demonstration.

"Why not me?" You may be asking. "Weren't YOU the coach?"

You would be right. It was my job, but I could not do it. "I can't take the hurdles!" I would have wailed, slightly embarrassed, had you asked me at the time. My husband was a former steeple chase runner; I knew he would not hesitate to do it.

Come demonstration day, both teams—OBHS and OGHS—came to the track to watch my husband hurdle and then try hurdling themselves. We set up two hurdles in different locations, one for the boys and one for the girls so they did not have to watch one another. The boys just ran up to the hurdle and "took" the hurdle. I was not even sure why training was necessary. They just hurdled.

The girls universally baulked and squealed, as I would have myself. Not one made it over at her first attempt. That evening, I asked my then-gangly 13-year-old son, a member of the boys' team, how it was that he knew how to take the hurdle. "I just had to," he said.

The girls were nervous. They saw their bodies as fragile and vulnerable, just as I did. They were capable runners, taller for the most part than their just-pubescent male counterparts, and more experienced on a competitive stage, but they protected themselves. Instead of disappearing in favor of their subjective intention to hurdle, the girls' bodies came forward in their consciousness. This is the presencing body that Leder's (1990) theoretical work enabled me to "see."

Fast forward a year or so: honors project completed (title: "'I Can't! I've Got My Period!' Menstrual Mythology: The Link between Disappearance and Feminine Movement"); I have been invited to write about it for a collection (a big deal for a simple honors graduate) (see Jutel, 2004); and I am getting ready to do a PhD. I am not quite sure what my topic will be, but I am confident that the way is going to become clear. I am still doing a few nursing shifts a week. I am in the dressing room of the neonatal ICU putting on my scrubs, ready to do my shift. My colleague Lesley is in the room with me, getting ready to go home. I am a few years younger than her, but I am almost 40. I am still a competitive runner and probably ran to work that day (it was all downhill from the house, as well as quicker and smarter than using the car). As I pulled off my top, Lesley looked at my skinny, muscled body and commented:

"You're so good!"
"Hunh?" I must have mumbled.
"Look!" she replied, as she pinched her own tummy, showing a modest amount of subcutaneous adipose tissue. "I'm BAD!"

That was it. Riding on the back of Young's (1980) feminine movement, and Leder's (1990) disappearing body, I had an *aha* moment about the subject of my PhD thesis. I would explore feminine self-scrutiny, that practice of carefully examining the body, of pinching, prodding, and stretching to discover and then presumably redress a continual parade of flaws: pluck your eyebrows, rouge your lips, do your steps, sit up straight!

But here I am also asking: How do we as women (in particular) come to see "truths" about our inner selves inscribed upon our bodies? Of course, the critical scholar should start by querying whether or not there even is an inner and an outer. But in this case, the idea that our respective moral qualities should inscribe themselves upon our abdomens was an irresistible matter to explore. My PhD was to be entitled "Visions of Vice: Appearance and Policy in Feminine Self-Scrutiny."

I undertook this study using a mishmash of cultural history, sociology, philosophy, and any other available technique I could get my hands on that could help me demonstrate how we saw correspondence between "inside" and "outside." I learned, for example, about the physiognomists who thought they could determine things like character, criminality, mental illness, and racial purity on the basis of the size of different body parts. Lavater (1855) generated a massive catalog in which he assigned personality traits to physical signs. "Can any benevolent, wise, or virtuous man, look, or walk, thus?" he wrote in his *Essays on Physiognomy* (plate IX), to caption an etching of a man of medium build, hands in pockets, tricorne under his arm, receding hairline and chin.

The phrenologists were drawn to the skull as their means for accessing inner truth. A prominent occipital bone might be, for example, a sign of "philoprogenitiveness (the capacity to love and care for children and small animals)" (Fowler and Fowler, 1857, p 54), while self-esteem would be evidenced by a prominent, rather than sloping, crown (p 81).

From the physiognomists to the phrenologists, as well as from the Renaissance portrait artists arranging marriages to the Victorians trying to irradicate the scourge of onanism (because masturbation "shows" in the complexion and in the shadows under the self-abuser's eyes), I sought to identify the (gendered) "duty to beauty" as a moral endeavor. Even advertisements for beauty products or exercises to "get that healthy glow!" caught my attention.

As I got close to submitting my thesis, my supervisor had some doubts about my approach. He wavered over the technique. "It's not really cultural history. You don't give enough context," he fretted. I was his first PhD student; this was my first PhD. Neither of us really knew. I wrote it like a book. (I *had* written books before: how-to running books.)

I would be nervous today if one of my students was as methodologically unspecific as I was at the time. Thank heavens MY supervisor was brave enough to let me forge ahead. I did have a sort of instinctive idea about what I was doing, or how it could be justified, that I called, probably incorrectly, *genealogy*. There was something about things that were done before and things that were done today that needed revealing. It was in line with the Māori whakapapa (Taonui, 2011), and slightly Foucauldian, but really it was something else.[1]

I had an exchange with Joan Brumberg, whose *Fasting Girls* (2000) was one of my secondary sources. I cannot remember exactly what I asked her, probably something about did she think that there was something in *anorexia mirabilis* that she saw reflected in contemporary eating disorders. She answered, "You DO know that my work is historical, right?" as if I were a journalist looking for a bite, having only read the back cover. Of course, I did, and I thought that made it still relevant today, but clearly not everyone did.

What was my sample? My population? Irrelevant, I thought. I was working with ideas, not "cases." The importance was in revealing how the inner–outer equation pervaded discourses, eras, and media. I would realize, almost a decade later, that I was looking for social patterns (Zerubavel, 2007). "Social pattern analysts," Zerubavel (2007) wrote, "are thus purposefully oblivious to the idiosyncratic features of the communities, events, or situations they study, looking for general *patterns* that transcend the specific instantiations" (p 133). It was Tom DeGloma, editor of this series (and a "Zerubavelian" like me), who sent me Zerubavel's article on social patterns. "We needed a way to describe this rich way of thinking about social phenomenon," he wrote. "Trust Eviatar to give us a methodological defense!" (T. DeGloma, personal communication, March 12, 2013).

Zerubavel's interpretive approach assembles pieces from broad-ranging sources and eras. "It is the search for cross-contextual similarity across seemingly dissimilar phenomena that so distinctly characterizes the formal sociological imagination" (2007, p 136), he explained in his article on social pattern analysis. It echoes, to my ears, the admonition of C. Wright Mills (1970), who wrote that "no social study that does not come back to the problems of biography, of history and of their intersections within a society has completed its intellectual journey" (p 6).

In addition to working with ideas, I also was using an interpretive, non-positivist methodology to overturn what I saw as a dogmatic overreliance on empirical method over interpretation in nursing scholarship, an aim that was progressively and irreversibly alienating me from my former colleagues (Jutel, 2008, 2012). Further, I was appalled at some of the highly celebrated empirical work I saw presented at American Sociological Association (ASA) conferences. The uncritical use of categories such as "race" to reveal social "problems" presented the same (worse) challenge that Blaxter (1978) brought to our attention in her article "Diagnosis as Category and Process," notably, that the "examination of the relevant systems of categorization and how they are used, or tolerated, or circumvented, may well demonstrate something of the nature of the practical activity concerned" (p 17). There is a long story behind race categories that bears telling.

Robin Wall Kimmerer (2021), member of the Citizen Potawatomi Nation, underlined this same conundrum, "between systems of categorization and how they are used" (Blaxter, 1978, p 17), when she commented that English is noun- rather than verb-based. Unlike many Indigenous languages, the speakers I saw at ASA conferences were sociologically resigned to using non-Indigenous, noun-based idioms that include taxonomic references to "race." Kimmerer imagined what an encounter between Linnaeus, the father of Western taxonomy, and Nanabozho, the great "namer" of the Potawatomi people, might look like. It probably looked something like a meeting between many of those empirical sociologists I am calling out and an aboriginal member of [fill in the blank with the precolonized name of any nation]. Awkward? Or mutually curious?

Rooted as they were in positivist epistemology, the disciplinary norms of nursing, which eschewed interpretive methods, and the uncritical empiricism of mainstream sociology too often put forth simplistic understandings of objectivity and validity premised on eliminating the researcher's subjective perspective (and embodied experience and location) from the research process. Feminist epistemologies (Smith, 1987; Collins, 1990; Haraway, 1991; Harding, 1991, 1993) as well as broader post-positivist interpretive and critical traditions in social theory (eg, Weber, 1949; Kuhn, 1962; see also Agger, 2013) have long problematized the possibility and desirability of evacuating the researcher's social location and experience—which arguably always begins from their embodiment—from the research process. Both the research methodology of my thesis and my guiding claim in this chapter that, whether we realize it or not, as scholars our embodied experience is at the root of our academic disciplines join in this tradition of challenging disembodied positivist epistemologies.

To finish the story of my own embodied journey to sociology, however, I must return to the PhD.

I did try to conform a little bit to what I thought a PhD must be about, and I wrote a concluding chapter that was a kind of policy review. I tried to pick out the enduring patterns from my big, trans-epochal, trans-media, trans-disciplinary project on the aesthetics of vice to see how they imprinted contemporary health policies concerned with weight. Probably the most important thing to come out of that in relation to the sociology of diagnosis (not yet a field, by the way) was how "overweight" was discursively constructed as a "thing" with its own symptoms, warning signs, and consequences, rather than simply, as my historical work had shown, a measure of deviation from a normative weight value.

Why it had become a diagnosis, I argued, had to do with the convergence of two important phenomena. As I wrote in my 2006 article in *Social Science and Medicine*, "the first is the belief in the neutrality of quantification, and the objectivity that measurement brings to qualitative description. The second is the importance attributed to normative appearance in health" (Jutel, 2006a, p 2268).

I came to realize that "thingness," which was at the root of the emergence of *overweight* as a category of disease, underpinned all diagnoses. I wondered: How do we come to see something as worthy of thingness and of assigning it a concordant label? I was drawn to this question of thingness by virtue of my curiosity and my job history. My first postdoc job was as a research fellow on a project relating to stillbirth in the pediatrics department. As I did the literature review for the primary investigator, I was struck by the fact that *stillbirth* was an almost meaningless term, given the variety of definitions across nations, and even states (Jutel, 2006b). Another historical diagnosis I stumbled across, *drapetomania*, categorizes a disease that causes slaves to run away. Both of these diagnoses (stillbirth and drapetomania) are examples of the political and cultural context in which diagnoses are conceptualized. The former underscores the fraught nature of pregnancy amid the pro-life/pro-choice movements, and the latter illustrates how diagnosis enacts and reinforces social power.

Thingness was also the basis for my reflection on Female Hypoactive Sexual Desire Disorder whose ontological status owed much to the pharmaceutical industry (Jutel, 2010). It was the perfect heuristic for revealing this encroachment of industry marketing on disease creation. I was looking for a way of revealing how the pharmaceutical industry messes with popular definitions of health and disease. I do not actually remember how I stumbled across this as an example, but it was powerful. In this case, an industry craving a pink Viagra and the potential windfall it could provide for shareholders was aggressively casting low libido as illness and pills as a solution (Jutel and Mintzes, 2017).

At this point, reader, if you believe my point of departure, in which I maintained that I would not embarrass you with intimate detail, you may surmise (or hope) that I am drifting away from my own embodied departure as I recount the range of conditions, experienced by other embodied beings, that were to become the focus of my scholarship. You would not be mistaken. I did not need to experience stillbirth or low libido to find the direction in which my focus on diagnoses would lead me. Indeed, even overweight was not a diagnosis I had ever confronted, yet it was my experience of running and my runner's body that led me to its discovery as more-than-a-label.

And, once discovered as an important point of critical reflection, *diagnosis* led me into the bodies of others: into the bodies of those who were stigmatized, effaced, categorized, and prioritized as a result of their diagnoses. Suzanne Fleischman (1999, p 6) wrote of and through her own diagnosis that "when a person suffers from a major illness, the affected organ or body part is never *just* a body part. Illnesses serve to activate the metaphoric and symbolic meanings that body parts take on in every culture." As a linguist facing her own, ultimately terminal, illness, she mused about the lexical resources for understanding disease. As she offered up her own body, discipline, and self, my own discipline found new branches.

Diagnosis is everywhere. It is the title, as well as topic, of a Netflix series, one that follows the trajectory of people without diagnoses for debilitating conditions, crowdsourcing candidate diagnoses to help. It is a narrative trope in fiction (Jutel, 2016). It is the focus of films and television shows (Jutel and Jutel, 2017). It infuses graphic novels and cartoons (Morrison et al, 2011). I read about "sick" buildings and bumble bees with Alzheimer's-like disease. Regular emotions are assigned disease labels (Horwitz and Wakefield, 2007), as are what we might have once considered "normal" behaviors (Conrad, 2007). Of course, at the same time, diseased states are also finding their way into normality (Scott, 1990; Kirk and Kutchins, 1992), as psychiatry, serving as the guardian of deviance and normality, defines both what is "bad" and what is "sick" (Conrad and Schneider, 1980; Rosenberg, 2006).

And as this takes place, I find myself returning to Drew Leder's work on the absent body. He writes, "While in one sense the body is the most abiding and inescapable presence in our lives, it is also characterised by its absence," and further, that "'freeing oneself' from the body takes on a positive valuation" (Leder, 1990, pp 1, 69).

I think about his theory through my own body. As a much older woman, I am now a cyclist rather than a runner. I call my mountain bike my "wheel chair"; it has wheels and I mainly sit on it. Thinking about the acquisition of any skill in cycling, say, taking a corner on a mountain trail, to start with, it is all in the body. I think about where I am going: I shift down well ahead of time, roll out around the corner, then bank around the turn, shoulder down, knee up. Whew! Made it. So many thoughts and bodily positions to keep in my mind. It is difficult. But, once the skill is acquired, I simply "take the corner." I lose my awareness of my knee, of the lines. I just ride.

And so it is in our disciplines as well. It is not that our embodied experiences are any less important. They remain pivotal, but they become, once more, experiences *qua* experiences as we use our disciplinary perspectives to open us to greater understandings of experiences beyond our personal reference.

This is how I understand the absent body. It is the focus on the intention (get around the corner) rather than on my body's stance in relation to the corner that allows me to boldly pursue my intentions. The same is true in academe. We start with ourselves and learn about what greater truths we can acquire beyond ourselves, our bodies, and then our disciplines. We riff off of the former to get to the latter. Then, and thenceforth, we have a solid frame for understanding myriad other conundrums.

The body is there, and then it vanishes. It was necessary, as it was on the bike, to have awareness in order to land, for many of us, on the scholarly direction that suits us. But, at the same time, we somehow have to shed that body and ride the bike with *biking* rather than *body* in the foreground. We have to get away from our bodies to do something even better.

At first glance, this idea of leaving the body behind might appear to replicate sociology's historically disembodied approach (Turner, 1984; Shilling, 2012). But I am arguing for something quite different from a totally missing body, or even the body as an unacknowledged "absent presence" (Shilling, 2012). I am asserting that we are embodied, but that we have to leave our own personalized space of embodiment to reap broader understandings of bodies at large. My uneventful menstrual history has, at the same time, little and everything to do with the fragilized female described historically by Vertinsky, explained by Young, theorized by me (using Leder), and witnessed at the track where my husband and I set up the steeple chase hurdles.

I do not think that my work has anything to do with my personalized embodiment any more. I hope it stays that way. Writing my last book on the diagnostic moment, I went through periods of magical thinking when I hoped that writing about serious diagnoses would not mean I would then have one. There. I have written that down. So far, so good. Have I jinxed anything? Yikes! And, *de nouveau*, I have critical distance that my departure from my own experience of myself allows me. I can go beyond my personal experience now that I have theorized it, transposed it, reshaped it, and taken it back.

Oh, and yes, at age 60-mumble, I can pinch my tummy fat; and because I am a sociologist, I can remember why I have to fight to remind myself that it does not mean I am bad.

**Note**

1 This is a traditional genealogical framework that "links all animate and inanimate, known and unknown phenomena in the terrestrial and spiritual worlds. Whakapapa therefore binds all things. It maps relationships so that mythology, legend, history, knowledge, tikanga (custom), philosophies and spiritualities are organised, preserved and transmitted from one generation to the next" (Taonui, 2011).

**References**

Agger, B. (2013) *Critical Social Theories* (3rd edn), Oxford: Oxford University Press.

Blaxter, M. (1978) 'Diagnosis as category and process: the case of alcoholism', *Social Science and Medicine*, 12: 9–17.

Blaxter, M. (2009) 'The case of the vanishing patient? Image and experience', *Sociology of Health and Illness*, 31(5): 762–778.

Brown, P. (1990) 'The name game: toward a sociology of diagnosis', *The Journal of Mind and Behavior*, 11(3–4): 385–406.

Brumberg, J.J. (2000) *Fasting Girls: The History of Anorexia Nervosa*, New York: Vintage Books.

Carel, H. (2015) 'With bated breath: diagnosis of respiratory illness', *Perspectives in Biology and Medicine*, 58(1): 53–65.

Collins, P.H. (1990) *Black Feminist Thought: Knowledge, Consciousness, and the Politics of Empowerment*, New York: Routledge.

Conrad, P. (2007) *The Medicalization of Society: On the Transformation of Human Conditions into Treatable Disorders*, Baltimore, MD: Johns Hopkins University Press.

Conrad, P. and Schneider, J.W. (1980) *Deviance and Medicalization: From Badness to Sickness*, Saint Louis, MO: The C.V. Mosby Company.

Dumit, J. (2006) 'Illnesses you have to fight to get: facts as forces in uncertain, emergent illnesses', *Social Science and Medicine*, 62(3): 577–590.

Engelmann, G.J. (1900) 'The President's address', *Transactions of the American Gynecological Society*, 25(1): 3–45.

Fleischman, S. (1999) 'I am ..., I have ..., I suffer from ...: a linguist reflects on the language of illness and disease', *Journal of Medical Humanities*, 20(1): 3–32.

Fowler, O.S. and Fowler, L.N. (1857) *The Illustrated Self-Instructor in Phrenology and Physiology*, New York: Fowler and Wells.

'Good data need good writing' (2005) *Nature Immunology*, 6: 1061.

Haraway, D. (1991) 'Situated knowledges: the science question in feminism and the privilege of partial perspective', in D. Haraway (auth) *Simians, Cyborgs, and Women: The Reinvention of Nature*, New York: Routledge, pp 183–202.

Harding, S. (1991) *Whose Science? Whose Knowledge? Thinking from Women's Lives*, Ithaca, NY: Cornell University Press.

Harding, S. (1993) 'Rethinking standpoint epistemology: what is strong objectivity?', in L. Alcoff and E. Potter (eds) *Feminist Epistemologies*, New York: Routledge, pp 49–82.

Horwitz, A.V. and Wakefield, J.C. (2007) *The Loss of Sadness: How Psychiatry Transformed Normal Sorrow into Depressive Disorder*, New York: Oxford University Press.

Jutel, A. (2004) 'Cursed or carefree? Menstrual product advertising and the sportswoman', in S.J. Jackson and D.L. Andrews (eds) *Sport, Culture and Advertising*, London: Routledge, pp 213–236.

Jutel, A. (2006a) 'The emergence of overweight as a disease category: measuring up normality', *Social Science and Medicine*, 63(9): 2268–2276.

Jutel, A. (2006b). 'What's in a name? Death before birth', *Perspectives in Biology and Medicine*, 49(3): 425–434.

Jutel, A. (2008) 'Beyond evidence-based nursing: tools for practice', *Journal of Nursing Management*, 16(4): 417–421.

Jutel, A. (2010). 'Framing disease: the example of female hypoactive sexual desire disorder', *Social Science and Medicine*, 70(7): 1084–1090.

Jutel, A. (2012) 'Commentary: method or madness? The dominance of the systematic review in nursing scholarship', *Aporia: The Nursing Journal*, 4(4): 52–57.

Jutel, A. (2016) '"The news is not altogether comforting": fiction and the diagnostic moment', *Perspectives in Biology and Medicine*, 59(3): 399–412.

Jutel, A. (2019) *Diagnosis, Truths, and Tales*, Toronto, CA: University of Toronto Press.

Jutel, T. and Jutel, A. (2017) '"Deal with it. Name it": the diagnostic moment in film', *Medical Humanities*, 43(3): 185–191.

Jutel, A. and Mintzes, B. (2017) 'Female sexual dysfunction: medicalizing desire', in B. Cohen (ed) *Routledge International Handbook of Critical Mental Health*, Abingdon: Routledge, pp 162–168.

Kimmerer, R.W. (2021) 'What can we learn without words?', *The Believer*, 18(1): 31–38.

Kirk, S.A. and Kutchins, H. (1992) *The Selling of DSM: The Rhetoric of Science in Psychiatry*, New York: de Gruyter.

Klawiter, M. (2004) 'Breast cancer in two regimes: the impact of social movements on illness experience', *Sociology of Health and Illness*, 26(6): 845–874.

Kuhn, T. (1962) *The Structure of Scientific Revolutions*, Chicago, IL: University of Chicago Press, 1970.

Lavater, J.C. (1855) *Essays on Physiognomy – Designed to Promote Knowledge and Harmony among Mankind* (15th edn), translated by T. Holcroft, London: William Tegg.

Leder, D. (1990) *The Absent Body*, Chicago, IL: University of Chicago Press.

Mills, C.W. (1970) *The Sociological Imagination*, Harmondsworth: Penguin Books.

Morrison, G., Quitely, F. and Grant, J. (2011) *All-Star Superman*, Burbank, CA: DC Comics.

Rosenberg, C.E. (2006) 'Contested boundaries: psychiatry, disease and diagnosis', *Perspectives in Biology and Medicine*, 49(3): 407–424.

Scott, W.J. (1990) 'PTSD in DSM-III: a case in the politics of diagnosis and disease', *Social Problems*, 37(3): 294–310.

Shilling, C. (2012) *The Body and Social Theory* (3rd edn), London: SAGE.

Smith, D. (1987) *The Everyday World as Problematic: A Feminist Sociology*, Evanston, IL: Northwestern University Press.

Stoddard Holmes, M. (2006) 'Pink ribbons and public private parts', *Literature and Medicine*, 25(2): 475–501.

Taonui, R. (2011) 'Story: Whakapapa-genealogy. Page 1. What is Whakapapa?', *Te Ara – The Encyclopedia of New Zealand*, available from: http://www.TeAra.govt.nz/en/whakapapa-genealogy/page-1.

Turner, B.S. (1984) *The Body and Society: Explorations in Social Theory*, Oxford: Blackwell.

Vertinsky, P.A. (1994) *The Eternally Wounded Woman: Women, Doctors, and Exercise in the Late Nineteenth Century*, Champaign: University of Illinois Press.

Weber, M. (1949) *The Methodology of the Social Sciences*, translated by E.A. Shils and H.A. Finch (eds), New York: Free Press.

World Health Organization (2009) 'International classification of diseases and related health problems (ICD)' [online], available from: https://www.who.int/standards/classifications/classification-of-diseases.

Young, I.M. (1980) 'Throwing like a girl: a phenomenology of feminine body comportment motility and spatiality', *Human Studies*, 3(2): 137–156.

Zerubavel, E. (2007) 'Generally speaking: the logic and mechanics of social pattern analysis', *Sociological Forum*, 22(2): 131–145.

# Index

## A

academic disciplines
  anthropology, disciplinary roots in cultural appropriation and othering 75
  biographical account of development of research field 13, 225–34
  conceptual, epistemic, or interpretive shifts in 2, 3, 19, 23–5, 44, 61, 160–1
  embodied experience and 13, 223–6, 228–9, 231–4
  emergence of during the Industrial Revolution 1
  epistemic authority, dominance, and legitimacy 49, 90, 93, 113, 231
  historical development of 1–5, 21–6, 45, 160–1, 223–4
  interdisciplinarity 48–50, 52, 55, 61, 62n6, 70
  positivism, in relation to ix–x, 2, 13, 21–2, 24, 231
  see also anthropology; Black studies; economics; medicine; psychology; public health; quantum physics; sociology; sociology of diagnosis; theoretical traditions
accountability 25, 137, 141, 142, 147, 192, 209
  see also gender, accountability to normative standards; self, as achievement
action
  acts of resistance 122, 150n3
  biological conditions of 2
  the body and xix, 1, 2, 5, 20, 31, 168
  capitalism and 123
  civil disobedience 203, 215, 219
  collective action 1, 26, 36, 99, 123, 207, 213
  conforming/disconforming 101, 144, 186, 219
  culture as epiphenomenon/condition of 22
  dance 99
  disciplinary 161, 178, 183, 186, 187
  discourse and narrative serve as "hermeneutic hooks" for 165
  disobedience 178
  dispositions and 78, 121, 171, 174n3, 189
  eating 168–9
  embodied experience and 204
  emotions and 184, 206
  *habitus* and 69, 78–9
  health outcomes and 121
  human 21, 22
  identity and 3, 61, 165
  as improvisational response 69

inactivity 118
instrumental 21, 38n3, 125
interpersonal dynamics and 194
interpretation and x, 105, 124, 134, 161, 183
intra-action, physicalist concept of 62n2
"ladylike" 186
lines/poles of action 27, 29, 31
lived body and 2
meaning and 2, 5, 6, 28, 31, 33, 37, 123
Migrant Trail Walk 211
"molecular action of art" 62n10
moralizing 109
narrative, power to direct action 38n3
*Nervous Conditions* 96, 99
obesity and corrective/preventative action 111
as object of sociological study 1, 2
as objective, observable behavior and practices 7, 22, 27, 33, 35–6, 66, 78–9, 97, 110
performative 3, 36
physical activity 139, 211, 226, 227
pragmatic 123, 231
pragmatist perspectives on 7, 33
praxis *see* praxeological approaches
protest 206
racism, institutional acts of 187
rational 22
religious devotion 161
routinized, everyday 6, 27, 139
sensible 72
social construction and 24–5
solidarity 219
song, embodied in action 62n8
speech acts 3
subjective 178
talk and 161
uncomfortable 211
*vocabularies of motive* and 159
"vulnerability" and 111
"witnessing" 171
see also behavior; interaction; intersubjectivity; motifaction; phenomenology; social action; symbolic interactionism
activism
  activists, white, middle-class, from the Christian left 202
  anti-SOA 216

# INDEX

breast cancer activism 11, 133, 134, 136, 138, 142
comfort/discomfort 213
cultural tools 203
embodied dynamics 203, 204
embodied tactics, to see/feel violence and expose injustices 213
embodied vulnerability and 203, 205, 206, 212, 213, 215, 219
fat activism 113, 118
high-risk 203, 205, 209, 212, 215, 217, 219, 220n2
interpretive effort and 212, 213, 214, 217, 219
Migrant Trail Walk and 209
"perceptual communities," activism, unsettling affect and the forging of 213
privilege, social and embodied 205, 214–15, 217, 218, 220n2
*sense* experiences, mediated by 206
US–Mexico border activism 209, 218
*see also* social movements; solidarity activism
aesthetics xii, 3, 33, 45, 68, 84, 113, 137, 140–4, 179
artistic sensibility and 141
Black girl dress aesthetics 184, 192–3
pleasure and 149
symmetry 137, 142
vice, aesthetics of 232
*see also* beauty; the senses
affect xi, 12, 13, 27, 37, 160, 206–7, 208, 211, 219
attention, directed by affective experience 205
bodily, sense experience and 205, 206–7
definition 220n1
embodied display of 210
embodied vulnerability and 203, 206–7, 209, 211–12, 215, 219
emotion, interpretive and signifying system of affect 205, 206–7
interaffectivity 6
modal thinking and sensitivity to 70, 79
physiological examples of 218
postmodernism and 24
power of 205, 214
sensemaking and 206–7, 214–15, 217
social meaning of 214
uncomfortable and unsettling 212, 213
*see also* emotion
Agawu, Kofi 75, 76, 83
agency 3–4, 31, 204, 219
appearance/disappearance of the body and 104
beauty and 135
Black bodies, colonialism and 91, 95, 104
Black girls' bodies and 183–4, 195, 104
bodily agency, constraining forces 31
bodily experience and 204
contingency of 183, 219
gender and 97–8, 104, 122, 135
health and 118, 122, 123, 124
individual agency, post-structuralist, deconstructionist, and postmodern emphasis of 4
mastectomy and 135
material agency 4

"neo-liberal politics" and 123
*Nervous Conditions* 91, 95, 97, 103, 104
"presence"/"dys-appearance" and 103
structure/agency relationship 135, 150n3, 195
Ahmed, Sara 59, 178, 217–18
Alcoff, Linda Martín 204, 217, 220n3
Alexander, Jeffrey C. 2, 6, 19, 20, 21, 22, 23, 25, 26, 27, 28, 29, 31, 37, 38n7, 39n11
American pragmatism xviii, 6
*see also* theoretical traditions, pragmatism
Anlo-Ewe people (southeastern Ghana) 9, 10, 66, 67, 68, 69, 75, 76, 78, 79–80, 84
caricatured as having an "uber sense" 76
sensorium 69–70
ways of knowing 10
*see also* language, Anlo-Ewe (language community in Ghana); *seselelāme*
anthropology
approach to the molecular 48
critique of 75
disciplinary roots in cultural appropriation and othering 75
psychological anthropology 68
psychology, disciplinary distinction from 83
sensory anthropology 69–70
sociology, disciplinary distinction from 22
Aphramor, Lucy 114, 115, 125
Aposhyan, Susan 66
Aristotle 47
artistic research
biomythographics of 48
embodied 9, 44, 48, 49, 60–1, 62n3
arts
artistic sensibility 141
capitalism and 60
decolonial art and the visibilization of molecular violence 48
"duty to beauty" and 229
humanities and 57
installation art centered on body image 148
"molecular action of art" 62n10
molecularity of identity evident in art 60
performative arts project and *seselelāme* 77
ASA (American Sociological Association) xviii, 231
Atkinson, Michael 110
attention
agency and 124
analytical 5, 6
attentional topography 5
beauty and 133, 135, 230
biographical disruption/repair 133, 170
Black girls and 189
bodily insistence and 213
bodily vulnerability and 205–6, 215, 217
the body, attentiveness and inattentiveness to 75, 79, 123, 159, 164, 167, 171–2
breathing and 170, 171
defamiliarized 95
desire and 99
disattention/inattention 5, 111, 159
eating and 168
embodied experience and 160

emotions, degree of attention to 73, 80
interpretive process and xii, 1, 5, 6, 7, 13, 69, 160
materiality and xviii, 5
meaning and xii, xviii, 6
music, attention to and increased bodily sensation 98
perceptual filtering and 95
physiological limits of 210
power and 12, 119, 124
presencing/copresencing 13, 160
as process of selection xviii
in religious life 160, 174
salience 5, 111
selective attention as cultural cognitive process linking meaning with materiality xviii
solidarity and 214
somatic 69, 80–1, 160
soul, attentional redirection to 164
yoga and 159, 164, 167, 168, 170–2

# B

Baker, Cynthia M. 62n14
Baker-Bell, April 185
Ball, Philip 58
Banting, William 112
Barthes, Roland 31, 39n10, 39n11
beauty
  in advertising 227
  agency, individual autonomy and 135
  anti-Black discourses and 193
  the beautiful and the sublime 30
  Black girls' bodies and 192
  Black hair 30, 31, 193, 194
  bodily form and function, in relation to 138–40, 144
  bodily movement, as fact of 139
  body projects and practices 30, 133, 134, 135, 192
  breast cancer activism and 11
  breast cancer as disruption of ideals of feminine beauty 133, 134, 139, 148, 149
  breast cancer recovery, meaning of beauty in 134–6, 137, 138, 142, 144, 149
  breastedness/breastlessness and 134, 137, 138, 140, 141, 143, 144, 149
  civility/incivility and 30
  consumer culture and 2
  disfigurement and 133, 137, 138, 139, 140
  "duty to beauty" as moral endeavor 229–30
  fashion-beauty complex 111
  feminist perspectives on 111, 134, 135, 137, 149
  gender and 11, 30, 133–50 passim, 192, 193, 227
  health and beauty industries 2
  identity and 134, 135, 142
  interpretation and 11, 134, 135, 136, 137, 139, 142, 144, 146, 149, 193
  mastectomy and beauty reinterpretation 11, 134, 135–6, 137–44, 149
  mastectomy and support for beauty reinterpretation 136, 144–9
  media 133, 143
  in medicine 11, 133
  natural/unnatural 193
  norms 11, 30, 111, 133, 134, 135, 136, 137, 139, 140, 141, 144, 149, 192, 193, 227
  pedagogies of "beauty"/"disgust" 30, 109
  queering of 149
  race and 30, 31, 192, 193
  scars and 137, 142–3
  symmetry and 137, 140–2
  talk, narratives of 137, 141, 142
  ugliness and 138, 139
  vanity 140–1
  visibility and 192
  yoga practice and feeling of 171
  see also aesthetics
Becker, Howard 173
behavior
  assignation of disease labels and 233
  behavioral approach/intervention 27, 113, 114, 120, 122, 191
  belonging in the classroom and 192
  bodyweight as proxy for 118, 119
  defamiliarization and 97
  embodied experience, influence on 204
  Euro-American ways of being and 66
  feelings, emotions as predisposition to behavior 78, 79
  instrumentalism, strategies of 21, 125, 189, 194
  Jezebel, controlling image and assumptions about Black girls' behavior 193
  "ladylike" behavior 186
  meaning construction: behavior as a conduit for 204; influence on behavior ix; as objective behavioral relation 33, 35, 36
  normative frames of "accountability" and 137
  obesity alarmism and healthism, focus on individual behavior 10, 110, 113, 114, 118, 123
  situational expectations of the educational setting and 189
  social structures and 121–2
  TWA (talking with attitude) 186
  see also action; interaction
Bell, Kristen 112
Bendelow, Gillian A. 19, 205
binary hierarchies 4
  binary cultural codes 28, 29
  binary sex-gender order 3, 4, 29, 32, 38–9n8, 51
  challenges to 4
  critique of 38n7
  ideality/materiality binary 8, 20, 22, 25, 49
  male/female binary coded as objectivity/subjectivity binary 38n6
  mind/matter 22
  moral valence, power of 29
  naturalization of 4
  nature/culture 4, 21, 25
  nature/history 25, 78
  nature/mind 21
  nonbinary 58
  objectivity/subjectivity 7, 8, 13, 20, 22–5, 27, 33, 36, 38n6, 231
  social construction of 29

# INDEX

structure/agency 124, 135, 150n3, 195, 219
subjectivity-idealism vs reason-society 22
  in Western philosophy 4
  *see also* body/mind dichotomy
biology/physiology
  biochemistry 44–50
  biological conditions of action 2, 100
  biological sex 22, 33, 225, 226
  biotic qualities of *seselelāme* 67
  cells 44, 45, 49
  essentialism 90, 122
  eyes 8, 28, 30, 82, 164, 167, 170, 186, 205, 229
  feminist materialisms and 4
  frameworks of meaning and 7
  hair 30, 31, 72–3, 135, 192, 193, 194
  hormones 47, 50
  lived body, in relation to 22
  men's health and 122
  menstruation 227
  molecular 45, 48
  morphology 73–4, 218
  muscle 81, 103, 138–40, 150n5–6, 170, 229
  *Nervous Conditions* 100
  neurobiology, neurosciences and 45, 66, 85n11
  physiognomy 22, 229
  physiology 45, 83, 115
  piloerection (goosebumps) 73
  racism and 91, 92
  as raw material 22
  skin 30, 34, 39n9, 48, 51, 68, 72, 80, 81, 91, 98, 102, 135, 138, 139, 178, 218
  stuff of life 64
  testosterone 46–7
  as unsociological matter 2
  *see also* body; breasts; DNA; materiality/ materialism/matter
Black bodies 88
  Black hair 30, 31, 192, 193, 194
  Black men's bodies 10, 88, 89, 91–2, 94, 95, 104
  Black women's bodies 10, 31, 34, 48, 88–90, 92–4, 104, 150n5
  colonialism and 10, 48, 89–105 passim
  docility, strategy and refusal 100, 189
  female strength 93, 150n5
  Floyd, George 88
  passivity, framing and resistance to 188, 190, 195
  skin 30, 34, 39n9, 48, 97, 178, 218
  targeted by police 88, 119, 218
  *see also* Black girls' bodies in educational settings; Blackness; race and racism
Black, David 38n3
  *see also* motifaction
Black girls' bodies in educational settings 12, 95–6, 100, 102–3, 178–95 passim
  agency 97, 104, 183–4, 195
  anti-Black discourses/practices 12, 179, 180–3, 188, 191, 192, 193, 194, 195
  Black talk, backtalk, sass 12, 179, 180, 184–8, 190, 192, 195
  Blackness 178, 189, 190, 191
  bodily negotiations interpreted from Black girls' own perspective 12, 179

body work 12, 181, 183
colonialism and 104
controlling images and 181, 182, 183, 186, 191, 192, 193, 194, 195nn3–4
discrimination 193
disrespect towards Black girls 186–7
dress code and appearance 12, 179, 180, 184, 192–4, 195
embodied reverse discourse 12, 181–3, 186, 188, 196n5
loudness and laughter 12, 179, 180, 184, 186, 187–8, 189, 190–2, 195
macrostructural constraints and microlevel interactions 183, 186, 192, 195
misogynoir 178, 179, 180–3, 184, 192, 194, 195, 195n1
mis/reading of Black girls' bodies in educational settings 179, 184–94
othering of 179, 180, 188
outsider status in classrooms 178, 192, 194
policing of Black girls 179, 180, 185–6, 187, 191–3, 195
quietness and silence 12, 102, 186, 188, 189–90, 192
racism 187, 188
school discipline and 178–9, 191, 195
sexuality 88, 98, 100, 102, 193, 194
stereotypes 187, 188, 190, 193–4, 195
symbolic interactionism 12, 183–4
teachers/students interactions 12, 179, 184, 185, 186–8, 189–90, 191, 192, 194, 195
TWA (talking with attitude) 186
*see also* Black bodies; Blackness; race and racism
Black Lives Matter 104, 119
Black studies 52, 57, 60, 62n8
Blackness 60, 180
  anti-Black discourses/practices 12, 60, 179, 180–3, 188, 191, 192, 193, 194, 195
  anti-Black linguistic racism 185
  "blaccent" 185
  "Black bitch"/"nigger bitch" 181, 182
  Black girls' bodies in educational settings 178, 189, 190, 191
  Black play 191, 196n7
  Black speech and Black volume as being unruly 191
  female controlling images 181, 182, 183, 186, 191, 192, 193, 194, 195nn3–4
  indigo and 48
  misogynoir 178, 179, 180–3, 184, 192, 194, 195, 195n1
  the molecular and 55, 56, 57
  "nigga" 182, 196n6
  performance of 191
  phenomenology of Blackness 89, 90–2, 104, 105
  racializing representations of Black people 180–1
  sound of 185, 191
  US 180–1
  *see also* Black bodies; Black girls' bodies in educational settings; race and racism
Blaxter, Mildred 223, 224, 231
Blumer, Herbert 2, 6

241

body
  abject, deviant, unruly 10, 110, 112, 138, 178, 193
  absence from sociological theory/disembodied approach 1, 19, 21–3, 234
  absencing/presencing and appearance/disappearance of the body 10, 13, 32, 88, 94, 99, 101, 103–5, 169, 189, 205, 227, 228, 229, 233–4
  agency and 3, 4, 31, 91, 95, 103, 104, 123, 204
  biological perspectives 2, 4, 7, 22, 33, 48, 90, 92, 122, 225–6
  brown bodies 59, 94, 218
  classed bodies 13, 125, 217
  commodification of 2, 92, 113
  corporeal schemas and 68, 81, 89, 91
    see also bodily ways of knowing; habitus
  discipline and control 2, 9, 10, 38n2, 92, 100, 101, 124, 161, 179, 182, 191, 195
  in early sociology 1–2, 19, 21–3
  "ecstatic" and "recessive" body 99, 103
    see also Leder, Drew
  food, diet, and the body 116, 166, 168–9, 213
  gender nonconforming 142, 148–9
  as ground of social experience and consciousness 204
  as ideality–materiality 8, 20, 37
  identity and 3, 9, 13, 53, 56, 92, 133, 149, 183, 217
  illness, disease and 100–3, 112, 133, 138, 142, 229, 233
  Indigenous bodies 70, 89
  as inscriptive surface 13, 21
  institutional, discursive, corporeal constitution 182
  interpreting the body 7–14
    see also interpretation
  interpretive "grasp on the world" 26
  malleability of 2, 25
  material agency 4, 32
  as material-semiotic xviii, 9, 55
  materiality of xviii, 2, 3, 4–5, 7, 8, 9, 10, 22, 25, 26, 27, 30, 31, 34, 36, 37, 53, 55, 56, 58, 84, 85n8, 89, 114, 123, 125, 140, 217
  meaning and matter 8
  medicalization of 113, 116, 123
  modification 8, 28, 35, 36, 182
  mortification 213
  mutability of 2, 3, 54
  as object separate from self 167
  ontology of 3–4, 19–20, 25, 48
  pleasure 89, 98, 99, 192
  self, body's role in construction of 8, 19, 25, 27, 33
  as situation 20, 26, 28, 37
  social collectivity, co-constituted by flesh and blood bodies 123
  as social fact worthy of study 25
  social movements and 149, 203–4, 213, 218
  social and symbolic construction of xviii, 3, 4, 7, 9, 14, 25, 27, 36–7, 88, 89, 90, 105, 112, 124, 159, 180, 182, 183

sociology of the body 20, 23, 27–8, 33, 37–8, 195
stigmatized 142, 193, 205, 233
as symbol 1, 3, 20, 31, 144, 167, 233
symbolic dimensions of 9, 11, 12, 22, 26–7, 35–7, 159, 161, 183
taken-for-granted medium 1
as text 31, 32
white bodies 31, 88, 92, 94, 104, 105, 115, 217
  see also biology/physiology; Black bodies; Black girls' bodies in educational settings; body projects; embodiment; female bodies; gender, gendered body/embodiment; lived body; male bodies; materiality/materialism/matter
body/mind dichotomy 4, 66, 83, 90
  Integral Yoga 158, 167, 171
  mind–body connection 37, 70, 73
  "mind–body problem" 80, 85n8
  mind as embodied 73
  mind versus matter 22, 49
  rational mind over the emotional body 112
    see also binary hierarchies; Cartesian dualism; Descartes, René; Integral Yoga, body/mind dualism
body politic 1, 2, 124, 186
body projects 3, 25, 30, 31, 110
  "beautifying" body projects 30
  male obesity and gendered "body project" 110, 112, 118
  physical body as project or work 31
    see also body work; Shilling, Chris
body studies 19, 89, 90–1
body work
  Black girls 12, 181, 183
  definition 3, 182
  embodied reverse discourse and 182
  male bodies 112, 113
  moral aspects of 3, 13
    see also body projects
Booth, Douglas 226
Bordo, Susan 24, 30, 31, 32, 39n9, 111, 135
Bourdieu, Pierre 6, 20, 29, 62n7, 90, 110, 122, 123, 160
  see also habitus; theoretical traditions, Bourdieusian/practice theory
breast cancer 33, 133, 150n4
  1998 Women's Health and Cancer Rights Act 150n1
  American Cancer Society, "Reach to Recovery Program" 133–4
  BRA-Day international 133–4
  BRCA gene variants (BReast CAncer) 136, 147
  breast cancer activism 11, 133–4, 136, 138
  breast cancer culture 147, 149, 150n4
  disruption of femininity and ideals of feminine beauty 33, 133, 134, 139, 148, 149
  embodiment of 33–4, 134, 142, 149, 150n4
  ideologies of femininity and 134
  imperative of concealment 133, 137, 138, 141, 145
  "Look Good Feel Better Program" 133–4
  narratives of recovery 11, 133–6, 137, 139–40, 142, 149
  previvors 147

restoration of femininity 33, 34, 133–4, 142, 144, 148
survivors 34, 136, 138, 143
*see also* breast reconstruction; breasts; mastectomy
breast reconstruction 34, 133–44, 137, 138–40, 141, 148–9, 150n1, 150nn6–7
autologous reconstruction 138, 139, 141, 150n6
cosmetic surgery 134, 135, 138, 139
as deformed and horrific 137, 138, 139, 141
flat closure and living flat 11, 34, 134, 135–6, 137, 138, 140, 141, 143, 144, 145, 147–9, 150n2
pressure to undergo reconstruction 144
queerness and flat closure 148
silicone implants 139, 150n7
*see also* breast cancer; breasts; mastectomy
breasts
femininity and 32, 33, 34, 133, 134, 138, 144, 147
"Frankenboobies" 137
material feeling and meaning 34
prosthetic 134, 140, 141, 145, 150n1
sexuality and 98, 146–7
as symbol 32, 33, 34, 133–4, 136, 137, 138, 144, 147, 148
symmetry 137, 140–2, 149
*see also* breast cancer; breast reconstruction; mastectomy
Broom, Dorothy 133, 138
Brown, Phil 223
Brumberg, Joan 230
Bull, Michael 70
Bunsell, Tanya 150n5
Butler, Judith 3, 25, 36, 37, 62n7, 204
Byrd, Jodi 53

## C

Campos, Paul 114, 115, 116–17
capitalism 1, 2, 23, 124
art production and 60
commodification and commoditization 2, 9, 67, 73, 77, 83, 84, 92, 113
consumer culture 2
health inequities and 119–25
industrial capitalism 1
macro-social factors impacting health 119
markets 67, 77, 119, 120, 148, 232
neoliberal capitalism 11, 119
race and 57, 59, 92
*see also* economics; Marxian perspectives
Carel, Havi 224
Carroll, Rebecca 184–5
Cartesian dualism 21, 83, 90, 99
*see also* Descartes, René
Champagne, Anne Marie xii, xviii, 1–18, 19–43, 67, 133
Chen, Mel Y. 47–8, 50, 62n4
Cheng, Anne Anlin 59
Chentsova-Dutton, Yulia E. 80–1
Cheyne, George 112
Chicago School 38n4
Classen, Constance 69
*collective consciousness* 36
colonialism 48, 53, 58, 89, 91–2, 100, 105

architectures of power 10, 90, 92, 93
British 93
Canada 115
colonial education 95–7, 103–5
decolonial art 48
gender and 10, 57, 89, 91–3, 103, 105
genocide 53
Indigenous 53, 89, 115
neocolonialism 67
norms 98, 100, 101, 104
patriarchy 89, 96, 100
postcolonial analytic perspectives xii, 10
postcolonial modernity 104
precolonial Nigeria 93
race and 53, 58, 67, 88, 91–7, 99, 102, 103
regimes of knowledge 48, 52
Sartre, theories of 95 *see also* Sartre, Jean-Paul
settler society 53
*see also* decolonization; gender, as colonial construct; gender on the post-colony; *Nervous Conditions*
Columbia University 38n4
commodification and commoditization *see* body, commodification of; capitalism, commodification and commoditization; globalization; male bodies, commodification of; *seselelāme*, commodification of
Conrad, Peter 113, 233
constructionism xiin5, 4, 5, 90
cultural construction of technoscientific knowledge 45
deconstructionism 4
dematerialized 4
gendered 44, 112, 122, 227
hermeneutic 31–3
material-semiotic construction of the body 9
materialization of "social facts" 25
molecular 44, 46
racialized 44, 180, 184, 185
strong constructionist perspectives, critique of 4–5, 9
*see also* social constructionism
Cook, Jennifer 162
cosmetic surgery 3, 135, 137
*see also* beauty; body projects; body work
COVID-19 pandemic xix, 62n4, 202
"dual COVID-19/obesity crisis frame" 109, 111, 113, 115, 118
Crawford, Robert 2, 114, 123, 125
critical race studies 9, 44–5, 55, 88, 217
critical studies 223, 227
CSM (critical studies on men) 110, 121–3, 124, 125
on health inequalities 119–20, 125
on obesity 112, 113–15, 123, 125–6
Crossley, Nick 27, 90, 91, 162, 204, 205
Csikszentmihalyi, Mihaly 173
Csordas, Thomas 2, 31, 69
Culp, Andrew 55
cultural sociology 6, 19, 20, 23, 26, 27–8, 30, 31, 32, 33, 35, 37, 38, 174n3
cultural and cognitive sociology xviii, 6, 85n9
Yale University's Center for Cultural Sociology xviii

*see also* SPCS (Strong Program cultural sociology); theoretical traditions, cultural sociology
cultural studies 48, 55
culture 19–20
  "absent presence" of culture and the body in early sociology 21–3
  body and society, as constitutive of 8, 26
  *collective-formative* interpretive framework and 5–6
  collective representations and 8, 21
  cultural analysis definition 34
  cultural analysis and perspective xii, 8, 27, 34–5, 55
  cultural appropriation 9, 67, 73, 75–6, 80, 83, 84, 85n10
  cultural codes 6, 8, 20, 28–31, 32, 33, 37
  cultural and cognitive schema 29, 68, 183, 205
  cultural discourse 9, 48, 111, 125, 180
  cultural forms 21, 31
  cultural history 229, 230
  cultural meaning 29, 30
  cultural model 68
  cultural phenomenology 69, 204
  cultural pragmatics 19, 38n1
  cultural psychology 80–1, 83
  cultural script 29
  cultural turn in sociology 25
  culture structures x, 25, 31, 32, 37
  cultures 53, 75, 90, 112, 115
  Durkheim's conception of 26
  emotion, cultural foundations of 6, 12–13, 37, 80, 205–6
  interpretation, signification and xii, 12–13, 26, 32, 68, 142
  *The Interpretation of Cultures* 34
  interpretive traditions, cultural approaches x, 6, 28, 31, 33, 68
  material culture 68
  matter, distinct from 2, 3, 4, 48, 49
  matter/meaning and xii, xviii, 3, 4, 5, 7, 8, 9, 14, 20, 21, 23, 25–7, 30, 31, 44, 45, 48, 49, 56, 57, 84, 135
  as "motifactional" force 20, 22, 36–7, 38
  postmodern crisis of meaning and cultural thematization of materiality and the body 23–6
  SPCS (Strong Program cultural sociology) and relative autonomy of culture 20, 28–31, 38
  as symbolic dimension of the body and social life 8, 19, 25, 27, 38
  visual culture 68
  *see also* anthropology; cultural sociology; cultural studies; meaning; ritual; SPCS (Strong Program cultural sociology); SPCS of the body and embodiment
culture, types of
  Black culture 191
  body-oriented consumer culture 112
  breast cancer culture 147, 149, 150n4
  gendered culture of slenderness 116
  "healthism" 125
  late-capitalist consumer culture 2
  popular culture 180, 182, 184, 224
  weight-loss culture 111
  Western culture 123
Cyr, Monica 115

**D**

Damasio, Antonio 66, 85n11
D'Andrade, Roy 68
Dangarembga, Tsitsi 10, 89, 92, 94–8
  *see also Nervous Conditions*
Dash, Julie 48
Davis, Kathy 3
decolonization 57
  decolonial art 48
  decolonial grammar of colors 60
  decolonial scholars 93
  decolonial thought 61
  *see also* colonialism; postcolonialism
deconstructionism *see* theoretical traditions: deconstructionism, literary criticism
DeFrantz, Thomas 54
DeGloma, Thomas ix–xiii, xviii, xix, 5–6, 230
Deleuze, Gilles 24, 44, 50–5, 56, 62n10
  *A Thousand Plateaus* 51–2
Descartes, René 84n2, 90
  *see also* Cartesian dualism
deviance 112–113
  deviant bodies 10, 100, 110
  in diagnosis 233
  weight/fat and 112–13
  *see also* body: abject, deviant, unruly; disability; othering
Dewey, John 37
diagnosis 13, 71, 134, 223–5, 232–3
  breast cancer 134, 136, 139, 141, 145, 147, 149
  of colonialism's effect 104
  embodiment and 233, 234
  overweight as a diagnostic category 232, 233
  racial categories and 231
  stories of 224
  "thingness" and the emergence of diagnoses 232
  *see also* sociology of diagnosis
Dilthey, Wilhelm 24, 32
disability 60, 79, 82, 118, 121
  able-bodied privilege 215
  disabilities, persons with 2, 79, 82
  *seselelāme* and 79, 82
discourse
  analytic perspective xii, 4–5, 24, 232
  anti-Black 12, 179, 180, 188, 193, 194
  biochemical discourse 48
  Black talk and voice, discursive misreading 185
  bodily detachment, as a means of cultivating 158, 164, 168
  body as "discursive tabula rasa" 27
  body, presencing discourses of 227
  body, as productive of 182
  body as site of discursive interpretation 161
  breast cancer discourse 133, 134, 146, 148, 149
  collective sentiment, social force and (discursive depth) 26, 35
  counternarrative and 12, 181
  cultural discourse 9, 48

# INDEX

discourse–practice interpretive interplay 161, 164, 165, 169, 173
discursive codification of race 179
discursive frameworks 5, 179
discursive knowledge 173, 180
discursive power 3, 6, 179, 180, 182, 183, 186, 192
discursive technologies 180
disfigurement, discourse of and reinterpretation as beautiful 137–8
dominant, hegemonic 12
embodied reverse discourse 12, 179, 181, 182, 183, 186, 195
feminine embodiment and beauty discourses 11, 135
health discourse 10, 122
as hermeneutic hooks 165
internet, online community as discursive space 136
interpretation/reinterpretation, as resource for 135, 142, 159
masculine discourse 123
militarized discourse 124
misogynoir 180, 181, 182, 184, 192, 195
modernity, discourses of 93
obesity and fat-phobic discourses 10, 11, 111, 112, 113, 114, 118, 125
as object of interpretive study/scholarship ix
post-structuralism and 3, 4, 24
practice, distinction between 159
racialized and gendered 12, 181, 183, 184, 185–6, 187, 188, 191, 192, 194, 195
racist discourses 92, 180–1, 188
sexist discourse 92
symbolic system and 27, 31, 37, 39n10, 55, 161
talk and 11, 172, 174n3
weaponization against Black people 180
"you are not the body" discourse 168
*see also* language; theoretical traditions, Foucauldian/discourse analysis
disidentification 135, 142, 149, 159, 169, 173
Douglas, Mary 1, 95, 160
Durkheim, Emile 2, 6, 25–6, 37
 *The Elementary Forms of the Religious Life* 21, 26, 35–6
 *see also collective consciousness*; SPCS (Strong Program cultural sociology); theoretical traditions, Durkheimian; totemism, *totemic principle*
Dzokoto, Vivian 80–1

# E

economics 2, 23, 25, 36, 61, 75, 109, 118–21
 Africa, economic extractive practices 84
 bodies within economies 96
 capital 36
 class analysis and economic theory 57
 economic determinism 25
 health systems and 109
 *homo economicus* 22
 Global North contexts 67, 84
 neoliberal capitalism and 11
 political economy 119
 power and 84, 124

race and "differential economy" of police intervention 218
race and gender as determinants of economic status 217
social action and 23, 25
socioeconomic status (SES) and health 118–21
sociology, interaction with 38n5
value 96
*see also* capitalism
education
 belonging/nonbelonging 97, 178, 179, 195
 *Brown v. the Board of Education* 39n9
 colonialism and 93, 95–6, 103–4, 105
 dissident body, production of 100
 equality, disparities in 178, 179, 188, 193
 as freedom 93, 96–7, 100, 104, 105
 gender-based oppression and 93, 98
 health outcomes and 121
 higher education, sociology departments and programs 2
 hostile educational experience 194
 as opportunity 95
 physical education 110, 111, 225
 socioeconomic mobility and 96–7, 98
 as transformation 96–7
 Western education 93, 96
 *see also* Black girls' bodies in educational settings; *Nervous Conditions*, colonial education
Elias, Norbert 6
embodied vulnerability *see* activism, embodied vulnerability and; attention, embodied vulnerability and; embodiment: embodied vulnerability, vulnerability and embodied awareness; solidarity activism, embodied vulnerability of
embodiment
 academic disciplines, research methods, and researcher embodiment 13, 47, 60, 114, 122, 208, 210, 211, 225, 231, 233–4
 anti-Black policies, singling out Black embodiment 193
 beauty and 134
 Black embodiment in relation to indigo plant 48
 Black girls' embodiment 179, 180, 181, 184, 188, 189, 192, 194
 Black presencing and 95
 body qua embodied situation 28
 colonialism as embodied memory/history 58
 colonization, embodied practices 93
 embodied artistic research *see* artistic research, embodied
 embodied belonging 89
 embodied cognition 204
 embodied consequences of trauma 114
 embodied difference 44
 embodied discourse 188
 embodied disposition 90
 embodied erasure 89, 99
 embodied experience 11, 13, 34, 99, 102, 142, 149, 159, 169, 171, 172, 173, 203, 204, 217, 219, 231
 embodied feeling, as predisposition to behavior 79

embodied human agency and healthier
societies 123
embodied knowledge 49, 142, 158, 172
embodied politic of survival 189
embodied practices of gender and sexuality 47
embodied privilege 215, 218, 220n2
embodied religious practices 160–1, 174
embodied reverse discourse 12, 181–2, 195
embodied social phenomena/structures 30, 110
embodied tactics for bearing witness to
violence 213
embodied versus spoken messages 195n2
embodied vulnerability 12, 13, 202–20 passim
embodied ways of knowing 9, 66
female/feminine and women's embodiment 11,
13, 134, 140, 141, 142, 149, 150n4, 181, 188,
192, 194, 218
grid/spectrum models of identity and
embodiment 58
as hermeneutical situation 37
invested with living value 32
as lived: lived experience, lived body, lived
corporeality 27, 31, 36
living flat: embodied honesty, freedom, and
authenticity 141, 148
living flat, extension of normative boundaries of
female embodiment 149
male/masculine and men's embodiment 115,
117, 123, 124
materiality and 45, 49, 56, 62n8, 123
meaning and 26, 27, 31, 33, 36, 37, 93, 219
mind as "inherently embodied" 73
racial and gender identities and 55, 216
recovery from breast cancer, restorations of
embodied self 138, 141
reversible relation with body 8
scientific understanding of 45
self-care, late-capitalist consumer culture and
embodied practices of 2
self and the social world, embodiment of 19, 25,
27, 37
solidarity, shared embodiment through
activism 203, 209–10
strong cultural sociology of 8, 27–8, 31, 37, 38
study of religion and 160
technique, identity, molecularity and 9, 47, 49,
57, 59, 62n8
TEPP (The Embodied Present Process™) 76
thought, reciprocal relation to embodiment 161
vulnerability and embodied awareness 13, 205, 218
wheelchair as extension of 79
women of color, embodied histories absent from
white feminist scholarship 89
*see also* biology/physiology; body; materiality/
materialism/matter; *seselelāme*
emotion
Black emotions 192
Black joy 192
*collective-formative* interpretive framework and 6, 13
as connection between culture and sensuous
form 37
embodied vulnerability and 207

embodied way of knowing, sensory-emotional
form 9, 66
"emotional labor" 6, 182
emotional meltdown 82–3
emotional rapture 82–3
emotional structure of classrooms 184
feelings of 70, 72, 79
feminine, coded as 38n6
*interactive-emergent* interpretive framework and 13
intuition and 78–9
meaning-making and 22, 27, 205–6, 214
as phenomenological experience of practice 160,
166, 169
as predispositions to behavior 78
*psychosocial* interpretive framework and 6
rational/emotional binary 4, 112
rhythm and 9, 70, 160
sensible life of the body and 67, 72, 78, 82, 214
*seselelāme*, as an emotional expression of self 72
shame 70, 115
social movements and 206
socio-emotional relationship 82, 83, 209
structures of feeling 27
as system of signification 206
TMMS (Trait Meta-Mood Scale Attention to
Emotion) 80
valence 27
*see also* affect; the senses; *seselelāme*
Engelmann, George J. 226
epistemology
Anlo epistemologies 70
anthropological 52
the body as epistemological resource 203, 205
civilizational difference 84
colonial sources of knowledge 52
constructionist tradition, epistemic challenge to
essentialist thought 90
disciplinary boundary work and 22
disembodied 231
embodied technique as epistemic 62n7
epistemic legitimacy, relation to ontological
force 49
epistemic modes xiiin2
epistemic positionality 60
epistemic shifts in understandings of the body 19
epistemic technique 51
feminist epistemologies 88, 231
interpretation and xiiin2, 7, 203
matter, onto-epistemologies of 48, 50
medicine, epistemic authority 113
the molecular and 58, 60
observant participation as epistemological
method 207
onto-epistemic cut separating technique and
identity, knowledge and power 61
positivist epistemology 22, 231
postmodern vs modern 24
quantitative methods, epistemic primacy of 44
social epistemology 45
Western epistemologies 89, 93
*see also* interpretation; knowledge production;
ways of knowing

# INDEX

Ernsberger, Paul 119
Eyerman, Ron 206

## F

Fanon, Frantz 10, 89, 91–2, 94–5, 217
  *Black Skin, White Masks* 91
  *The Wretched of the Earth* 94–5
Featherstone, Mike 23, 24
Felski, Rita 135, 149
female bodies
  athleticism 13, 138, 139, 147, 150n5, 225–6, 228, 233
  "being a good native girl," effect on body 105
  binary sex-gender order and 29, 39n8, 51, 56, 91, 93
  biological sex 22, 29, 33, 225, 226
  Black female bodies 10, 12, 31, 34, 48, 79, 88–105 passim, 150n5, 178–96 passim
  cisgender 29, 133, 140, 147, 150n4, 236
  colonialism and 10, 48, 92–5, 99, 100, 104–5
  construction of 12, 33, 38n6, 92, 93, 100, 134, 144
  cosmetic modification 8, 30, 135, 137, 229
  damage 105, 190
  dancing 98–100
  disappearance of 10, 89, 94, 96, 99, 101, 103–5, 190, 192, 227, 228, 229
  discourse and 11, 12, 92, 93, 111, 133, 134, 137, 146, 148, 149, 180–6, 188, 192, 193, 195
  disfigurement 133, 137, 138, 139, 140
  feminist thought and 89, 93–4, 105, 105n1, 110, 111, 112, 117, 134–5, 137
  form vs function, prioritization of 138–40
  frailty 13, 92, 226–8, 234
  gendering of 12, 30, 55, 89, 92–5, 105, 117, 136, 150nn4–5, 186, 192, 194, 217
  hysteria 100
  illness 100–3, 121, 232
  interpretation of 32, 34, 79, 89, 94, 105, 134, 137, 139–40, 142–6, 149, 166, 178–80, 190–3, 195, 212–14, 217–18
  male bodies, in relation to 11, 29, 47, 91, 94, 96, 97, 110, 115, 121, 122, 143, 150n4, 217–18, 228
  menstruation 226–7, 234
  molar/molecular and 51–2
  movement 139, 226, 227, 228, 229
  muscle and strength 93, 138, 139, 140, 150n5, 229
  normative/nonnormative 11, 31, 32, 89, 98, 111, 134, 136, 137, 138, 142, 144, 145, 148, 149, 150n4–5, 227
  obesity 11, 110, 116, 117
  organic theory of native woman's body 94
  pleasure and enjoyment in 10, 98, 99, 103, 105, 149
  presencing of, making visible 13, 89, 94, 95, 96, 103–5, 142, 188, 190, 192, 227, 228, 234
  queer 138, 147–8
  self-scrutiny of 229
  sexuality 89, 98, 144, 146–7, 192
  slenderness, tyranny of 111
  smell of 97
  speaking through the body 100–1, 186
  vulnerability 115, 142, 218
  white women's bodies 92, 94, 104, 217, 218
  *see also* beauty; Black girls' bodies in educational settings; breast reconstruction; breasts; gender; mastectomy; *Nervous Conditions*; transgender
femininity
  Black femininity 181, 186, 188, 191, 193
  breast cancer, disruption/restoration of femininity and ideals of feminine beauty 33, 34, 133–4, 139, 142, 144, 148, 149
  breast cancer and ideologies of femininity 134
  breasts as most visible physical marker of 134
  fat, feminization of 116, 117
  feminine movement 227, 228, 229
  gender discourse and 11, 192, 193
  health: perceived as feminine issue 123; conflation with normative feminine beauty 137
  heterosexuality and 147
  homosexuality and 147
  LGBTQ and queer perspectives 148
  masculinity, in relation to 29, 116, 117, 123
  normative feminine embodiment 11, 134, 142, 144, 150n4
  norms 31, 32, 133, 134, 137–40, 142, 144, 148, 150n5, 181, 186, 188, 191, 195
  symbolic constructions of 13, 33–4, 38, 116, 117, 123, 227
  white femininity 181
  *see also* beauty; Black girls' bodies in educational settings; breast cancer; breast reconstruction; breasts; female bodies; gender; mastectomy
feminism 3, 88
  on beauty 135, 149
  Black feminism 89
  Bourdieu's neglect of 122
  critical race feminism 217
  Deleuzian feminism 51
  feminist epistemologies 231
  feminist materialisms/neomaterialisms 4, 5
  feminist scholarship 4, 110, 111, 112, 113, 117, 134–5, 137, 149
  Lacanian and Freudian feminism 7
  postcolonial feminism 10, 92
  second-wave feminism 23
  Western feminism 93
  white feminism 88–9, 94, 105
  *see also* theoretical traditions: Black feminism, feminist/gender theory, feminist materialism
fitness 3, 164
  male bodies and 110, 112
  medicine, biomedical gaze and fitness regimes 82, 110
  obesity and 110, 112, 115, 117
  *seselelãme* and 9, 73, 74, 76, 82
  social fitness, civilizing bodies 112, 115, 123
  in yoga as "way of being" 164
  *see also* body projects; health
Fleischman, Suzanne 224, 233
Floyd, George 88
Foucault, Michel 3, 6, 29, 37, 62n7, 90, 230
  *The History of Sexuality* 29

Fowler, Lorenzo N. 229
Fowler, Orson S. 229
Frank, Arthur W. 2, 23, 36, 182, 195
Friedman, Asia xii, xviii, 1–18, 29, 67, 213
Friedman, Samuel R. 120

# G

Gard, Michael 109, 111, 113
Geertz, Clifford xiiinn, 4–5, 20, 31, 34–5, 36, 68, 160, 209
  *Interpretation of Cultures* 34–5
gender 3, 5, 10
  accountability to 137, 141, 142, 147, 192
  binary sex-gender order 3, 4, 29, 32, 38–9n8, 47, 51, 92–3, 124
  as colonial construct 89, 105
  *doing gender* 6
  gender justice 88, 123, 125
  gender nonconforming body 142, 148–9
  gender performance 3, 191, 192
  gendered body/embodiment 3, 9, 10, 55, 61, 89, 92, 94, 100, 105, 110, 111, 115, 116, 117, 136, 137, 150nn4–5, 186, 193, 215–17, 218
  male/female binary coded as objectivity/subjectivity binary 38n6
  norms/ideologies of 3, 11, 31, 32, 89, 99, 111, 133, 134, 135, 136, 137, 140, 142, 147, 148, 149, 150nn3–4, 150n9, 191
  race and gender as material and substantial identities 55–6
  social construction of 3, 88, 89, 90, 116, 135, 227
  testosterone, gender, and sexuality 46–7, 50
  *see also* femininity; gender on the post-colony; masculinity; transgender
gender on the post-colony 10, 89, 105
  British colonialism 93
  colonial patriarchy 89, 95, 96, 100, 102
  gendering the colonial body 92–4
  gendering operates in parallel ways to racialization 92–3
  intersectional phenomenological approach 10
  literature as organic theory 94–5
  *see also Nervous Conditions*
genealogy 7, 91, 230, 235n1
Germov, John 116
Geurts, Kathryn Linn 9–10, 66–87
  *Culture and the Senses* 75
Ghanaian *see* Anlo-Ewe people (southeastern Ghana)
Giddens, Anthony 2, 3
Gimlin, Debra 3, 25, 182
Gingras, Jacqui 115
Giugni, Marco 204
globalization 23
  *seselelãme* and 67, 69, 73–7
Global North 9, 66, 67, 73, 75, 77, 80, 82, 83, 84, 202
  *see also* colonialism; globalization; postcolonialism
Global South 67, 88, 202
  *see also* colonialism; globalization; postcolonialism

Goffman, Erving 2, 3, 6, 25, 27, 29, 36, 116, 179, 183, 184, 195n2
Gordon, James S. 66
Gough, Brendan 112, 113, 116
Gould, Deborah 205–6, 214, 220n1
Graham, Hilary 121
Greedharry, Mrinalini 10, 88–108
Green, Kyle D. 162, 165, 174n3
Greene, Kevin J. 75
Griffith, R. Marie 158, 161
Grosz, Elizabeth 38n6, 51
Guattari, Félix 44, 50–5, 56, 62n10

# H

*habitus* 6, 55, 62n8, 69, 78
  definition 69, 78
  religious habitus 161
  *see also* Bourdieu, Pierre
HAES® (Health-At-Every-Size) 114, 118, 125
Haraway, Donna 225
Hardey, Michael 112
Haupt, Adam 84, 85n10
health
  1980 Black Report 120
  agency and 118, 122, 123, 124
  behavioral focus 110, 113, 114, 118, 120–3, 124, 125
  breasts, softness and meanings of wellness 34
  capitalism and 2, 11, 119, 120, 122, 123, 124, 125
  diagnosis 224, 232–3
  health inequalities 10–11, 118–23, 124–5
  importance of normative appearance 232
  individual responsibility and 119, 120, 121, 122, 125
  inequity 111, 114, 117, 118–22, 123, 124, 125
  macro-social factors impacting health 119, 120
  medicalization of 11, 113, 116, 123
  men, masculinities, and health 10, 109–26 passim
  morality and 109, 113, 118, 121, 229
  neoliberalism and health inequalities 119–20, 121, 123, 124–5
  social justice and 119, 121, 122, 123, 125
  UK 120, 121
  US 111, 119, 120
  yoga and 164, 165, 166, 192
  welfare state and 120
  *see also* breast cancer; diagnosis; obesity; obesity and male bodies; public health; sociology of diagnosis
healthism 114, 122, 125
Heidegger, Martin 90
hermeneutics 8, 24, 33–4
  body as hermeneutical situation 20, 37
  hermeneutic reconstruction of meaning 20, 28, 30, 31–4, 38
Integral Yoga, "hermeneutic hooking" 165–6

# INDEX

maximal/minimal interpretation and 35
*see also* interpretation; meaning; research methods, critical hermeneutic; SPCS (Strong Program cultural sociology); theoretical approaches, hermeneutic
Hochschild, Arlie 6
Holmes, Stoddard 224
*homo economicus* 22
hooks, bell 186, 188
Houchen, Diedre 191
Howes, David 68, 69, 70, 78–9, 85
Husserl, Edmund 90

## I

identity
　asymmetry, identity as incommensurable substance 58, 61
　beauty and 133, 134, 135, 136
　body and 3, 9, 55, 56, 61, 149, 173, 183, 217
　categorical vs modal thought and 9, 70, 78–9
　categories of 3, 46, 52, 56–7, 217
　collective, shared identity 6, 36, 46, 206
　cultural forces and xi, 23
　disidentification 135, 138, 142, 149
　disruption and loss of 133, 147, 148, 149
　DNA as "molecule of identity" 46
　embodied xviii, 13, 59, 149
　gendered 13, 47, 50, 55–7, 60, 116, 134, 147, 181, 189, 217
　identity politics 52, 54, 56, 60, 89
　Indigenous identity 53, 56
　Integral Yoga, bodily detachment/disidentification 11–12, 157, 158, 159, 161, 168, 169, 171–2, 173
　internet and 136
　interpretation and xviii, 51, 89, 137–8, 142, 149
　intersectionality 50, 57, 60, 179
　Jewish 56, 60, 61n1
　mastectomy, disidentification processes 135, 138, 142, 149
　material basis 9, 46, 47, 51, 55–6, 58, 59, 61, 217
　"material-semiotic" 9, 46, 47, 50, 55
　molar 52
　mutability 47, 51, 54, 55, 58, 59, 61
　nonbinary, non-gridded 58
　onto-epistemic relation between knowledge, power, identity, and technique 59, 60, 61
　power and 3, 52, 54, 57, 60, 61, 135, 180
　race and gender as material and substantial identities 9, 46, 47, 51, 53, 55–6, 58, 61
　racial identities 9, 46, 47–8, 51, 55–62, 92, 96, 180, 181
　religious, spiritual, yogic practices and 160, 164, 165, 173
　*seselelāme* and Anlo-Ewe identity formation 69
　social movements and 206
　spectrum, continuum, and grid models of identity 56, 60, 61, 165
　symbolic basis ix, 9, 36, 56, 60, 92, 135, 181, 183
　technique/identity, mutual construction 9, 46, 50, 51, 53–4, 57–9, 61
　transgender identity 47 *see also* transgender
　*see also* the molecular
Integral Yoga 11–12, 172–4
　attachment to/identification with the body 157, 158
　bodily detachment/disidentification 11–12, 157, 158, 159, 161, 168, 169, 171–2, 173
　body/mind dualism 158, 167, 171–2, 173
　body as object: metaphor, analogy, and practical enactment 159, 166–9
　description of 162
　Eternal Self 157, 171
　Hatha Yoga 157, 162, 163, 164, 166, 169, 172–3
　"hermeneutic hooking" 165–6
　instructors 154, 158, 163–5, 167, 169–72
　language, power of 157, 158, 165, 169–70, 172–3
　primary goals of 162
　reciprocal influences of embodiment and thought 161
　*satsang* ("spiritual dialogue") 163, 167
　savasana (corpse pose) *170*
　Self/"True Self" 12, 158, 159, 167, 168, 169
　Self/"True Self," embodied experience of 171–2, 173
　*shat kriyas* 166–9
　spiritual formation and progress 158, 159, 163–7, 168–9, 173
　Surya Namaskar (sun salutation) 155, *156*, 157, 158
　*sutra neti* 167–8, 174n7
　symbolic–somatic interplay 11, 159, 161, 173–4
　talk in situ 12, 159, 174
　"theology of the body" 12, 158, 159
　verbal instruction and cues 12, 157, 158, 159, 164, 169–72, 173
　vocabularies of motive and transcendent goals 159, 163–6
　"We are not the body" 155, 158, 168
　*yoga nidra* ("deep relaxation") 159, 165, 166, 170–2, 173
　yogic diet 166, 168–9
　*see also* Integral Yoga Institute
Integral Yoga Institute 162, 163, 164, 166, 168, 172, 173
　goals of 162, 164
　Integral Yoga altar 155
　teacher training manual 168, 169, 171–2
　teacher training program 155, 157, 158, 162–3, 165–6, 167, 172, 174n1
　TTs (teacher trainees) 155, 157, 158, 163, 165–6, 167, 169, 172
　*see also* Integral Yoga
interpretation
　academic disciplines as interpretive frameworks 13
　affect and emotion, interpretive relationship 12, 13, 206, 218
　Arunta rite of passage, interpretation of 35–6
　beautification practices as focal sites for interpretation 192
　bodies up for interpretation 203, 217, 218

bodily practices and 11, 13, 158, 159, 161, 166, 168, 172, 173, 203
body as interpretive medium, conduit, resource 37, 136, 144, 161, 204, 213
body's dependency on 8, 20
collective/shared 25, 159, 172
as concept for thinking about the body 5, 7
culture structures and 32, 33
as description/explanation x, 1, 34–6
discourse as interpretive space/framework 5, 10, 27, 136, 149, 179, 180, 185–6
discursive–interactionist interpretive framework 183–4
ethnography: interpretive benefits 162; participant observation and interpretive inquiry 207, 208
European beauty aesthetics and interpretation of Black styles 193
as focal metaphor 5
fuses matter with meaning 21
gendered bodies and 10, 29, 89, 94, 124, 136, 137, 144, 178, 185, 186, 191, 215–18
hermeneutics 24, 31–4, 165, 166
historical contingency and 74, 179, 183
interpreting the body 7–14
interpretive authority, positionality, and validity 10, 12, 23, 24, 37, 179, 191, 231
interpretive communities: Integral Yoga 158, 162, 164, 173; online 136, 143–4; protest 206
"interpretive epistemic mode" xiiin2
interpretive filters 11, 137
interpretive frameworks 6, 143, 173, 183, 186, 191, 212
interpretive labor 13, 212, 215
language and the interpretation of somatic experience 12, 173
literary form and 94
meaning-making and xi, xii, xiiin2, 5, 6, 7, 8, 12, 24, 28, 30, 31, 34, 160–1, 204, 213–14
minimal/maximal interpretation *see* maximal interpretation
misinterpretation of Black girls and Blackness 12, 179, 185, 186, 189–91, 194
misogynoir as anti-Black interpretive repertoire 179, 195
nonpositivist 231
oppression and victimhood, interpretive lens 89
phenomenology and 13, 105, 160
postmodernism and 4, 23–4
power/powerful contexts and 5, 7, 10, 29, 30, 118, 146, 179, 191, 215
as process involving: classification 20; interplay between discourse and practice 161, 169; selection/deselection 1, 5; signification 32; *technique* and *identity* 9
raced bodies and 10, 89, 94, 178, 187, 190, 193, 215–18
reflexive engagement with xi, 8
reinterpretation 12, 23, 89, 105, 110, 124, 125, 159, 163–5, 166, 196n5, 215
reinterpreting beauty 11, 134–8, 140–9
relationality and 90

schemas 183, 205
scholars' interpretive approaches: to narratives 174n3; to religious practices 160–1
*seselelāme*, as an interpretive template 68
*see also seselelāme*, interpretive distortion of
social interaction and 11, 12, 134, 146, 149, 179, 183, 191
social movements as resource for interpreting embodied experience 203, 204
social privilege as interpretive framework 214
sociology as *interpretive* science ix, 1, 2, 5, 23, 26, 31, 36, 37
solidarity, interpretive instantiations of 203, 212
systems of xii, 12, 27, 32, 134
talk as interpretive link between yoga practice and Integral Yoga's symbolic world 158, 167
*thick description* 35
vocabularies of motive and 159, 163–5
war on obesity, weight/fatness and 110, 111, 114, 118, 124
Zerubavel, Eviatar, interpretive approach 230
*see also* attention, interpretive process and; epistemology; Interpretive Lenses in Sociology; knowledge production; meaning; SPCS (Strong Program cultural sociology); theoretical traditions; ways of knowing
Interpretive Lenses in Sociology 5–7
*collective-formative* 5–6, 8, 9, 10, 11, 12, 13
*interactive-emergent* 6, 8, 10, 11, 12, 13
*psychosocial* 6–7, 8, 10
intersectional analysis 10, 89, 179, 195
interdisciplinary intersectionality 48–9, 52, 55, 61, 62n6, 62n9
intersectional discursive frames 184
intersectional subjugations 178, 179
*see also* theoretical traditions, intersectional
intersubjectivity
individualism, in contrast to 82, 83, 84
*interactive-emergent* interpretive lens 6, 8, 10, 11, 12, 13
interaffectivity 6
intercorporeality 6, 13, 183
as interpretive process by which the body comes to know itself 90–1
interrelationality 26, 173
men's intersubjective meanings 123
*seselelāme*'s intersubjectivity 9, 80–3, 84, 85nn8–9
*see also* social interaction; symbolic interactionism

# J

Jamison, Andrew 206
Jay, David 143
Jewel (singer/songwriter) 134, 138
Jewishness 56, 57, 60
Johnson, Boris 109–10, 113
Johnson, Mark 66, 73–4
Johnston, Erin F. 11–12, 155–77
Joseph, Nicole 186, 187, 188, 192
Jude, Julia 67, 76–7
Jutel, Annemarie 13, 223–37
*Diagnosis: Truths and Tales* 224

# INDEX

## K

Kimmerer, Robin Wall 231
King, Tiffany Lethabo 48, 62n8
Knorr Cetina, Karin 49, 61n2
knowledge production 9, 13, 45, 46, 58, 142, 158, 172, 180, 182
 *see also* epistemology; ways of knowing
Komabu-Pomeyie, Sefakor 9–10, 66–87
Koonce, Jacqueline 186
Kristeva, Julia 138

## L

Lakoff, George 66, 73–4
language
 affect, emotions and 205–6
 Akan (language community in Ghana) 71
 Anlo-Ewe (language community in Ghana) 66, 68, 75, 77, 82
 anti-Black linguistic racism 185
 *backtalk*, as embodied reverse discourse 186
 "blaccent" 185
 Black voice and vernacular 184–5, 188–9, 191
 body idiom, shared vocabularies and meanings of the body 184
 chemistry, language of 54, 58, 59
 conceptual framework for interpreting somatic experience 12
 embodied messages 195n2
 Integral Yoga, power of language 157, 158, 165, 169–70, 172–3
 language of diagnosis 224, 233
 linguistic double consciousness 185
 linguistic model, verbocentrism of 68
 linguistic orientation and "brown" racialization 59
 linguistic turn in sociology 23
 linguistics 3, 23, 224
 materialization of social facts and 25
 misogynoir, linguistic use and Black female identity 180–1
 non-Indigenous idioms 231
 rhetoric 30, 46, 109, 112, 135, 180
 *seselelāme*, linguistic interpretation, translation, and appropriation of 68, 73, 74, 78, 80, 82
 Shona (language community in Zimbabwe) 97
 silence: as an embodied politic of survival for Black girls 188–90; making the body speak 100, 102–3, 186; refusal 188
 social construction of the body/identity and 3, 4, 7, 57, 184, 217
 talk, cultural sociological approaches to 174n3
 talk in situ 12, 159, 174
 talking about the body, interpretive salience of 155, 157, 158, 161, 167, 169, 172
 Twi (language community in Ghana) 71
 *see also* discourse; semiotics; signification; symbols/symbolization
Laplantine, François 67, 70, 72, 84, 84n2
 *Life of the Senses* 70
Latour, Bruno 6, 26

Lavater, Johann Caspar 229
Leder, Drew 32, 234
Lei, Joy L. 190, 193
LGBTQ community 147–8
lived body 2, 22, 27, 33, 36, 37, 88, 120, 123
 lived experience 4, 9, 13, 27, 30, 31, 94, 173, 205, 217
 somatic inversion and 160
 *see also* affect; body; embodiment; phenomenology; the senses
Lizardo, Omar 6–7, 158, 162
Lohan, Maria 110, 121–2, 124
Lupton, Deborah 109, 113, 115, 123
Lyotard, Jean-François 23, 60

## M

Macon, Anna-Lisa F. 193
male bodies
 Black men's bodies 10, 89, 91, 94, 95, 104
 commodification of 113
 deviant 110, 113, 124
 "health" discourse and 112–13, 124
 as machines 112
 white male bodies 115
 *see also* masculinity; obesity and male bodies
Marxian perspectives
 Marxist formulations of class 57
 materialist critique of ideology 23
masculinity
 discredited masculinities 110, 112, 116
 masculine domination 110, 116, 117, 122, 125, 218
 men, masculinities, and health 121–3
 norms, myths, and symbols of 11, 112, 123–4
 privilege of 38n6
 social construction of masculinities 116–17
 as status shield 11, 118
 toxic masculinity 52
 as unmarked category 29
 *see also* male bodies; obesity and male bodies
mastectomy 8, 11, 28, 33–4, 133–4, 136, 137, 142, 145–6, 149
 agency 135
 beauty reinterpretation 11, 134, 135–6, 137–44, 149
 bilateral 136, 140, 143, 145, 147–8
 communities of experience and supportive daily interactions 11, 134, 136, 142–3, 149
 contralateral 136
 disfigurement discourse 133, 137
 disidentification, processes of 135, 138, 142, 149
 family interactions 34, 136, 144–6, 149
 "Flat and Fabulous" 143
 form and function 137, 138–40, 149
 gender nonconforming body and social stigma 142, 148–9
 imperative of concealment 133, 137, 138, 140, 141, 144, 145
 LGBTQ community 148
 living flat after 11, 34, 134–49, 150n2
 meaning of beauty in breast cancer recovery 134–6

normative beauty 11, 133, 134, 135, 137, 141, 144, 149
normative feminine embodiment 11, 134, 142, 144, 150n4
normative ideologies of gender 135, 150n3
prosthetics 134, 141, 145, 150n1
queerness, proximity to 144, 146–9
"Scar Project" 143
scars 133, 137, 139, 142–4, 149
sexuality and sexual attractiveness 146, 147
symmetry aesthetics 137, 140–2, 149
unilateral 136, 142
*see also* breast cancer; breast reconstruction; breasts
materiality/materialism/matter
academic disciplines and approaches to 2, 4–5, 13, 21–3, 45, 48–9, 69–70, 223, 224–5, 234
binary oppositions and *see* binary hierarchies; body/mind dichotomy
body, materiality of 2, 4–5
boundaries between meaning and matter 3
breast reconstruction and 33–4
constructionism and 3, 4, 5, 9
definition of 49
embodied technique 49, 62nn7–8
as essence or substance 3, 9, 44
feminist materialisms/neomaterialisms 4
fusion of meaning and matter 8, 27, 31, 37
material affordance 30, 37
material agency 4
material conditions of power and inequality 7, 10, 30, 57–8
material-cultural fasciae/webs of meaning 26, 32
material determinism 5
material-semiotic and material-symbolic perspectives 9, 27, 46, 47, 50, 55
material specificity 4, 10, 57–8
materialist explanation for health inequity 120, 122
meaning and matter *see* meaning, meaning and matter
new materialisms 6, 45, 53, 55, 62n8
as passive 9, 22, 47, 90
physical character of thought 67
pleasures of 10, 24, 57, 98–9
postmodern crisis of meaning and 23–6
post-structuralism, matter as an effect of power 3
prostheses (prosthetics) 134, 141, 145, 150n1
race and gender as material and substantial identities 55–6
the senses and sensation 24, 26, 27, 38, 66, 68, 69–70, 72, 78, 79, 82, 90–1, 98, 100, 139, 160, 169, 173
song, materiality of 49, 62n8
*see also* biology/physiology; body; body/mind dichotomy
Mauss, Marcel 62nn7–8, 90, 160
maximal interpretation 20, 28, 34–7, 38
definition 35
minimal/maximal interpretations, difference 35–6
*see also* Reed, Isaac Ariail

Mbembe, Achille 92
McCulley, Susan 73–4, 76, 77
McNaughton, Darlene 112
McWhorter, John 185, 196n6
Mead, George Herbert 2, 6, 21, 22
meaning
activation of meaning through illness 233
affect and 27, 210, 211, 214, 217
approaches to xi, xviii, 6, 8, 10, 19, 20, 27, 31–5, 68, 160–1, 203–4
beauty, meaning of the breast in cancer recovery 134–5, 138, 149
behavior as a conduit of meaning 204
behavioral relation between objectivities 33
binaries, relations of difference/opposition and 3, 12, 29, 38n7, 51
body idiom 184
body work and 182
collective, shared systems of ix, xi, 5, 6, 11, 19, 22, 24, 25, 26, 32, 33, 36, 37, 161, 183, 172, 184, 212–14
collective representations and 8, 29, 36, 37, 38
as core structures of self and identity ix
cultural codes and 6, 8, 30, 32
culture and 19, 22, 25, 29, 30, 31, 32, 36, 37, 38n7, 55
discourse and ix, 11, 12, 27, 37, 55, 161, 173, 174, 174n3, 182, 183
embodiment, embodied experiences/practices and 12, 20, 27, 31, 32, 33, 34, 37, 59, 93, 161, 172, 173, 182, 203, 204, 218
gender/race and 7, 10, 11, 12, 29, 32, 47, 55, 89, 93, 111, 123, 134, 135, 217
hermeneutic reconstruction of 20, 24, 28, 30, 31–4, 38
history of slavery and the meaning of blackness 60
how bodies take on meaning xii, 3–4, 8, 12, 19–21, 27, 30–3, 36–7, 142, 161, 178, 182–4, 213, 217, 233
imagination and 37
indican, biochemical molecule and the meaning of blackness 48
"landscapes of meaning" 20, 28, 35 *see also* Reed, Isaac Ariail
meaning and matter xii, xviii, 3–4, 5, 7, 8, 9, 20, 21, 25, 27, 30–4, 37, 47, 48, 55, 59, 89, 111, 161, 174
meaninglessness: free play/experimentation, variety, and the flattening of meaning 24, 30, 59, 232
*moles*, meaning of 51
objective/subjective ix, 24, 25, 33, 36, 69, 70, 78, 123, 161, 173, 174, 183, 214
poles of meaning delimit lines or poles of potential action 31
postmodern crisis of meaning 23–6
power and 3, 5, 6, 7, 10, 27, 29, 30–1, 32, 51, 60, 182, 183, 218
process of signification 26
as psychic structures 6
religious frameworks and 213–14

religious practice and 160, 174, 174n3
*seselelāme*: distortions of its organic meanings 67; meaning of 78
sign and 32, 38n7, 135
as social force 23, 184
social meanings 34, 35, 183
sociophysiological 10
SPCS (Strong Program cultural sociology), meaning-centered approach to body and embodiment 20, 22, 33, 36, 37
symbolic interaction and 12, 183
symbols and 3, 7, 8, 19, 20, 21, 27, 30, 31, 34, 36, 37, 38, 55, 160, 161, 174n3, 233
*thick description* cultural analysis and 34, 35
ubiquity of 30, 32
webs of meaning 32, 33, 36, 68, 111
*wellness*, meanings of 34
*see also* interpretation; signification
meaning-making ix, 6, 7, 14, 20, 25, 28, 30, 34, 37, 38n2, 219
medicine xii, 11, 22, 66, 82
critiques of 113, 118
epistemic authority of 113
surveillance medicine 113, 117
*see also* diagnosis; health; public health; sociology of diagnosis
Merleau-Ponty, Maurice 19, 25, 62n8, 69, 90–1, 204
*Phenomenology of Perception* 91
metaphor 5, 22, 33, 38n3, 50, 51, 82, 84, 118, 159, 161, 166–9, 233
Miles, Brittney 12, 178–201
Millard, Jennifer 135
Miller, Christopher 52–3, 54, 60
Miller, William Ian 178
Mills, C. Wright 159, 230
mind–body dualism *see* binary hierarchies; body/mind dichotomy; Descartes, René; Integral Yoga, body/mind dualism
misogynoir 178, 179, 180–3, 184, 192, 194, 195, 195n1
modernity 1, 2, 23–4, 69, 89, 92, 93, 96, 104, 118
the molecular
"biomythography" of racialized molecules 48, 60
Blackness and 55, 56, 57
critical race theory 9, 44–5, 55
Deleuzo–Guattarian concept of the molecular 50–4
DNA 45–7, 50
embodied artistic research *see* artistic research, embodied
embodied technique 49, 57, 62nn7–8
hard and soft molecules 45–50
interdisciplinary intersectionality 48–9, 52, 55, 61, 62n6
knowledge production processes, circular 9, 46
lead and mercury (metals) 47–8
material-semiotic perspective 9, 46, 47, 50, 55
molecular theory of identity 44, 46, 47, 54, 58–60
molecularization of race and identity 51–5
molecules as materially and socioculturally constructed 9, 44, 45–8, 50

molecules of *technique-identity* 9, 46, 47, 55–7, 58–9
performance studies 9, 44, 58
quantitative methods, epistemic primacy of 44
race as concept of technique/identity 57
race and gender as material and substantial identities 55–6
radical asymmetry of 9, 44–5, 54–61
romance of the molecular 50–5
as technique and identity 9, 46, 51, 53–4, 57, 59, 61
technique as knowledge 9, 44, 46, 47, 50
technoscientific knowledge/practices 9, 44, 45–50, 53, 57
technoscientific knowledge, racial and gender hierarchies behind 45–8, 50, 55
testosterone 46–7, 50
Monaghan, Lee F. 10–11, 109–32
morality 5, 9, 25–6
body, meaning and moral valence 5, 30–1, 36, 38n6
body work and 3, 13
Christian morality 98
"duty to beauty" as moral endeavor 229–30
health and 118, 121
interpretation/meaning and ix, 5, 20, 31
moral significance of the molecular 9
motifaction and 20, 38n3
SPCS of the body and embodiment, moral aspects 26, 27, 29, 31, 36–7, 38
Morris, Edward W. 186, 187
Morris, Monique 189
motifaction 20, 22, 36–7, 38, 38n3
motif and 22, 38n3
power of 36, 38n3
*see also* Black, David
Muñoz, José Esteban 59, 135
Myers, Natasha 44, 45
myth 22, 31, 36, 37, 235n1
"biomythography" 48, 60, 62n5
myths of masculinity 123–4

**N**

NAACP (National Association for the Advancement of Colored People) 182
Nair, Supriya 96
neoliberalism 67, 119–20
"color-blind" neoliberal racism 181
health inequalities and 119–20, 121, 123
neoliberal capitalism 11
patriarchy and 110
*Nervous Conditions* (Tsitsi Dangarembga) 10, 89, 95–6, 104–5
agency 97, 103, 104
ambivalence 96, 103–4
Anna 97
Babamukuru 95, 96, 97, 98, 100–4, 105
Black Zimbabwean women 89, 94
Blackness, phenomenology of 89, 90–2, 104, 105
Chido 95, 97, 99, 105
colonial Christianity 95, 98, 100, 102
colonial education 96–8, 100, 102–5

dancing and pleasure 98–100
defamiliarization 95
Fanon, Frantz and 10, 89, 91–2, 94–5
girls' bodies and colonial power 10, 90
Maiguru 95, 97–8, 100–1, 103
Ma'Shingayi 95, 100, 104
mission school 95–7, 101, 102
nervous condition 94–5, 96, 100, 104–5
Nhamo 95, 97, 105
Nyasha 10, 89, 95–6, 97, 98, 99–102, 103, 104, 105
as organic theory of the native woman's body 10, 94
physical body's disappearance and colonized womanhood 10, 94, 99, 101, 103–5
postcolonial awareness 104
regulating "good native girls" 98–100, 103, 105
sexuality 89, 91, 92, 98, 100
sick bodies: hunger, longing, and wasting away 100–3
Tambu 10, 89, 95–101, 102–4, 105
*see also* gender on the post-colony
Norwood, Kristen 208
Nunn, Nia Michelle 194

## O

obesity
  2008 great Financial Crisis and 109
  BMI 111, 113, 116–17
  childhood obesity 111–12, 113, 116, 117
  crises and 109, 111
  critical studies on 112, 113–15, 119, 120, 123, 125–6
  as discursively constructed rather than deviation from normative weight values 232
  "dual COVID-19/obesity crisis frame" 109, 111, 113, 115, 118
  fitness and 110, 117
  framing of obesity as epidemic/public health crisis 10, 109, 111–15
  gender inequality in body norms 116, 117
  obesity alarmism 10, 124
  "obesity-survival paradox" 113
  overweight as category of disease 113, 232
  sociology of diagnosis on overweight 232, 233
  stigma and discrimination related to 114, 115, 116
  war on obesity 109, 110, 111, 118
  war on obesity, critique of 114–15, 118
  *see also* health; obesity and male bodies; public health
obesity and male bodies 10–11, 110, 123–6
  discredited masculinities 110, 112, 116
  gendered "body project" 110, 112, 118
  "health" discourse as means of controlling socially deviant bodies 10, 110, 112
  medicalization of men's bodies as "overweight" 112–13, 115–16
  medicalized calls to fight fat/weight 111–13
  men, masculinities, and health 121–3
  obesity epidemic rhetoric 112–13
  obesity warmongering 110, 115–16, 118

social construction of masculinities and 116–17
stigma 116
surveillance medicine 113, 117
symbolic violence 110, 117
war on obesity as expression of masculine domination 110, 116, 117, 124
*see also* health; masculinity; obesity; public health
Olssen, Mark 3
Ong, Bie Nio 120
ontology 25, 28, 48, 49, 59, 62n9, 84, 232
  biomythographic ontology 60
  culture and matter, ontological distinction between 48
  deontologisation/reontologisation of race 50–1, 57–8
  embodied vulnerability as an ontological given 204
  movement as ontological ground of the body 3–4
  "object-oriented ontology" 62n9
  ontological force 49
  ontological traditions 66
  ontological uncertainty 24
  "ontological wonder" 53
  social ontology of the body 19–20
  technoscientific ontologies 45, 50
othering 75, 179, 180, 188
  in-groups vs out-groups 7
  nonbelonging 97
  outsider 173, 178, 192, 193
  stigmatized 193
Oyewùmí, Oyèrónké 92, 93

## P

Parsons, Talcott 2, 22, 38n5
Passy, Florence 204
Patchay, Sheena 100
patriarchy 3, 89, 110, 188
  colonial patriarchy 89, 95, 96, 98, 100, 102
  neoliberalism and 110
perception xviii, 6, 66, 69, 81, 84n2, 98, 99, 204
  of Black children 187
  bodily discomfort as way of perceiving state violence 213
  breast reconstruction, perceived imperative 150n7
  disappearance of the body and 227
  disrespect and disruption, perceptions of 185
  gendered perceptions of overweight/obesity 117
  interoception 80, 81, 83
  intuition 79
  invisibility and 190
  lived body/experience and 37, 217
  material specificity of the body and 10
  Merleau-Ponty and the phenomenology of 91, 204
  "perceptual communities" 213
  perceptual filters 6, 29
  perceptual reframing of the body 159
  perceptual selection 1
  proprioception 81
  recessive body and 99
  ritual and 160
  self-presentation, self-perception of 194
  sensation and 69, 90

social values and 69
"visceral perception" 85n8
visceroception 81
*see also* epistemology; interpretation; knowledge production; phenomenology; the senses; ways of knowing
performance studies 9, 44, 58, 60
Petersen, Alan 115
phenomenology 7, 10, 19, 24, 95, 105n1
   Blackness, phenomenology of 10, 89, 90–2, 94, 104, 105, 217
   body studies, phenomenological tradition of 19, 89, 90–1, 205, 217
   corporeal schema 89, 91
   cultural phenomenology 69
   Merleau-Ponty's phenomenology of perception 90–1, 204
   phenomenological ground of *seselelāme* 9
   phenomenology of illness 224
   phenomenology of race and racism 89, 90–4, 104–5, 217
   poles of action 29, 31
   religious practices as phenomenological experience 160
   reversibility, phenomenology of 31, 34
   social movements, phenomenological approach 13, 204, 219
   sociogeny 91
   *see also* theoretical traditions, phenomenology
Pickett, Kate 119
Pitts-Taylor, Victoria 3, 4, 7, 134, 136
positivism ix, 1–2, 21, 24, 50
   critique of 13, 50, 231
   positivist epistemology 22, 231
postcolonialism xii
   postcolonial awareness 104
   postcolonial criticism 92
   postcolonial feminism 10, 92
   postcolonial literature 89, 96
   postcolonial modernity 104–5
   *see also* decolonization; gender on the post-colony; *Nervous Conditions*
postmodernism 4, 23–4
   postmodern crisis of meaning 23–6
   postmodern *egalité* 24
   theorization of the body and 20, 25–6
   *see also* theoretical traditions, postmodernism
post-structuralism 3, 4, 24, 26, 50, 56
power 27
   body/materiality and power 4, 5, 9, 10
   colonial power 89, 92–3
   diagnosis and power 223–4
   discursive power 3, 180, 182, 183
   embodied vulnerability and social power 205, 211, 215
   Foucault, Michel on 3, 6, 29
   institutional power 7, 216–17
   intersectionality and power 52, 55, 122, 124, 178, 179, 216–19
   meaning/language and 7, 29, 30–1, 49, 50, 55, 59–61, 67, 135–6, 142, 149
   molar/molecular distinction and power 52, 54
   reverse discourse 188
   social research and power 209
   subject as an effect of power 3
   symbolic relations of power 30
   teacher/student power dynamics 179, 184
   ubiquity of 29–30, 32
pragmatism *see* American pragmatism; theoretical traditions, pragmatism
praxeological approaches 19, 24, 33, 38n2
   *see also* American pragmatism; pragmatism; theoretical traditions: Bourdieusian/practice theory, performance studies, performativity
Preciado, Paul 47, 63n3
psychology 68, 69, 80–3, 84, 84n2, 85nn8–9
   experimental psychology 81
   "mind–body problem" 80, 85n8
   psychoanalysis xiii, 91, 92
   psychoanalytic perspectives xviii, 6, 22, 91, 92
   psychological anthropology 68
   *seselelāme*, in academic psychology 80
   therapy 66, 76, 84
   social psychology 80
   sociology, in contradistinction to 22, 83
public health
   framing of "excess" weight/fat as public health crisis 111–12, 113, 114–15
   "stigma system" 120
   *see also* health

## Q

quantum physics 4–5
queer 60, 138, 144, 146–9

## R

Raby, Rebecca 194
race and racism
   anti-Black discourses 12, 179–80, 185–6, 188, 193–4
   "color-blind" neoliberal racism 181
   deontologisation/reontologisation of race 50–1, 57–8
   DNA and 45–6
   ethnicons 57, 60, 62n14
   gendering operates in parallel ways to racialization 92–3
   metal lead and 47–8
   molecularization of race and identity 51–5
   phenomenology of race and racism 89, 90–4, 104–5, 217
   race categories 3, 50, 55–6, 60, 89, 231
   race and gender as material and substantial identities 55–6
   race as technique/identity 46, 51, 53–4, 57
   racial consciousness 10, 91, 185, 218
   racial differences 5
   racial discrimination and cultural signification 30
   racial identities 46, 47–8, 51, 57, 92
   the racial as molecular materiality of technique/identity 51–7
   racial normalization 31

racialization 3, 9, 12, 30, 46, 47–8, 55, 59, 62, 75, 84, 88, 89, 91, 92, 94, 100, 104, 180–1, 185, 190–3, 202, 215
racialized bodies 10, 55, 57, 88, 89, 91, 92, 95, 104, 105, 180, 188, 192, 193, 195
racist tropes 180, 192
school discipline and 181
structural racism 11, 119
see also Black bodies; Black girls' bodies in educational settings; Blackness, the molecular and
Rajan-Rankin, Sweta 10, 88–108
rational choice 2
rational actor 21, 22, 23
rationality 1, 4, 21, 22, 23, 38n6, 67, 69, 77, 83, 90, 91, 92, 112
Reed, Isaac Ariail x, xiiinn2–3, xiiin5, 20, 28, 32
Rehabilitation Act (1973) 2
relationality 68, 82
gender relations, relational power context of 122
identity formation and 69, 116
knowing the self and 90
relational approach to the study of the body 70
socialization, relational selves 70
see also intersubjectivity; social interaction; symbolic interaction
religion and spirituality
colonial Christianity 95, 98, 100, 102
embodied religious practices 160–1, 173, 174
solidarity activism and 209, 212, 213–14
the symbolic in religious practices 37, 160, 174n3
symbolic/somatic interplay in religious practice 11, 161, 174
"theologies of the body" 161
see also Integral Yoga
research methods
biomythography as 62n5
critical hermeneutic 57
embodied 203, 211, 219
embodied artistic 60–1
embodied vulnerability and 13, 203, 206, 207–11
empiricism of mainstream sociology 231
ethnography 13, 45, 75, 111, 116, 158, 162, 207, 208, 216, 219
experimental 44, 60
historical development of sociological methodologies 2
interviews 34, 116, 136, 162–3
narrative analysis xi
"observant participation" 207
participant observation 162–3, 207
positivism 2, 22, 230–1
"practice as research" 60
psychological 80–2
qualitative ix, x, 208
quantitative ix, 55
research ethics 209
semiotics xi
social pattern analysis 230
Strong Program cultural sociology methodological commitments 20, 28

technoscientific 50, 57
*thick description* 35
reverse discourse 181–2, 196n5
Black girls' bodies, embodied reverse discourse 12, 181–3, 186, 188, 195, 196n5
body work and 182
definition 196n5
Riediger, Natalie 115
ritual 8, 21, 28, 34, 36, 93, 160, 213
Robertson, Roland 21, 22, 23, 25
Robertson, Steve 110, 121, 122, 123, 124
Rodriguez, Dylan 206
Rosenberg, Charles 233
Rosenberg, Jordy 53
Russo, Chandra 12–13, 202–22

**S**

Saldanha, Arun 50–1
Sartre, Jean-Paul 91, 94–5
Satchidananda, Swami 155, 162, 172
Scambler, Graham 118, 119, 120, 122, 125
Schneider, Joseph W. 113, 233
Scott-Samuel, Alex 110, 119–20
self
agency and 3–4, 183, 204
as an achievement 25
beauty and 135
biographical disruption of 33, 133–4, 147–8
body as mutable outer representation of 3
embodied self 25, 31–2, 33, 36, 138, 210
Integral Yoga, eternal/"True Self" 12, 157, 158, 167, 168, 169, 171–2, 173
inward Black self 190
narrative, discourse, meaning and the self ix, 161, 183
power and the self 3
protean reinvention of 24
race, heightened awareness and 218
as rational actor 22
religious practices and 160
self-actualization 3
self-care 2
self-expression 3
see also SPCS of the body and embodiment, self and society as reciprocally constituted through the physical body; subjectivity
semiotics xi, xii, 3
affordances of the physical body and 30, 31, 34, 37, 135
material-semiotic perspective 5, 6, 9, 31, 46, 47, 50, 55
mimesis 34
see also language; signification; symbols/ symbolization
the senses
aesthetic experience and 33, 141–3
*Culture and the Senses* 75
the five-senses model 70
*Life of the Senses* 70
mind/body dualism and 90
*Phenomenology of Perception* 91
pleasure and 24, 78, 98

# INDEX

sensation/sensory experience 24, 27, 68, 69, 70, 78, 79, 98, 139, 160, 169
sensemaking 12–13, 203, 206–7, 212, 219
sense/sensory studies 69–70, 85n5
sensibility and 31, 32
the sensible 67, 72, 74, 83
sensible objects 69
sensorium 69–70
sensory-emotional 9, 66, 82
smell 160, 178
touch 31–2, 34, 72
*see also* aesthetics; embodiment; materiality/materialism/matter, the senses and sensation; sound; vision; voice
*seselelāme* 9, 10, 66–7, 83–4, 85n6
  in academic parlance 68–70, 83
  in African everyday terms 67–8, 70–3, 82
  Anlo-Ewe speakers' interpretation of 78–80, 82
  Anlo-Ewe ways of knowing 10, 66
  in Black Atlantic worlds 68
  as bodily ways of knowing 9, 67, 68, 69, 70, 74, 79–80
  Bourdieu's *habitus* and 69, 78
  categorical thinking and 70, 72, 76, 77, 84
  commodification of 9, 67, 73, 77, 83, 84
  as concept "everything is connected" 67, 77
  cultural appropriation of 9, 67, 73, 75–6, 80, 83, 84
  emotional dimensions of 9, 66–7, 72–3, 78, 82–3
  fitness and 73, 74, 76, 82
  Global North use of 9, 66–7, 73–7, 80, 82, 83, 84
  globalization and 67, 69, 73–7
  as globally reaching "family of related cultural models" 68
  interpretive distortion of 9, 67, 73–7, 80, 82, 83, 84
  intersubjectivity and 9, 82–3, 84
  modal thinking and 70–3, 77, 78–9, 84
  New Age and 67, 74
  as opposed to euro-American ways of being 66
  as pan-African foundational schema 68
  psychology and 80–3, 85nn8–9
  sensory studies 70, 85n5
  *see also* Anlo-Ewe people (southeastern Ghana)
sexuality
  Black girls' bodies 98, 193, 194
  Christian morality and 98
  colonialism and 89, 91, 92, 100
  as cultural category 7, 52, 56
  Female Hypoactive Sexual Desire Disorder 232
  mastectomy and 146, 147
  misogynoir discourses and black female sexuality 181, 192
  *Nervous Conditions* 98, 100
  testosterone, gender and 47
Shepherd, Philip 67, 74, 75–6, 77
  *Radical Wholeness* 74, 75
Shilling, Chris 2, 3, 5, 19, 22, 160, 161, 182, 183–4, 234

Shore, Brad 68
sight *see* the senses; vision
signification 20, 26, 30, 32, 39n11
  emotions as system of signification 206
  form/content 32, 36
  frailty, Falstaff's flesh in Shakespeare's *Henry IV* as signifier of 112
  interpretation and 32
  materiality of 39n10
  muscles, racially signified 150n5
  reverse discourse, use of dominant discourse signifiers in 196n5
  sign 20, 24, 26, 32, 35, 36, 38n7, 39nn10–11, 44, 50, 53
  significant gestures 30
  signified 31, 32
  signifier 32, 36, 39n10, 196n5
  "signifyin(g)" 68
  signifying structures 35
  surface/depth 26, 31, 32
  vanity, breast reconstruction as signifier of 141
  *see also* interpretation; meaning; semiotics; symbols/symbolization
Simmel, Georg 2, 21–2
Sivananda, Swami 155, 162
Sledge, Piper 11, 133–54
Smith, Philip 6, 20, 23, 25, 26, 27, 28, 31, 38n7
social action ix, 2, 20, 22, 24, 38, 183
  the body, in theories of 22
  cultural codes and 30
  as cultural performance 38n1
  economic-cum-social action 23, 25
  meaning, power and 31
  "motifactional" force and 20, 22, 36–7
  postmodernism and 24
  semiotic significance of ix
  *see also* action; behavior; social interaction; symbolic interactionism
social constructionism
  body, social construction of 7, 14, 88, 90, 117, 124, 134
  Cartesian dualism and 90
  childhood 111
  gender, social construction of 31, 33, 46–7, 105, 117, 133, 139, 144, 148–9, 150n5, 179, 181, 192, 227
  masculinities, social construction of 11, 46–7, 116–17, 124
  molecules as materially and socioculturally constructed 9, 44, 45–8, 49, 50
  obesity 119–20
  race 31, 48, 180, 181, 192, 195
  social constructionism/phenomenology comparison 105n1
  *see also* theoretical traditions, social constructionism
social interaction ix, 11, 20, 21, 144, 149, 150n5, 178
  avoidance of 178
  creative resistance through 150n3
  family/parent–child interactions 10, 34, 136, 144, 146

257

interpersonal "communities of experience" and 11, 149
"maneuverability" and bodily negotiation 12, 183
mediating role of breastedness/breastlessness in intimate social interactions 144, 146
microlevel 11, 12, 179, 183
misogynoir, interactional contexts 180, 182
reassembling the social and 26
teachers/students interactions 12, 179, 184, 185, 186–8, 189–90, 191, 192, 194, 195
*see also* intersubjectivity; relationality; social action; symbolic interactionism
social justice 121, 123, 125, 208
social movements
affect/emotion in 205–6, 209, 214, 219
Black Lives Matter 104, 119
the body in 13, 203, 204
civil rights and 2, 119
civil rights movement 2, 181
disability rights 2
feminist/women's movements 2, 23, 88, 93, 105, 110–11, 113, 117, 118, 232
as knowledge projects 206
religion in 213–14
School of the Americas Watch 202
social movements as *sensemaking* projects 13, 203, 204, 206, 215, 219
social movement studies 203, 204, 206, 209, 210
US/Mexico border justice movement 202, 207–8
Witness Against Torture 202
*see also* activism; solidarity activism
sociology
American Sociological Association (ASA) xviii, 231
body and 1–7, 21–3
body, absence from sociological theory/disembodied approach 1, 19, 21–3, 234
"carnal sociology" 162 *see also* Crossley, Nick
classical and early sociology 1–2, 4, 6, 20, 21–3, 25
cognitive sociology/approaches xviii, 6, 85n9, 206
contemporary sociology 20, 23, 38
corporeal turn in 2–3, 19, 23
cultural sociology xviii, 6, 8, 19–38 passim, 174
distinction from other scientific disciplines 1–2, 22–3, 83
embodied/disembodied sociological approach 114, 208, 231, 234
interpretation/interpretive endeavor ix–xii, 1, 2, 27, 28, 31, 37, 118, 208
macro-sociology/macro-social perspectives 25, 38n1, 116, 118, 119, 125, 183
medical sociology 10–11, 110, 118–23
micro-sociology/micro-social perspectives 25, 124
modern sociology 22–3, 24, 37, 70
neo-modern context 25, 38
phenomenology, sociological treatments of 204
physical duress, sociological perspective on 209
physical matter and 2
positivism and 1–2, 21, 22, 231

postmodern 4, 23–6, 37
postwar sociology 21
*process*, attention to 5–7
professionalization of 21, 38n4
psychoanalytic sociology xviii
as scientific discipline 21–3
semiotic turn in 3
sociological critique 125
sociological imagination 230
sociological models of identities as labels or axes 58
sociology of the body 20, 23, 27–8, 33, 37–8, 195
*see also* Interpretive Lenses in Sociology; research methods; sociology of diagnosis; SPCS (Strong Program cultural sociology); theoretical traditions
sociology of diagnosis 13, 223–5, 232–4
crowdsourcing diagnosis 223, 233
diagnosis is everywhere 233
drapetomania 232
Female Hypoactive Desire Disorder 232
gender and 225–30
language of diagnosis 224, 233
low libido as illness 232
overweight 232, 233
pharmaceutical industry marketing and disease creation 232
self-diagnosis 223
social patterns 230
stillbirth 232
"thingness" and diagnosis 232
*see also* diagnosis; health; sociology, medical sociology
solidarity activism 12–13, 202–3, 207, 213, 215, 218, 219
affect and emotion 12–13, 205–6, 214
arrests and jail time 206, 213, 215
civil disobedience 203, 215, 219
contesting US policies 202–3, 207–8, 213
desert pilgrimage 203, 206, 207, 213–14
embodied *practices* and *feelings* of solidarity 203, 212–13, 219
embodied vulnerability 12–13, 203, 204–7, 212, 215, 219
embodiment of 202, 203
fasting 203, 206, 213–14
high-risk activism 203, 205, 209, 212, 215, 217, 219, 220n2
interpreting labors 13, 211–15
interpreting raced and gendered bodies 215–19
Migrant Trail Walk 13, 202, 207–15
observant participation 202, 207, 210–11
phenomenological approach 13, 204–205
physically demanding protest 203, 205, 206, 207, 211, 212, 213, 215
privilege based on race, gender, class 13, 205, 214–15, 217, 218, 220n2
religious and spiritual practices 209, 212, 213–14
School of the Americas Watch 202, 215–16
social movements as *sensemaking* projects 13, 203, 206, 212–15, 219
solidarity witnessing 12, 13, 203, 219

# INDEX

US security state  205, 215, 216, 219
US state violence  203, 213, 215, 217, 218, 220n2
Witness Against Torture  202, 213
*see also* activism; research methods, embodied vulnerability and; social movements
Solomon Linda, "Mbube" song  85n10
sound
  Black girls' sonic performances  191, 192
  laughter  155, 157, 188, 190–2, 195
  quiet  189–90, 191
  as signifier  39n10
  silence  171, 188–90, 210
  soft vocal tone, association with whiteness  191
  "sonic flutters" and racialized understandings of accented speech  185
  *sounding* Black  185, 195
  volume/loudness, gendered and racialized stereotypes  186–8, 190–2, 194
  *see also* the senses; voice
Spatz, Ben  9, 44–65
  *Blue Sky Body*  62n6
  *What a Body Can Do*  62n7
SPCS (Strong Program cultural sociology)  6, 8, 27, 28, 29, 31, 36–8
  critique of  28–9, 38n7
  cultural sociologist, task of  26
  Durkheim, Emile and  26
  *see also* SPCS, methodological commitments; SPCS of the body and embodiment
SPCS, methodological commitments
  hermeneutic reconstruction of meaning  20, 28, 30, 31–4, 35, 37, 38
  maximal interpretation  20, 28, 34–7, 38
  relative autonomy of culture  6, 8, 20, 28–31, 38
  *see also* SPCS (Strong Program cultural sociology); SPCS of the body and embodiment
SPCS of the body and embodiment  8, 20–1, 23, 26, 27, 37–8
  breast cancer-related mastectomy (example)  8, 28, 33–4
  changing brown eyes to blue with contact lenses (example)  8, 28, 30
  cultural codes  6, 8, 20, 32, 33, 37
  ideality/materiality binary  8, 20, 22, 25, 37
  interpretive methodology of  28–37
  meaning and  19–20, 27–38
  meaning-centered approach to body and embodiment  20, 22, 33, 36, 37
  moral aspects  26, 27, 29, 31, 36–7, 38
  ritualized tooth extraction (example)  8, 28, 35–6
  self and society as reciprocally constituted through the physical body  8, 27, 37, 38
  structuration of bodily meaning  8, 27
  subjectivity/objectivity binary  8, 20, 22, 25
  symbolic dimension of the corporeal and lived body  19, 25, 26, 27, 30, 31, 35, 36–7
  *see also* SPCS (Strong Program cultural sociology)
Stoltz, Dustin S.  38n7
Strauss, Claudia  68

Strong Program in cultural sociology  *see* SPCS (Strong Program cultural sociology)
structuralism  3, 53, 56, 62n13
subjectivity
  academic disciplines, biographical account  13, 225–34
  Black subjectivities  179–80
  body and self  3, 13, 22, 23, 25, 179
  postmodernism and  24–5
  religious practices and  160
  researcher's embodied subjectivity  13
  *seselelāme*, intersubjectivity  9, 82–3, 84
  subject formation  24–5, 38n2, 92
  subjectivity-idealism vs reason-society  22
  subjectivity/objectivity binary  8, 20, 22, 25
  *see also* intersubjectivity; self
symbolic interactionism  6, 12, 22, 137, 150n3
  Black girls' bodies in educational settings  12, 183–4
  Society for the Study of Symbolic Interaction  xviii
  *see also* Blumer, Herbert; Mead, George Herbert; theoretical traditions, symbolic interactionism
symbols/symbolization  8, 11, 19, 30, 34
  as background against which bodies and social action are observed  35
  body as material/natural symbol  1, 3, 8, 11
  body as site of explicit symbolism  161
  breasts as symbol of female value  144
  *collective-formative* interpretive framework and  5–6
  emblematization  21, 36, 142
  icons and  36, 39n10
  as ideal vs instrumental resource  20, 38
  identity and  55
  illness, activation of symbolic meanings of the body  233
  Integral Yoga and symbolic/somatic interplay in religious practice  11, 159, 161, 173–4
  interpretive sociology and  2
  intuitive symbolic reality  39n11
  living reality and  25–26
  masculinized symbols  112
  prayer ties, symbolism of  212, 213
  religious practices understood symbolically  160, 174n3
  reversibility with matter  31
  social-symbolic field, symbolic "distinctions" within  29
  *subjective* matter, symbolic foundations of  22
  symbolic asymmetries, power, and violence  7, 67, 84, 110, 117
  symbolic basis of economic-cum-social action  23
  symbolic dimensions of the body  3, 7, 8, 9, 11, 12, 14, 19, 20, 25, 26, 27, 30, 31, 35, 36–7, 88, 89, 90, 105, 112, 124, 144, 159, 161, 180, 182, 183, 184
  symbolic dimensions of social life  8, 25–6, 31
  symbolic relations of power, reciprocal relation to meaning  7, 30

symbolic–somatic interplay 11, 159, 161
symbolic system 11, 12, 27, 37, 117
symbolic webs, fasciae, ligatures, connective tissues 21, 27, 32, 35, 68
symbolic worlds 158, 160
symbolization and meaning-making 30
*see also* semiotics; signification; symbolic interactionism; totemism

## T

TallBear, Kim 45–6, 50
Taonui, Rāwiri 230, 235n1
technique 9, 27, 44, 47, 58, 167
  technique/technology and identity 47
  academic disciplinary technique 229, 230
  embodied 49, 62nn7–8
  epistemic technique 51
  gender as technique 62n3
  identity and 46, 47, 50, 51, 53–4, 56–61
  Indigenous technique (knowledge and ways of being) 53
  literary 95
  molecules of 9, 46, 54
  representational techniques 1
  techniques of the body 90, 160
  "techniques of the self" 47
technology 1, 2, 23, 31, 45, 49, 121, 134, 179, 180
theoretical traditions x–xii, xviii, 5–8, 9
  Black feminism 89, 105n1, 181, 188
  Bourdieusian/practice theory 6, 19, 20, 29, 33, 36, 69, 78, 90, 122, 123, 160
  classical sociological 1, 2, 4, 6, 21, 22
  cognitive sociology 6, 85n9
  critical race theory 9, 44, 55, 88, 217
  cultural sociology 6, 8, 20, 26, 27–38, 85n9, 174n3
  deconstructionism 4
  Durkheimian 1, 2, 6, 21, 25–6, 35–7, 209
  embodied artistic research 9, 44, 48, 49, 60–1, 62n3
  feminist/gender theory 3–5, 6, 10, 51, 57, 62n3, 76, 88–9, 90, 92–4, 105, 110, 111, 112, 134–5, 137, 149, 217, 225–6, 231
  feminist materialism 4–5
  Foucauldian/discourse analysis 3, 6, 29, 62n7, 90, 122–3, 179, 230
  hermeneutic 20, 24, 28, 31–4, 37
  intersectional 10, 49–50, 52, 55, 62n6, 62n9, 89, 178–9, 184, 195, 217–18
  literary criticism 224
  Marxian 23, 57
  modern 23–5, 37, 38, 69, 70
  performance studies 9, 44, 58, 60
  performativity xii, 3, 8, 22, 36, 45, 62n8
  phenomenology 7, 10, 13, 19, 24, 69, 76, 85n7, 89, 90–2, 94, 105, 105n1, 204–5, 217, 219, 224
  postcolonial xii, 10, 89, 92
  postmodernism 4, 20, 23–6, 37
  post-structuralism 3–4, 24, 26, 50, 56
  pragmatism 6

psychoanalysis xiii, 6, 10, 91–2
social constructionism 7, 88, 90, 105n1, 227
subaltern studies 93
symbolic interactionism 6, 12, 19, 22, 137, 150n3, 183–4
Weberian 2, 6, 21, 22, 38n5, 231
*see also* Interpretive Lenses in Sociology
totemism 21, 36
  *totemic principle* 36
transgender 47, 60, 142, 143, 148, 149, 150n4
Turner, Bryan 2, 20, 38n5, 85n9, 234
Turner, Paaige 208
Turner, Terence 23

## V

van der Riet, Pamela 138
Vannini, Phillip 3, 6, 138, 150n3
Vargas, João Costa 202, 207
Vertinsky, Patricia A. 226–7, 234
vision
  embodied disposition as a way of seeing experience 90
  scars, seeing surgical results 143
  seeing, socially patterned by experience and action 161
  *seselelāme* as an emotional expression of seeing 72
  *see also* the senses
voice 12, 172, 184, 185, 189, 195, 225
  *see also* the senses; sound
vulnerability *see* solidarity activism

## W

Wacquant, Loïc 158, 162
Waskul, Dennis 3, 6, 138, 150n3
ways of knowing 45, 90
  protest tactics, affect, embodied vulnerability and 205–6, 213
  *seselelāme* as bodily way of knowing 9, 10, 66–8, 70, 74, 76, 79, 80, 82, 84
  *see also* epistemology; interpretation; knowledge production; perception
WCHP (Weight-Centered Health Paradigm) 112, 113, 114, 118
Weber, Max 2, 6, 21, 22
Weinberg, Darin 90
Weitz, Rose 142, 143
Well Now project 114, 125
West, Candace 6, 137, 141
whakapapa 230, 235n1
Wiest, Julie B. ix–xiii, xviii, xix, 5–6
Wilderson, Frank 56, 62n13
Wilkinson, Richard 119
Williams, Gareth H. 121
Williams, Lauren 116
Williams, Robert 110, 121, 122, 123, 124
Williams, Simon 19, 205
Winchester, Daniel 160, 161, 162, 165, 167, 174n3, 174n5
Winfrey, Oprah 31

Wolfe, Patrick  58
Wright, Jan  111, 113
Wun, Connie  179, 186–7, 189, 190
Wuthnow, Robert  161, 174n3

**Y**

yoga  *see* Integral Yoga
*Yoga Journal*  162

Yogaville  162
  *see also* Integral Yoga
Young, Iris Marion  227, 229, 234

**Z**

Zerubavel, Eviatar  6, 230
Zimmerman, Don H.  6, 137, 141

www.ingramcontent.com/pod-product-compliance
Lightning Source LLC
Chambersburg PA
CBHW051532020426
42333CB00016B/1883